A HISTORY
OF EVANGELICALISM

THE DISRUPTION
OF EVANGELICALISM

THE AGE OF TORREY, MOTT,
McPHERSON AND HAMMOND

GEOFFREY R. TRELOAR

INTER-VARSITY PRESS
36 Causton Street, London SW1P 4ST, England
Email: ivp@ivpbooks.com
Website: www.ivpbooks.com

First published 2016

British Library Cataloguing-in-Publication Data
A catalogue record for this book is available from the British Library.

ISBN: 978–1–78359–432–0
eBook ISBN: 978–1–78359–558–7

Set in Garamond 11/13pt
Typeset in Great Britain by CRB Associates, Potterhanworth, Lincolnshire
Printed and bound in Great Britain by CPI Group (UK) Ltd, Croydon, CR0 4YY

Inter-Varsity Press publishes Christian books that are true to the Bible and that communicate the gospel, develop discipleship and strengthen the church for its mission in the world.

IVP originated within the Inter-Varsity Fellowship, now the Universities and Colleges Christian Fellowship, a student movement connecting Christian Unions in universities and colleges throughout Great Britain, and a member movement of the International Fellowship of Evangelical Students. Website: www.uccf.org.uk. That historic association is maintained, and all senior IVP staff and committee members subscribe to the UCCF Basis of Faith.

CONTENTS

To the memory of
Sir Marcus Loane KBE (1911–2009)
Anglican Archbishop of Sydney (1966–82)
and Primate of Australia (1978–82)

And to my friends
Brian Dickey, Mark Hutchinson, Bob Linder, Darrell Paproth
and Stuart Piggin, who are the makers of the tradition
of evangelical historiography in Australia

ACKNOWLEDGMENTS

Although intended to stand alone if required, this survey of evangelicalism in the English-speaking world in the early twentieth century takes its place in a series intended to cover the history of the movement from its beginning in the eighteenth century down to the present at the opening of the twenty-first. Although fourth in the sequence, this volume is the last to be published. It has therefore had the very considerable advantage of access to the others, and also to the history of global evangelicalism by Mark Hutchinson and John Wolffe. These works have made it possible to view the collective experience of early twentieth-century evangelicals in the setting of the whole history of the evangelical movement. At first sight, the theme of 'disruption' strikes a discordant note with the 'rise', 'expansion' and 'dominance' described in the previous volumes of the series, and with the 'globalization' outlined in the last. In fact, it enables an appreciation of the predicament and achievement of the evangelical men and women of this era.

For understandable reasons, the early twentieth century has not been popular with students of the history of evangelicalism. It certainly seems to lack the features that evangelicals have valued – revival, heroic missionary endeavour, compelling theological formulation and successful movements of social reform. In consequence it has been regarded as a time of decline and failure, ridden with theological uncertainty, internal conflict, loss of evangelistic drive and political ineffectiveness. With few exceptions, studies of the period have concentrated on fundamentalism, the peculiarities of premillennial speculation and the birth of modern Pentecostalism. Against the prevailing pattern of interpretation, this account proffers a more positive assessment of the early twentieth-century evangelical experience by recognizing the achievement of the evangelicals of a troubled era in the light of the enormous world events and changing social structures with which they had to contend. One consequence is a move away from the polarization model that has dominated study of this period to an emphasis on the commonalities and trends taking place within a shared tradition as it adjusted to a world setting very different from that which had favoured 'rise', 'expansion' and 'dominance'. The seemingly chaotic variety of evangelicalism has been a frustration to scholars with their penchant for clarity and precision. But it is the salient feature of evangelicalism and must duly be accommodated in scholarly consideration of the movement. The preference for attending to diversification and filiation around shared commitments and tasks in the following account seeks to respect this aspect of its history.

In taking this approach, a clear understanding of the phenomenon of evangelicalism remains as elusive as ever. But this is perhaps to accept the amorphous and dynamic nature of the movement. The people who call themselves evangelicals identify with an entity constituted by social as well as theological elements that can be understood in diverse ways and to which commitment can be made in varying degrees. They do not join an organization with clearly defined terms of membership and rules for operating (although many evangelicals have attempted to establish both, not least during the early twentieth century). The spectrum model utilized in this study represents an attempt to accommodate the range of evangelical opinion and behaviour at the same time as recognizing its inherent fluidity and even instability. If it means that some surprising names turn up in the ranks of early twentieth-century evangelicals, that will be because evangelicalism at this time was broader and more contingent than those who have come later would like it to have been. Indeed, the attempt to make it more delimited has been an important consequence of the disruption of evangelicalism.

The resources for writing the history of evangelicalism in the early twentieth century are seemingly limitless and certainly defy the capacity of a single student. The 'select bibliography' below lists the sources on which the present study is explicitly based. If it cannot be exhaustive, it does aspire to being representative. It is also intended as a standing invitation to others to engage with an era that, in its impact on the condition of conservative Protestantism in the contemporary world, is no less significant than the times of great evangelical achievement.

Several aspects of my usage require clarification. *Fin de siècle* as a shorthand term for the period covered in part 1 picks up the notion of 'the long nineteenth century' (1815–1914) and conveys a sense of the inheritance of the early twentieth century from the 'dominance' of the mid-Victorian years. The term 'social gospel' is capitalized only when referring to the movement in America which was given that designation. In part 2, what became 'the Great War' is referred to as 'the war'. In part 3 it is 'the War' in recognition of the reification of the experience in the process of remembrance. Throughout the book 'ecumenist' is used for the evangelical instinct for solidarity to avoid confusion with the ecumenical movement (referred to as 'ecumenicalism') that took shape from 1910 with the substantial involvement of evangelicals. The John Treloar mentioned in chapter 10 was my great-uncle. I never met him, but awareness of his committed Methodism came to me directly from his son, Alan, who edited his father's *Anzac Diary*. Every effort has also been made to obtain copyright permission to use the moving poem by G. H. Edwards Palmer quoted on page 138.

In drawing this project to a close, I have many debts to acknowledge. Inter-Varsity Press (and its senior commissioning editor, Philip Duce) has been a forbearing and supportive publisher. The energetic assistance of the in-house editor, Rima Devereaux, and of the copy editor, Eldo Barkhuizen, has meant that the outcome is less imperfect than it might have been. David Bebbington and Mark Noll, the general editors of the series, have responded to earlier versions of these chapters with helpful critiques and encouragement. They deserve the credit for whatever merits the book may have but none of the blame for the shortcomings that remain. My colleague at the Australian College of Theology, Graeme Chatfield, manfully read the near-final version of the manuscript and provided the much-needed encouragement of the educated reader. Along the way, Stuart Piggin at Robert Menzies College, Macquarie University, Ian Walker at the Kensington Colleges, UNSW, and Mark Harding at the Australian College of Theology have upheld the place of this project in the life of those institutions. Many friends and colleagues (some of whom are personally unknown to me) have either given or loaned materials that have expanded my understanding of what early twentieth-century evangelicalism encompassed. They are too numerous to name, but I will never forget their generosity. The book could not have been written without my access to the splendid library at Moore College in Sydney. Julie Olsten and her team members have been unfailing in their support of a project well outside their normal sphere of responsibility. Funding from the Ingram-Moore Estate enabled two periods of research in British libraries, while a grant from the Canada Council made possible access to the treasures in the libraries around the University of Toronto. During the gestation period of this book, I have had the good fortune to be associated with the preparation of three doctoral theses that have enriched my understanding of the history of evangelicalism. In this connection I am very glad to be able to thank John Gascoigne, Hugh Chilton, David Furse-Roberts and John McIntosh. The Evangelical History Association of Australia – where I have encountered the scholarship and friendship of Peter Bentley, Keith Sewell, Stephen Chavura, Meredith Lake and Laura Rademaker – has been a source of nourishment and fellowship in scholarship over many years. My greatest personal debt, it almost goes without saying, is to my wife Linda who has borne the 'opportunity cost' of a scholarly project pursued in the time left over from the duties of other roles with unfailing love and generosity. She joins with me in acknowledging through the dedication what this book owes to the tradition in which I have lived and worked.

ABBREVIATIONS

ABQ	*American Baptist Quarterly*
ACW	*Australian Christian World*
AEGM	Anglican Evangelical Group Movement
AHR	*American Historical Review*
AHSDSJ	*The Anglican Historical Society Diocese of Sydney Journal*
AP	*Aldersgate Papers*
AQ	*American Quarterly*
BDE	*Biographical Dictionary of Evangelicals*, ed. Timothy Larsen, David Bebbington and Mark A. Noll (Downers Grove: IVP Academic, 2003)
BHH	*Baptist History and Heritage*
BJRULM	*Bulletin of the John Rylands University Library of Manchester*
BQ	*Baptist Quarterly*
BR	*Biblical Review*
BRQ	*Biblical Review Quarterly*
BS	*Bibliotheca sacra*
BST	*Bible Student and Teacher*
BW	*Biblical World*
BWC	*Baptist World Congress*
C	*The Christian*
CH	*Church History*
Ch	*The Churchman*

CHC8	Sheridan Gilley and Brian Stanley (eds.), *Cambridge History of Christianity*. Vol. 8: *World Christianities c.1815–c.1914* (Cambridge: Cambridge University Press, 2006)
CHC9	Hugh McLeod (ed.), *Cambridge History of Christianity*. Vol. 9: *World Christianities c.1914–c.2000* (Cambridge: Cambridge University Press, 2006)
CHR	*Canadian Historical Review*
CMS	Church Missionary Society
ConsQ	*Constructive Quarterly*
CQ	*Congregational Quarterly*
CWP	*Christian World Pulpit*
EAQ	*Evangelical Alliance Quarterly*
EC	*Evangelical Christendom*
EcMC	*Ecumenical Missionary Conference* (London: Religious Tract Society/American Tract Society, 1900)
EMC	*Ecumenical Methodist Conference*
EvQ	*Evangelical Quarterly*
FCC	*Free Church Chronicle*
FH	*Fides et Historia*
HJ	*Historical Journal*
HomR	*Homiletic Review*
HTR	*Harvard Theological Review*
IBMR	*International Bulletin of Missionary Research*
ICC	*International Congregational Council*
ICM	*Islington Clerical Meeting*
IMC	International Missionary Council
IRM	*International Review of Missions*
JAH	*Journal of American History*
JAS	*Journal of Anglican Studies*
JBEM	*Journal of Broadcasting and Electronic Media*
JEH	*Journal of Ecclesiastical History*
JES	*Journal of Ecumenical Studies*
JPH	*Journal of Presbyterian History*
JRH	*Journal of Religious History*
JSH	*Journal of Social History*
JSS	*Jewish Social Studies*
L	*Lucas: An Evangelical History Review*
LQHR	*London Quarterly and Holborn Review*
LQR	*London Quarterly Review*
MBC	*Mundesley Bible Conference*

MC	*Modern Churchman*
MRW	*Missionary Review of the World*
NZJBR	*New Zealand Journal of Baptist Research*
NZJH	*New Zealand Journal of History*
ODNB	*Oxford Dictionary of National Biography* (Oxford: Oxford University Press, 2004–16)
OH	*Ontario History*
Pn	*Pneuma: The Journal for the Society of Pentecostal Studies*
PTR	*Presbyterian Theological Review*
RAC	*Religion and American Culture*
RCW	*Record of Christian Work*
RE	*Review and Expositor*
RPC	*Proceedings of the . . . General Council of the Alliance of the Reformed Churches Holding the Presbyterian System*
RSCHS	*Records of the Scottish Church Historical Society*
SC	*Southern Cross*
SCH	*Studies in Church History*
SCM	Student Christian Movement
SVM	Student Volunteer Movement
TCBH	*Twentieth Century British History*
VC	*Victorian Churchman*
VE	*Vox Evangelica*
WBC	*World Baptist Congress*
WD	*World Dominion*
WMM	*Wesleyan Methodist Magazine*
WS	*War and Society*
WSCF	World's Student Christian Federation
WTJ	*Wesleyan Theological Journal*
YMCA	Young Men's Christian Association
YWCA	Young Women's Christian Association

PART 1: *FIN DE SIÈCLE* (C.1900–1914)

1. THE EVANGELICAL WORLD C.1900

At the Ecumenical Missionary Conference in 1900 the American President William McKinley, a devout Methodist, asked rhetorically in relation to Christian missions, 'Who can estimate their value to the progress of nations?' His own answer to the question was already something of a commonplace:

> Their contribution to the onward and upward march of humanity is beyond all calculation. They have inculcated industry and taught the various trades. They have promoted concord and comity, and brought nations and races closer together. They have made men better.[1]

McKinley's celebration of the impact of missions was part of a larger panegyric to the nineteenth-century achievements of evangelicalism as an uplifting force in the world and eager anticipation of its prospects for the new century to come.[2] Turn-of-the-century commentators looked back on an era of unprecedented

---

1. *Ecumenical Missionary Conference New York 1900*, 2 vols. (London: Religious Tract Society, 1900), I, 40.

2. E.g. W. Douglas Mackenzie, *Christianity and the Progress of Man As Illustrated by Modern Missions* (Edinburgh: Oliphant, Anderson & Ferrier, 1898); A. T. Pierson, *Forward Movements of the Last Half Century* (London: Garland Publishing, 1984 [1905]).

scientific and technological development, immense material advancement and increases of wealth. To these secular advances they added their own grounds for satisfaction – progress of evangelism at home and abroad, the spread of the holiness movement, and the success of their many philanthropic and social-service activities. Viewing the world as a field for the transformative effects of the Christian gospel, and swept along by *fin de siècle* fervour, evangelicals entered upon the new century confident that it would be 'the great religious and Christian century' extending the 'forward movement' they discerned in recent history.[3]

Evangelicalism as a global movement

The buoyancy of the turn-of-the-century commentators assumed the spread and rise to 'dominance' of the evangelical movement traced in the three previous volumes of this series. Over the century and a half since its beginnings, evangelicalism had spread with the expansion of the British Empire and the westward movement of the American frontier to become a distinctive feature of English-speaking civilization. Following the rediscovery of the Great Commission by evangelicals in the 1790s, missionary activity had also established an evangelical presence in Asia, the Pacific and western and southern Africa.[4] By 1900 there were some 80 million people who were at least nominally evangelical Christians – approximately 60% of all Protestants – distributed over all the main regions of the world.[5]

Because of the number and spread of its adherents, evangelicalism in 1900 was a genuinely global religion.[6] Yet the great concentration of evangelicals was

---

3. E.g. 'The New Century's Religion', *SC* (8 Feb. 1901), 157, reproduced from *Exchange*.
4. Martin I. Klauber and Scott M. Manetsch (eds.), *The Great Commission: Evangelicals and the History of World Missions* (Nashville: B&H Academic, 2008).
5. Todd M. Johnson et. al., 'Status of Global Christianity, 2015, in the Context of 1900–2050', *IBMR* 39.1 (Jan. 2015), 29.
6. Mark Hutchinson and John Wolffe, *A Short History of Global Evangelicalism* (Cambridge: Cambridge University Press, 2012); Donald M. Lewis and Richard V. Pierard (eds.), *Global Evangelicalism: Theology, History and Culture in Regional Perspective* (Downers Grove: IVP Academic, 2014). The figures in this paragraph are based on the statistics in David Barrett et al. (eds.), *World Christian Encyclopedia: A Comparative Survey of Churches and Religions in the Modern World*, 2nd ed., 2 vols. (Oxford: Oxford University Press, 2001), I, 4, 12–15, 81, 139, 170, 386, 540, 675, 772, which are derived from a slightly lower calculation of the total of world evangelicals (75 million).

in the English-speaking regions. Of the approximately 35 million evangelicals in Europe, some 20 million lived and worked in Great Britain and Ireland. Similarly, of the 2.5 million evangelicals in Oceania, about 2 million were in Australia and New Zealand. In the United States around 32 million evangelicals represented 42% of the population, while in Canada 1.5 million evangelicals made up 25% of the total. Numerically and proportionately evangelicals were a significant presence in the English-speaking world.

The great majority of these evangelicals belonged to recognized Protestant churches. By 1900 this adherence evinced two main patterns.[7] From the first, evangelicals were a presence within denominations. Thus there were evangelical Anglicans throughout the Anglican communion, and Presbyterian evangelicals in the churches of Scotland. The churches of the 'old dissent' that began in the seventeenth century – Baptists, Congregationalists and Quakers – had also become increasingly evangelical in orientation. Lutherans remained somewhat distinct but had much in common with evangelicals because of their shared origins in the Reformation. As it gathered momentum, evangelicalism also created its own denominations. The Methodists were the first. They in turn divided into numerous subgroups – Primitives, Bible Christians, and many more. In the nineteenth century the Brethren, the Churches of Christ, holiness churches and the Salvation Army emerged. Black churches also appeared in southern Africa and in America.

Most evangelicals were able also to look beyond their own church grouping to the larger connection with other evangelicals. Not itself a church with a set order, as a new development in the history of Christianity during the eighteenth century, evangelicalism engendered an 'ecclesial consciousness' that embraced churches and other Christian organizations.[8] For evangelicals 'the church' was the body of true believers, united by a common experience of grace and devotion to Christ as saviour, wherever they were to be found. Unity consisted in a shared openness to the Bible and its teaching, spiritual friendship and cooperation in common causes, especially mission. This ecclesiology was the basis of the 'ecumenism' that characterized the movement. In addition to being transnational, evangelicalism was transdenominational.

This capacity for wider affinities had important organizational consequences. Apart from sympathizing with one another, the men and women of the

---

7. David W. Bebbington, *The Dominance of Evangelicalism: The Age of Spurgeon and Moody* (Leicester: Inter-Varsity Press, 2005), 51–62.

8. Bruce Hindmarsh, 'Is Evangelical Ecclesiology an Oxymoron? A Historical Perspective', in John G. Stackhouse (ed.), *Evangelical Ecclesiology: Reality or Illusion?* (Grand Rapids: Baker Academic, 2003), 15–37.

evangelical diaspora came together in parachurch organizations that became a distinctive feature of the movement. The first was the British and Foreign Bible Society, founded in 1804 for the printing and distribution of Bibles at home and abroad. Missionary organizations such as the Church Missionary Society (CMS) established branches in all the main English-speaking lands. The Evangelical Alliance, the YMCA, and the YWCA, began in the middle decades of the nineteenth century and rapidly created global networks. In the second half of the nineteenth century both the Woman's Christian Temperance Union and Francis E. Clark's Christian Endeavour followed their example. The globalizing effect of these endeavours was enhanced by the tendency of the evangelical churches also to organize internationally.[9] By 1900 the globe was populated by evangelical organizations and churches that facilitated the circulation of literature, reproduced patterns of piety and served common causes across national and physical boundaries.

This spread of evangelical culture created a natural unit, what would now be called a sacriscape.[10] Its development and operation were facilitated by rapidly improving communications and travel technologies. A striking illustration is *Southern Cross*, a weekly published in Melbourne (almost as far away from the major metropolitan centres as it was possible to go) by the Methodist W. H. Fitchett, renowned author of *Deeds That Won the Empire* (1897).[11] While the primary focus of this pan-evangelical newspaper was the state of Victoria, it also reported extensively on news throughout Australia and the evangelical world beyond. A large part of the substantial content was material reproduced from a wide range of northern-hemisphere periodicals such as *The Christian*, *The Sunday School Times* and *The Outlook*. Fitchett's presentation of the evangelical

---

9. For these developments, see Alan P. F. Sell, *A Reformed, Evangelical, Catholic Theology: The Contribution of the World Alliance of Reformed Churches, 1875–1982* (Grand Rapids: Eerdmans, 1991); David Hempton, *Methodism: Empire of the Spirit* (New Haven: Yale University Press, 2005); Richard V. Pierard (ed.), *Baptists Together in Christ 1905–2005: A Hundred Year History of the Baptist World Alliance* (Falls Church: Baptist World Alliance, 2005).

10. David Lyon, 'Wheels Within Wheels: Glocalization and Contemporary Religion', in Mark Hutchinson and Ogbu Kalu (eds.), *A Global Faith: Essays on Evangelicalism and Globalization* (Sydney: Centre for the Study of Australian Christianity, 1998), 47–68.

11. Robert D. Linder, 'William Henry Fitchett (1841–1928): Forgotten Methodist "Tall Poppy"', in Geoffrey R. Treloar and Robert D. Linder (eds.), *Making History for God: Essays on Evangelicalism, Revival and Mission in Honour of Stuart Piggin* (Sydney: Robert Menzies College, 2004), 197–238.

experience in the Antipodes as part of the global evangelical culture through acquaintance with the literature and events of the evangelical world at large was made possible by the telegraph. Fitchett also travelled periodically between Australia and England. In doing so, he was like other evangelical leaders who moved around a growing constituency at increasing speeds and in ever greater comfort. More and more evangelicals operated extensively within a domain they regarded as a coherent whole.

The transnational and transdenominational aspect of evangelicalism is the first indication of its nature. It was primarily a movement, an increasingly connected and integrated, but still a loose assemblage, of people, organizations and denominations.[12] This impulse arose from a combination of doctrinal convictions, a common heritage, similar aspirations and tendencies, and similar practices. Human sinfulness, salvation by faith in the atoning death of Christ and the authority of the Bible furnished a pool of essential beliefs. The heritage incorporated the Reformation, Puritanism, Pietism and, by 1900, the 150-year history of evangelicalism itself. Aspirations and tendencies included the desire to lead a holy life and to win the world for Christ. Practices included hymn singing, personal Bible study and similar styles of worship. Easily transportable as evangelicals moved across borders and from one community to another, these commonalities engendered the capacity to create the cross-denominational organizations that sought to turn aspiration into achievement. Such organizations in turn fostered a sense of belonging to a community committed to social service and, above all, to evangelism and mission. In the American context the movement has been described as 'the evangelical denomination'.[13] As a loose agglomeration held together globally by similar commitments, it is perhaps more fittingly described as 'the evangelical coalition'.[14]

Evangelicalism as a tradition of belief

Because of the amorphous character of the movement, evangelicalism as it existed in 1900 may be understood as a widespread and highly influential

---

12. Cf. Stuart Piggin, 'Towards a Bicentennial History of Australian Evangelicalism', *JRH* 15.1 (1988), 20–37.

13. George Marsden, 'Introduction: The Evangelical Denomination', in George Marsden (ed.), *Evangelicalism in Modern America* (Grand Rapids: Eerdmans, 1984), vii–xix.

14. As by Bebbington, *Dominance of Evangelicalism*, 57.

tradition of Protestant Christianity descending from 'the evangelical impulse' of the eighteenth century.[15] 'Tradition' has not been used much in discussions of evangelicalism, probably because of its ambiguity and possible confusion with the Roman Catholic usage, which sees 'tradition' as the teaching of the church (as opposed to the teaching of the Bible). However, it is also a broad sociological concept that refers to the creations of human thought and action handed down from the past to the present. These creations may change over time but retain the essential elements. Thus a tradition is 'a temporal chain ... a sequence of variations on received and transmitted themes. The connectedness of the variations may consist in common themes, or the contiguity of presentation and departure, and in descent from a common origin'.[16] Such a conception is readily applicable to evangelicalism as a pattern of Christian belief and practice intentionally reproduced by its adherents across the generations.

By providing a lens through which to view the movement as a whole, the leading advantage of attending to 'the evangelical tradition' is the coherence it affords to the feature that most strikes (and sometimes frustrates) scholars, the seemingly endless variety within evangelicalism. In the recognition of endogenous factors, 'changes which originate within the tradition and are carried out by persons who accept it', and exogenous factors, changes 'in response to changed circumstances of action',[17] it provides a method to explain this variety as the result of the interaction of the internal dynamics of evangelicalism itself with different settings and changing circumstances. Perhaps most importantly, tradition also provides a framework for tracing filiation from the eighteenth-century root, a process that intensified during the *fin de siècle* years.

While there have been many attempts to identify the conceptual content – the 'endogenous factors' – of the evangelical tradition, the set of characteristics adopted for this series is what is now widely known as 'the Bebbington quadrilateral'. Four interlocking characteristics are posited by David Bebbington as the enduring qualities of evangelicalism over the near 300 years of its history.[18] Conversionism (the belief that lives need to be changed by coming to faith in Christ for salvation), biblicism (reliance on the Bible for knowledge about God, salvation and the nature of the world), crucicentrism (trust in the self-sacrificial

---

15. Frank M. Turner, *John Henry Newman: The Challenge to Evangelical Religion* (New Haven: Yale University Press, 2002), ch. 1.

16. Edward Shils, *Tradition* (London: Faber & Faber, 1981), ch. 1, with quotation on 13.

17. Ibid. 213, 240.

18. First in David W. Bebbington, *Evangelicalism in Modern Britain: A History from the 1730s to the 1980s* (London: Unwin Hyman, 1989), esp. 1–17.

death of Christ on the cross for the redemption of the world and its people) and activism (the insistence that commitment is properly expressed in action) have been its defining features. These four components embrace smaller, local and even factious groups of Christians as well as the evangelical mainstream. These other groups add colour, variety and complexity to an already diverse phenomenon. Timothy Smith compared the movement to a kaleidoscope; Bebbington himself refers to 'the evangelical mosaic'.[19] Both metaphors aptly describe the motley assemblage of evangelical organizations, denominations, churches and individuals linked by an underlying pattern of belief, attitudes and conduct in the turn-of-the-century anglophone world.

Of the many responses to the Bebbington quadrilateral,[20] perhaps the most valuable came from the Canadian historian George Rawlyk, for whom it was not so much the four components themselves that are important as the way they have interacted.[21] Ever present, the four components have not always been equally determinative of evangelical culture. Their ebb and flow goes a long way towards explaining how evangelicalism – in a way always the same, yet frequently appearing in different lights – changes over time. To some extent Rawlyk had been anticipated by George Marsden's notion of 'conflictual priorities within pan evangelicalism' in America. As 'competing priorities', 'they are elaborated, emphasized and combined with considerable variation by diverse evangelical groupings, producing significant internecine rivalry'.[22] What is true within the movement in America is true of the movement as a whole. The prevailing balance of the different components largely determines the character of the movement at any one point in time.[23] As well as describing

---

19. Bebbington, *Dominance of Evangelicalism*, 52, 57.
20. E.g. Michael A. G. Haykin and Kenneth J. Stewart (eds.), *The Emergence of Evangelicalism: Exploring Historical Continuities* (Nottingham: Apollos, 2008), esp. the chapters by G. J. Williams and Timothy Larsen; and Charlie Phillips et al., 'Roundtable: Re-examining David Bebbington's "Quadrilateral Thesis"', *FH* 47.1 (2015), 44–96.
21. George Rawlyk, 'Introduction', in George Rawlyk (ed.), *Aspects of Canadian Evangelicalism* (Montreal: McGill-Queen's University Press, 1997), xiii–xxv.
22. Rob Warner, *Reinventing English Evangelicalism, 1966–2001: A Theological and Sociological Study* (Milton Keynes: Paternoster Press, 2007), 19–20.
23. A similar approach is taken by Stuart Piggin in his account of Australian evangelicalism as an interaction of 'Spirit', 'Word' and 'World', *Spirit, Word and World: Evangelical Christianity in Australia*, rev. ed. (Brunswick East: Acorn Press, 2012).

the phenomenon of evangelicalism, the Bebbington quadrilateral has become
a heuristic for understanding the fluctuations of its history.

The Rawlyk–Marsden proposal gives salience to a suggestion from the sociologist Rob Warner for how evangelicalism has been driven by its own inner
forces. For the period 1966 to 2001 in England, he posits a 'biblicist-crucicentric
axis' and a 'conversionist-activist axis' as 'twin and rival axes ... that energise
the dynamic of evangelical rivalries, experiments and evolution'.[24] Whatever the
merits for the context to which it is applied, Warner's suggestion shows how
the components of evangelicalism not only wax and wane but also combine to
produce varying emphases and changing permutations within the movement.
While other combinations are also possible, for individuals and collectively,[25]
identification of these two axes greatly assists the interpretation of what
happened in evangelicalism in the early decades of the twentieth century.

The interpretative value of Warner's axes emerges when brought into contact
with another approach to understanding the history of evangelicalism. Two
main currents have been identified in the broad flow of evangelical life since
its eighteenth-century beginnings.[26] Out of the orthodoxy of Reformation
Protestantism came the disposition to doctrinalism that, in a drive for theological
conformity, has continually manifested itself as adherence to 'the Scripture
principle', codification in systematic theology and confessions and disputation
which sustain a separatism that runs counter to evangelical ecumenism. From
the reaction against deadening orthodoxy came a revivalist strand that was
primarily interested in experiential piety, a high moral and devotional life, and
cooperation in works of love, service and missionary outreach. Rationalistic
doctrinalism favours the biblicist-crucicentric axis; pietistic revivalism, the
conversionism-activism axis. Evangelicalism has been at its best when the two
dispositions have been held together, as by such 'middle men' as Jonathan
Edwards and John Wesley. But, while evangelicals have rarely if ever been
swayed by one tendency to the exclusion of the other, preferences for theology
and piety have often been sources of tension and even open conflict as the

---

24. Warner, *Reinventing English Evangelicalism*, 19–20.
25. David Furse-Roberts, 'The Making of an Evangelical Tory: The Seventh Earl of
    Shaftesbury (1801–1885) and the Evolving Character of Victorian Evangelicalism',
    PhD thesis, University of New South Wales, 2015, observes the operation of a
    biblicist-activist axis in the life and work of Lord Shaftesbury.
26. W. R. Ward, *The Protestant Evangelical Awakening* (Cambridge: Cambridge University
    Press, 1992); Stuart Piggin, 'Historical Streams of Influence on Evangelical Piety',
    L 18 (1994), 5–19.

importance and content of right belief and practice has been contested. This continued to be the case early in the twentieth century. The great flourishing of the missionary movement and concomitant evangelical ecumenism before 1914 owed much to the revivalist tendency. It was subverted in the 1920s and 1930s by an upsurge of fundamentalism as an expression of the doctrinalist tendency in evangelicalism. To a large extent this was why the conversionist-activist axis was determinative in the first half of the era (c.1895–1914) and the biblicist-crucicentric axis in the second half (c.1919–1940).

Political, social and cultural landscapes

While most of the discussion of the Bebbington quadrilateral has focused on the endogenous factors driving the history of the evangelical tradition, as Bebbington himself laboured to point out, this history has also been shaped by external conditions. If evangelicals were not entirely 'of the world', they remained 'in the world', and, as members of local, national and increasingly international communities, reacted to the immediate political, social and cultural situations in which they attempted to live out their faith. An examination of the various world settings in which the evangelical movement came to expression both sets the scene for the history of the movement in the early decades of the twentieth century and also points to the larger forces – the 'exogenous factors' – to which the evangelicals of the era were subject.

The increasing interconnectedness and integration of the evangelical world coincided with and reflected the new pattern of internationalism emerging from around 1815, and especially after 1870.[27] In the final decades of the nineteenth century European governments and the rising nation state of America looked to imperialism as a tool of increasing national prestige and securing economic and strategic interests. Of these the United Kingdom of Great Britain and Ireland, which since the sixteenth century had eclipsed Spain, Portugal and France, was around 1900 still the pre-eminent world power. A union of England, Scotland, Wales and Ireland, it generated enormous wealth and exercised a prodigious influence over the emerging world economy as the first industrial nation. It also controlled the largest empire in human history, encompassing about one-fifth of the world's population, while command of the oceans enabled it to push its power well beyond the limits of its formal domain. The

---

27. C. A. Bayly, *The Birth of the Modern World 1780–1914* (Malden, MA: Blackwell Publishing, 2004).

fact that these four small countries exercised dominion over such a large proportion of the world's surface and its people was a source of wonder that, in a Darwinian age, bred a belief in the superiority of the Anglo-Celtic people. With it went the twin beliefs in a national mission and providential purpose of varying degrees of definiteness and intensity. As the response to the outbreak of war in 1914 was to show, evangelicals readily absorbed these ideas into their own synthesis.

By 1900 the British Empire included four additional major anglophone societies – Canada, Australia, New Zealand and South Africa. All were monuments to the success of the British imperial project. As the wide use of English testified, the imposition of British civilization and control on wilderness in these regions was more or less complete. Despite setbacks in the 1880s and 1890s, local economies prospered and become enmeshed in the evolving world economy. Stable social and political orders had been established. Having achieved self-government, politically all were liberal democracies, in some respects more advanced than the British system. Large numbers of emigrants from Britain and Ireland continued to come, so that English, Scottish, Welsh and Irish traditions were perpetuated. Schools, universities and other institutions replicated British norms and procedures. The broad cultural and political homogeneity of 'Greater Britain' provided an environment in which the same form of Christianity could thrive, while the voluntarism inherent in the prevailing ideal of 'a free church in a free state' favoured evangelicalism.[28]

While somewhat different culturally, not dissimilar in the main lines of its political and economic development was the USA, which had broken away from Britain in the eighteenth century. Having grown from 16 to 45 states, and from about 8 million to almost 100 million people in the course of the nineteenth century, it was the rising power of the *fin de siècle* world. Following the fratricidal agony of the Civil War (1861–5), rapid industrialization, accompanied by massive urbanization and immigration, transformed the country. War with Spain in 1898 signified the beginning of embroilment in wider world affairs. At the same time a growing 'informal empire', arising from the spread of American values and institutions, was feeding a sense of responsibility for the moral leadership of the world.[29] Its predominantly evangelical religion was one of the forces through which this influence was exercised. The controversial English

---

28. Hilary Carey, *God's Empire: Religion and Colonialism in the British World, c. 1801–1908* (Cambridge: Cambridge University Press, 2011).

29. Ian Tyrrell, *Reforming the World: The Creation of America's Moral Empire* (Princeton: Princeton University Press, 2010).

Nonconformist journalist W. T. Stead recognized the significance of these developments and perceptively forecast that the twentieth would be America's century.[30]

Because of its large following as a transdenominational movement, evangelicalism was a dominant religious force in these societies at the turn of the century.[31] Its standing as a public religion stemmed from the conversionism and activism of the evangelical creed that engendered the intention of shaping the beliefs and conduct of other people. Not all evangelicals aspired to high levels of overt public engagement, but as citizens all were an 'embedded presence', affirming their societies as well as seeking to redeem and improve them. They operated key institutions (including their churches), mobilized people and resources for various ends, commented on public affairs, worked for social betterment and participated in politics. As a result, they came to exercise significant influence both directly and indirectly. If the peak of this 'cultural authority', which David Bebbington characterizes as 'dominance', had passed by 1900, it remained significant and early twentieth-century evangelicals expected it to continue. The maintenance and defence of cultural authority was one of the leading drivers of their public life.[32]

Modernization and the disruption of evangelicalism

In addition to the political, social and economic structures of the host societies, the major cultural forces of the English-speaking world also acted on evangelicalism to shape its history. The first, it is now well established, was the Enlightenment.[33] The birth and infancy of evangelicalism in the eighteenth century as a reasonable and optimistic expression of Protestantism was a response to its tenets and values. The new temper that came over the movement

30. W. T. Stead, *The Americanization of the World, or, the Trend of the Twentieth Century* (New York: Garland Publishing, 1972 [1902]).

31. Exemplified in Stuart Piggin and Robert D. Linder, '*The Fountain of Public Prosperity*': *Evangelical Christians in Australian History*. Vol. 1: *1740–1914*, forthcoming.

32. See Frank M. Turner, *Contesting Cultural Authority: Essays in Victorian Intellectual Life* (Cambridge: Cambridge University Press, 1993), for the concept of cultural authority.

33. E.g. Mark A. Noll, *The Rise of Evangelicalism: The Age of Edwards, Whitefield and the Wesleys* (Leicester: Apollos, 2004), 140–141; Bebbington, *Dominance of Evangelicalism*, chs. 4–5.

in the early decades of the nineteenth century was due to the overlay of the Enlightenment inheritance by the influence of Romanticism. Intensified supernaturalism expressed as high views of biblical inspiration, commitment to holiness, the faith principle and fervent eschatological speculation are traceable to this source. The Enlightenment commitment to rationality and the Romantic attachment to emotion and imagination did not always sit well with one another. Over time the elements constituting the evangelical belief system were pushed to new emphases and drawn into synthesis with new concerns by the coexistence of these very different cultural forces. Around 1900, evangelicals were still in the grip of the tensions between the major cultural flows of their world.

At the turn of the century evangelicalism was changing again as it adapted to a new major influence arising from the contemporary world setting. From about 1870 the movement came increasingly under the influence of the cluster of forces historians and sociologists have called 'modernization'. Primarily these forces were capitalism, industrialization, urbanization and nationalism. Their many offshoots included consumerism, mass communication, large-scale population movements from the old world to the new, and the resultant cultural pluralism. Building since the sixteenth century, they came together synergistically in the final decades of the nineteenth to produce the emerging liberal democratic states and mass societies in which *fin de siècle* evangelicalism functioned. In many ways this development was unfavourable for the evangelical movement. In addition to difficult new social and demographic conditions, the leading religious concomitant was secularization, the disposition to understand the world solely by empirical enquiry and rational calculation, an outlook at odds with the supernaturalism fundamental to the evangelical standpoint.[34] Such was its progress by 1900 that the tide of evangelical sociocultural influence, at its high-water mark in the middle Victorian years, had turned.

The increasing sway of naturalistic and materialistic approaches to life raises the question of the extent to which evangelicals were modern people. The 'either-or' logic of the discourse of modernity initiated at the time by the German sociologist Max Weber sets all evangelicals as holders of a supernaturalistic *Weltanschauung* (world-philosophy) against the modern world. Yet few withdrew from the world, and most engaged with it to some extent. They made use of scientific knowledge and technical innovation, appreciated the advantages of rational arrangements in their organizations, and used reason to explain and promote their outlook. This combination of seemingly inconsistent attitudes

---

34. Robert B. Mullin, *Miracles and the Modern Religious Imagination* (New Haven: Yale University Press, 1996).

and behaviours is accommodated by the recently identified phenomenon of 'multiple' or 'alternate modernities'.[35] Evangelicals represent a not unusual 'enchanted modernity'. At the turn of the century it was quite common to interact with science at the same time as finding satisfaction in religious or quasi-religious experience. Evangelicals could be both religious and modern. Yet in their reactions to emerging modernity there were differences among them.[36]

For one group the interaction with the modern world was largely instrumental and utilitarian. They welcomed and made good use of the new transport and communication technologies to maximize their reach and effectiveness in their efforts to preach the gospel and build up their constituencies. However, they almost entirely rejected the new currents of thought shaping the modern world. In their religion strong opponents of the new critical methods of Bible study, men such as the Irish-English policeman Robert Anderson and the American lawyer Phillip Mauro were the anti-modern evangelicals. Their ranks were dominated by those deeply influenced by the intense supernaturalism fostered by Romanticism. Most distinctly they included many of the premillennialists who emerged in the course of the nineteenth century. In the new century 'anti-modern' evangelicals largely became fundamentalists.

Other evangelicals were open to the intellectual forces shaping the contemporary world. For them it was important as a matter of Christian faithfulness and personal integrity to adjust their thinking in the light of the ascertained truth of the day while retaining (at least in their own minds) their evangelical identity. At the time (and ever since) others have not been so ready to allow their self-designation as evangelicals. Certainly they often pushed the boundaries of evangelicalism and caused much dismay. Men such as the Canadian Anglican Henry Cody and the Australian Presbyterian Andrew Harper were the 'modern' evangelicals. In the interwar years they came out as 'liberal evangelicals' or 'evangelical liberals'.[37]

---

35. Michael Saler, 'Modernity and Enchantment: A Historiographic Review', *AHR* 111.3 (2006), 692–716.

36. Thirty years after its appearance, J. D. Hunter, *American Evangelicalism: Conservative Evangelicalism and the Quandary of Modernity* (New Brunswick: Rutgers University Press, 1983), remains the most substantial study along sociological lines.

37. Kenneth Cauthen, *The Impact of American Religious Liberalism*, 2nd ed. (Lanham, MD: University Press of America, 1983); William H. Katerberg, *Modernity and the Dilemma of North American Anglican Identities, 1880–1950* (Montreal: McGill-Queen's University Press, 2001); Matthew Bowman, *The Urban Pulpit: New York City and the Fate of Liberal Evangelicalism* (Oxford: Oxford University Press, 2014).

Probably the majority of evangelicals fitted into neither category. They were not reactionaries; nor were they innovators. While aspiring to retain the received faith, they were prepared also to move as far as necessary with the times. Eschewing controversy, they acquiesced in diversity and addressed differences by forbearance and negotiation. Continuity within order was their distinct preference. Occupants of this broad position were the 'modernizing' evangelicals. The Scottish Presbyterian James Orr and the Southern Baptist E. Y. Mullins were their outstanding representatives. Little studied,[38] their collective importance is demonstrated by the only well-known case, American Presbyterianism.[39] In this denomination the clash between the anti-moderns and the moderns created a contest for the support of the majority 'loyalist' group in the middle. If less overt, a similar contest for the allegiance of the centrist evangelicals was a feature across the movement through the early decades of the twentieth century.

The emergence of these positions reveals that modernization diversified the *fin de siècle* evangelical movement to produce an ever-increasing pluralism. With important exceptions, previous historiography has represented the positions of turn-of-the-century Protestants as more settled and definite than they really were. This has meant that the transitional nature of evangelicalism during this era has gone unappreciated at the cost of overlooking its fluidity and complexity. Neglect of centrist evangelicals has given undue prominence to the other groups (particularly the anti-moderns) and, in turn, to acceptance of polarization as the determining dynamic of the era.

A means of accommodating both diversification and the transitional nature of turn-of-the-century evangelicalism is a spectrum model that recognizes a continuum of opinion within the evangelical tradition. The movement clearly included a conservative right wing and an innovative left wing with a broad centre of moderates more or less committed to change according to the matter in hand. Various combinations may be described as 'centre-right' or 'centre-left' to clarify the leaning and the range of particular positions. The spectrum also allows for difference within each broad category. Not all fundamentalists were the same;

---

38. Douglas Jacobsen and William V. Trollinger, Jr. (eds.), *Re-forming the Center: American Protestantism, 1900 to the Present* (Grand Rapids: Eerdmans, 1998), is a plea for recovery of the centrist position.

39. Bradley J. Longfield, *The Presbyterian Controversy: Fundamentalists, Modernists, and Moderates* (New York: Oxford University Press, 1991); William J. Weston, *Presbyterian Pluralism: Competition in a Protestant House* (Knoxville: University of Tennessee Press, 1997); *Leading from the Center: Strengthening the Pillars of the Church* (Louisville: Geneva Press, 2003).

liberals varied in the degree of their liberality; and the centre was broad. Not even recognition of a 'third party' is sufficient to accommodate the complexities of a period the study of which has been dominated by the 'two party' approach.

The fluidity of a spectrum model also facilitates asking questions about evangelical identity that have seldom been addressed. At what point does a non-evangelical become an evangelical (as in the case of the English Congregationalist P. T. Forsyth) or, more pressingly, a liberal evangelical become so 'liberal' or 'modernist' that he or she ceases to be an evangelical (as with the English Congregationalist C. J. Cadoux)?[40] Who decides the answers to these questions of religious identity, and on what basis? Should contemporary polemics be allowed to do so? In fact, the spectrum enables management of difficult cases such as that of the American Harry E. Fosdick. In his lifetime other evangelicals regarded him as 'the Moses of modernism'.[41] Yet Fosdick was an avowed evangelical, although of an intentionally modern type. Similarly E. W. Barnes, a notorious 'modernist' Anglican bishop of the 1930s and 1940s, openly identified with liberal evangelicalism in the early part of his career.[42] His case illustrates that this could be a stopping-off point for some as they passed out of the movement altogether.

A further complexity arises because evangelicals could move along the spectrum on specific issues. The Canadian Methodist Albert Carman was as conservative on the biblical question as he was radical in social matters.[43] Still others changed their standpoint. W. H. Griffith Thomas, a centrist evangelical initially, became a fundamentalist, but then returned to the centre.[44] Some dropped off the spectrum altogether: extreme separatists from the right to become outright sectaries; others from the left, to become liberal modernists. At least one person (the Welshman D. R. Davies) dropped off and then returned.[45]

---

40. Elaine Kaye, *C. J. Cadoux: Theologian, Scholar, Pacifist* (Edinburgh: Cadoux Family and Edinburgh University Press, 1988).

41. Robert M. Miller, *Harry Emerson Fosdick: Preacher, Pastor, Prophet* (New York: Oxford University Press, 1985), vii.

42. John Barnes, *Ahead of His Age: Bishop Barnes of Birmingham* (London: Collins, 1979), 132–134.

43. Nancy Christie and Michael Gauvreau, *A Full-orbed Christianity: The Protestant Churches and Social Welfare in Canada 1900–1940* (Montreal: McGill-Queen's University Press, 1996), 21–22.

44. Katerberg, *Modernity*, ch. 5.

45. D. R. Davies, *In Search of Myself: The Autobiography of D. R. Davies* (London: Geoffrey Bles, 1961).

The wide continuum encompassed by the evangelical tradition by 1900 reveals the extent to which *fin de siècle* evangelicalism had already been affected by the modern world order. Its political, social and intellectual conditions were profoundly disruptive of the conditions under which evangelicalism had risen to the high point of its cultural influence during the Victorian era. Disruptiveness in this context is understood as the impact of events and developments that challenged the continuation of the expectations, structures and processes by which *fin de siècle* evangelicals framed their world as they faced the future.[46] They experienced this disruptiveness in three closely interrelated ways.

The most obvious was the sequence of 'extraordinary' events, from the effects of which there was no escape. The early twentieth century was an era of major world crises – principally the two world wars and the Great Depression. Their devastating political, sociocultural and economic effects perpetuated across the years from 1900 to 1950 a turbulent outward setting to which evangelicals were obliged to respond. No generation of evangelicals since the era of the French Revolution had been called on to face disturbing world events of this magnitude.

Disruptiveness also occurred from without as diminishing cultural authority. The result of loss of standing in contemporary society, it involved facing new claimants for popular adherence in the modern world: from inside Protestantism, the 'new theology' and the 'new evangelism'; from the wider world, such forces as the 'new nationalism', the 'new leisure' and the 'new psychology'. Its accretive effects were felt in lost ground in debates about matters such as Sunday observance and education, which signified the loss of imperium, the right to speak decisively in matters to do with society and culture.[47] Early twentieth-century evangelical leaders expected to have the same influence as their grandfathers and fathers, and were often bewildered, disappointed and resistant when it was withheld. The recovery of cultural authority persisted as a powerful motivating force among evangelicals through the early decades of the twentieth century.

Another 'ordinary' event causing disruptiveness was the diversification that engendered an ever-deepening pluralism within the movement. Early twentieth-century evangelicals were the recipients of an order that, in a set of shared beliefs and expectations, still provided the basis of cooperation in the form of 'the evangelical coalition'. This was subverted in the half century after 1900 as

---

46. Hendrik Vollmer, *The Sociology of Disruption, Disaster and Social Change* (Cambridge: Cambridge University Press, 2013).

47. See Owen Chadwick, *The Secularization of the European Mind in the Nineteenth Century* (Cambridge: Cambridge University Press, 1975), for the concept of imperium.

forces from within obfuscated evangelical identity and altered the balance between the separatist and ecumenist tendencies inherent in the movement more in favour of separatism. As they faced major world events and contended for restored cultural authority, evangelicals had to reckon with – and often exacerbated – the divisions of diversity.

The diversity and range of evangelical responses to these 'extraordinary' and 'ordinary' events are evident in the lives of the four figures – three men and one woman – chosen to reflect the dynamics of the period. As if to foreshadow the beginning of the age of disruption, the dominant figures of the previous era of 'dominance' died within a few years of one another on the eve of the new century, C. H. Spurgeon in 1892 and D. L. Moody in 1899. Nobody of the same stature arose until Billy Graham and John Stott after 1945. Yet evangelicalism in the early twentieth century was not bereft of notable leaders. Reuben Archer Torrey (1856–1928) was an international revivalist and early fundamentalist leader; John Raleigh Mott (1865–1955), the principal missionary statesman and evangelical ecumenist of the day; Aimee Semple McPherson (1890–1944), the founder of a Pentecostal denomination and a religious entrepreneur who attained filmstar-like celebrity; and Thomas Chatterton Hammond (1877–1961), a centre-right theologian and publicist. All were recipients of the evangelical tradition as it existed around 1900, but each responded to and transmitted it differently. Other leaders, such as J. Gresham Machen or P. T. Forsyth, might have been selected, but the juxtaposition of these four careers illustrates the diversification of evangelicalism, its loss of cultural authority, the weakening of evangelical ecumenism and the confusion of evangelical identity in an age of new challenges and difficulties that saw the movement become more marginal to its host societies but survive as a vigorous force within Christianity itself. Their stories are the stories around which the disruption of evangelicalism in the first decades of the twentieth century can be narrated and analysed.

2. REVIVAL, REVIVALISM AND MISSIONS

From the beginning of the history of the movement, life as an evangelical was thought to begin with the conversion of the individual, that point of decision at which the offer of salvation by faith in Christ was accepted with all of its consequences.[1] At once the product and the means of the awakenings of the 1730s and 1740s, this understanding gave rise among evangelicals to preaching for repentance as a standard practice and the perennial hope of further revival, the conversion of large numbers of people in a community at more or less the same time. Understood initially in the eighteenth century as 'a surprising work of God', the result of divine agency, early in the nineteenth century conversion was reframed by Charles G. Finney as 'a work of man', a shift that resulted in revivalism, the organized attempt to bring about conversion on a large scale by human effort. In a further development in the final quarter of the nineteenth century, the techniques of revivalism were adjusted to the conditions of modern cities by D. L. Moody and his many imitators throughout the English-speaking world. Simultaneously with these developments, the modern missionary

---

1. Editors' 'Introduction' in Mark A. Noll, David W. Bebbington and George A. Rawlyk (eds.), *Evangelicalism: Comparative Studies of Popular Protestantism in North America, the British Isles, and Beyond, 1790–1990* (New York: Oxford University Press, 1994), 3–5.

movement moved towards the point of commitment encapsulated in the controversial slogan 'the evangelization of the world in this generation'. However understood, action to bring about conversion at home and abroad was not only a hallmark of *fin de siècle* evangelicalism but stamped it at the time as an intensely proselytizing religion.

Although still generally accepted as the principal means by which people were brought into the movement, around 1900 conversion was much discussed by evangelicals. On the one hand, there was a deep and pervasive concern that preaching for conversion had fallen into a lull, the number of conversions was declining, and church attendance was falling. The need in many minds was for an intensification of conversionist activism in the form of 'a great forward movement' with a sharp spiritual and evangelistic focus, both locally and globally. Behind this call, as ever, was the revival hope. On the other hand, the reality and nature of conversion came under the disruptive scrutiny of 'the new knowledge', principally in the nascent psychology of religion that presented conversion as a natural process subject to empirical observation, rational analysis and improvement.[2] For the evangelicals who took this critique seriously, it raised the question of whether the received understanding of conversion – particularly as it was practised in contemporary urban revivalism – was viable. Perhaps in the modern world other recruitment strategies – especially religious education – would be sounder and more productive. Differences about the incidence and means of conversion were among the leading issues faced by evangelicals as they contemplated the future of the churches and of world Christianity in the new century.

Revival and revivalism

Among the results of this concern with the state of contemporary conversionism was a widespread determination to begin the new century with a great forward movement that would be, in the words of one enthusiast, a 'mighty, world-wide, permanent movement, that shall sweep the world before it'.[3] The first attempt to realize this aspiration was the simultaneous mission organized by the Free Church Council in Britain for all the major population centres in

---

2. Ann Taves, *Fits, Trances, and Visions: Experiencing Religion and Explaining Experience from Wesley to James* (Princeton: Princeton University Press, 1999), pt. 3.

3. D. S. Gregory, 'The Forward Movement – How to Be Brought About', *HomR* 40.6 (1900), 560–565 (quotation on 562).

the first months of 1901.[4] Hailed as a great success, the British example was
followed as far away as Sydney before the year was out. In the meantime
a 'Twentieth Century Gospel Campaign' had been organized in New York
City. Among the results was the appointment by the Presbyterian Church of
the United States of a Special Committee to stimulate the evangelistic work
of the Church. Its efforts gave rise to sustained, systematic evangelism all over
the country that inspired varying degrees of emulation in other evangelical
churches.[5] In addition to special missions, the local churches themselves were
urged to maintain the work of evangelization as part of their culture, and the
Record of Christian Work identified those that did so as 'good churches'. A renewed
emphasis on organizing and preaching for conversion was a marked feature of
early twentieth-century evangelicalism.

An answer to the prayers of evangelicals for a new revival came from an
unexpected quarter early in 1902. In the previous year Reuben Archer Torrey,
Moody's successor as both pastor of the Avenue Church and principal of the
Bible Institute in Chicago, was invited by the Evangelisation Society of Australasia
to conduct a mission in Victoria.[6] Interpreting the invitation as God's call to lead
a worldwide revival, Torrey crossed the Pacific, conducting evangelistic meetings
in Hawaii, Japan and China on his way to Australia. He was joined in Melbourne
by songster Charlie Alexander, and the success of the mission that followed was
hailed throughout the evangelical world.[7] Invitations to conduct similar missions
flooded in. As a result Torrey and Alexander crossed to New Zealand, where
they conducted meetings from Wellington to Invercargill. From here they sailed
to Britain, stopping for a six-week campaign in India and Ceylon along the way.
From 1903 to 1905 Torrey and Alexander conducted missions in the major
population centres of England, Scotland, Wales and Ireland, culminating in a

-----

4. Reported in successive numbers of the *Free Church Chronicle* for 1900 and 1901.
   For the setting, see David W. Bebbington, 'Evangelism and Spirituality in Twentieth-
   Century Protestant Nonconformity', in Alan P. F. Sell and Anthony R. Cross (eds.),
   Protestant Nonconformity in the Twentieth Century (Carlisle: Paternoster Press, 2003),
   184–215.

5. Ford C. Ottman, *J. Wilbur Chapman: A Biography* (New York: Doubleday, Page,
   1920), 120–126.

6. Roger Martin, *R. A. Torrey: Apostle of Certainty* (Murfreesboro: Sword of the Lord
   Publishers, 1976); Kermit L. Staggers, 'Reuben A. Torrey: American Fundamentalist,
   1856–1928', PhD thesis, Claremont Graduate School, 1986.

7. Extensively reported in *The Christian* from June to Nov., 1902. See also 'The Revival
   in Australia', *MRW* (Nov. 1902), 861.

five-month campaign in London from February to June, 1905. By now hailed as 'the new Moody', Torrey was back in North America early in 1906 to conduct missions in Chicago, Toronto, Philadelphia, Atlanta and Ottawa. By the time their mission had run its course, Torrey and Alexander had circled the globe, the first evangelists in the history of Christianity to do so in a single campaign. Along the way they led the evangelical world in a revival of revivalism.[8]

In their work in Britain, the United States and Canada, Torrey and Alexander were the beneficiaries of the remarkable revival that swept across Wales from late 1904 and through 1905.[9] Having taken a highly successful mission in Cardiff in October 1904, their publicists claimed credit for its beginnings. In fact, the first stirrings had occurred earlier in the year, and its leader, the enigmatic Evan Roberts, had experienced the visions that convinced him God would work in Wales and 'in all the world' in the previous spring and summer. The Welsh Revival was also an event of a different order. Direct leadership and organization were minimal, and crowded revival meetings all over Wales were characterized by spontaneous prayer, praise and testimony. By the end of 1905, 100,000 men and women had been added to the Welsh churches and society had been uplifted as a wave of sobriety and moral transformation swept the country. The perception that this was a genuine revival also made it an international event. The news was spread by the same print networks that had earlier proclaimed 'the Australian revival', and the curious came from near and far to see for themselves. In the next few years Welsh evangelists, missionaries and émigré ministers promoted the work of the revival. At the same time Welsh revival phenomena were sought and experienced throughout the evangelical world and provided a great stimulus to further revivalism.[10]

Against the background of the great stir caused by the Welsh Revival, Torrey and Alexander carried on their work on both sides of the Atlantic for another two years. But in mid-1906 the partnership – possibly always under strain because of Alexander's commercial activities – broke up, ostensibly because of illness befalling Alexander's new wife, Helen Cadbury. Having resigned the

---

8. George T. B. Davis, *Torrey and Alexander: The Story of a World-Wide Revival* (New York: Fleming H. Revell, 1905). See also J. Kennedy Maclean, *Triumphant Evangelism: The Three Years' Mission of Dr Torrey and Mr Alexander in Great Britain and Ireland* (London: Marshall Bros, n.d.).

9. R. Tudur Jones, *Faith and the Crisis of a Nation: Wales 1890–1914*, ed. Robert Pope, trans. Sylvia Prys Jones (Cardiff: University of Wales Press, 2004), chs. 12–13.

10. Noel Gibbard, *On the Wings of the Dove: The International Effects of the 1904–5 Revival* (Bridgend: Bryntirion Press, 2002).

Chicago Avenue Church pastorate, Torrey went his own way as an evangelist for the next few years, although never again on the same level. Alexander too continued on his own, among other things launching the Pocket Testament League in 1907, but when he teamed up with John Wilbur Chapman (1859–1918) early in the next year, the early twentieth-century upsurge in international revivalism was given another boost.

Chapman, to whom the mantle of global revivalist now passed, was another of Moody's protégés and had become a full-time evangelist after several pastorates and a term as the Secretary of the American Presbyterian General Assembly Committee on Evangelism.[11] Following campaigns in America and Canada culminating in the great Boston Simultaneous Mission of 1909, Chapman and Alexander burst on to the wider international scene with a four-month mission in Australia. From here they conducted a tour of the mission stations of the Philippines, Hong Kong, China, Korea and Japan. They began 1910 with meetings in North America before crossing to Britain for a major summer campaign, a pattern repeated the following year. In 1912–13 Chapman and Alexander spent eighteen months in Australia and New Zealand. After a summer break at home they next campaigned in Scotland over the winter of 1913–14. Because of the outbreak of war in August, a mission in London in October 1914 was the last of the Chapman–Alexander campaigns outside America. Nevertheless, the duration, extent and impact of their revivalist activity surpassed that of Torrey and brought pre-war international revivalism to its high point of endeavour and achievement.

Although they were the most spectacular examples of their kind, the evangelistic enterprise of Torrey, Chapman and Alexander was augmented by numerous other evangelists whose labours were faithfully reported each week in *The Christian* and *Record of Christian Work*. Of the many who plied their evangelistic trade across national borders, the most noteworthy was the appointed missioner of the National Council of the Evangelical Free Churches, 'Gipsy' Smith, who conducted frequent missions in North America, South Africa and Australasia, as well as his native Britain.[12] Several women, among them the converted Jewish woman Emilia Baeyertz,[13] were also part of the international circuit. Many

11. John C. Ramsey, *John Wilbur Chapman: The Man, His Methods and His Message* (Boston: The Christopher Publishing House, 1962).

12. [Gipsy Smith], *Gipsy Smith: His Life and Work by Himself* (London: National Council of the Evangelical Free Churches, 1906).

13. Robert Evans, *Emilia Baeyertz Evangelist* (Hazelbrook, NSW: Research in Evangelical Revivals, 2007).

others operating domestically supplemented the campaigns of international visitors. Most spectacularly in America the remarkable career of Billy Sunday, an independent evangelist since 1896, was well underway in the pre-war years.[14] Refusing invitations to hold meetings in other countries on several continents, Sunday still managed to preach to more people in more cities than anybody else in history to that point. At home and abroad revivalist activity proclaimed the high importance of conversionism in early twentieth-century evangelicalism.

Aims and techniques of revivalism

Viewed as a whole, this revivalism was disparate and uncoordinated. At the same time it was connected by several shared aims and purposes.[15] Of course it represented the response of contemporaries to the perennial evangelical imperative to preach the gospel. Above all it was a response to the call for more conversions that echoed down the early years of the new century. But giving it urgency and social salience were the deficiencies evangelicals perceived in the church and society of their day: the marked decline in spiritual interest; secularization and mechanization of church life; lessening of preaching of sin and salvation; and decreasing church membership. Subsidiary purposes, such as the 'Canadianization' and 'Americanization' of new immigrants, were a further response to the conditions of modern life and reflect the evangelical presumption of the need for the Christianization of society.

As contrived moments of crisis, revivalist meetings were so ordered and regulated that they have been likened to a ritual.[16] In fact, as contemporaries realized, the Torrey and Chapman meetings were more in line with the rational methods of American 'big business'. They opened with a period of heartfelt singing usually involving a locally raised mass choir. This was followed by prayer, a collection for expenses, a Scripture reading and then some announcements, all of which used local clergy as far as possible. Community interest was

---

14. Lyle W. Dorsett, *Billy Sunday and the Redemption of Urban America* (Grand Rapids: Eerdmans, 1991).

15. Much scholarship is summed up in Michael J. McClymond, 'Issues and Explanations in the Study of North American Revivalism', in Michael J. McClymond (ed.), *Embodying the Spirit: New Perspectives on North American Revivalism* (Baltimore: Johns Hopkins University Press, 2004), 1–46.

16. One of the features identified by Russell E. Richey, 'Revivalism: In Search of a Definition', *WTJ* 28.1–2 (1993), 165–175.

cultivated further by taking requests for prayer, answering questions placed in the question box and hearing testimonies of those affected by the meetings. The culmination was the sermon that concluded with a call to 'come out' for Christ. Those who were interested were then invited to stay for an 'after meeting' at which the need to decide was pressed further. Very often there was an enquiry room, but whether or not in a dedicated space, personal workers now intervened to provide counsel, and to encourage both signing an enquirer's card and joining a local church. In presenting the gospel to the modern world, nothing was left to chance to secure lasting decisions for Christ.

Other features showed how revivalism had been brought up to date. Behind the scenes the revivalists and their supporters made the most of the resources of the contemporary world. Communication technology enabled the networking that spread the news of revival and extended the campaigns geographically. The steamship facilitated travel across the face of the globe, while the steam train permitted rapid movement from one venue to the next. The meetings were well advertised, and they also demanded and often received extensive coverage in the secular press that underlined their importance and extended their reach. Major public buildings with the best facilities – such as the Exhibition Building in Melbourne, the Albert Hall in London, and Massey Hall in Toronto – at or near the centre of large concentrations of people were used instead of churches. Where suitable venues could not be found, contemporary construction technologies allowed the erection of makeshift buildings such as the temporary tabernacles in South London and on the Strand.

As a growing body of scholarship is making clear, the focus of revivalism was the city, the major demographic artefact of modernity.[17] Although this was an extension of the enterprise begun in the 1870s by Moody, Torrey and especially Chapman devoted much thought to adapting received techniques to ensure their continuing effectiveness.[18] Of these the simultaneous mission was

---

17. Janice Holmes, *Religious Revivals in Britain and Ireland 1859–1905* (Dublin: Irish Academic Press, 2000); Margaret L. Bendroth, *Fundamentalists in the City: Conflict and Division in Boston's Churches, 1885–1920* (New York: Oxford University Press, 2005); Eric R. Crouse, *Revival in the City: The Impact of American Evangelists in Canada, 1884–1914* (Montreal: McGill-Queen's University Press, 2005); Thekla E. Joiner, *Sin in the City: Chicago and Revivalism 1880–1920* (Columbia: University of Missouri Press, 2007).

18. R. A. Torrey (ed.), *How to Promote and Conduct a Successful Revival* (London: Andrew Melrose, 1898); J. Wilbur Chapman, *Present-Day Evangelism* (New York: Baker & Taylor, 1903).

the principal innovation. With saturation coverage calculated to yield maximum results, this was a method by which a city was divided into sections, with revival meetings conducted at the same time in each section. Tried first in London and Melbourne, it was brought to its high point of development by Chapman in Chicago in 1910. He worked the city along these lines for six weeks using no fewer than 60 evangelists to help him run some 1,500 meetings. Missions were sustained over long periods, from several weeks to many months, to ensure that all had the opportunity to hear. By such wide-reaching methods the claims of the gospel were asserted over the modern city.

In spite of ostensible attempts to de-emphasize the front-line revivalist, Torrey and Chapman emerged nevertheless as the defining feature of the enterprise. While it suited them to publicize their continuity with Moody, in fact they represented a new style of evangelist. University educated, their demeanour was calm and reasonable. They also cultivated a personal style that countered criticism that revivalism was sensational and unintellectual. Torrey was stiff and formal, to the point of pomposity. Unlike the self-effacing Evan Roberts, he exalted his own authority and insisted on the rightness and rectitude of his views. Chapman was less bombastic in his public persona but equally commanding and fervent. In contrast with the homespun Moody, they projected an image of Christian belief as reasonable and fitting for the educated person of the day.

For Torrey and Chapman, revivalism was a major undertaking in public rhetoric. In a manner reflecting the democratic polities of the English-speaking world, they recognized the right of the individual to choose and take a side in determining the future. As the centrepiece of the meetings, their sermons used structured argument sustained by remorseless logic in line with the scientific temper of the times. Such preaching was different from Moody's in content as well as style.[19] Whereas the eirenic Moody had found the blandishments of heaven to be a better incentive for drawing men and women into the kingdom, Torrey now placed new emphasis on hell and hellfire. Against those who downplayed or doubted its importance, he stressed the awful reality of hell and everlasting damnation as the clear teaching of Jesus and the Bible. Less theologically combative than Torrey, Chapman also insisted that there was no hope for those who failed to come out for Christ.[20] In line with the vogue for

---

19. See Jonathan M. Butler, *Softly and Tenderly Jesus Is Calling: Heaven and Hell in American Revivalism, 1870–1920* (Brooklyn, NY: Carlson Publishing, 1991), esp. ch. 3.

20. R. A. Torrey, *Revival Addresses* (London: James Nisbet, 1903); J. Wilbur Chapman, *Evangelistic Sermons* (New York: Fleming H. Revell, 1922), esp. 'Eternity' and 'Prepare to Meet Thy God'.

empiricism in the modern world, Torrey and Chapman presented rational people with the facts they had to face.

Despite this severity, from Melbourne to Montreal, from Launceston (in Tasmania) to London, large crowds squeezed into capacious venues night after night. In Toronto in January 1906, for example, some 220,000 people (some of whom would have gone to the meetings more than once) out of a population of 250,000 attended the 25-day campaign. At the time it was not uncommon to write down these crowds as consisting mainly of churchgoers. Yet the numbers attending were too large to represent mostly the professional classes and self-employed artisans who supported the churches, and observers hastened to point out that many were evidently working class. Given the place of evangelical Christianity in English-speaking society, one reason for the undoubted popularity of revivalism was the appeal of the familiar and reassuring. Large crowds also made the meetings the biggest 'event' in town to which admission was free. The conversions, which included such colourful figures as champion boxers Jim Burke in Tasmania and Alfred Allen in Canada, added to the drawing power of revivalism. Along with continuing support for the evangelical message, curiosity, the allure of popular piety and the excitement of a large community event contributed to the success of international revivalism across the populations of the cities of the English-speaking world.

However, Alexander provided the main attraction.[21] The songster, whose words reinforced those of the preacher, had been an established part of the revivalist presentation since Ira D. Sankey had accompanied Moody in the 1870s. But, like Torrey and Chapman, Alexander was an innovator.[22] He refused to depend on the proven 'Sankeys' and created his own collection of *Revival Songs*. Easy to sing and learn, they made the music enjoyable. To the musically educated they could seem vulgar, but to the masses they had great appeal. For the music Alexander greatly preferred the piano to the traditional organ, and he had the good fortune to find in the Australian Robert Harkness a pianist with the flair to provide whatever accompaniment his whimsy called for. Alexander also changed the role of the song leader. Having introduced both mass choirs and audience participation, he came out from behind the melodeon and conducted with vigorous arm actions. Often playing off one part of the audience against another and rebuking lacklustre performance, his familiarity could cause offence. But, by drilling audiences, he drew out the group solidarity inherent in the gospel

---

21. Helen C. Alexander, *Charles M. Alexander: A Romance of Song and Soul-Winning* (London: Marshall Brothers, 1920).

22. Mel R. Wilhoit, 'Alexander the Great: Or, Just Plain Charlie', *Hymn* 46.2 (1995), 20–28.

message. Comparison of the Alexander presentation with the music hall was not uncommon but, without compromising conversionist intent in the interest of popularity, Alexander brought revivalism into step with contemporary entertainment.

Another reason for success was extensive cooperation among contemporary evangelicals. In Melbourne all the evangelical bodies worked as one to stage the simultaneous mission and showed what could be accomplished by united action. Elsewhere Baptists, Methodists, Congregationalists, Salvationists and others similarly put aside the denominational differences that defined them and worked together to maximize the impact of mass evangelism. Anglican evangelicals encountered difficulty, as their church would not endorse popular revivalism. But individuals such as the Australian Bishop E. A. Langley, who actually led the mission in Bendigo, ignored denominational disapproval and threw themselves into the work. Early twentieth-century revivalism was a singular achievement of the evangelical 'coalition' inherited from the nineteenth century.

Conversionism contested

But not all evangelicals went along with what was being done in the name of conversionism. At the same time as its methods were being used more extensively than ever before, revivalism came under increasing criticism. At the turn of the century even its principal object, conversion itself, had become a matter for doubt. The 'new birth', once typically regarded as the unpredictable and inscrutable work of the Holy Spirit, was caught up in the belief that everything in the modern world was susceptible to scientific investigation. From the psychological analysis of religious experiences pioneered by William James came the view that regeneration occurs in definite ways for identifiable reasons, like other mental phenomena.[23] The de-supernaturalizing effect of this claim challenged the notion that Christian experience must begin with an infusion of divine life discontinuous with past consciousness. Now a matter for empirical study, conversion was being reframed as a natural phenomenon, a change that created new possibilities for religious proselytizing.[24]

---

23. E.g. O. C. Helming, 'Modern Evangelism in the Light of Modern Psychology', *BW* 36.5 (1910), 296–306; Theodore Gerald Soares, 'Some Psychological Aspects of Regeneration', *BW* 37.2 (1911), 78–88.

24. E.g. Frederick Morgan Davenport, *Primitive Traits in Religious Revivals: A Study in Mental and Social Evolution* (New York: Negro Universities Press, 1968 [1905]).

The impact of the 'new psychology' on conversionism was felt most keenly on the left wing of the movement where the American Methodist George A. Coe took the lead in developing an alternative approach to evangelical recruitment.[25] Coe spoke for those who, like himself, had found the traditional experience of transformation through conversion unattainable. After a period of deep reflection and research through the 1890s, he determined that religion could be taught and embraced by a conscious decision to espouse its tenets and practices. This new approach was recognized as a development of the view first articulated by Horace Bushnell in the late 1840s that religious growth is natural in a nurturing environment characterized by direct teaching and human example.[26] It gave rise to the religious education movement that Coe promoted over the next two decades with the aim of enabling children to grow up as Christians. Directed in its own way to conversion and religious experience, this was touted by him and his associates as a new and better form of revival.

Although the position was never clear cut, these new perspectives found a measure of sympathy within the left wing of the evangelical movement.[27] In these quarters the claim was that, in order to be in step with the direction of modern thinking, it was necessary to recognize that 'conversion' is an entirely normal event wholly explicable in terms of psychological antecedent and the laws of life. Candidates for the ministry illustrated the grounds for this thinking by providing evidence of the rising importance of gradually increasing enlightenment and conviction in their experience.[28] Change along these lines was more a matter of embracing an ideal and following an example than of repentance to receive personal salvation.

This shift in outlook had important practical consequences. Among the clergy, weakened conversionist zeal led to preaching that focused on ethics and good works. Against the background of decreasing church membership, more traditional evangelicals were alarmed. They reasserted the aggressive evangelism practised in contemporary revivalism with a definite call to repentance and

---

25. Matthew Bowman, *The Urban Pulpit: New York City and the Fate of Liberal Evangelicalism* (New York: Oxford University Press, 2014), ch. 6.

26. E.g. 'Education vs. Revivals, or Education and Revivals?', *BW* 25.5 (1905), 323–326.

27. E.g. George Jackson, *The Fact of Conversion* (New York: Fleming H. Revell, 1908); Newton H. Marshall, *Conversion, or the New Birth* (London: National Council of Evangelical Free Churches, 1909).

28. Kenneth D. Brown, *A Social History of Nonconformist Ministry in England and Wales, 1800–1930* (Oxford: Clarendon Press, 1988), 49–55.

amendment of life as the clear teaching of Scripture and the great need of the day.[29] But even where the traditional approach was advocated, there was some assimilation to the new perspective on conversion. Even in the conservative *The Fundamentals* it could be maintained, 'God is scientific', so that the work of evangelism, it followed, was done most effectively when it conformed to the methods he had established.[30] Conversion as 'a surprising work of God' was no longer quite the evangelical shibboleth it had once been.

New ways of thinking about conversion also had an impact on the message. By the turn of the century a 'new evangelism' had arisen. This was in part the legacy of the Scot Henry Drummond who, as yet another protégé of D. L. Moody and a highly successful student evangelist, could hardly be ignored. From the traditional evangelicalism of his youth Drummond had moved to a more modern standpoint that relied less on scriptural and creedal authority than on scientific thought and method.[31] As with other contemporary innovations (to be examined in chapters 3 and 4) the change involved several important theological shifts. Drummond saw God more as Father than Judge, Christ more as friend and exemplar than as Advocate and Saviour, and sin more as specific aberrations of conduct than a state of fallenness. His 'new theology' in no way lessened his passion for evangelistic work, but it did require the 'new evangelism' to meet the needs of the age.[32] In method it left less to reason than imagination, while in content it concentrated on the life of Christ rather than the atonement. Salvation in turn required not a change of status but of character, while those who refused to embrace it were regarded not as destined for hell but as having lost a chance to live. The 'new evangelism' still required a decision, but there was no prescribed method. The need was to enter the life of Christ, but

---

29. E.g. Arnold R. Whately, 'Conversion and Modern Thought', *Ch* 20.7 (1906), 413–422; 'Conversion and Modern Needs', *Ch* 24.6 (1910), 436–445; James H. Hodson, 'Living Questions. Is the Methodist Pulpit Evangelistic?', *WMM* 136.2 (1913), 99–100.

30. H. M. Sydenstrecker, 'The Science of Conversion', in George Marsden (ed.), *The Fundamentals: A Testimony to the Truth*, 12 vols. in 4 (New York: Garland Publishing, 1988 [1912–15]), III (VIII: 64–73).

31. Mark J. Toone, 'Evangelicalism in Transition: A Comparative Analysis of the Work and Theology of D. L. Moody and His Protégés, Henry Drummond and R. A. Torrey', PhD thesis, University of St Andrews, 1988, ch. 5.

32. Henry Drummond, *The New Evangelism and Other Papers*, 2nd ed. (London: Hodder & Stoughton, 1899), ch. 1; George Adam Smith, *The Life of Henry Drummond* (London: Hodder & Stoughton, 1899), app. 1, esp. 486–488.

each individual could do so by a different way. Although somewhat vague, Drummond's popularity showed this approach had wide appeal.[33]

Advocacy of the 'new evangelism' met with equally strong advocacy of the old. In 1905 the American Baptist A. C. Dixon, soon to be the pastor of the Moody Church in Chicago, provided a programmatic statement, inspired in part by recent revival events in Wales, Australia, Great Britain and America and supported by his own ministries on both sides of the Atlantic.[34] In general he urged reliance on revelation, not human thought. Against the 'new evangelism' he reasserted the need for 'the new birth'. None of the mooted alternatives – reliance on the spirit of the age, amelioration of environments, philanthropy, morality or working with children – was adequate or effective. It was especially mistaken to believe people could be made Christian by education, an approach Dixon dismissed as 'a pagan theory of evolution from beneath'. This standpoint had consequences for action. It was 'not enough to be evangelical', he insisted; 'we must be evangelistic'. 'The real need of the day', he continued, 'is re-emphasis of sudden, instantaneous conversion, a crisis with a view to a process of growth. There is no growing into it, but there is immense growth in it.' On this the prospects for revival depended: 'Without the preaching of the doctrine of the Atonement and individual conversion, there never was and never can be a revival worthy of the name.' How best to bring people to faith was becoming a source of deep difference within the evangelical movement.

Yet evangelicals at large were not necessarily comfortable with this strident reassertion of older views and, from about 1905, an unmistakable reaction against the latest wave of revivalism set in. Of course criticism was not new, but there were new criticisms. At first the reaction was partly personal. Torrey's imperious manner and dogmatism easily offended.[35] In Britain it was also claimed that he came without proper authority, and was therefore 'unapostolic'. If this perspective reflected the hierarchical nature of British society and found little

33. E.g. Silvester Horne, 'The New Evangelism', *FCC* (Feb. 1900), 63–64; Walter Rauschenbusch, 'The New Evangelism', in William R. Hutchison (ed.), *American Protestant Thought in the Liberal Era* (Lanham, MD: University Press of America, 1968), 108–116.

34. A. C. Dixon, *Evangelism Old and New: God's Search for Man in All Ages* (New York: Garland Publishing, 1988 [1905]), *passim* and 168, 154–155, 168 and 39 for the quotations that follow.

35. This paragraph is based on T. Rhondda Williams, *The True Revival Versus Torreyism* (London, 1905); Crouse, *Revival in the City*, 90–96, 100; Holmes, *Religious Revivals*, 184–195.

resonance elsewhere, more general was the objection to reliance on method, which made the revivalist's work seem more material than spiritual and failed to allow for the diversity of human response. Exception was taken to both the aggression and seeming commercialism of his campaigns, while the message, especially in its biblical literalism and emphasis on hell, was condemned as reactionary and perpetuating outmoded notions. Its effect was also said to be controversial and divisive, and although large numbers came to the meetings, it did not attract the genuine outsider. Torrey's new revivalism was regarded by opponents as unhelpful and unproductive.

For all the thrill it produced, even the Welsh Revival had its critics. Early in 1905 Peter Price, minister of Bethania Congregational Church, Dowlais, stirred up controversy by claiming there were two revivals taking place in Wales.[36] The true revival was the result of some years of presenting Jesus Christ, as saviour of the world, and the person and work of the Holy Spirit. At the same time a bogus revival was being led by Evan Roberts, whose language belied pretension to being endowed with divine attributes. Later in the year Roberts, with whom the revival tended to be identified, was said to be psychologically unstable and misusing his gifts. Other psychological excesses attracted attention, and there was much concern about emotional excitement. After the revival had passed, disillusionment set in. While it had led to net gain in church membership, large numbers of converts had dropped out. The results of revivals, it was said, did not last.[37]

What was said about events in Wales reflected the gathering strength of the case against revivalism that built in the immediate pre-war years.[38] As Chapman returned to various places, the necessity for further campaigns was questioned, particularly as they seemed less and less productive. Decision cards were revealing that fewer new people were being added to the churches, so that the efficacy of revival meetings was increasingly questioned. Fewer ministers were prepared to support them as the value of the cost and time involved became more doubtful. The meetings themselves were said to be dull and uninspiring, and even the music, now dismissed as 'ragtime', was losing its appeal. With the cities seemingly as wicked as ever, the social impact of revivalism was also seen as minimal. Progressive evangelicals, still offended by the use of the techniques

---

36. Tudur Jones, *Faith of a Nation*, 312–314, 333, 361.

37. J. Vyrnwy Morgan, *The Welsh Religious Revival 1904–5: A Retrospect and a Criticism* (London: Chapman & Hall, 1909), 45–46, chs. 3 and 4.

38. Richard James Anderson, 'The Urban Revivalists, 1880–1910', PhD thesis, University of Chicago, 1974, chs. 6–7.

of mass persuasion, were also concerned that the teaching and emphasis of the revivalist were out of step with the times, even barbaric.[39] And of course the great awakening did not come. Together with more attention to the quickening of the life the churches already possessed, other methods (such as personal and pastoral evangelism) seemed to offer a better approach.[40] In any case, it was being said that good results could not be produced in a hurry and revivalism seemed an unstable basis on which to rest the spiritual fortunes of the soul.[41] Although it continued up to the outbreak of war and beyond, confidence in revivalism was on the wane.

Despite the criticism, evangelicals did not give up on revivals and revivalism. As they wrestled with the perceived indifference of the great mass of the population, because of its recent history revivalism still stood out as the primary method of reaching the people. After more than a decade of renewed activity, moreover, the crowds continued to come and conversions were made. Indeed, it was around this time that in the large cities of America's north-east Billy Sunday brought *fin de siècle* urban revivalism to its highest point of appeal and impact. Moreover, some of the converts, most notably Oswald Smith in Toronto, brought new energy and commitment to the task as they themselves began to work for the conversion of others. In any case, the revival hope abided, having been boosted by events in Wales in 1904–5 and further stimulated by the jubilee celebrations of the 1859–60 revivals.[42] Furthermore, revivalism served purposes other than straight-out conversionism, particularly in North America, where, at a time of high levels of immigration and urbanization, it was seen as an instrument of naturalization, and also a solution to the moral and social problems of the rapidly expanding cities. Elsewhere the benefits for public life were also appreciated. As the English Wesleyan Methodist minister C. Ensor Walters declared, revivals were not only the means by which Christianity made its mightiest advances.[43] Their social effects would solve any problems. The revival hope persisted not only as the means of bringing large numbers of people to conversion but also as a means by which evangelicals made their mark on society.

---

39. 'The Next Revival', *FCC* 10.115 (1908), 133–134; John Humphry, 'Our Attitude Toward Revivalism', *HomR* 64 (1912), 455.
40. E.g. 'Evangelists and Their Critics', *ACW* (27 Nov. 1908), 7; Charles W. Andrews, 'Living Questions. Evangelism: One by One', *WMM* 136.11 (1913), 815–817.
41. W. H. Wynn, 'Rhapsodic Conversion', *HomR* 56 (1908), 58.
42. E.g. 'Revival Reminiscences', *C* (31 Dec. 1908), 16; Archibald G. Brown, 'Prayer and True Revival', *EC* (Jan.–Feb. 1909), 19–21; 'The Passing Year', *C* (30 Dec. 1909), 11.
43. C. Ensor Walters, 'How to Reach the Masses', *FCC* 11.22 (1909), 36–37.

Missions

Since the era of its 'expansion' in the late eighteenth century, the other side of
the conversionist impulse in evangelicalism was the commitment to foreign
missions. To prosecute the task evangelicals typically created voluntary societies
such as the CMS or established missionary arms to their churches. In the course
of the nineteenth century this pattern was reproduced in the settler societies of
'Greater Britain', once mission fields themselves, as they absorbed the missionary
world view imported from Britain. As new sending societies they became part
of the Anglo-American missionary culture that was informed by the dualism
underlying the charge to Christendom to evangelize heathen non-Christendom.[44]
Although sustained by this perennial evangelical motivation, enthusiasm for
missions waxed and waned across the nineteenth century.[45] In its closing decades,
however, there was a spectacular upsurge in missionary enthusiasm. New organizations were created – most notably the Student Volunteer Movement for
Foreign Missions and the World's Student Christian Federation. More missionaries were sent out than ever before, and generally they were recruited from the
higher and better-educated social classes. Numerical and social transformation
was accompanied by geographical expansion as missions were extended into
new areas. Although as ever driven by a committed minority, at the turn of the
century missions were central to the conversionist ideology and enterprise of
evangelicalism.

 The evangelical commitment to missions was strongly reaffirmed at the Ecumenical Missionary Conference held in New York early in 1900. It was badged
'ecumenical' 'because the plan of campaign which it proposes covers the whole
area of the inhabited globe', and evangelicals left their stamp on the proceedings.[46]
Their leading missionary societies were represented, as were the faith missions
which had sprung up in the later nineteenth century. Most importantly, evangelicals dominated the discussion of 'general principles'. Speakers included the
American Baptist theologian Augustus Strong, Eugene Stock of the CMS and
Hudson Taylor of the China Inland Mission. Each in his own way echoed the

---

44. For New Zealand, see now Hugh Morrison, '"It Is Our Bounden Duty": Theological
  Contours of New Zealand's Missionary Movement, 1890–1930', *IBMR* 29.3 (2005),
  123–128; '"A Great Australasian Scheme": Australian Influences on New Zealand's
  Emerging Protestant Missionary Movement, 1885–1922', *FH* 38.2 (2006), 87–102.
45. Brian Stanley, *The Bible and the Flag* (Leicester: Apollos, 1990).
46. *EcMC* I, 10; Thomas A. Askew, 'The New York 1900 Ecumenical Missionary
  Conference: A Centennial Reflection', *IBMR* 24.4 (Oct. 2000), 146–154.

reminder of Bishop E. R. Hendrix of the Methodist Episcopal Church that
the reason for missions is Christ's command to give the gospel to every creature,
and his insistence that 'the church has no other purpose in existence; no other
end to serve . . . but this great end of giving the gospel to the world'.[47] Appealing
to history, the American Presbyterian J. I. Vance observed that the nineteenth-
century progress of missions undertaken for this purpose was 'the supreme
endorsement of God'.[48] At a time when social-service reasons were advocated,
fin de siècle evangelicals insisted on the evangelization of the world as the primary
purpose of the Protestant missionary movement.

The timetable of world evangelization was set by the speaker who concluded
the section on 'general principles'. John R. Mott, General Secretary of the
World's Student Christian Federation, spoke for the 'large and increasing number
of Christians who believe not only that it is the duty of the Church to evangelize
the world *in this generation*, but also that it is possible to accomplish the task'.[49]
Coined by A. T. Pierson, 'the evangelization of the world in this generation'
had already been adopted as its 'watchword' by the Student Volunteer Movement for Foreign Missions (SVM) from which its influence had spread.[50] As a
missionary slogan it was controversial. The German missiologist Gustav
Warneck in particular criticized its apparent haste, superficiality, confusion
of human effort with God's purpose and, above all, its eschatological notion of
hastening the second coming. In his New York speech Mott rebutted Warneck's
critique. The evangelization of the world now meant

> to give every person an adequate opportunity to know Jesus Christ as personal Saviour
> and Lord. We do not mean the conversion of the world in this generation. We do not
> imply a hasty or superficial preaching of the gospel. We do not use the expression as
> prophecy. It calls attention to what may and ought to be done, not necessarily to what
> is actually going to occur.[51]

Still a global call for individual conversion, gone were the earlier millennial
overtones and the confident schemes for its accomplishment. Mott provided
further reassurance by insisting on the retention of traditional missionary

47. *EcMC* I, 73, 74.

48. Ibid. 85–87.

49. Ibid. 95–103. The emphasis has been added to the quotation from 95.

50. Dana Robert, 'The Origin of the Student Volunteer Watchword: "The
    Evangelization of the World in This Generation"', *IBMR* 10.4 (1986), 146–149.

51. *EcMC* I, 95.

methods such as education, distribution of literature and medical work. But, coupled with confidence in the power of the watchword to motivate and enable those who heeded its call, he also emphasized the obligation of the present generation to proclaim the Christian message. Later in the year Mott expanded his case in a book-length treatment in which he identified the difficulties of the task but indicated what might be done to overcome them.[52] Largely as a result of his efforts, the watchword was widely accepted as the epitome of the contemporary task of missions.

In the years following the New York Conference Mott was to become one of the most influential church leaders of the early twentieth century. Converted at Cornell under the influence of the Englishman J. E. K. Studd, even the circumstances of his conversion suggested the world outlook that was to characterize his career.[53] Like Torrey and Chapman he was connected with Moody, having come under his influence at a Northfield Convention, where he committed his life to missionary work. Regarding himself primarily as an evangelist, he was also a modern man like them in making the most of the technologies of travel and communication to pursue a global mission. His world tours, of which eventually there were to be five, made him an even more striking example of the expansionist outlook of contemporary American evangelicalism. In other respects he was most unlike Torrey. Optimistic and open to progressive schemes, he was not fired by premillennial urgency. More a strategist than a theologian, his message was about Jesus and the possibilities of living rather than about heaven and hell. While firm and decisive, he was also cooperative and statesmanlike. These qualities made him the leader of men and women of a similar cast of mind, particularly those similarly influenced by the watchword. As such he emerged as possibly the principal representative of the broad centre of the evangelical movement in the early years of the twentieth century.

Mott's argument that missions should take advantage of the opportunities offered by the state connection indicates that, for all its ambiguities, *fin de siècle* evangelicals were comfortable with empire and functioned easily within its framework.[54] Yet, even as the New York Conference celebrated more than a century of missionary achievement, events were occurring that loosened the

---

52. John R. Mott, *The Evangelization of the World in This Generation* (London: Student Volunteer Missionary Union, 1900).

53. Mott's life is chronicled in C. Howard Hopkins, *John R. Mott 1865–1955: A Biography* (Grand Rapids: Eerdmans, 1979).

54. James G. Greenlee and Charles M. Johnston, *Good Citizens: British Missionaries and Imperial States, 1870–1918* (Montreal: McGill-Queen's University Press, 1999).

connection between missions and empire. The Boer War in South Africa (1899–1902) brought few gains and many disappointments for missions. In China the loss of some 200 Protestant missionaries and 30,000 national Christians during the Boxer Rebellion, together with criticism of missions from politicians at home, dramatically underscored the disadvantages of association with a foreign power on the field. A few years later the victory of Japan in its war with tsarist Russia marked the arrival of an aggressive nationalism in Asia that heralded increasing resistance to Western influence. All of these developments were part of an early twentieth-century transformation that made the connection with empire look more a hindrance than a help to the cause of Christian missions. Its leaders began looking more to ecumenical cooperation and reliance on their own resources as the means to achieving their goals.

Against this background in the early years of the new century Mott saw his task increasingly as mobilizing home support for the realization of the vision of world evangelization. His insistence on the disparity between unprecedented opportunity and the inadequate response pinpointed the dilemma of contemporary missions. According to the conventional wisdom that effectiveness in missions depended more on people than money, its resolution depended in part on recruiting the necessary personnel. Despite spectacular recent increases in the number of volunteers, many more were seen to be needed to realize the possibilities on the mission fields of the world. Mott estimated that about 25,000 additional recruits were required to achieve an acceptable ratio of one missionary to every 25,000 people in the unevangelized world. He believed this was a number the colleges and universities of Christendom could supply over a 20-year period. The churches were the other important component of the home base. Mott pressed the ministers in particular to take the lead in recruiting for the worldwide task.[55]

The other side of the necessary home support for missions was financial. By 1900 Mott had already shown himself adept at raising the support of modern capital for his movements and projects, but was gratified when the home support for foreign missions was taken to a new level by the formation in America of the Laymen's Missionary Movement in 1907, which enabled 'activist men of faith' to bring their business expertise to the cause of mission funding.[56]

---

55. John R. Mott, *The Home Ministry and Modern Missions: A Plea for Leadership in World Evangelization* (London: Hodder & Stoughton, 1905), esp. 144.

56. This paragraph is based on David G. Dawson, 'Funding Mission in the Early Twentieth Century', *IBMR* 24.4 (Oct. 1994), 155–158; 'Mission and Money in the Early Twentieth Century', *JPH* 80.1 (2002), 29–42.

Conventions and conferences held all over the country had a spectacular impact on the foreign mission work of the American church, with financial support increasing by 87.5% between 1904 and 1914. Looking back, Mott judged it to be 'the most significant development in world mission during the first decade of the present century'.[57] But its success was against the trend. Elsewhere missionary giving was in decline, so that by 1908 the United States replaced Britain as the largest contributor to foreign missions. Although per capita giving for church members was low, only here did actual support approach the rhetoric about the importance of foreign missions.[58] The drive to evangelize the world was limited by the available financial resources.

The need to find the best way to organize and fund the task of world evangelization in the face of a less conducive world order was uppermost in the minds of Mott and his coterie of supporters as they made the arrangements for the next major missionary conference to be held in Edinburgh in 1910. A threat by non-evangelical Anglicans to secede because proselytism of Catholics, Orthodox and Oriental Christians was originally envisaged as part of Christian mission was sufficient for the organizers to accept a narrowing of their vision in order to secure a pan-Protestant conference.[59] By acquiescing in a restriction to non-Christian populations, only evangelicals had to live with a violation of the basic conference principle that no participants be required to compromise matters of earnest conviction. Inclusive evangelicals such as Mott were prepared to be pragmatic in the cause of world evangelization.

The purpose of the conference was indicated by its full title and its method. It was the 'World Missionary Conference to Consider Missionary Problems in Relation to the Non-Christian World'.[60] For ten days in June 1910 representatives of the major missionary agencies debated the reports of the eight commissions appointed to investigate leading issues facing the world missionary movement. Its achievement was to create in the Continuation Committee a structure to effect the ongoing international cooperation that conference delegates presumed

---

57. John R. Mott, *Five Decades and a Forward View* (London: Harper & Brothers, 1939), ch. 2, esp. 30.

58. *World Missionary Conference, 1910. Report of Commission VI. The Home Base of Missions* (Edinburgh: Oliphant, Anderson & Ferrier, n.d. [1910]), esp. 146–160.

59. Brian Stanley, 'Defining the Boundaries of Christendom: The Two Worlds of the World Missionary Conference, 1910', *IBMR* 30.4 (Oct. 2006), 171–176.

60. Brian Stanley, *The World Missionary Conference, Edinburgh 1910* (Grand Rapids: Eerdmans, 2009). Andrew Walls, *The Cross-Cultural Process in Christian History* (New York: Orbis Books, 2002), ch. 3.

was the key to world evangelization. In the *International Missionary Review* and *The Moslem World* it also established the means to maintain the scientific investigation required for sound missionary planning and strategy. Confident that the Conference had made the arrangements to realize the vision of the transmission of the gospel to the non-Western world, Mott declared at its close, 'The end of the Conference is the beginning of the conquest. The end of the planning is the beginning of the doing.'[61]

Although the full spectrum of contemporary Protestant opinion had been represented, the Conference was, as its most recent historian has pointed out, 'an overwhelmingly evangelical gathering'.[62] With evangelicals having taken the principal part in its organization, the Conference provided them with a further opportunity to lead the church in mission. Having largely drafted and then edited the report of Commission I, 'Carrying the Gospel to All the World', Mott was a deft and authoritative chairman, while Joseph Oldham was an efficient (although silent) secretary. For other evangelicals Edinburgh 1910 was a moment to speak and act before the wider church. The American secretary of the SVM in India, Sherwood Eddy, the Scottish theologian James Denney, and the British CMS missionary to Cairo, Egypt, Temple Gairdner were among those who addressed the evening meetings. With their devotional leadership, W. H. Findlay of the Wesleyan Methodist Missionary Society and Handley Moule, Bishop of Durham, contributed to the spiritual power and sense of oneness that pervaded the proceedings. When it came to perpetuating its achievement, the Conference turned again to Mott and Oldham, appointing them as chairman and secretary of the Continuation Committee. Mott summed up the message and spirit of the Conference for the whole church through *The Decisive Hour of Christian Missions*, which he wrote for use in mission study circles in the days immediately before and after the Conference,[63] while Oldham became foundation editor of the *International Review of Missions*. Edinburgh 1910 not only marked the high point of *fin de siècle* missionary activism and willing-ness to work with others in the cause of world evangelization; it was perhaps also the last flash of the evangelical 'dominance' of the churches inherited from the late Victorian era.

---

61. *World Missionary Conference, 1910. The History and Records of the Conference Together with Addresses Delivered at the Evening Meetings* (Edinburgh: Oliphant, Anderson & Ferrier [1910]), 347; W. H. T. Gairdner, *'Edinburgh 1910': An Account and Interpretation of the World Missionary Conference* (Edinburgh: Oliphant, Anderson & Ferrier, 1910), 266–268.

62. Stanley, *World Missionary Conference*, 90.

63. John R. Mott, *The Decisive Hour of Christian Missions* (London: CMS, 1910).

For all the excitement and energy it generated, Edinburgh 1910 did not resolve the missiological debate simmering within the evangelical movement in the early years of the twentieth century. At one end were those who were saying that the object of missions was to permeate host societies with Christian ideas for their transformation.[64] Agencies such as schools and hospitals would be at once instruments for Christianization and civilization. At the other end were those who still insisted that preaching for conversion was the sole purpose of missionary enterprise. Occupying the broad middle ground was the synthetic view represented by the American Presbyterian Robert Speer.[65] Like Mott, Oldham and many others, he maintained that missions were primarily evangelistic in their purpose at the same time as being fully committed to the social goals of the gospel. Believing that cooperation was necessary to Christianize the world, these centrist evangelicals were also now supportive of the incipient ecumenical project.

Paralleling the increasing complexity of missionary motivation was the question of the relation of Christianity to other religions, which the encounter on the mission field made inescapable. No evangelical was prepared to endorse the non-Christian religions without qualification, but, against those who dismissed these religions altogether, there was a growing realization that there was more to be said for them than traditionally allowed.[66] At a time of much theorizing about the conflict of faiths, the Scottish Indologist John Nicol Farquhar's fulfilment theory – which maintained Christianity does not oppose but brings to completion the world's highest religions – offered an influential if controversial way of reconciling the seemingly absolute claims of the gospel with the religions of the missionary world.[67] Once a matter of some certainty,

----

64. E.g. James L. Barton, *Human Progress Through Missions* (New York: Fleming H. Revell, 1912).

65. Robert Speer, 'Foreign Missions a Constructive Interpretation of Christian Principles', *ConsQ* 1.3 (1913), 544–570; Richard V. Pierard, 'Evangelical and Ecumenical: Missionary Leaders in Mainline Protestantism, 1900–1950', in Douglas Jacobsen and William V. Trollinger (eds.), *Re-forming the Center: American Protestantism, 1900 to the Present* (Grand Rapids: Eerdmans, 1998), 150–171.

66. E.g. *World Missionary Conference, 1910: Report of Commission IV. The Missionary Messsage in Relation to Non-Christian Religions* (Edinburgh: Oliphant, Anderson & Ferrier, 1910).

67. Kenneth Cracknell, *Justice, Courtesy, and Love: Theologians and Missionaries Encountering World Religions, 1846–1914* (London: Epworth Press, 1995), esp. 167–173.

loss of clarity about the scope and purpose of missions was, like the debate about conversion, a sign of the increasing differentiation within early twentieth-century evangelicalism.

Conclusion

Whatever complexity had emerged, preparations for the 1914 Chapman–Alexander campaign in London and the work of the Continuation Committee from Edinburgh 1910 indicated that the momentum of *fin de siècle* conversionist activism was maintained right up until the outbreak of war. Written against this background, John Mott's *The Present World Situation* recognized that the moment was precarious, but it also presupposed the great achievement of the previous twenty-five years as the springboard to further evangelistic success.[68] In doing so, it was an expression of the high point of aspiration and organization reached by evangelicals as they dared to aim at 'the evangelization of the world in this generation'. If attainment of the goals eluded them, the turn of the century was nevertheless an era of considerable achievement. A band of international and local revivalists typified by Torrey, and a small army of missionaries and a coterie of outstanding leaders of whom Mott was the most distinguished, made use of the resources of the contemporary world to cover more ground and bring the message of salvation to more people than ever before. Motivated by the basic impulse to preach the gospel, given urgency by declining church adherence and perceptions of falling levels of Christian devotion coupled with a sense of the needs, dangers and opportunities of the times, and sustained in the revival hope by the revival in Wales and other points around the globe, *fin de siècle* evangelicals took conversionist zeal to an unprecedented level. Although far from fruitless, their efforts did not produce mass conversions at home or on the mission field to constitute the much cherished 'awakening'. While no doubt they were disappointed that it did not come in their day, this did not mean these evangelicals had failed. All along, the emphasis in their thinking was the responsibility of proclamation that might be left to produce its own results. In this respect they had no equals in the previous history of the evangelical movement.

Although it was a time of great achievement, this commitment to taking the gospel to the world was not uncontested among evangelicals. Both the

---

68. John R. Mott, *The Present World Situation: With Special Reference to Demands Made upon the Christian Church in Relation to Non-Christian Lands* (London: SCM Press, 1915).

motivation and the means of conversion at home and abroad were closely scrutinized through the *fin de siècle* years. The result was the emergence of differences of opinion about the necessity for conversion and alternative proposals for how evangelicals should propagate the message of salvation. These differences reflected rising tensions within the movement. Men such as Mott, broad minded and eirenic, looked for cooperation in a common cause, while others, such as Torrey, aggressive and uncompromising, were unconcerned about the potential of difference for division. However foreboding for the future, the impact of this diversity was minimal. Evangelism was still a task that brought evangelicals together. Indeed, part of the achievement of the era was the Edinburgh Missionary Conference, a triumph of evangelical ecumenism. Setting in motion the dialogue and cooperation that within a generation produced the ecumenical movement in Protestantism showed that the days of evangelical 'dominance' were not quite over.

3. THE LIFE OF FAITH

Adherence to evangelicalism, whether by conversion or by socialization and education, was just the beginning. Throughout the history of the movement, the evangelical impulse to reproduce authentic New Testament Christianity sustained the expectation that 'conversion' would mark the commencement of a new life characterized by the application of faith to the whole of the believer's life. For early twentieth-century evangelicals, this life of faith was epitomized as 'consecration', the term frequently coupled with 'conversion'.[1] At once the product of evangelical beliefs and the demonstration of those beliefs, consecration was what A. T. Pierson called 'the present tense' of the believer's life, and it lasted until death.[2] Evangelical experience in this 'tense' was primarily a matter for the individual, but it was also social. As a part of their 'lived religion', evangelicals were expected to interact with others who had had the same experience, and to participate in the institutions and collectives which directed their experience into public activity. In these settings they were inducted into practices and habits of mind that, in their social dimension, constituted a religious culture with its own symbols, rituals, taboos, processes and boundaries by which life

---

1. E.g. F. S. Guy Warman, 'The Essentials of Evangelicalism', *Ch* 24.58 (1910), 750–758.
2. A. T. Pierson, *The Believer's Life: Its Past, Present and Future Tenses* (London: Morgan & Scott, 1905), 7, 9, 53–57.

was interpreted and structured.[3] As a religious culture, evangelicalism was defined as much by its attitudes and practices as by its distinctive beliefs. Coming to expression with seemingly unlimited variety, there was nevertheless an underlying sense of order that delimited the evangelical experience. Part of this order was the expectation that the experience of evangelicals would be both truly spiritual and practical, and thus a sign of the reality and depth of conversion. The life of faith was a test as well as a regimen.[4]

By the turn of the century, the life of faith was also under extensive consideration by evangelicals. Their concern was in part a response to perceptions of neglect. Present-day evangelicals were widely thought to be less assiduous in cultivating the life of faith than those who had gone before. The interest was also due in part to the perennial aspiration to make the life of faith more effective. As its own history showed, the life of faith as experimental religion committed to the maintenance of spiritual vitality contained the seeds of self-renewal and transformation. This was also the time when it, like conversion, became a subject for scientific observation as psychologists of religion looked to evangelicalism as one of the principal manifestations of religious experience, a development which again suggested malleability and improved management. Much was at stake as evangelicals insisted against the outside world that theirs was a genuine encounter with the living God, which challenged the moral and spiritual failings of the age.

Evangelical devotionalism

Basic to the life of faith as practised at the turn of the century was strong devotional discipline. As new adherents were soon informed, setting aside time each day for religious reading and reflection was not only a requirement of evangelical life but also a condition of success.[5] It provided an opportunity to seek God's leading for every activity of the day and to ask for his blessing upon

---

3. Evangelicalism as a religious culture is addressed by David W. Bebbington, 'Evangelicalism and Cultural Diffusion', in Mark Smith (ed.), *British Evangelical Identities Past and Present*. Vol. 1: *Aspects of the History and Sociology of Evangelicalism in Britain and Ireland* (Eugene: Wipf & Stock, 2008), 18–34.

4. On the life of faith generally, Ian M. Randall, *What a Friend We Have in Jesus: The Evangelical Tradition* (London: Darton, Longman & Todd, 2005).

5. E.g. R. A. Torrey, *How to Make a Success of the Christian Life* (London: James Nisbet, n.d.).

it. Perhaps the best-known contemporary example of a widely advocated practice was 'the morning watch' promoted by John Mott and the organizations he led.[6] The importance of such devotions was underlined by repeated protests against the failure of contemporaries – allegedly distracted by the pressures of modern life and the attractions of pleasure seeking – to give devotions the time they warranted.

The need for direction and support in the devotional life sustained a large literature. Contemporary evangelicals took advantage of a burgeoning print culture and cheap publication costs to flood their market with books and periodicals offering guidance for this key practice. The doyen of writers at this time was the South African Andrew Murray who still had sixteen years to live in the new century. A rising star was the Scottish Baptist Oswald Chambers, who went on to produce the classic *My Utmost for His Highest* (published posthumously in 1924). Another newcomer who began to make his mark from the end of the first decade of the century with a steady flow of devotional writing from a different standpoint was the American Harry E. Fosdick. With a view to enriching evangelical experience, these writers produced an extensive literature on the life of faith, which was unprecedented in volume, refinement and diversity.[7]

This diversity was reflected in the prescriptions for devotional practice. Those on the right, who persisted in viewing the world as the scene of transcendent spiritual struggle, required a significant allocation of time (at least half an hour) at the beginning of the day in quiet surroundings. Writers on the left, adjusting to modern intellectual and social conditions, preferred a flexible approach, with shorter bursts of devotional engagement at almost any time and in any place. One perspective required a disciplined method of achieving contact with God in order to build up the spiritual reserves necessary to get through the day. The other was more inclined to gaining propulsion continually from the ever-present God. Historian Rick Ostrander has likened these methods of drawing spiritual energy to a 'battery' and a 'windmill'.[8]

This diversification was especially evident in Bible reading, the first indispensable devotional practice for evangelicals in the life of faith. In 1914 William

---

6. E.g. John R. Mott, *The Morning Watch and Bible Study for Personal Spiritual Growth* (Melbourne: SCM Press, n.d.).

7. W. M. Douglas, *Andrew Murray and His Message* (Belfast: Ambassador Publications, 1998 [1926]); Harry E. Fosdick, *The Living of These Days: An Autobiography* (London: SCM Press, 1957).

8. Richard Ostrander, 'The Battery and the Windmill: Two Models of Protestant Devotionalism in Early-Twentieth-Century America', *CH* 65.1 (1996), 42–61.

Souper, the Presbyterian Church of England minister at Battersea Rise, reiterated for his generation the basic evangelical conviction 'Next to Christ
Himself the Bible is our most precious and priceless possession.'[9] For most
evangelicals the Bible's authority derived from its status as the Word of God
requiring absolute trust and unquestioned obedience. With varying degrees of
sophistication, this perspective favoured a literal reading, non-differentiation
of the parts and proof-texting. Other evangelicals (as chapter 4 will show) more
in touch with the results of literary and historical study, preferred to see the
Bible as a record of religious experience. As such, it was a guide to the patterns
of individual behaviour and of historical development through which God
works, and its power derived from internalizing these patterns and putting them
into practice.[10] While it allowed for a more nuanced reading and differentiation
of the parts, this change of approach required no reduction in commitment to
the authority of the Bible and belief in its spiritual power. Early twentieth-
century evangelicals were no less devoted to the Bible in their spiritual lives than
were their predecessors, but more and more their biblicism encompassed
different meanings and expectations.

The impact of modern knowledge was also evident in the attempts of evangelicals to use the Bible to determine what Christ, their 'most precious and
priceless possession', meant for the life of faith.[11] Evangelicals rejected the
'Christless Christianity' of contemporary theological speculation and insisted
on the facticity of the biblical presentation of Christ as the eternal Son of God
who became man.[12] In practice this meant three things.

First, as God in humanity, Jesus was the revelation of the being and nature
of the Almighty. *Fin de siècle* evangelicals were caught up in the reconsideration
of conceptions of God in the light of science, which had given rise to a new
emphasis on divine immanence and posed the problem of finding the balance
with divine transcendence. Whatever its other consequences, the debate led to
a heightened awareness of God as the father of all humanity. The American
missionary statesman Robert Speer drew out what this meant for the life of

---

9. William Souper, 'Christ and the Scriptures in the Life and Thought of To-day',
   MBC 1914, 150.
10. For the impact of biblical scholarship, William Newton Clarke, *Sixty Years with
    the Bible: A Record of Experience* (New York: Charles Scribner's Sons, 1909).
11. E.g. Augustus H. Strong, 'The Greatness and the Claims of Christ', *WBC 1905*,
    52–64; William E. Barton, 'The Person of Jesus Christ', *ICC 1908*, 54–62; Peter
    T. Forsyth, *The Work of Christ* (London: Hodder & Stoughton, 1910).
12. W. Radcliff, 'The Deity of Christ', *RPC 1913*, 89–94, with quotation on 90.

faith: 'if God is our own Father let us love Him more and trust Him more and please Him more'.[13]

Second, evangelicals also looked to the humanity of Jesus and generally welcomed the contemporary emphasis on the incarnation and the quest for the historical Jesus.[14] From different points along the spectrum of opinion, their own writers produced studies of his life and work. These studies illuminated the facts on which their experience was based and confirmed Jesus' status as 'the supreme teacher'.[15] He was also their exemplar. Kansan Charles M. Sheldon's novel of 1896, *In His Steps, Or What Would Jesus Do?*, won wide acclaim for its portrayal of the results of recognizing Jesus as the pattern of what people might do and become. The life of faith still entailed following the teaching and example of Jesus.

Third, evangelicals trusted in Christ as the saviour of humankind. While in some quarters its influence had given way to other interpretations, at the turn of the century substitutionary atonement was still the basis of the evangelical belief system. But it was more than an objective doctrinal fact to be received gratefully. In that Christ's death set a pattern that demanded a response from his followers, it was also subjectively a force for life. As an act of self-sacrifice, it was a spur to similar consecration. Gratitude for what God had done in Christ could also furnish the motivation for lives of devoted service. Above all, as the Scottish Presbyterian H. R. Mackintosh pointed out, lives fashioned by the cross were the means of commending Christ to others: 'The world will be persuaded of the efficacy of the death of Jesus when it sees His followers acting in the Spirit (*sic*) of that death.'[16] Depending on the emphasis, the focus on the cross had numerous applications for private and public life.

Evangelicals also looked to Jesus as the recipient of prayer, the second basic practice of the devotional life, singly and in groups, privately and in public. It was conceived as conversation with God, the means of responding to his word spoken in the Bible, and the source of spiritual energy. No evangelical would

---

13. Robert Speer, *Christ and Life* (New York: Fleming H. Revell, 1901), 213–214.

14. E.g. J. D. Jones, 'The Christ of History and the Christ of Experience', *MBC 1908*, 227–238.

15. E.g. Robert Speer, *Studies of the Man Christ Jesus* (New York: YMCA Press, 1896); George Jackson, *The Teaching of Jesus* (London: Hodder & Stoughton, 1903), with quotation on 13; Harry E. Fosdick, *The Manhood of the Master* (New York: Association Press, 1914).

16. H. R. Mackintosh, 'The Cross and Present-Day Religion', *RPC 1913*, 98. For the social implications of the Atonement, see chapter 5 below.

have disagreed with the assessment of its importance made by the editor of the *Evangelical Alliance Quarterly*: 'As no live creature can continue without breathing, so the individual Christian cannot continue without praying.'[17] In holding to this assessment, evangelicals had withstood the scepticism of the previous generation and now presented answered prayer as the empirically based answer to scientific criticism of prayer.[18] The effect was to intensify the traditional presentation of prayer by writers on the right such as Torrey as the cause of objective effects in the world. They asserted that not to set aside time to pray along approved lines was nothing less than disobedience to God. Yet subtle differentiation was taking place. While no less responsive to the biblical injunction to pray, the evangelical left made available an approach more in harmony with the idea of divine immanence. Supporters thought of petitionary prayer as a request for particular attentions of the ever-present God. Its domain, however, was more properly spiritual and its effect on the world came chiefly through the transformation of the person praying. John Mott's endorsement of Harry Fosdick's *The Meaning of Prayer* signified the acceptability of this recalibration at least to the evangelical centre.[19]

As standard practices and running along well-developed lines, Bible reading and prayer were a pressure for conformity. At the same time they remained indicative of the individualism and open-endedness of the evangelical impulse. As their penchant for testimony suggests, evangelicals expected God to deal with people one by one, occasionally with surprising results. The brothers Norman and Kenneth Grubb grew up in the shadow of their uncle, the turn-of-the-century missionary hero and very conservative C. T. Studd, who frequently spoke about his own eccentric religious experience and matched it with an equally unusual career. The 'Bible-soaked' Norman followed a similar pathway but devotional reading in the mystics (especially William Law and Jacob Boehme) following a time of spiritual crisis led to the discovery of 'the Universal Christ' and 'a vast enlargement of heart and mind'. Far from plumbing the depths of divine immanence, the less theologically reflective and highly pragmatic centre-left Kenneth relied on an uncomplicated biblicism that was sufficient to sustain a missionary career in South America, the presidency of the CMS and eventually involvement in the World Council of

---

17. 'Editorial Notes', *EAQ* 11 (Jan. 1902), 183–84.
18. Rick Ostrander, *The Life of Prayer in a World of Science: Protestants, Prayer, and American Culture 1870–1930* (Oxford: Oxford University Press, 2000).
19. Harry E. Fosdick, *The Meaning of Prayer* (New York: Association Press, 1915), esp. vii–viii.

Churches.[20] Such cases confirm that evangelical devotionalism, as well as reproducing evangelical culture as expected, could always take the movement in
new and surprising directions.

Churchgoing and anti-Catholicism

A further biblical principle recognized by evangelicals was that, while nurtured
mainly in private, the life of faith should be expressed publicly. Salvation
by faith in Christ created a bond with other believers, which it was natural
to express by association, but also produced a solidarity, with benefits and
responsibilities.[21] For this reason the third basic practice of the life of faith
was churchgoing.[22] Every Sunday evangelicals came together for the meetings
and worship services of their churches. In many cases they attended midweek
meetings as well. In various ways their churches were the scene of the worship,
celebration of Holy Communion and teaching of the Word through preaching
that cultivated the life of faith. But evangelicals not only received nurture and
support; because the church was a sphere of service where believers could
add their own endowment to the whole, they were expected also to give. The
American Presbyterian Henry Sloane Coffin spoke for the whole movement when he summed up this reciprocal relationship: 'The Christian is
dependent upon the Church for his faith, his growth, his usefulness.'[23] As the
sites of their principal gatherings, the churches were largely the means of
shaping and organizing the thought and conduct of early twentieth-century
evangelicals.

---

20. Norman Grubb, *C. T. Studd: Cricketer and Pioneer* (London: Religious Tract Society,
     1933); *Once Caught, No Escape: My Life Story* (London: Lutterworth Press, 1969),
     ch. 6 (quotations on 171, 167); Kenneth Grubb, *Crypts of Power: An Autobiography*
     (London: Hodder & Stoughton, 1971), ch. 5.
21. E.g. J. H. Shakespeare and R. H. Fitt, 'The Spirit of Brotherhood in the Church',
     BWC 1911, 308–319.
22. This section draws on Charles D. Cashdollar, *A Spiritual Home: Life in British and
     American Reformed Congregations, 1830–1915* (University Park, PA: Pennsylvania State
     University Press, 2000); J. Michael Utzinger, *Yet Saints Their Watch Are Keeping:
     Fundamentalists, Modernists, and the Development of Evangelical Ecclesiology, 1887–1937*
     (Macon, GA: Mercer University Press, 2006), pt. 1.
23. Henry Sloane Coffin, *Some Christian Convictions: A Practical Restatement in Terms
     of Present-Day Thinking* (New Haven: Yale University Press, 1915), 183.

Perhaps more than anything else, the expansive 'ecclesial consciousness' of evangelicals (described in chapter 1) accounts for two important countervailing tendencies within the evangelical movement. On the one hand, evangelicals at large were deeply committed to their own churches. In myriad ways – in polity, role of the clergy, theological emphases, styles of worship, forms of evangelical life, recruitment, membership requirements, and attitudes towards the wider community – these churches differed from one another. While compatible with alignment with the evangelical tradition, their differences were not matters of indifference. In conjunction with the force of specific issues and personalities, they sustained a separatism that continually spawned new churches. Recent additions to the ranks of evangelical denominations included the Salvation Army, the Christian and Missionary Alliance and a plethora of holiness churches. These were followed early in the new century by the Church of the Nazarene and the Pentecostal churches. Because evangelicals were not greatly troubled by denominational disparity, 'church' remained the point at which the diversity of the movement was most visible.

On the other hand, their 'ecclesial consciousness' sustained the tendency to evangelical ecumenism. The shared experience of salvation enabled evangelicals to come together across denominational borders in friendship and cooperation. Shared experience and outlook enabled provision for the life of faith in arrangements for joint prayer meetings and intercession, periodicals such as *The Christian* which was directed to all who shared an interest in revival and revivalism, and in innumerable Bible, prophecy and holiness conferences all around the evangelical world. In some cases they allowed a measure of reunion within evangelical churches. In Scotland in 1900, for example, the United Presbyterian Church and the Free Church of Scotland came together to form the United Free Church. Around the same time branches of Methodism in Canada, Australia, New Zealand and England similarly combined largely to combat the problems of vast distances in the settler societies. Organic union was never seriously contemplated by early twentieth-century evangelicals but they continued to operate non-denominational structures and pursue common strategies to deal with particular situations and needs along the lines set in an earlier age by parachurch agencies such as the British and Foreign Bible Society, whose centenary was celebrated in 1904. The decline of the Evangelical Alliance in America was a reminder that cooperation could not always be maintained.[24] Nevertheless,

---

24. Philip D. Jordan, *The Evangelical Alliance for the United States of America, 1847–1900: Ecumenism, Identity and the Religion of the Republic* (New York: Edwin Mellen Press, 1982).

although under pressure from time to time, working together as 'the evangelical coalition' remained a feature of evangelical experience into the twentieth century.

Because the boundaries of their shared culture were undefined and porous, evangelicals demarcated them as circumstances required. The emergence of Christian Science towards the end of the nineteenth century was one such occasion. As a new form of religious life, Christian Science was rejected by evangelicals on the grounds that, by denying the reality of matter, sin, Satan, the life and crucifixion of Jesus, the second coming and prayer, it was a negation of the biblical view of God, the world and humanity.[25] These objections showed that the boundaries were primarily theological, but as a defence of the elements of the life of faith they evince social characteristics as well. The same mix of conceptual and social limits was evident in hostility to Catholicism, Roman and Anglican, the evangelical opposition with the longest lineage and greatest emotive power.

Historians argue that by 1900 anti-Catholicism in English-speaking society at large had begun to abate.[26] If this view is correct, evangelicals were an exception to the larger pattern. The anti-Catholicism that had long been a part of the evangelical heritage from the Reformation was maintained by the agitation of organizations such as the Protestant Truth Society, created late in the nineteenth century to protect Protestant identity from Catholic encroachment.[27] A succession of events intensified this feeling in the new century. The Royal Commission into Ecclesiastical Discipline in 1906, and the beginnings of a movement for change to the Anglican Book of Common Prayer, sharpened awareness of the prospect of betrayal from within the Church of England.[28] In 1908 a publicly assertive Eucharistic Congress in London posed afresh the threat of Roman Catholicism to English national identity. Similarly the proposal to revise the Sovereign's accession oath in 1910 by removing disclaimers against Catholic doctrine such as Transubstantiation was a powerful reminder of the ever-present danger of the weakening of Protestantism.[29]

---

25. E.g. James M. Gray, *The Antidote to Christian Science, Or How to Deal with It from the Bible and Christian Point of View*, 4th ed. (New York: Fleming H. Revell, 1907).
26. John Maiden, *National Religion and the Prayer Book Controversy, 1927–1928* (Woodbridge: Boydell Press, 2009), 'Introduction'.
27. Martin Wellings, 'The First Protestant Martyr of the Twentieth Century: The Life and Significance of John Kensit (1853–1902)', *SCH* 30 (1993), 347–358.
28. Reactions in *ICM 1907. The Royal Commission Report and the Duty of Evangelical Churchmen* (London, 1907), and traceable thereafter in *The Churchman*.
29. 'Notes' and 'The Royal Declaration', *EC* (July–Aug. 1910), 77–79.

For other reasons anti-Catholicism was an important part of the environment throughout the evangelical world. Because of its dominant French
Catholic culture, the province of Quebec in Canada was a special case.
Similarly in Ireland, where the Protestant Reformation had been rejected,
Roman Catholics constituted the majority of the population. Both they
and the Protestant minority maintained strictly observed religious identities,
with the result that sectarian division was endemic to the everyday culture of
the Irish people.[30] Evangelicals – mainly Presbyterians and Methodists, with
some Anglicans – were distinctly non-Roman in their religion and opposed
to the conception of the Irish nation as Catholic. Ongoing agitation for Irish
Home Rule sustained widespread sympathy for Ulster Protestantism. Irish immigration during the nineteenth century transplanted these religious differences
between Protestants and Catholics to cities in other parts of Britain and
the settler societies of 'Greater Britain' and America.[31] Notwithstanding the
encroachment of 'high church' practices on church culture, even beyond
the Anglican churches,[32] overt hostility towards Catholicism remained a
defining part of the evangelical way of life, contributing to the sectarianism
of the societies in which evangelicals lived, but also strengthening their own
shared identity.

History and eschatology

History was another source of identity for evangelicals in the life of faith. From
the Bible they received a providentialist framework for understanding world
history into which they had fitted their own stories.[33] In the *fin de siècle* years they
extended this part of their tradition by writing historical accounts of persons,
institutions, denominations, groups and factions, the movement and the church

30. Donald Akenson, *Small Differences: Irish Catholics and Irish Protestants 1815–1922*
    (Montreal: McGill-Queen's University Press, 1988), esp. 140–147.

31. Philomena Sutherland, 'Sectarianism and Evangelicalism in Birmingham
    and Liverpool', in John Wolffe (ed.), *Protestant–Catholic Conflict from the
    Reformation to the Twenty-First Century* (Houndmills: Palgrave Macmillan, 2013),
    132–165.

32. D. W. Bebbington, *Evangelicalism in Modern Britain: A History from the 1730s to the
    1980s* (London: Unwin Hyman, 1989), 203–207.

33. Stuart Piggin, 'Evangelicalism and Contemporary History: The Revival Chronicles
    of the 1740s', *L* 14 (1992), 1–26.

itself.[34] These histories grounded evangelicalism by establishing lineages from Christian beginnings, the Reformation and the evangelical revival itself. They celebrated achievement, reinforced beliefs and values, justified attitudes and conduct, and adumbrated desirable futures. They did so by affirming the continued progress of the gospel, God's use of means rather than direct intervention and his sovereignty over all things. While marred by the defects that inevitably attend confessional and apologetic agendas, the shared narrative of the histories vindicated evangelicals' status as agents of gospel progress and countered discouragement in the face of dismissal by the modern world.

One reason for the uplifting effects of historical thinking by evangelicals was its cosmic scope. The Bible took their interest beyond the mundane and fixed their attention on the parousia, the second coming of Christ, as the destination of history. That Jesus would come again and make all things right was an assurance held in common by all evangelicals. Their eschatological orientation included an interest in the millennium, an end time of liberation from godless worldliness lasting a thousand years before the end foretold in Revelation 20. While perhaps once a 'non-essential' evangelical doctrine, in the course of the nineteenth century it had risen in importance in the minds of an influential minority. Attitudes to the millennium divided evangelicals into two main camps.

Since the beginning of the movement, the standard view of the end times among evangelicals was that Christ's return would follow the millennium. Post-millennialism was still widely influential around 1900, in large measure because it chimed with the optimistic mood of the *fin de siècle*.[35] In this perspective, modern civilization was seen as a blessing, pregnant with great possibilities as the providential plan was realized. Science and technology were signs of the benevolence of God and bearers of his will for the world. His activity in history was therefore through observable and rational means. The role of Christians was to work with these means, lead faithful lives and in particular to evangelize the world. Similarly, the church was God's agent to bring in the kingdom that would be established on earth but continue into eternity. These attitudes seemed to provide the warrants for use of rational management, business-like organization

---

34. Notable histories and biographies written at this time include J. Wilbur Chapman, *The Life and Work of Dwight L. Moody* (London: James Nisbet, 1900); Eugene Stock, *A History of the Church Missionary Society: Its Environment, Its Men and Its Work*, 3 vols. (London: CMS, 1899); G. R. Balleine, *A History of the Evangelical Party in the Church of England* (London: Longmans, Green, 1908).

35. James H. Moorhead, *World Without End: Mainstream American Protestant Visions of the Last Things, 1880–1925* (Bloomington: Indiana University Press, 1999).

and scientific expertise. Although time was bounded, the associated notions of ongoing process and indefinite improvement meant that there was little reason to think that the end was near. Although the new century soon brought evidence that the future would not be untroubled, the prospect of the end of history was less discussed in this segment of eschatological thinking than it had been a generation or two previously.

While still the generally held view of the end times, increasingly post-millennialism was challenged by the view that placed the second coming before the millennium.[36] Premillennialism had been a rising force within the evangelical movement since the 1820s, but across the second half of the nineteenth century it was urged with greater definitional clarity, historical particularity and emotional intensity. In this perspective modern civilization was a cause of deep *Angst*, with the present age becoming worse and worse. Science and technology were a denial of the supernatural and the bases of unbelief and secularism. Although transcendent, God was no less active in history, but the providential plan was one of decline leading to crisis. The role of Christians was again to be faithful, especially by preaching the gospel that offered deliverance from this sinful order. Even the church from this standpoint was condemned as unfaithful and under God's judgement. Only divine intervention in the second coming could bring in the millennium. If the sense of the end had diminished in postmillennialism, in premillennialism it was intensified and dramatized. History was therefore far from benign, but pretensions to cultural authority arose among premillennialists from understanding history's true meaning and dispensing the means to an appropriate response. Such was the appeal of premillennialism that, by the turn of the century, it had become the characteristic position of the evangelical centre-right, attracting even mainstream figures such as the Englishman Handley Moule, from 1901 the Bishop of Durham.[37]

An important development within the premillennial camp that came to prominence with the publication of the *Scofield Reference Bible* in 1909 was

---

36. The remainder of the section is based on Matthew A. Sutton, *American Apocalypse: A History of Modern Evangelicalism* (Cambridge, MA: Belknap Press, 2014), ch. 1; Crawford Gribben and Andrew R. Holmes (eds.), *Protestant Millennialism, Evangelicalism and Irish Society, 1790–2005* (Houndmills: Palgrave Macmillan, 2006).

37. Joel A. Carpenter (ed.), *The Premillennial Second Coming: Two Early Champions* (New York: Garland Publishing, 1988); John B. Harford and Frederick C. MacDonald, *Handley Carr Glyn Moule, Bishop of Durham: A Biography* (London: Hodder & Stoughton, n.d. [1922]), 296–297.

dispensationalism.[38] This refinement differed from traditional premillennialism in maintaining that all of the prophecies about the latter days were still to be fulfilled. Begun by one of the early leaders of the Brethren, the Irish-born John Nelson Darby, this 'futurist' premillennialism divided history into eras or dispensations according to the development in God's plan each embodied. The scheme posited a radical disjunction between Israel and the church, and held that the present era of the church was a parenthesis. It also introduced the expectation of the rapture, an earlier stage of Christ's return when he would come for the believers of the present dispensation, resurrecting dead Christians and snatching away the living. This expectation meant in effect that Christ would come twice, first and secretly to rapture his chosen and secondly to inaugurate the millennium. Populist, strident, defensive and even separatist, premillennial dispensationalists challenged the evangelical movement as a whole by their claim to be the true representatives of biblical teaching. By the time war broke out in 1914, disagreement about how the Bible should be read as the key to history was probably the most powerful solvent acting on the 'evangelical coalition'.

Gender and race

Outwardly the evangelical devotional life and the life of the churches as places of spiritual development were intended for all. In neither were there acknow-ledged distinctions between men and women. This was in keeping with the Reformation doctrine of the priesthood of all believers and the general expect-ation that all would participate in the life of the movement. Yet, at the operational level, the churches appeared to be male dominated. They were led by men, and the great majority of writers were men. However, in the course of the nineteenth century the role of women in evangelicalism changed in that they became predominant in number and influence. These apparently contradictory features of the movement reflected the gender traits of *fin de siècle* evangelical culture and also the inevitable effect of social structures on the life of faith.[39]

At the turn of the century the life of faith was certainly being masculinized. Coming out for Christ was strikingly presented by the revivalists as the manly

---

38. R. Todd Mangum and Mark S. Sweetnam, *The Scofield Bible: Its History and Impact on the Evangelical Church* (Colorado Springs: Paternoster Press, 2009).

39. This section draws on Sarah C. Williams, 'Evangelicals and Gender', in Donald M. Lewis and Richard V. Pierard (eds.), *Global Evangelicalism: Theology, History and Culture in Regional Perspective* (Downers Grove: IVP Academic, 2014), 270–295.

thing to do. The life that followed – the life of resisting the temptations of the
world, remaining true to Christian commitment and engaging in service – was
similarly promoted as fitting for men. A range of influences and motives came
together to produce this exaltation of masculinity within contemporary evangelicalism. It was clearly a response to the so-called 'woman problem', the
domination of contemporary Christianity by women. It was also intended to
counteract sloth and weakness, which were said to be among the effects of
urbanization. As the missionary leaders pointed out, only more robust male
qualities would be able to make the most of the opportunities of the *fin de siècle*
world. Around 1900 the militarism of the churches in the high Victorian years
had blended with muscular Christianity to produce a religiosity calculated both
to appeal to men and also to make use of their distinctive qualities.[40]

This emphasis on masculinity was a channel for the contemporary upsurge
of conversionist evangelicalism as a high-demand religion. The mission field
was promoted as the preferred career choice for a life of manly service. Against
the tendency to see it as effeminate, the ministry too was presented as a sphere
for the application of Christian manliness. But, plainly, these occupations were
neither available to nor suitable for all. The ideal was transferrable to any walk
of life, such as politics, the law and business.[41] Similarly evangelical men were
also expected to meet the demands of faith in their domestic life. Male responsibility at this level included establishing and maintaining a home, protecting and
providing for it, and overseeing its spiritual life. Raising sons to responsible
adulthood was an extension of this role, which provided for the future of the
family, the church and society at large. This wide-ranging aspect of the evangelical male's life subverts the dichotomy at the root of the historiographical
stereotype that there were 'separate spheres' for men and women. Public life
was important for evangelical men, but private life was no less so.

Recognition of the importance of the evangelical woman for modern
Christianity further weakens the 'two spheres' stereotype.[42] As the embodiment

40. Clifford Putney, *Muscular Christianity: Manhood and Sports in Protestant America, 1880–
    1920* (Cambridge, Mass.: Harvard University Press, 2001); Ann Taves, 'Feminization
    Revisited. Protestantism and Gender at the Turn of the Century', in M. Bendroth
    and L. Brereton (eds.), *Women and Twentieth-Century Protestantism* (Urbana: University
    of Illinois Press, 2002), 304–324.

41. Deryck W. Lovegrove (ed.), *The Rise of the Laity in Evangelical Protestantism* (London:
    Routledge, 2002), 'Introduction'.

42. Chiefly by Callum Brown, *The Death of Christian Britain: Understanding Secularisation
    1800–2000* (London: Routledge, 2001), ch. 4.

of piety in her role as wife and mother, the future of evangelicalism was seen to depend on her. To the extent that this reproduced the moral qualities on which society depended – thrift, honesty, sobriety, self-discipline – the female sphere was necessary for the well-being of the public domain. For this reason the woman's role was not circumscribed by the home, but it remained a vital site for the exercise of evangelical spirituality. Women themselves, it was thought, wished to be wives, mothers and homemakers.

Exalting the home and domestic life did not of course preclude active participation in their churches. As individuals and through their own organizations, women contributed to church life. The Woman's Missionary Union of the Southern Baptist Convention, formed in 1888 to support missionary work at home and abroad, demonstrated the capacity of women in church life while upholding the gender conventions of their denomination.[43] Other organizations, such as the YWCA and the Mothers' Union, provided women with opportunities to use their gifts and skills.[44] The deaconess movement, widely embraced in the 1890s, provided a recognized institutional role in the churches for women.[45] More tellingly, exaltation of the domestic ideal seemed to require wider engagement by women. The Woman's Christian Temperance Union – begun in 1883 – pushed into the public sphere to protect home life from the destructive effects of alcohol.[46] Social needs on the mission field enabled women to function as teachers, social workers, nurses and even as doctors. Certainly their churches were a bridge from the home to the world beyond.

At the turn of the century the evangelical movement seemed also to provide considerable scope for women to exercise genuine leadership. With ordination still not generally open to women, the leadership of churches was not an option.

---

43. Paul Harvey, 'Saints but Not Subordinates: The Woman's Missionary Union of the Southern Baptist Convention', in Bendroth and Brereton, *Women and Twentieth-Century Protestantism*, 4–24.

44. Anne O'Brien, *God's Willing Workers: Women and Religion in Australia* (Sydney: University of New South Wales Press, 2005), esp. 68–73.

45. Karyn-Maree Piercy, 'Patient and Enduring Love: The Deaconess Movement, 1900–1920', in John Stenhouse and Jane Thompson (eds.), *Building God's Own Country: Historical Essays on Religions in New Zealand* (Dunedin: University of Otago Press, 2004), 196–208.

46. Ian Tyrrell, *Woman's World/Woman's Empire: The Woman's Christian Temperance Union in International Perspective, 1880–1930* (Chapel Hill: University of North Carolina Press, 1991).

By admitting women to unusually prominent leadership roles, the Salvation Army was perhaps one exception that proved the rule. But apart from the churches women took a number of significant parts. Nearing the end of her life in 1900, Josephine Butler had led a movement for political and social reform for more than a quarter of a century. The 'woman evangelist' Emilia Baeyertz was a prominent revivalist from about 1880 to the mid-1920s. Where manifest giftedness was matched with opportunity, within the limits of organizational constraint, the cause of the gospel demanded that women be allowed to make their contribution.[47]

The attitudes of the time towards race had a much greater limiting effect than gender on the evangelical way of life as a reproduction of New Testament Christianity. This was in part because, on the surface, race was not a pressing issue in English-speaking societies. Rarely avowedly racist but luxuriating in their national, British and Anglo-Saxon identities, turn-of-the-century white evangelicals largely accepted the racial assumptions of the communities in which they lived. The presumption of white supremacy was readily bolstered and directed by their sense of the call from Providence to Christianize and civilize the world. There was some awareness of Acts 17:26 and what it might mean for racial relations. But around 1900 it made little practical difference, even in those places where the race question could not be ignored.

With white people dominant in their communities, African Americans and dispossessed indigenous populations throughout 'Greater Britain' were largely segregated or marginalized and often impoverished. These people generally fitted in with the social arrangements prescribed by whites. They were obliged either to accept paternalistic provision in their religious lives or to form their own churches, which developed along several different lines. Some African Christians embraced the ideals of 'Ethiopianism' and adhered to the beliefs and practices of the white churches under native leadership. African American churches tended to create their own expressions of evangelicalism characterized by otherworldliness blended with practicality, conservative beliefs and their distinctive worship and music. Evangelicals were among those who crossed or minimized racial divides to bring salvation and social amelioration, but overall the life of faith in the early twentieth century was too bound up with white

---

47. Andrew Mark Eason, *Women in God's Army: Gender and Equality in the Early Salvation Army* (Waterloo: Wilfrid Laurier University Press, 2003); Robert Evans, *Emilia Baeyertz Evangelist* (Hazelbrook, NSW: Research in Evangelical Revivals, 2007).

supremacy to counter the racist ideology of English-speaking societies in the name of Christ.[48]

Holiness

For all evangelicals – male and female, of all ethnic groups – the aim of the life of faith was spiritual and moral progress towards a Christlike perfection. Such progress was to be expected from growth in understanding and deepening of experience resulting from devotional discipline. The theological term for this development was 'sanctification'. While a biblical concept, its meaning had always been much debated in the evangelical movement.[49] Interpreted narrowly, it referred to growth in holiness; more broadly, it meant spiritual advancement and increased effectiveness. Importantly sanctification denoted continuation of the reality of conversion, and furnished thereby assurance of salvation.

However understood, the principal obstacle to sanctification was sin, taken at the turn of the century to mean primarily a general condition of rebelliousness against God and particular acts of disobedience to the moral and spiritual teaching of the Bible. The functioning of evangelicalism as a social activity meant too that contemporary taboos were also presented as sin. While not condemned by all evangelicals, primarily these were consumption of alcohol, dancing, card playing and gambling in all its other forms. As the strictures of the revivalists made clear, avoidance of these behaviours was effectively a condition of participation in the movement. Evangelical leaders worried that the sense of personal sin was in decline, but they derived some reassurance from a rising awareness of national sin.[50] Combating sin in all of its forms was the perennial condition of spiritual vitality and effectiveness, for the

---

48. Steve De Gruchy, 'Religion and Racism: Struggles Around Segregation, "Jim Crow" and Apartheid', in *CHC9*, 385–400; Ogbu Kalu, 'Africa', in Lewis and Pierard, *Global Evangelicalism*, 125–165; Nancy Christie and Michael Gauvreau, *Christian Churches and Their Peoples, 1840–1965: A Social History of Religion in Canada* (Toronto: University of Toronto Press, 2010), ch. 3; Allan Davidson, *Christianity in Aotearoa: A History of Church and Society in New Zealand*, 3rd ed. (Wellington: Education for Ministry, 2004), chs. 5, 13; John Harris, *One Blood. 200 Years of Aboriginal Encounter with Christianity: A Story of Hope* (Sutherland: Albatross Books, 1994), ch. 9.

49. Stanley N. Grundy (ed.), *Five Views on Sanctification* (Grand Rapids: Zondervan, 1987).

50. E.g. R. C. Gillie, 'Problems of the Spiritual Life', *RPC 1913*, 208–209.

movement as a whole in relation to society at large as well as for individual participants.

During the final decades of the nineteenth century the desire for progress in the life of faith gave rise to an intense interest in the condition of holiness that continued to grow in the *fin de siècle* years.[51] Understood primarily as inward moral perfection and outward devotion and service, like almost everything else within the contemporary evangelical movement, the attainment of holiness was understood in a variety of ways. The oldest expression of the ideal was the word-centred understanding descending from Calvin and the Puritans. As maintained by evangelicals in the Reformed stream, holiness was a matter of perennial struggle to obey the commands and cultivate the virtues of the Bible, shunning sin and seeking Christlikeness. A creation of evangelicalism itself was the seemingly more hopeful Methodist view originating with John Wesley. Although now referred to increasingly as 'full salvation', 'entire sanctification', according to which, after a period of striving, sin and sinfulness could be eradicated from the human heart by love of God and other people, remained the dominant view among Methodists around 1900. The most recent expression was the blend of the Reformed and the Wesleyan approaches promoted in the final decades of the nineteenth century through the Keswick movement. Received in an instant, 'sanctification by faith' (like conversion itself) turned on giving up personal effort and trusting in Christ. It did not entail the eradication of sin, but it did involve a definite transaction with God in which the believer undertook to rest in supernatural power to diminish sin in his or her life. Its slogan 'let go, and let God' explains its appeal.

Although it never replaced the others, the rising dominance of the Keswick approach was evident in its internationalization at the turn of the century.[52] Having been held since 1875 in the lakeside village of Keswick in the north-west of England, around 1900, conferences reproducing its brand of spirituality were spreading through the evangelical world. In Britain counterparts to Keswick were established throughout England, Scotland, Wales and Ireland. From around 1890 it was taken abroad. The evangelist George Grubb planted it in Australia at Geelong in Victoria in 1891. In 1903 the Katoomba Convention was established for Sydney. The hegemonic nature of Keswick spirituality was

---

51. Bebbington, *Evangelicalism in Modern Britain*, ch. 5; *Holiness in Nineteenth-Century England* (Carlisle: Paternoster Press, 2000). The ideal found its most able expositor in Peter T. Forsyth. E.g. Peter. T. Forsyth, *Christian Perfection* (London: Hodder & Stoughton, 1899).

52. Charles Price and Ian Randall, *Transforming Keswick* (Carlisle: OM Publishing, 2000).

shown by the way it took over the Northfield Conference established in 1886 by D. L. Moody, largely under the influence of English speakers such as F. B. Meyer and George Campbell Morgan during the *fin de siècle* years. In 1913 Charles Trumbull established an American version. This network of conferences, together with the flood of literature it produced, spread the Keswick ideal of 'holiness by faith' around the world in a form of evangelical cultural diffusion surpassed at the time only by the movement's hymns. It also provided the framework for the development of the victorious life ideal and the exaltation of character, both of which were promoted extensively in the conventions and evangelical educational institutions. The promised benefits were the evangelical virtues of spiritual capacity and effectiveness: within, in the overcoming of sin; and without, in lives of Christian service.[53]

Despite its pervasiveness, the new holiness teaching did not go uncontested. Among the legacies left by J. C. Ryle when he died in 1900 was his book on holiness, first published in 1877 and enlarged two years later.[54] While he doubted whether 'higher life' meetings actually produced increases in practical holiness, Ryle opposed Keswick's vague language, severance of the nexus between conversion and consecration and the prospect of attaining perfection in this life. In their place he reasserted the traditional Reformed understanding of the life of faith as relentless personal exertion directed by specific biblical teaching. Above all he upheld the view that the sinful nature is improved under the influence of the Holy Spirit over the Keswick claim that it is replaced by the indwelling Christ. The case against the 'very dubious' conceptions of Keswick was sustained in the first decades of the twentieth century by the Princeton Seminary professor Benjamin Warfield. Like Ryle, he opposed any suggestion of a 'second conversion' and displacement of the need for struggle and perseverance. Despite the claim to 'higher life', he contended further that Keswick fed off superficial views of sin and sinning and offered a weak view of holiness as 'mere ease in Zion'. Perhaps worst of all, its transformation of 'trust' into a 'work' made it a paradoxically man-centred approach and negated its own claim to 'complete dependence on God'.[55] Although prepared to attend higher-life conferences,

---

53. Douglas W. Frank, *Less Than Conquerors: How Evangelicals Entered the Twentieth Century* (Grand Rapids: Eerdmans, 1986).

54. J. C. Ryle, *Holiness: Its Nature, Hindrances, Difficulties and Roots* . . ., enlarged ed. (London: William Hunt, 1879); Bebbington, *Evangelicalism in Modern Britain*, 170–171; *Dominance of Evangelicalism*, 194–197.

55. Benjamin Warfield, *Perfectionism*, 2 vols. (New York: Oxford University Press, 1931), II, 463–558 (quotations on 555).

other evangelicals – Torrey among them – preferred the idea of continual struggle over the apparent passivity of Keswick teaching as the true biblical teaching. Against its rising popularity, Reformed evangelicals continued to make available a vigorously argued alternative to the Keswick version of 'scriptural holiness'.

Baptism of the Holy Spirit and the birth of modern Pentecostalism

A significant effect of the holiness milieu and its quest for spiritual renewal and power in the later nineteenth century was an intense interest in the Holy Spirit, the more remarkable for its neglect in other traditions of Christianity. Beginning with the Methodist William Arthur's *The Tongue of Fire* (1856), there was subsequently a remarkable flow of books on the subject from the evangelical presses, which came to something of a climax around 1900. This burgeoning literature was a sign that a large cohort of *fin de siècle* evangelicals, intent upon success in the life of faith, was determined to recover the theology and presence of the Holy Spirit.[56]

An important by-product of this pneumatological interest was talk about 'pentecostal experience', and in particular about the New Testament idea of the 'baptism of the Holy Spirit'.[57] While some evangelicals denied that this experience was still available, others were equally insistent that modern-day believers could receive the baptism. Yet, as with holiness, this conviction supported rival proposals for what was involved. In mainstream Wesleyan teaching, the baptism of the Holy Spirit was the name given to the post-conversion crisis experience that brought the will of the believer into a state of complete conformity with the will of God. Newly presented in Pentecostal language, this was what John Wesley had called 'perfect love', and it was available to all believers who sought it. This perspective spawned a more radical interpretation that differentiated between sanctification and the baptism of the Spirit as two distinct works of grace. The shift accommodated greater emphasis on spiritual gifts and power, and eventually produced a 'three blessings' interpretation (conversion, sanctification and the baptism). At the same time more Reformed evangelicals narrowed the perspective by interpreting the baptism as a 'special enduement for service'

---

56. Grant Wacker, 'The Holy Spirit and the Spirit of the Age in American Protestantism, 1880–1910', *JAH* 72 (1985), 45–62.

57. Donald Dayton, *Theological Roots of Pentecostalism* (Metuchen, NJ: Scarecrow Press, 1987), ch. 4.

rather than as a cleansing experience.[58] But, more important than the differences themselves was the discussion that sustained the preoccupation with the doctrine. *Fin de siècle* evangelicals were intent on tapping the full meaning of the baptism of the Holy Spirit.

Evangelical perspectives on baptism in the Holy Spirit were differentiated still further on the very first day of the twentieth century. At the Bethel Bible School and Healing Home in Topeka, Kansas, the founder and principal, Charles Fox Parham, laid his hands upon Agnes Ozman. He later recalled: 'I had scarcely completed three dozen sentences when a glory fell upon her, a halo seemed to surround her head and face, and she began speaking in the Chinese language and was unable to speak English for three days.' In the days that followed, the students of the Bethel Bible School are reported to have spoken in twenty-one known languages. It was an episode of some significance for world Christianity in the twentieth century. Although anticipated by similar events in Portland, Victoria, in the 1870s and at a camp meeting in Cherokee County, North Carolina, in 1896, it marked the advent of the baptism of the Holy Spirit as evidenced by speaking in tongues as a new feature in the evangelical tradition, and the beginning of modern Pentecostalism.[59]

While it began in the American Midwest, the decisive development in the rise of Pentecostalism took place from 1906 to 1909 at Azusa Street in Los Angeles, where one of Parham's protégés, the black holiness preacher William Seymour, conducted well-attended spontaneous and emotional meetings that often ran continuously from early morning until late at night. The meetings, which were characterized by tongues speaking and other ecstatic behaviour as well as disregard for conventional racial distinctions, were hailed as a second Pentecost and interpreted as the revival that would inaugurate the end times and the return of Christ. In the wake of the recent revival in Wales, thousands from all over the world flocked to Azusa Street as word of what God was doing spread largely through the reports in Seymour's own periodical *The Apostolic Faith* and those of participant-observer Frank Bartleman. Azusa Street became the symbolic centre of incipient Pentecostalism.[60]

---

58. John Fea, 'Power from on High in an Age of Ecclesiastical Impotence: The "Enduement of the Holy Spirit" in American Fundamentalist Thought, 1880–1936', *FH* 26.2 (1994), 23–35.

59. Vincent Synan, *The Century of the Holy Spirit: 100 Years of Pentecostal and Charismatic Renewal, 1901–2000* (Nashville: Thomas Nelson, 2001), ch. 3 (quotation on 44).

60. Joe Creech, 'Visions of Glory: The Place of the Azusa Street Revival in Pentecostal History', *CH* 65.3 (1996), 405–424.

Many of the thousands of visitors who flocked to Azusa Street to witness
the apparent restoration of New Testament Christianity returned to their
churches and began their own revivals. In other cases the connection was more
substantial. While Florence Crawford broke away from Azusa Street, her experience enabled her to establish an independent church in Portland, Oregon.
William Durham, baptized at Azusa Street, set up an important Pentecostal
ministry in North Avenue, Chicago, which had a deep influence on the development of Pentecostalism in Canada. News of the outpouring of the Holy
Spirit also stimulated isolated revivals at numerous points around America
that had no direct contact with Azusa Street. Directly and indirectly Azusa
Street engendered a small but distinct Pentecostal subculture in American
evangelicalism.[61]

It was by no means an isolated phenomenon. Pentecostalism began in Canada
from the Hebden Street Mission in Toronto, so named after its founder, Ellen
Hebden, who had the new experience of Spirit baptism in private in November
1906. Australian Pentecostalism was similarly indigenous. It commenced in 1908
when Janet Lancaster, having been baptized in the Spirit, established the Good
News Hall in North Melbourne as a centre of preaching, evangelism and mission.
The seminal point in Britain was All Saints Church in Sunderland where the
rector, Alexander Boddy, who had his experience of Spirit baptism in Christiania
in Norway, conducted annual Whitsuntide conventions for those in sympathy
with tongues speaking. A product of the pervasive holiness culture in evangelicalism, Pentecostal outbursts occurred around the world independently of
Azusa Street.[62]

The rapid spread of Pentecostalism reflected the appeal of the new
movement. Much has been made of the lower-class origins of the first Pentecostals.[63] For these men and women Pentecostalism was ostensibly compensation
for social and economic deprivation. This sociological observation explains the
adherence of some, but not all, for the appeal of Pentecostalism transcended

---

61. Grant Wacker, *Heaven Below: Early Pentecostals and American Culture* (Cambridge, MA:
    Harvard University Press, 2001).

62. Barry Chant, *The Spirit of Pentecost: The Origins and Development of the Pentecostal
    Movement in Australia 1870–1939* (Lexington: Emeth Press, 2011); James Robinson,
    Pentecostal Origins: Early Pentecostalism in Ireland in the Context of the British Isles (Milton
    Keynes: Paternoster Press, 2005); Michael Wilkinson (ed.), *Canadian Pentecostalism:
    Transition and Transformation* (Montreal: McGill-Queen's University Press, 2009).

63. Classically by Robert Mapes Anderson, *Vision of the Disinherited: The Making of
    American Pentecostalism* (New York: Oxford University Press, 1979), esp. chs. 7, 12.

class differences.[64] Similarly, while many of the early leaders were not accomplished, others were highly educated and already well established in society. Alexander Boddy was an Anglican clergyman, while the British evangelist Smith Wigglesworth was a successful small businessman. Their stories indicate that they were drawn by the phenomena of the movement. Its manifest spiritual vitality provided what they had looked forward to as members of holiness communities. Ecstatic and other physical expression satisfied emotional needs not otherwise catered for in experiential evangelicalism. Reproduction of phenomena described in the Bible proffered an experience of authentic biblical religion. Construction of Pentecostalism as fulfilment of eschatological prophecy added a sense of personal and collective importance among Pentecostals. These primitivist impulses were both served and spread by the peripatetic preaching and teaching that facilitated the emergence of networks. Meetings such as the Bradford Convention, which began in 1909, fulfilled a propagating function similar to that of Keswick and its many offshoot conventions. Intensified experientialism coupled with the entrepreneurial and organizational flair of capable leaders engendered the early effulgence of Pentecostalism.

From the first, Pentecostalism added to the diversity of the evangelical movement. Subgroups rapidly emerged because disagreements over doctrine and experience were both rife and passionate.[65] Further impetus to definition and organization came from the fierce opposition of other evangelicals. In England the reaction was almost immediate.[66] Most of it came from within the holiness community itself, where proponents of different interpretations of the baptism of the Holy Spirit condemned the new view. In time more doctrinally attuned evangelicals such as Robert Anderson joined the charge. In America, although slower to come, the criticism was no less vehement.[67] The polemic against 'the tongues movement' ran along five main lines: (1) as a Pentecostal experience it was trivial and inauthentic; (2) it was satanic rather than a real work

---

64. The remainder of the paragraph is based on Timothy B. Walsh, *To Meet and Satisfy a Very Hungry People: The Origins and Fortunes of English Pentecostalism, 1907–1925* (Milton Keynes: Paternoster Press, 2012), esp. sects. 1, 2.

65. Edith L. Blumhofer, *The Assemblies of God: A Chapter in the Story of American Pentecostalism*, 2 vols. (Springfield: Gospel Publishing House, 1989), I, chs. 9–10.

66. Timothy B. Walsh, '"Signs and Wonders That Lie": Unlikely Polemical Outbursts Against the Early Pentecostal Movement in Britain', *SCH* 41 (2005), 410–422.

67. Grant Wacker, 'Travail of a Broken Family: Evangelical Responses to Pentecostalism in America, 1906–1916', *JEH* 47.3 (1996), 505–528; Blumhofer, *Assemblies of God*, I, ch. 8.

of God; (3) an overreaction against worldliness, it was fanaticism; (4) it was also carnal and especially weakened the commitment to marriage; and (5) above all, its understanding of the baptism of the Holy Spirit was mistaken. Of course Pentecostals had answers to each charge, but evangelicals at large were unpersuaded. As Pentecostals made their bid to join the wider evangelical community, it closed ranks against them as it had done earlier against other 'aberrant' developments such as Christian Science. Although at this point existing only on the margins, the birth of Pentecostalism produced a new layer of diversity and a further source of tension within the *fin de siècle* evangelical movement.

Conclusion

At the turn of the century evangelicals evinced a way of life that demonstrated how the consequences of conversion are appropriated individually and collectively. They did so by the practice of a devotional ethic that turned on dedication of time for Bible reading, prayer, churchgoing and association with like-minded men and women, all of which were understood in the context of an eschatological interpretation of history. Sustaining this pattern of behaviour were the twin motives of countering neglect and the desire to realize the fullness of spiritual power and effectiveness. The resultant culture was an extension of conversion not only as the means of bringing conversion to completion, but also as a presentation to the wider society of a better way than that society's perceived indifference to Christianity, love of luxury in an age of rising consumerism and preoccupation with pleasure seeking. These drivers engendered a period of high levels of spiritual engagement and innovation that produced new perspectives and practices in the life of faith.

Although a further sign of the liveliness of *fin de siècle* evangelicalism, the increasing diversity of the movement also fuelled tendencies to separatism that undermined the evangelical synthesis. Innovation was interpreted by some as faithlessness. Of the new developments, the most significant for the longer term was Pentecostalism. Although still only a tiny fragment of the evangelical movement by 1914, it demonstrated the capacity of evangelicalism to generate new expressions of the life of faith that were unsettling for the majority of adherents. For the present the most important was millennial speculation, which at one and the same time maintained tension with the sociocultural environment and also challenged evangelicals more interested in adapting their religion to modern conditions. Like Pentecostalism, but over a wider front, it evinced afresh the dynamism and creativity of evangelicalism but also its inherent instability.

The effect, however, was offset by other aspects of evangelical identity – principally entrenched anti-Catholicism – that encouraged the ecumenist tendency of evangelical culture and helped to hold the evangelical coalition together. Such currents and countercurrents were not uncommon in the flow of the life of faith, but during the *fin de siècle* they sustained a vibrant if contentious religious culture as evangelicals worked out the consequences of conversion in the modern world in both formal religious settings and the mundane circumstances of their daily lives.

4. THEOLOGICAL NARROWING AND BROADENING

From the beginning the evangelical impulse spawned a distinctive theology as the movement's best minds analysed the experience of conversion, the life of faith and received Christian doctrines. If none had surpassed the first great evangelical intellectual, Jonathan Edwards, for acumen and its first great leader, John Wesley, for range of coverage, others had continued the task of theological reflection over the following century and a half. This was due in part to the need for clarity. Christian belief must be intelligible, compelling and readily applicable to life. It was also due in part to the need to maintain their theological tradition for transmission to new generations of teachers and ministers, and to educate their communities in the precepts of evangelical belief and culture. In their own way the intellectuals were activists, reaching out to society by elaborating evangelical theology with a view to defending and extending the influence of evangelicalism on their communities.

Around 1900 there was no other area of evangelical life that felt the disruptiveness of modernization more keenly. The 'new knowledge' of the day embodied a far-reaching transformation of human thought that presented a profound challenge to the presumptions of evangelical thought and culture. It included the 'higher criticism', which opposed the view of the Bible as the unique Word of God with an alternative reading as a collection of historically contingent documents. Scientific naturalism challenged the two-tiered universe presupposed by divine transcendence with a unitary system governed by natural law. The new discipline of comparative religion and the incipient social sciences made the uniqueness of Christianity harder to maintain. Together these developments undermined the supernaturalism at the heart of the evangelical system and prompted within Protestant Christianity a divergence between modernists and anti-modernists that pulled evangelicals in opposite directions. Intellectually the movement was probably better placed to deal with the crisis than at any previous point in its history. For the modernization of theological and biblical scholarship had coincided with the professionalization of the clergy and the upgrading of theological education.[1] As a result there were more evangelical theologians and Bible scholars at work in a greater number of church colleges and other academic institutions in the anglophone world than ever before. In carrying out the normal functions of evangelical theology, their particular responsibility was to secure the continued salience and authority of evangelical thought and teaching at a critical juncture.

Narrowing: towards fundamentalism

What many at the time would have taken as the traditional evangelical view of the Bible was strongly reasserted by Torrey. Part of his revivalist presentation was a pugnacious series of 'Bible Study' addresses titled 'Why I Believe the Bible is the Word of God'. Torrey's ten reasons grounded the belief that the Bible is inspired and inerrant, and thus truthful, entirely trustworthy and, interpreted literally, plain in its message. According to this assessment, the Bible offered certain knowledge in a comprehensive account of the world and God's relationship with humanity.[2] It positioned Torrey for his life and ministry, enabling him to speak with the authority of God in drawing out the teaching of the Bible for belief and practice. Having flirted with higher criticism early in his career, Torrey sustained a vigorous polemic against it for the rest of his life.[3] His

---

1. D. G. Hart and R. Albert Mohler, Jr. (eds.), *Theological Education in the Evangelical Tradition* (Grand Rapids: Baker Books, 1996).

2. R. A. Torrey, *Ten Reasons Why I Believe the Bible Is the Word of God* (Chicago: Bible Institute Colportage Association, 1898); *What the Bible Teaches: A Thorough and Comprehensive Study of All the Bible Has to Say Concerning the Great Doctrines of Which It Treats* (London: James Nisbet, n.d. [1898]).

3. Timothy E. W. Gloege, 'A Gilded Age Modernist: Reuben A. Torrey and the Roots of Contemporary Conservative Evangelicalism', in Darren Dochuk et al. (eds.), *American Evangelicalism: George Marsden and the State of American Religious History* (Notre Dame: University of Notre Dame Press, 2014), 199–229.

standpoint provided reassurance throughout the evangelical world. The Reverend A. Madsen reported as one of 'the golden beams' of the 1902 mission in Launceston, Tasmania:

> The simple appeal to Bible authority – not some clipped and isolated text, but the Gulf Stream of biblical teaching . . . has come as an irresistible inspiration to many of us preachers . . . The Divine Book will be preached in Launceston for years to come with a stronger conviction of its supreme and final authority.[4]

Like-minded leaders similarly promoted the dogmatic reading of the Bible in early twentieth-century evangelical communities around the world with force and dedication.[5]

This strident presentation of biblical authority was not confined to the popular side of the movement. At the Presbyterian Princeton Seminary in the decades spanning the turn of the century, the Professor of Didactic and Polemic Theology, Benjamin B. Warfield, built a strong intellectual defence of biblical inspiration as the authoritative basis of theology and Christian living. As he developed the case he was able to applaud Torrey's setting forth of the teaching of the Bible, but also found it necessary to suggest it could be done better by a truly inductive approach in place of the superficial aggregation of apparently relevant texts in Torrey's *What the Bible Teaches*.[6] In a series of more measured but no less assertive works, he presented the high view of inspiration and its effects in both its varied scriptural expressions and the unity of its historical development. Like Torrey, the target of Warfield's polemic was the higher criticism, but (in line with his conviction that the calling of Christianity was to reason its way to dominion) his aspiration was to meet defective with better scholarship, particularly by arguing from a starting point of Christianity as a supernatural, not a natural, religion. Again, in maintaining this position he was not alone. At Princeton his colleagues – John D. Davis and Robert D. Wilson for the Old Testament, William P. Armstrong and Caspar Wistar Hodge, Jr., for the New, and Geerhardus Vos for Biblical Theology – also presented a high

---

4. *The Torrey–Alexander Souvenir: A Complete Record of Their Work in Australia. A Special Souvenir Number of the 'Southern Cross'* (10 Sept. 1902), 56.

5. Kathleen C. Boone, *The Bible Tells Them So: The Discourse of Protestant Fundamentalism* (Albany: State University of New York Press, 1989).

6. 'R. A. Torrey', in Mark Noll (ed.), *The Princeton Theology 1812–1921: Scripture, Science, and Theological Method from Archibald Alexander to Benjamin Breckinridge Warfield* (Grand Rapids: Baker Books, 1983), 299–301.

view of biblical revelation in its various facets.[7] Bridging the domains of the
academy and populist evangelicalism, the work of the Princeton scholars was
welcomed in other parts of the world, mainly through *The Princeton Theological
Review* by which historic, particularly Reformed, Christianity was upheld and
propagated.

If not quite at one about what it meant, Torrey and Warfield were similarly
intent on defending this commitment to an inerrant Bible. The combination
of their militancy with belief in the absolute authority of Scripture and the
underlying suspicion of modern knowledge and intellectual processes represented an important development within the evangelical movement. It readily
appealed to a large and varied constituency of evangelicals – conservatives in
the main evangelical churches, Reformed propositionalists, premillennialists,
Brethren, Pentecostals – united on the right wing of the movement by the
need for an unambiguous conception of biblical authority. It has been
common to give the name 'proto-fundamentalism' to this *fin de siècle* disposition to protest against the undermining of biblically based orthodoxies
and traditions by theological innovation and adaptation. Given that fundamentalism emerged after the First World War, the term is anachronistic. The
implication that full-blown fundamentalism was the inevitable consequence
makes it also teleological. Historically it is more appropriate to speak of the
'fundamentalist impulse', a term that does not foreclose different out-
comes. Building since the 1870s, by 1900 it was a rising force in the evangelical
world.

Although the fundamentalist impulse was felt universally among evangelicals,
it was not experienced uniformly. Around 1900 it was most conspicuous and
developed in America where it was encouraged by the twin traditions of sectarian
dissent and 'unopposed revivalism'.[8] An amalgam of biblical infallibilism,
revivalist soul-winning, dispensational premillennialism and holiness pietism, it
was expressed beyond the local level through Bible study meetings and prophecy
conferences and had given rise to a loose group identity among leaders such as
A. C. Dixon, Charles Blanchard, James Gray, Isaac Haldeman and, of course,
Torrey. One of the group, the unaffiliated Arno C. Gaebelein, before 1914 still
'a leader with few followers', made explicit the disruptiveness inherent in

---

7. James H. Moorhead, *Princeton Seminary in American Religion and Culture* (Grand
   Rapids: Eerdmans, 2012), chs. 10–11.

8. George M. Marsden, *Fundamentalism and American Culture: The Shaping of Twentieth-
   Century Evangelicalism 1870–1925*, rev. ed. (Oxford: Oxford University Press, 2006),
   esp. xxiv, 223 for the quotation.

emerging fundamentalism when he called for separation from the worldly church.[9]

In Britain, where the fundamentalist impulse had been felt for much of the nineteenth century as a sense of embattlement in the face of liberalism (political and theological) and Catholicism (Roman and Anglican), primarily among Anglican evangelicals and Brethren, it was less definite. An intense super-naturalism, expressed as a commitment to the verbal inspiration of the Bible, premillennialism, Moodyist revivalism and Keswick spirituality, was non-controversial. More moderate and less influential than its American counterpart, around the turn of the century the fundamentalist impulse in Britain was more a presence than a force in the life of the evangelical churches.[10] By that time it had emerged throughout 'Greater Britain', in part because of the immigration of evangelical clergy and lay people from the UK and Ireland. In the colonies evangelicals evinced the same loyalty to their denominations that prevailed in their home countries.[11] Even in Canada, where the influence of the United States was strong, the British connection was determinative. Although inter-denominational alliances took shape to defend the Bible and related causes, here as elsewhere the separatism of the impulse was contained by the Protestant consensus.[12] At this stage more assertive than aggressive, the fundamentalist impulse was not yet a threat to the integrity of the evangelical movement.

Broadening: towards liberal evangelicalism

Not all evangelicals felt the same need to reject biblical higher criticism and the modern approach to knowledge it represented. Even within revivalist evan-gelicalism the line from D. L. Moody included the expansive Henry Drummond as well as Torrey. Drummond's influence was one reason for this alternative

---

9. Ibid. 127.

10. Ian S. Rennie, 'Fundamentalism and the Varieties of North Atlantic Evangelicalism', in Mark Noll et al. (eds.), *Evangelicalism: Comparative Studies of Popular Protestantism in North America, the British Isles, and Beyond* (New York: Oxford University Press, 1994), 333–350.

11. John Stenhouse, 'Fundamentalism and New Zealand Culture', in Bryan Gilling (ed.), *'Be Ye Separate': Fundamentalism and the New Zealand Experience* (Hamilton: University of Waikato and Colcom Press, 1992), 1–23.

12. Ronald Sawatsky, '"Looking for That Blessed Hope": The Roots of Fundamentalism in Canada, 1878–1914', PhD thesis, University of Toronto, 1985.

response becoming particularly strong in Scotland where it also coincided with
vivid memories of the condemnation of the Old Testament specialist William
Robertson Smith in the early 1880s.[13] In the final decades of the nineteenth
century numerous Scottish scholars in varying degrees found ways to emulate
Drummond and Robertson Smith by embracing the new biblical scholarship
in conjunction with substantially orthodox belief and received evangelical piety.
Outside Scotland, this combination appealed to those seeking ways of remaining
evangelical while also keeping in step with contemporary ideas and culture,
especially in relation to the problems raised by biblical criticism. Its advent,
announced on the eve of the *fin de siècle* by English Congregationalist R. W. Dale,
established a broadening dynamic in evangelicalism to countervail the narrowing
effect of the fundamentalist impulse.[14]

A lead in modern biblical interpretation within evangelicalism was provided
by Presbyterian Old Testament scholars. George Adam Smith in Scotland,
Charles Briggs in America and others elsewhere incurred the ire of their
denominations by producing major works of scholarship exhibiting the methods
of modern scholarship to counter the danger to faith in the modern world
posed by literal and unhistorical reading.[15] They also published general statements explaining how the critical approach enhanced the religious teaching
of the Bible. Smith in particular drew out the connection between scholarship
and the life of faith as a critical enterprise involving 'interests and responsibilities
which are not merely scholastic or historical, but thoroughly evangelical –
concerned with faith, and the assistance of souls in darkness, and the equipment
of the Church of Christ for her ministry of God's Word'.[16] Other Presbyterians
were not always convinced, and Smith and Briggs both faced heresy charges in
their denominations. The fact that neither was convicted indicated a growing

---

13. David W. Bebbington, *Evangelicalism in Modern Britain: A History from the 1730s to the
    1980s* (London: Unwin Hyman, 1989), 184–186.

14. R. W. Dale, *The Old Evangelicalism and the New* (London: Hodder & Stoughton,
    1889).

15. Matthew Bowman, *The Urban Pulpit: New York City and the Fate of Liberal
    Evangelicalism* (New York: Oxford University Press, 2014), ch. 3; Andrew R. Holmes,
    'Biblical Authority and the Impact of Higher Criticism in Irish Presbyterianism,
    ca. 1850–1930', *CH* 75.2 (2006), 343–373; Michael Gauvreau, *The Evangelical Century:
    College and Creed in English Canada from the Great Revival to the Great Depression*
    (Montreal: McGill-Queen's University Press, 1991), ch. 5.

16. George A. Smith, *Modern Criticism and the Preaching of the Old Testament* (London:
    Hodder & Stoughton, 1901), 23–28 (28 for the quotation).

acceptance that the evangelical tradition could be broadened to accommodate the new approach to the Bible.

Bringing biblical Christianity into due relation with modern knowledge was part of a larger task, the nature of which was clarified by its ablest advocate, the English Congregationalist P. T. Forsyth. As he readily confessed, the impulse was his own conversion:

> There was a time when I was interested in the first degree with purely scientific criticism. Bred among academic scholarship of the classics and philosophy, I carried these habits to the Bible . . . It also pleased God by the revelation of His holiness and grace, which the great theologians taught me to find in the Bible, to bring home to me my sin in a way that submerged all the school questions in weight, urgency and poignancy. I was turned from a Christian to a believer, from a lover of love to an object of grace. And so, whereas I first thought that what the churches needed was enlightened instruction and liberal theology, I came to be sure that what they needed was evangelization, in something more than the conventional sense of that word.[17]

So understood, evangelization called for presenting the gospel in and through a modern theology. Avoiding mere accommodation required embracing the modern without capitulating to liberalism. Forsyth kept the two apart by understanding liberalism as 'the theology which begins with some rational canon of life or nature to which Christianity has to be cut down or enlarged' and the necessary 'modern positivity' as 'a theology that begins with God's gift of a super-logical revelation in Christ's historic person and cross, whose object is not to adjust a contradiction but to resolve a crisis and save a situation of the human soul'. The difference, which for Forsyth was infinite, centred on the estimate of Christ: 'For positive theology Christ is the object of faith; for liberal He is but its first and greatest subject, the agent of a faith directed elsewhere than on Him.'[18] The distinction allowed the marrying of new developments in science and biblical studies with the traditional evangelical message, and made out a pathway that an increasing number of *fin de siècle* evangelicals were keen to take. Their task was to modernize evangelicalism theologically, an agenda that called for numerous applications and admitted of varying degrees. By about 1910 the term 'liberal evangelical' was established in Anglican evangelical

---

17. Peter T. Forsyth, *Positive Preaching and Modern Mind* (London: Hodder & Stoughton, 1907), esp. chs. 4, 6–7 (281–283 for the quotation).

18. Ibid. 210.

discourse as a convenient description of those undertaking this task and was coming into wider use.[19]

Evangelical biblical scholarship

The coexistence of the narrowing and broadening tendencies at the turn of the century produced several important effects in evangelical thinking about the Bible. One was the continuation of the debate about biblical higher criticism that became a major site for the diversification of the evangelical tradition.

Anti-modern opponents of criticism on the right charged that it was far from new and merely echoed the rationalism of the past.[20] With some inconsistency they also claimed that critical methods and conclusions were novel. Why, they asked, should the testimony of generations of believers be so readily set aside? In its approach to the supernatural (especially reports of miracles) and the value of ancient traditions, higher criticism, they said, was excessively sceptical. Its speculativeness was exposed by the absurdity of the results produced by application of the method in areas where the results could be more readily tested. Its naturalism and evolutionism could never accommodate the biblical history, which was by definition exceptional. For many the authority of Christ settled the matter. It was a clear choice between 'Christ or the Critics'. The consequences of criticism were also serious. It led to loss of faith in the truthfulness of scriptural Christianity; it vitiated Bible reading by making the Bible a book for a scholarly elite; it was a hindrance to preaching and a burden to evangelism; it even portended moral collapse. On this side of the argument higher criticism was antagonistic to Scripture, faith and ultimately social well-being.[21]

Modern upholders of criticism countered that it was inherent in the structures of evangelical thought. Principles inherited from the Reformation – the

---

19. Martin Wellings, 'The Anglican Evangelical Group Movement', in Andrew Atherstone and John Maiden (eds.), *Evangelicalism and the Church of England in the Twentieth Century: Reform, Resistance and Renewal* (Woodbridge: Boydell Press, 2014), 68–88.

20. This and the next paragraph are based on Martin Wellings, *Evangelicals Embattled: Responses of Evangelicals in the Church of England to Ritualism, Darwinism and Theological Liberalism 1890–1930* (Carlisle: Paternoster Press, 2003), ch. 4.

21. E.g. Robert Anderson, *The Bible and Modern Criticism* (London: Hodder & Stoughton, 1902); *Psuedo-Criticism or the Higher Criticism and Its Counterfeit* (New York: Fleming H. Revell, 1904).

right of private judgement, the importance of an open Bible and the priesthood of all believers – led in this direction. The commitment to truthfulness exalted by their Victorian parents and grandparents made it a moral issue as well. Criticism was further commended by the achievements of a 'reverent' approach to the New Testament, where the findings of the Cambridge Triumvirate of Lightfoot, Westcott and Hort, particularly against the radical theories of the Tübingen School, were a source of reassurance.[22] In turn the methods used to achieve these results could hardly be withheld from the more problematic field of Old Testament studies. The idea of progressive revelation facilitated reconciliation with modern knowledge by explaining miracles and the unscientific world view of the Old Testament as the poetic memories of a primitive nation that no longer had to be accepted as factual. Similarly the moral problems presented by the Old Testament were attributable to the underdeveloped notions of God of the ancient Israelites. The upholders also urged the benefits of criticism for evangelical religion. An answer had been supplied for the difficulties of which 'free thinkers' had long made sport, and emphasis on the spiritual development of the Hebrew people gave the Bible a new vividness and relevance to contemporary life. Somewhat unrealistically, the proponents of evangelical biblical criticism expected that the new approach would bring the Bible back into common use.

Although the debate was protracted, support for critical approaches to the Bible in some measure was widespread.[23] The upshot was the opening of a broad centre of opinion on the biblical question. For those who occupied a middling position on this wide spectrum, the anti-modern narrowers and the modern broadeners alike were cause for anxiety. The Church Missionary Society statesman Eugene Stock represented the arguments of these modernizing evangelicals when, in an eirenicon intended to bridge the gulf between extreme positions, he urged that the status and authority of the Bible were not necessarily compromised by criticism. Ultimately, he said, 'only good can come from the critical studies of devout and good men' and interpretations of Scripture do need to be revised from time to time.[24] The traction of this argument was evident in the warm reception given even by the anti-moderns to criticism that supported

---

22. Geoffrey R. Treloar, 'The Cambridge Triumvirate and the Acceptance of New Testament Higher Criticism in Britain, 1850–1900', *JAS* 4.1 (2006), 13–32.

23. E.g. *EMC 1901*, 146–164; *EMC 1911*, 238–262; *ICC 1908*, 345–352; *RPC 1904*, 38–66; *RPC 1909*, 210–230; and *WBC 1905*, 128–142.

24. Eugene Stock, *A Plain Man's Thoughts on Biblical Criticism* (London: Longmans, Green, 1911); *My Recollections* (London: James Nisbet, 1909), 396–399.

their own standpoint.[25] Celebration of biblical archaeology as a source of objective data controlling the speculation of critics was a further sign of the gradual blurring of the distinction between the dogmatic and higher-critical readings of the Bible.[26]

For some turn-of-the-century evangelicals this development (especially finding, as criticism seemed to require, the due relation between the human and divine elements in Scripture) called for modification of the categories of biblical authority.[27] With their commitment to an 'either-or' standpoint, this was change that anti-modernists such as Torrey and Warfield could not allow. If anything, their insistence on inerrancy in the face of its increasing repudiation represented a hardening of the case for verbal inspiration. But broadeners of varying stripes operated along the lines urged by Stock. More and more they accepted that it was the writers rather than the words that were inspired. There was also a rising preference for the view that the Bible *tells of* the revelation of God rather than actually *being* the revelation. Corresponding to these changes was the debate over whether the Bible *was* or *contained* the Word of God. W. H. Griffith Thomas, for a time editor of *The Churchman*, reflected the growing diversity on the biblical question by arguing that both formulae were necessary adequately to comprehend the phenomenon of the Bible.[28] Behind these semantic manoeuvrings was a shift to experience, pre-eminently of the Bible's writers, but also of its readers, as the locus of religious authority. By such means evangelicals found ways to enable the Bible to function as the authoritative basis for Christian life and thought at the same time as applying modern critical methods to its interpretation.

The results of these adjustments were well represented in the work of the Scots James Orr and James Denney, both colleagues of George Adam Smith at the Glasgow College of the United Free Church. Viewing the Bible as the record of the supernatural revelatory acts of God with its inspiration consisting not in inerrancy but in a demonstrably high degree of historical and factual accuracy, Orr sustained a discriminating encounter with the rising volume of

---

25. E.g. Reception of the work of Sir William Ramsay: 'The Stronghold of Holy Scripture', *C* (4 Mar. 1915), 11; T. J. Pulvertaft, 'Professor Ramsay and the Trustworthiness of the New Testament', *EC* (Mar.–Apr. 1915), 66–68.

26. E.g. M. G. Kyle, 'The Recent Testimony of Archaeology to the Scriptures', *RPC 1909*, 163–168.

27. On this issue H. D. MacDonald, *Theories of Revelation: An Historical Study 1860–1960* (London: Allen & Unwin, 1963), has not been surpassed.

28. W. H. Griffith Thomas, *Methods of Bible Study* (London: Marshall Brothers, n.d.).

biblical scholarship of the *fin de siècle* era.[29] Of particular importance in this respect was *The Problem of the Old Testament* (1906), a massive review of the previous thirty years of research, which, while accepting many 'proven results' of criticism, rebutted the Graf-Wellhausen hypothesis, the widely accepted basis of critical reconstructions of the Old Testament history. While probably the most extensively published evangelical writer of the era, Orr was nevertheless regarded even by 'believing critics' as too conservative. His colleague James Denney occupied a position further to the left.[30] In a private letter, written in 1902 against the background of the Adam Smith heresy case, he wrote of the need to 'persuade people who are alarmed not to close their minds in impatience, but to face the kinds of questions criticism raises and to meet them with the composure of intelligence and the assurance of faith'. The non-inerrantist, non-infallibilist approach of his writing, he maintained, enhanced the Bible as a means of grace and vehicle for the gospel. While both Denney and Orr could be objects of suspicion, many within the movement were grateful for their leadership in the difficult task of mediating biblical criticism.

Certainly their teaching and example cleared the way for accepting the practice of genuine biblical scholarship among evangelicals themselves. The outstanding scholar from within the movement in this era was the Primitive Methodist A. S. Peake, Tutor at Hartley College in Manchester from 1892 until his death and the first holder of the Rylands Chair of Biblical Exegesis at Manchester University from 1904.[31] Peake readily identified himself with the advanced criticism enshrined in the work of the Anglicans Lightfoot and Old Testament scholar S. R. Driver and sought to build on their achievement.[32] In the pre-war years his prolific writings included commentaries on the Old Testament books of Job (1905), Jeremiah (1910) and Lamentations (1912) and the New Testament epistles to the Hebrews (1902) and Colossians (1909). He also outlined his position in *A Critical Introduction to the New Testament* (1909) and *The Bible: Its Origin, Its Significance and Its Abiding Worth* (1913). Peake's utilization of higher-critical methods was rooted in the conviction that they enabled the Word of God to be more clearly heard. His personal piety and wide engagement

---

29. Glen C. Scorgie, *A Call for Continuity: The Theological Contribution of James Orr* (Macon, GA: Mercer University Press, 1988), esp. 85–101, ch. 8.

30. James M. Gordon, *James Denney (1856–1917): An Intellectual and Contextual Biography* (Carlisle: Paternoster Press, 2006), esp. 154–155 for the quotation below.

31. J. T. Wilkinson, *Arthur Samuel Peake: A Biography* (London: Epworth Press 1971).

32. Arthur S. Peake, *Recollections and Appreciations* (London: Epworth Press, 1938).

with church life and Christian causes led one of his contemporaries to sum up his standpoint as representing 'the not impossible combination of Modernist and Evangelical'.[33]

While few others were willing or able to straddle this difficult divide, Peake was joined in the enterprise of advanced biblical study by a diverse range of evangelical scholars around the world. In 1912 the conservative American Presbyterian, J. Gresham Machen, in the early stages of a career at Princeton, urged the necessity of consecrated biblical scholarship as a contribution to the larger task of winning back the culture for Christ.[34] Also in America, the Southern Baptist A. T. Robertson was another who combined deep Christian devotion with a commitment to advanced learning capable of producing *A Grammar of the Greek New Testament in the Light of Historical Research* (1914) and his important commentary on 1 Corinthians (1911).[35] The Anglican H. E. Ryle (son of J. C. Ryle) and the Australian Andrew Harper produced Old Testament scholarship from a standpoint similar to that of Peake in England and Australia. While none of these scholars was of quite the same calibre as Peake, their output – alongside that of Adam Smith, Orr and Denney – showed that, in the early years of the twentieth century, the practice of believing biblical criticism was emerging across the spectrum of evangelical opinion.

Evangelical theology

The broadening project envisaged by Forsyth and others extended beyond the task of biblical interpretation to theological restatement.[36] As the biographies of the era make clear, evangelical theologians saw themselves confronted by a dual challenge. From within, they were called to revise static doctrinal conceptions in the face of modern notions of historical development and to deal

---

33. Quoted in Martin Wellings, 'Peake, Arthur Samuel', in *BDE*, 512–514.
34. J. Gresham Machen, 'Christianity and Culture', in D. G. Hart (ed.), *J. Gresham Machen: Selected Shorter Writings* (Phillipsburg: P&R Publishing, 2004), 399–410.
35. Edgar V. McNight, 'A. T. Robertson', in W. A. Elwell and J. D. Weaver (eds.), *Bible Interpreters of the Twentieth Century: A Selection of Evangelical Voices* (Grand Rapids: Baker Books, 1999), 93–104.
36. This section draws on Dale A. Johnson, *The Changing Shape of English Nonconformity, 1825–1925* (New York: Oxford University Press, 1999), esp. 125–128, 152–153, 159–160; Alan P. F. Sell, *Nonconformist Theology in the Twentieth Century* (Milton Keynes: Paternoster Press, 2006).

with the decline of Calvinism, which was seen as unbendingly restrictive. From
without, their task was to respond to the 'new theology', the many sided attempt
to repackage Christian thought in terms of the major intellectual currents of
the day, philosophical idealism, materialist science and liberalism in its German
and Anglo-American forms.

Of the specific tasks facing the theologians, the challenge of science did not
loom so large as it had in the aftermath of Darwin's *Origin of Species* (1859).[37] At
the turn of the century biology was still the main area of concern, and some
anti-moderns continued to rage against evolution. Torrey was again the representative figure with his denunciation of evolution as unproven and unscientific.[38]
This opposition found some support from within the scientific community
from the likes of the Anglican evangelical Sir Ambrose Fleming. But an acceptance of evolution was now common among evangelicals. Even Benjamin
Warfield supported an evolutionary perspective if limited to matters of scientific
observation, while others – moderns and modernizers – shifted to a new natural
theology in which evolution was nothing more than the unfolding of the divine
plan and the argument from design remained more or less intact.[39] Others, James
Orr and P. T. Forsyth among them, were more cautious, speaking out against
accommodations that excluded major themes of Scripture such as the Fall and
sin and the application of evolution to humanity itself. While there was some
doubt about whether the reconcilers had really understood the issues,
the nineteenth-century concern about the materialism of science had been
overtaken by a more positive assessment that, within proper limits, assigned
science a place in the evangelical tradition as promoting a spiritual understanding
of the world.

The times also called for guidance through the new explorations of contemporary German liberal theology, especially those of Albrecht Ritschl and
his followers.[40] Ritschlianism, by the end of the nineteenth century the dominant

---

37. Papers by Mark Noll and David Bebbington in David N. Livingstone et al. (eds.),
    Evangelicals and Science in Historical Perspective (New York: Oxford University Press,
    1999); David N. Livingstone, *Darwin's Forgotten Defenders: The Encounter Between
    Evangelical Theology and Evolutionary Thought* (Grand Rapids: Eerdmans, 1987).

38. *Torrey–Alexander Souvenir*, 73.

39. E.g. W. F. Adeney, *A Century's Progress in Religious Life and Thought* (London: Methuen,
    1901), 102–103; David N. Livingstone and Mark Noll, 'B. B. Warfield (1851–1921):
    A Biblical Inerrantist as Evolutionist', *JPH* 80.3 (2002), 153–171.

40. E.g. R. Mackintosh, 'Recent Philosophy and Christian Doctrine', *ICC 1908*, 76–84,
    esp. 79–80.

theology in Germany, where it was encountered by several young English-speaking evangelical theologians, was recognized as a commendable attempt to present Christianity in the light of scientific naturalism. Its theory of 'value judgements' held that God is not known in himself but only in his effects on (or worth for) people. These effects are revealed in the work of Christ and appropriated by faith. While it was important to use the most rigorous historical criticism in reconstructing the Jesus of history, the scientific consciousness as such cannot affirm or deny the value judgements of faith. Locating religious knowledge as a matter not for the intellect alone but for the whole person was perceived as a gain.

But there were aspects of Ritschl's teaching that evangelicals could not accept. James Orr led the charge with two main criticisms.[41] In its wish to rid theology of metaphysics, Ritschlianism was too subjective. Evangelicals preferred to retain the objective certainty on which they based their faith. The disposition to collapse everything into love in Ritschl's view of justification and reconciliation undermined the need for forgiveness and minimized the operation of grace. Orr's critique was representative of the evangelical response to Ritschl, but a more positive assessment was proffered by the self-styled 'liberal-evangelical' Alfred Garvie, soon to be Professor at the Congregationalists' New College, London. In his view the Ritschlian theology should be valued for its commendation of the Christian faith in a setting in which it was losing its hold on the cultured men and women of the age. The theory of value judgements in particular put the objects of faith beyond the criticisms of science and philosophy, so that, as he affirmed, 'over against the suspicions and surmises of criticism we can put the certainties of our experience of Christ's saving power'.[42]

Contested adjustments of evangelical thinking to science and theological liberalism led on to some reconsideration of the character of God and the nature of his relation with the world. A way forward was shown from the left by the Scottish Congregationalist A. M. Fairbairn, who directed attention to Jesus' consciousness of God's Fatherhood and his own Sonship as a principle that envisaged collective as well as individual salvation and overcame the moral objections to the judicial view of the God–world relation of Calvinism.[43] At the turn of the century the English Methodist J. Scott Lidgett set himself the

---

41. James Orr, *The Ritschlian Theology and the Evangelical Faith* (London: Hodder & Stoughton, 1897).

42. Quoted in Johnson, *Changing Shape of English Nonconformity*, 212–213, n. 59.

43. Ibid. 149–150.

task of establishing Fatherhood in Christian thinking, not by replacing the governmental interpretation with the paternal, but by holding the two together and reordering the priority.[44] With Fatherhood as primary, God's motive and method in creation and redemption became clear as self-giving love leading to life. This 'both-and' perspective set his formulation apart from liberal Protestantism, whose exaltation of love excluded penal views of the atonement. However, despite the synthesis between the old and the new, to his critics Scott Lidgett seemed also to break with evangelical teaching. Finding the place for divine immanence in a tradition that had exalted transcendence remained a difficult undertaking.

While the proposals of liberal Protestantism were filtered at leisure by the scholars, the need for a response became pressing when they came before the wider public in the 'new theology' controversy of 1907–12. The centre of the storm, which was followed closely all around the evangelical world, was the Congregational minister of the City Temple in London, R. J. Campbell.[45] Reflecting the vogue for philosophical idealism, Campbell stressed the concept of divine immanence. This priority led to a this-worldly focus and an insistence on the essential identity of humanity and God. One corollary was the initial importance of the testimony of the Holy Spirit within, so that individual judgement was exalted over the authority of the biblical revelation. Campbell also played down the importance of doctrine and argued that traditional teachings about the Fall, the atonement, salvation, and the punishment of sin 'were not only misleading but unethical'. Jesus, in this presentation, was 'the best of men', and human sympathy rather than clear and forceful doctrine made for vigorous church life. Campbell kept up this teaching for the next couple of years and won a large following. But his ideas were an affront to evangelical opinion and met with vigorous resistance, especially from fellow Nonconformists.[46] Worn down by the onslaught of the orthodox, Campbell himself in time abandoned the 'new theology' and (shockingly in the eyes of some) entered the Church of England late in 1915. His case stood as a perpetual reminder of

---

44. J. Scott Lidgett, *My Guided Life* (London: Methuen, 1936), ch. 9.

45. E.g. Reports in *The Outlook*, the newspaper of the Presbyterian and Methodist Churches of New Zealand; Keith Robbins, 'The Spiritual History of the Rev. R. J. Campbell', in his *History, Religion and Identity in Modern Britain* (London: Hambledon Press, 1993), ch. 10 (quotation below on 143).

46. E.g. Charles H. Vine (ed.), *The Old Faith and the New Theology: A Series of Sermons and Essays on Some of the Truths Held by Evangelical Christians, and the Difficulties of Accepting Much of What Is Called the 'New Theology'* (London: Sampson Low, Marston, 1907).

the tendency of the 'new theology' to pantheism and the dangers of too free a handling of received evangelical truth.[47]

These needs for restatement and reassessment created an environment in which a large number of theologians across the spectrum of evangelical thought and opinion flourished. Those who had taken a leading part in responding to the problems of the day – Orr, Forsyth, Denney, Garvie, Scott Lidgett – were joined in Britain by Robert Mackintosh and W. B. Selbie. Among Anglicans Handley Moule, at the time Principal of Ridley Hall, Cambridge, wrote *Outlines of Christian Doctrine* (1894), while W. H. Griffith Thomas maintained a steady flow of writing on both sides of the Atlantic following his *The Catholic Faith: A Manual of Instruction for Members of the Church of England* in 1904. In America Augustus Strong, William Newton Clarke and William Adams Brown provided syntheses of the old and the new.[48] In their own domains the Canadian Methodist Nathaniel Burwash, author of a two-volume *Christian Theology on the Inductive Method* (1904), and the Southern Baptist E. Y. Mullins, whose *magnum opus* was *The Christian Religion in Its Doctrinal Expression* (1917), were important leaders. Probably at no previous point in the history of the movement had so many writers produced such a volume of high-quality theological writing to instruct their constituency. The 'new theology' of the *fin de siècle* stimulated something of 'a golden age' in evangelical theology.

Consolidation of positions

One effect of the crisis caused by the 'new theology' controversy was to precipitate action at the conservative end of the movement for the defence of evangelical Christianity. In the belief that they would 'have a mighty influence on the Church and the world',[49] public gatherings fashioned after the indignation meetings arising from 'the Nonconformist conscience' were held in Britain and 'Greater Britain' to testify 'to firm adherence of the Bible as the infallible Word of God' and to uphold 'its authority as supreme on all matters concerning

47. E.g. 'The New Orthodoxy', *Ch* 24.54 (June 1910), 406–407; 'The Unchangeable Gospel – and the "New Theology"', *C* (23 June 1910), 23.

48. Augustus H. Strong, *Outlines of Systematic Theology Designed for the Use of Theological Students* (Philadelphia: American Baptist Publication Society, 1908); William Newton Clarke, *An Outline of Christian Theology* (Edinburgh: T. & T. Clark, 1907); William Adams Brown, *Christian Theology in Outline* (New York: Charles Scribner's Sons, 1906).

49. 'Meetings for Testimony to Fundamental Truth', *EAQ* (1 Apr. 1905), 51–52.

spiritual life'.[50] At one such Bible defence meeting in Melbourne the controversial Anglican C. H. Nash typified the bombast of these occasions:

> it may be that the scholarship and learning of our day will hand over the Scriptures to be crucified by the world. But we believe in Christ, who passed through the gate of death to a glorious resurrection; and, if we believe that about Him, we need not fear about them.[51]

The Evangelical Alliance also organized its eleventh international conference in 1906 as 'a national and international testimony to the integrity of God's Word' and to 'unswerving adherence to the faith of the Gospel'.

These meetings built on the work of the Bible Leagues. The first had been formed in Britain in 1892 in response to the Baptist John Clifford's modernizing *The Inspiration and Authority of the Bible*, 'to promote the Reverent Study of the Holy Scriptures, and to resist the varied attacks made upon their Inspiration, Infallibility, and Sole Sufficiency as the Word of God'.[52] An American counterpart followed in 1903, together with a Canadian auxiliary in 1906.[53] It organized periodic public conventions for the promulgation and defence of its principles, and its journal, *The Bible Student and Teacher*, published to propagate the best methods and results of Bible study 'to stem the rising tides of unbelief in the Bible as the written Word of God', achieved an international circulation of 6,000 copies per month.[54] Travelling representatives were also appointed to promote the standpoint of the League. In the years before the outbreak of the First World War conservative evangelicals came out into public space to contend for the authority and influence of the Bible.

Other steps taken to consolidate their position included the foundation of Bible colleges for the propagation of the traditional understanding of the Bible as the Word of God.[55] The establishment of Moody's Bible Institute in

---

50. 'The Labour of Others', *EC* (Apr.–May 1907), 58.

51. C. H. Nash, 'Christ and the Holy Scriptures', *VC* (9 Aug. 1907), 321–324, with the quotation on 324; Darrell Paproth, *Failure Is Not Final: A Life of C. H. Nash* (Sydney: Centre for the Study of Australian Christianity, 1997).

52. Bebbington, *Evangelicalism in Modern Britain*, 187.

53. Marsden, *Fundamentalism and American Culture*, 118.

54. 'League Notes and Points', *BST* XII (Apr. 1910), 321–322.

55. Virginia L. Brereton, *Training God's Army: The American Bible School, 1880–1940* (Bloomington: Indiana University Press, 1990); John G. Stackhouse, Jr., *Canadian Evangelicalism in the Twentieth Century: An Introduction to Its Character* (Toronto: University of Toronto Press, 1993), ch. 3.

Chicago in 1886 provided the model. In the United States another twenty-eight such colleges were founded in the years down to the First World War. Similar institutions were founded elsewhere as the Bible Training Institute in Glasgow (1892), the Toronto Bible College (1894) and the Mission and Bible College in Sydney (1916). Set up at about the same time and for much the same reason, the Bible colleges aimed to supplement the work of the seminaries by producing a large force of biblically knowledgeable laypeople with the practical skills for effective Christian ministry at home and abroad. At the centre of the curriculum was 'the whole (English) Bible' taught with a Torrey-like inductive approach. With their anti-modern aspirations, they rapidly institutionalized the fundamentalist impulse and stood as bulwarks against broadening trends in biblical interpretation. As the case of the Bible Institute of Los Angeles (founded in 1908) shows, they also became centres for the teaching of dispensationalism.[56]

In an age of programmatic statements staking out theological positions,[57] evangelicals at the conservative end of the movement also wrote to fortify and commend their beliefs. The most influential volume of the era was of course the *Scofield Reference Bible* of 1909, already discussed in chapter 3. Other right-of-centre evangelicals also attempted to shore up their position. The Evangelical Alliance, for example, launched a 'Tractarian Movement', a series of pamphlets to counteract 'the new theology'.[58] Its writers included Robert Anderson, James Orr and Anglicans J. E. Watts Ditchfield and H. W. Webb Peploe. Their subjects ranged over such matters as *The New Apostasy*, *Salvation*, *Miracles* and *Man in Relation to God*.

Some of these writers were also involved in the best-known contemporary undertaking of the kind. *The Fundamentals*, a series of twelve paperback booklets published between 1910 and 1915, came about when Californian oil magnate Lyman Stewart recruited A. C. Dixon to assemble 'the best and most loyal Bible

---

56. Daniel W. Draney, *When Streams Diverge: John Murdoch MacInnis and the Origins of Protestant Fundamentalism in Los Angeles* (Milton Keynes: Paternoster Press, 2008), ch. 3.

57. E.g. *Lux Mundi* (1889), *Contentio Veritatis: Essays in Constructive Theology by Six Oxford Tutors* (1902); *Essays on Some Theological Questions of the Day by Members of the University of Cambridge* (1905); *Foundations: A Statement of Christian Belief in Terms of Modern Thought* (1913); *Essays Catholic and Critical* (1926).

58. 'Alliance Tractarian Movement', *EC* (May–June 1907), 62 (with advertisement titled 'Evangelical Alliance Tractarian Movement Versus "New Theology"' on the inside back cover).

teachers in the world' to produce a great 'Testimony to the Truth'.[59] Dixon drew on the revivalist network centred on Chicago to create a team of American authors to carry out this agenda. He supplemented the team by including writers from Britain, Canada and Germany known to favour the broad programme. They came together as representatives of the evangelical 'coalition' to present a wide-ranging statement and commendation of evangelical Christianity as a contribution to a wider discourse about the essentials of Christian belief.[60] The primary theme was the Bible and its authority in relation to the inroads of modern knowledge. Criticism was not dismissed out of hand, only its misuse. Nor was inerrancy uniformly asserted. The real object of attack was secularism, the evacuation of the supernatural from the world and consideration of its ways. Sent out free of charge to English-speaking Protestant pastors, theological professors and every conceivable category of Christian worker for whom addresses were available to ensure its universal consideration, *The Fundamentals* reaffirmed the evangelical commitment to a theology and religion based upon the Bible as a supernatural revelation of God and his will for humankind.

The broadeners were not yet so well organized as the conservatives, probably because they were neither so numerous nor so anxious about the course of events. But there were signs that they too were learning to come together to further their ends. In England in 1906 a small group of Anglican evangelicals to be known as 'the Liverpool Six' formed with a threefold intention: to provide a study network for those who were 'braver spirits' in theological terms; to secure recognition from the leaders of the evangelical party; and to cooperate more extensively in the institutional life of the Church of England.[61] Their intention was to replace the negations of the older generation of evangelicals with a positive policy. By the end of 1907 similar groups had been formed in twelve centres around the country, and the first of what became biennial conferences had been held. While these activities remained private, their

59. *The Fundamentals* is best read in the edition of George Marsden (1988). The best informed account of the project is now Timothy E. W. Gloege, 'Consumed: Reuben A. Torrey and the Construction of Corporate Fundamentalism', PhD thesis, Notre Dame University, 2007.

60. For this reading, Geoffrey R. Treloar, 'The British Contribution to *The Fundamentals*', in David Bebbington and David Ceri Jones (eds.), *Evangelicalism and Fundamentalism in the United Kingdom During the Twentieth Century* (Oxford: Oxford University Press, 2013), 15–34.

61. Eric Smith, *Another Anglican Angle. Liberal Evangelicalism: The Anglican Evangelical Group Movement 1906–1967* (Oxford: The Amate Press, 1991).

popularity indicated that they met a need, and the desire for a more open and positive type of evangelicalism led to steady expansion down to the outbreak of war in 1914. Around 1912 the movement became more formal with the adoption of a constitution. It proclaimed the Group Brotherhood as an association of clergy seeking to interpret the fundamental principles of evangelicalism 'in relation to modern life and thought', an aspiration that comprehended the study of the Bible, religious experience, social and ethical problems, and churchmanship. By this time the Brotherhood and its aspiration had also been taken abroad. In 1909 J. C. Wright, chairman of the first conference, was appointed Archbishop of Sydney, and he in turn appointed two other group members, David Davies and A. E. Talbot, as Principal of Moore College and Dean of Sydney respectively.

While they were unable to produce anything with either the circulation or galvanizing effect of the *Scofield Reference Bible* or *The Fundamentals*, the broadeners also issued volumes that sought to stake out their position. Individuals issued a steady flow of books with proposals for adjustment of evangelical teaching for the times.[62] These were accompanied by a rising tide of collective statements. Among Anglicans the Group Brotherhood produced a series of *English Church Manuals* and *Anglican Church Handbooks*. While the first series was addressed to matters of Anglican faith and practice, the second provided a mediating stance on critical and theological issues with works assimilating what one contributor called 'credible modern research'. In 1911 the English Congregationalist W. B. Selbie organized a symposium on the doctrine of the church with a view to promoting the substantial (if not organic) unity of evangelicals and, ultimately, through the appeal to history and experience, to authenticate 'Evangelical religion'.[63] Three years later a group of Methodists, all avowedly loyal to the evangelical tradition, brought out *The Chief Corner-Stone: Essays Towards an Exposition of the Christian Faith Today* with a view to harmonizing the Christian doctrines of salvation with the modern outlook.[64]

By the middle of the second decade of the new century the broadening impulse had reached such a stage of maturity that attempts were made to

---

62. E.g. D. S. Cairns, *Christianity in the Modern World* (London: Hodder & Stoughton, 1906); Henry Sloane Coffin, *Some Christian Convictions: A Practical Restatement in Terms of Present-Day Thinking* (New Haven: Yale University Press, 1915).

63. W. B. Selbie (ed.), *Evangelical Christianity: Its History and Witness* (London: Hodder & Stoughton, 1911).

64. W. T. Davison (ed.), *The Chief Corner-Stone: Essays Towards an Exposition of the Christian Faith for To-Day* (London: Charles H. Kelly, 1914).

formulate the liberal evangelical position. Two manifestos of 1915, one by the English Anglican E. A. Burroughs and the other by the American Presbyterian Henry Sloane Coffin, enunciated as principles the ideas and commitments that had shaped incipient liberal evangelicalism over the preceding twenty-five years or so.[65] It was liberal, in general, because of its acceptance of open enquiry and the need for theological restatement on the grounds that revelation under the guidance of the Holy Spirit was ongoing; and, in particular, because of its acceptance of the new knowledge about the Bible arising from measured and reverent criticism. It remained evangelical in its insistence on the Bible as the authoritative expression of God's life with men, Jesus as the unique saviour of the world, the cross as the power of God for the world's salvation, and continuity with apostolically minded people from the time of Christ and, more particularly, with the church descended from the Reformation. Underneath its stated aims – truthfulness, evangelism of the thinking men and women of the day, vital religious experience and education, strengthening of the church and promotion of church unity, and social regeneration – was a commitment to the recovery of the power and authority of evangelicalism. For this reason liberal evangelicals differentiated themselves from conservatives who were tied to outdated formulations, creeds and rituals. Perhaps more importantly, they set themselves against radical modernists who, by reducing the supernatural claims of religion to metaphor, were intent on breaking with the past without concern for the damage to the church. By the end of the *fin de siècle*, a clearly defined modern position had emerged on the left wing of the evangelical movement.

A mediating stance in relation to the Bible was also proclaimed by the *International Bible Encyclopaedia* (1915), edited by James Orr. Its aim was to provide a comprehensive and accurate work 'in every way adequate to the exacting requirements of teachers in colleges and theological seminaries and Bible schools, clergymen, and all others who desire to be familiar with the Holy Scriptures and those themes of doctrine, criticism, and scholarship which are directly related to them'.[66] To achieve this end it embodied 'the best scholarship and newest knowledge', an aspiration achieved by drawing on the learning of America, Britain, 'Greater Britain' and continental Europe. The professed standpoint was

65. [E. A. Burroughs], 'Liberal Evangelicalism: What It Is and What It Stands for', *Ch* 29 (Mar.–Aug. 1915), 193–200, 277–285, 371–379, 439–448, 513–521, 602–609; Henry Sloane Coffin, *The Practical Aims of a Liberal Evangelicalism: Closing Address, May 18th, 1915* (New York: Union Theological Seminary, 1915).
66. James Orr (ed.), *The International Standard Bible Encyclopedia* (Chicago: Howard-Severance, 1915), preface, vii–xii (xii and viii for the quotations).

'a reasonable criticism', a position that allowed positive and constructive criticism and use of the aids it brought to understanding 'the sacred Word'. Its several editions indicate that the *Encyclopedia* served an important need over a long period. As the new century unfolded, evangelical theologians and scholars made distinct modernizing efforts to reconcile traditional piety with up-to-date biblical and theological knowledge.

Yet, despite the constructive intention behind these undertakings, in the years immediately before the Great War of 1914–18 the anxiety of the era had also begun to generate the disruptiveness always likely to result from differentiation on biblical and related questions. A sign of this reaction came in 1910 when 22 student members of the Cambridge Inter-Collegiate Christian Union (CICCU), a product of the Moody missions to Britain, voted to disaffiliate from the Student Christian Movement (SCM) by a majority of 17 to 5.[67] Although other issues were involved, the basic cause was difference over biblical interpretation. Whereas the SCM was open to new views about the Bible, CICCU held to the traditional understanding and deeply distrusted higher criticism. The direction it wished to take is indicated by its inviting Torrey to conduct a University mission in the following year, and by reconstituting the Cambridge Voluntary Union following withdrawal from the British Student Volunteer Missionary Union.[68] More was at stake than the intransigence of a handful of students in one corner of the evangelical world. The disposition to take a separate stand in the name of biblical faithfulness spread as the students of 1910 became leaders at various points around the world.

This fissiparity was paralleled by the controversy in Canadian and British Methodism over the appointment of George Jackson to the chair of Homiletics and Pastoral Theology at Didsbury College in Manchester.[69] Jackson had made

---

67. *Old Paths in Perilous Times: An Account of the Cambridge Inter-Collegiate Christian Union* (n.p.: 1913) with the revisionist interpretation of Jonathan Thacker and Susannah Clark, 'A Historical and Theological Exploration of the 1910 Disaffiliation of the Cambridge Inter-Collegiate Christian Union from the Student Christian Movement', unpublished paper presented at the 'Evangelicalism and Fundamentalism in Britain' conference in Oxford in Dec. 2008.

68. See Marcus L. Loane, *Archbishop Mowll: The Biography of Howard Kilvinton Mowll Archbishop of Sydney and Primate of Australia* (London: Hodder & Stoughton, 1960), 43–55, esp. 52; J. C. Pollock, *A Cambridge Movement* (London: John Murray, 1953), chs. 14–15.

69. David W. Bebbington, 'The Persecution of George Jackson: A British Fundamentalist Controversy', *SCH* 21 (1984), 421–433.

a name for himself as a preacher, first in Edinburgh, and then in Toronto, where he went on to hold the chair of English Bible at Victoria University from 1909 to 1913. His Fernley Lecture to the 1912 Wesleyan Conference in England, published as *The Preacher and the Modern Mind*, caused intense controversy. Accordingly his appointment to Didsbury was opposed on the grounds that he had abandoned biblical infallibility, a dangerous characteristic in one charged with the task of preparing men for the ministry. With the failure of their efforts to block the appointment, Jackson's opponents banded together and formed the Wesley Bible Union in 1913, a permanent organization to contend for the faith as the only way of saving Methodism from modernist apostasy.[70] As Britain moved into the war years, the Wesley Bible Union's attack broadened to include anything subversive of the Bible and traditional Methodist beliefs. Some Methodists were unable to acquiesce even in the conclusions of mainstream biblical criticism.

Among the American churches the early years of the twentieth century were a period of relative calm following the theological storms of the 1880s and 1890s.[71] Yet there were some stirrings that portended a more troubled future. For the Baptists the perceived liberalism of the School of Theology at the recently established University of Chicago caused a large group to leave the Illinois Baptist Convention to join the Southern Baptist Convention in 1907. Six years later moderate conservatives founded the Northern Baptist Seminary in Chicago to provide an alternative to the University. Similarly, Northern Presbyterians, alarmed by the liberal tendencies of ministerial candidates from Union Theological Seminary, persuaded the General Assembly of 1910 to adopt a five-point declaration of 'essential and necessary' doctrines. Requiring ordination candidates to affirm these doctrinal minima established not only a means by which conservatives could test their orthodoxy but also a potential battle line between conservatives and liberal members of the denomination.

Conclusion

Theological activity furnishes yet another reason for regarding the turn of the century as one of the periods of genuinely noteworthy achievement in the

---

70. Martin Wellings, 'Methodist Fundamentalism Before and After the First World War', in Bebbington and Ceri Jones (eds.), *Evangelicalism and Fundamentalism*, 76–94.

71. Marsden, *Fundamentalism and American Culture*, ch. 13, esp. 117; Bradley J. Longfield, *The Presbyterian Controversy: Fundamentalists, Modernists, and Moderates* (New York: Oxford University Press, 1991), 23–25.

history of evangelicalism. Across the movement as a whole there was during the *fin de siècle* years more formal biblical scholarship and creative theology than at any previous era. Further, the general standard of evangelical biblical and theological scholarship was unmatched, and in men such as A. S. Peake and P. T. Forsyth the movement produced outstanding contributors to their respective fields. If it is objected that such scholars belong to the centre-left, men of the calibre of James Orr and Benjamin Warfield point to the contribution made by representatives of the centre-right. In geographical extent too, early twentieth-century evangelical theological scholarship was without precedent. As erstwhile colonial societies matured and church life developed, pockets of theological activity such as Toronto and Melbourne emerged and nurtured the likes of Andrew Harper, who were able from a distance to contribute to the larger culture of evangelical understanding of the Bible and theology.

Driving this flourishing of evangelical theology was the attempt to defend, explain and make effective evangelical biblicism in the modern world. Above all, its leading thinkers sought to present evangelicalism in a manner that would win and maintain the adherence of the people of their societies. The underlying anxiety about loss of cultural authority produced different approaches to a shared commitment, which again added to the diversity of the movement. Uncertainty about biblical authority gave rise to the narrowing of the funda-mentalist impulse, which in turn produced forceful polemical statements of the ostensibly traditional position. Emerging alongside the fundamentalist impulse was acceptance of the need for a measure of broadening to allow the methods of biblical criticism their due place and some restatement of received theological positions. While sustained by hopefulness about the possibilities of a modern-izing programme, what these tasks entailed covered a wide range of views and operations, and produced such differences of opinion on specific issues. The effect was not only further diversification of the evangelical movement but also competition for the support of evangelicals who, while committed to their tradition, felt the tensions of the modern world. Yet even where the pull towards separation was strong, the divisiveness of difference was limited by the char-acteristic evangelical commitment to cooperation in pursuit of common ends. As both *The Fundamentals* and the *International Bible Encyclopedia* showed, at the end of the first decade of the twentieth century, the evangelical coalition was functioning effectively to produce responses to 'the new theology'. At the same time controversy and fragmentation were a sign of the fragility of a movement in transition. Nevertheless, called on to make good their position as never before, *fin de siècle* evangelicals sustained a vigorous discussion of their beliefs as the key point of interface with their societies.

5. A SOCIAL GOSPEL?

If conversionism and theology were two bridges from the private and church lives of evangelicals to society at large, social activism was another.[1] This was the result from very early in the history of the movement of the application to public life both of what they learned from reading their Bibles and of the reflective and analytical powers developed in cultivating their spirituality. These impulses led to participation in various reform activities and philanthropic societies as evangelicals sought to enforce the ethics of the gospel. Their capacity to lead civilization and shape culture was shown by the historic high point of these movements of protest and reform, the abolition of slavery in the British Empire finally achieved in 1833, a work that was extended by the 'abolitionists' in the United States over the next thirty years. The language and methods of the anti-slavery campaigns were carried over into other causes as evangelicals grappled with a wide diversity of social and humanitarian needs caused by the processes of modernization. Wide-ranging engagement with society continued to build because it served basic evangelical ends. Practices perceived as sinful, an obstruction to the spread of the gospel or out of step with Protestant Christianity moved evangelicals to protest and campaign for reform. Across the second half of the nineteenth century such was

---

1. Brian Stanley, 'Evangelical Social and Political Ethics: An Historical Perspective', *EvQ* 62.1 (1990), 19–36.

the increase of sociopolitical involvement of evangelicals as the categories of what was integral to the gospel broadened that social activism was a further dynamic of *fin de siècle* evangelicalism.

For many reasons the interaction of *fin de siècle* evangelicals with society was the area where the disruptiveness of modernization was most visible.[2] With their own observations further informed by such early social scientific investigations as Charles Booth's *Life and Labour of the People in London* (1889–1903) and Seebohm Rowntree's account of working and living conditions in the northern English city of York, *Poverty: A Study in Town Life* (1903), they were unsettled by the magnitude of the problems and their own lack of understanding of how to achieve remedies. They were also confronted by powerful secular ideologies of reform and, from within Christianity, the so-called Social Gospel, which, in America, was the Christian component of the Progressive Movement. Expressions of ambivalence and uncertainty on the matter have persuaded some historians to discern a decline in early twentieth-century evangelical social commitment. This interpretation has been favoured by definitions of the Social Gospel that marginalize evangelicals.[3] In fact, the Social Gospel, understood at the time as 'the application of the teaching of Jesus and the total message of Christian salvation to society, the economic life, and social institutions . . . as well as to individuals',[4] was sufficiently wide ranging for them easily to be considered a part of it. As in other facets of the movement, disruptive influences were a stimulus to commitment and activity lest evangelicals forfeit their legitimate role and influence in the contemporary world.

Early twentieth-century evangelical social activism

Turn-of-the-century evangelicals strongly (re)affirmed their commitment to the social application of the gospel. Pastors delivered sermons on the many aspects

---

2. For the background, see John Maloney and David Thompson, 'Christian Social Thought', in *CHC8*, 142–153.

3. Paul T. Phillips, *A Kingdom on Earth: Anglo-American Social Christianity, 1880–1940* (University Park, Pa.: Pennsylvania State University Press, 1996), xvi–xx; William R. Hutchison, *The Modernist Impulse in American Protestantism* (Durham: Duke University Press, 1992), 164–174.

4. By the American Shailer Matthews in 1921, quoted in Ronald C. White, Jr., and C. Howard Hopkins, *The Social Gospel: Religion and Reform in Changing America* (Philadelphia: Temple University Press, 1976), xi.

of the subject and exhorted their people (in the words of the emerging New York City fundamentalist John Roach Straton) 'to plant the cross of Christ in their homes, schools, businesses and town halls'.[5] Theologians and teachers wrote numerous books analysing contemporary social problems, explaining relevant biblical teaching and advocating various responses, while articles about social Christianity were a regular feature in evangelical newspapers and periodicals. Speeches were made and resolutions passed on social subjects at conferences and meetings. The prayers of evangelical communities included petitions for the correction of social abuses and the redemption of society. The social rhetoric of early twentieth-century evangelicals was at least the equal of that of previous generations.

To a large extent what was done supported what was said. In his turn-of-the-century celebration of evangelical progress, Arthur T. Pierson reported 'rescue work of magnitude, both as to the effort and its results, probably beyond any other period of history'.[6] In Pierson's account the philanthropic works warranting this judgement were the Salvation Army and the American Volunteers, the Mission to Deep-sea Fishermen, and the Jerry McAuley Mission and the Florence Crittenton Mission to the indigents and prostitutes of New York respectively. A proper survey would have gone much further, for evangelical social ministries covered a bewildering variety of causes and concerns.[7] All around the evangelical world urban-based evangelical social welfare work begun in the nineteenth century continued into the twentieth without fanfare. It included provision of food and shelter, medical services and physical relief, holiday and fresh-air programmes, work and skills training for the unemployed and, in the settler societies, support for immigrants.[8] Rescue work for prisoners and prostitutes was supplemented by ongoing pressure for penal reform and opposition to 'the white slave trade', the well-organized traffic in young girls. The turn of the century saw no diminution in the quantity and range of evangelical social endeavour.

5. John Roach Straton, *The Salvation of Society and Other Addresses* (Baltimore, 1908), 24, quoted in Gary Scott Smith, *The Search for Social Salvation: Social Christianity and America, 1880–1925* (Lanham, MD: Lexington Books, 2000), 406.

6. Arthur T. Pierson, *Forward Movements of the Last Half Century* (London: Garland Publishing, 1984 [1905]), 351.

7. E.g. Josiah Strong, *Religious Movements for Social Betterment* (New York: Baker & Taylor, 1900).

8. Norris Magnusson, *Salvation in the Slums: Evangelical Social Work, 1865–1920* (Metuchen, NJ: Scarecrow Press and the American Theological Library Association, 1977).

Although the extent of evangelical social ministries attests a broad consensus on the social question, this aspect of the movement was no less diverse and contested than others. On the left, the social application of the gospel was often the priority. While this position could have the appearance of a departure from evangelicalism, it was not unusual for it to be underpinned by a traditional piety or affirmation of the necessity of personal conversion. The American Josiah Strong, moved by a changing social and intellectual environment, was among the first to advocate 'the social interpretation of Christianity'.[9] After promoting social reform in tandem with evangelism as General Secretary of the American branch of the Evangelical Alliance for more than a decade, he left in 1898 to form the League for Social Service (later called the American Institute for Social Service) in order to expedite social change through research, education and direct advocacy. This was no break with his evangelical past. Strong presented the emphasis on social Christianity as a further stage in the development of the revivalist tradition and a requirement for the next awakening in America.[10] He was surpassed in his advocacy of social Christianity only by fellow American Walter Rauschenbusch, author of a succession of influential books beginning with *Christianity and the Social Crisis* in 1907.[11] A product of the German-Baptist tradition of piety, which he never abandoned, Rauschenbusch was always primarily a pastor, concerned for the well-being and spiritual life of his flock. In the face of pervasive social sin the great need was for a revival of genuine Christian ethics made possible by conversion and renovation of the soul by God. His message that Jesus came to save the human race as well as the individual was intended to complete evangelicalism, not replace it. While they may have tested the boundaries of theological orthodoxy, Strong and Rauschenbusch presented social transformation as an extension of spiritual rebirth.

Similar elevations of social Christianity were taking place elsewhere in the English-speaking world at about the same time. For Canadians such as Samuel Chown, T. Albert Moore, Hugh Dobson and C. W. Gordon, commitment to the new social Christianity was a means of making the gospel effective and thus

---

9. Donald K. Gorrell, *The Age of Social Responsibility: The Social Gospel in the Progressive Era, 1900–1920* (Macon, GA: Mercer University Press, 1988), 11–13, 31–32.

10. Josiah Strong, *The Next Great Awakening* (New York: Baker & Taylor, 1902).

11. Rauschenbusch's 'evangelical-liberal faith' is a theme of the most recent biography, Christopher H. Evans, *The Kingdom Is Always but Coming: A Life of Walter Rauschenbusch* (Grand Rapids: Eerdmans, 2004). See also Matthew Bowman, 'Sin, Spirituality, and Primitivism: The Theologies of the American Social Gospel, 1885–1917', *RAC* 17.1 (2007), 95–126.

an instrument for Christianizing a rapidly changing Canada.[12] The Wesleyan Samuel Keeble led English Nonconformists in promoting the capacity of a Christian spirit of love, goodwill and brotherhood to transform all the social relationships of humanity informally through literary work and institutionally through the Wesleyan Methodist Union of Social Services, which he helped to found.[13] For laypeople too society could be the preferred domain for the practical application of their faith. The Welshman Joseph Branch was a committed Calvinistic Methodist, a member of the Independent Labour Party and chairman of the Briton Ferry Rural District Council, who devoted his life to achieving better housing for the workers.[14] For a variety of reasons some evangelicals appeared to put the social gospel first.

On the right wing of the movement, social ministry could be deprecated. For some of these evangelicals, opposition to social ministry was not a matter of principle but merely of priority. They did not have enough time for this as well as spiritual work. Revivalist Torrey is a prime example. He was not uncaring. In the early stages of his career he served as President of the International Workers' Association, the leading Protestant social service organization of the era in America.[15] However, after his emergence as an international evangelist, social and welfare work was decidedly subordinate to the task of preaching the gospel. Similarly pragmatic was the Welshman W. T. Glyn Evans. His claim that the church's only mission was to equip people for the next world arose from concern about the divisiveness of social and political questions.[16]

But others were more definite in their outlook. They argued that the problems of society were too complex for the churches. In any case such a concern might be counterproductive: the secularizing effect of social engagement could cause

12. Nancy Christie and Michael Gauvreau, *A Full-orbed Christianity: The Protestant Churches and Social Welfare in Canada 1900–1940* (Montreal: McGill-Queen's University Press, 1996).

13. David Thompson, 'The Christian Socialist Revival in Britain: A Reappraisal', in J. Garnett and C. Matthew (eds.), *Revival and Religion Since 1700: Essays for John Walsh* (London: Hambledon Press, 1993), 273–295.

14. Robert Pope, *Building Jerusalem: Nonconformity, Labour, and the Social Question in Wales, 1906–1939* (Cardiff: University of Wales Press, 1998), 102.

15. Timothy E. W. Gloege, 'A Gilded Age Modernist: Reuben A. Torrey and the Roots of Contemporary Conservative Evangelicalism', in Darren Dochuk et al. (eds.), *American Evangelicalism: George Marsden and the State of American Religious History* (Notre Dame: University of Notre Dame Press, 2014), 199–229.

16. Pope, *Building Jerusalem*, 152–153.

the churches to lose their influence. Some English evangelical Anglican clergy considered greater social involvement unnecessary in the light of improving social conditions or even as demonically inspired distraction.[17] For other evangelicals, mainly premillennialists such as Cyrus Scofield and Isaac Haldeman, works for social improvement were a waste of time. Christ's return was imminent; working for the salvation of men and women while there was still opportunity was paramount. Further, the hope of social improvement was a mirage. Efforts to remedy social problems by the churches were dismissed as the postmillennial error of supposing that improving the world would help bring in the millennium.[18]

Easily the most populated position was the broad centre. For evangelical centrists, distinctly religious activity and social ministry went together. The need to keep them in harness was repeated many times by *fin de siècle* evangelicals from all parts of the world. In 1904 the American Presbyterian minister J. D. Gold spoke for this standpoint when he referred to the indissolubility of the union:

> It would seem unnecessary to couple the Church of Christ, verbally, with Social Reform, for what God has joined together, we must not think of as existing apart. The Church cannot be conceived as standing outside of the social life of the nation or community. It seems to take hold of social questions quite naturally, as claiming its own . . .[19]

Many agreed with Gold on the simple need to keep the two aspects of Christian work together. It was a marriage more or less of equal partners. Others asserted that social ministry was definitely subordinate to preaching for individual redemption. Whatever their precise view, these evangelicals believed that individual regeneration provided the impetus for altruism. As converts were nurtured in the faith and educated in social problems, they would go to work to improve living conditions, not just in individual acts of charity but by participation in movements for social reform as well. As the Indianapolis Methodist Worth M. Tippy indicated, this dynamic could apply 'to the home, to social customs, to the organization of industries, to education, to government, to

---

17. David W. Bebbington, *Evangelicalism in Modern Britain: A History from the 1730s to the 1980s* (London: Unwin Hyman, 1989), 213–214.

18. Smith, *Search for Social Salvation*, 380. Matthew Sutton, *American Apocalypse: A History of Modern Evangelicalism* (Cambridge, MA: Belknap Press, 2014), 32–34.

19. J. D. Gold, 'The Church and Social Reform', *RPC 1904*, 163.

diplomacy, to literature and the fine arts, to the correction of social evils, etc., as well as to the eternal welfare of human hearts'.[20] Moreover, as the number of such socially conscious Christians grew, they would have a greater impact on society. This was why Tippy could forecast, 'if these two elements be preached together, they will issue some day . . . into a redeemed society'. Not only was their Christianity inconceivable without social ministry; for these evangelicals their hopes for the future of society were staked on it.

While it would be convenient to equate the rejection of social ministry with the theological right and the priority of social ministry with the left, evangelical attitudes to social Christianity defy neat categorization. While there were those who concentrated almost exclusively on theological questions, no example of a liberal evangelical rejecting social ministry has been located, but those subject to the fundamentalist impulse were frequently advocates of social works. The Canadian Methodist Albert Carman was one extreme conservative on the biblical question who was equally vehement on the need for social ministry.[21] The revivalists, who are often thought to have placed all their emphasis on saving souls, could add a social dimension to the traditional evangelical message of individual conversion.[22] Emerging American fundamentalists Mark Matthews and William Bell Riley both contributed to reform efforts.[23] Even within the socially cautious Keswick movement the idea of Christian service could be broadened to include welfare activism.[24] As the network that took shape around William Holmes Howland in late nineteenth-century Toronto shows, premillennial thinking could also support the view that social should go hand in hand with personal improvement as a means of bearing Christian testimony and preparing for the return of Christ for the final judgment.[25] Even among anti-modern evangelicals, individual and social salvation were combined in a 'salvationist ideology' of reform. Relatively few *fin de siècle* evangelicals had no social interest.

---

20. Quoted in Gorrell, *Age of Social Responsibility*, 29–30.
21. Christie and Gauvreau, *A Full-orbed Christianity*, 21–22, 209–210.
22. Smith, *Search for Social Salvation*, 25–26.
23. Ferenc Szasz, *The Divided Mind of Protestant America, 1880–1930* (Tuscaloosa: University of Alabama Press, 1982), 58–61, with other examples.
24. Ian M. Randall, 'Spiritual Renewal and Social Reform: Attempts to Develop Social Awareness in the Early Keswick Movement', *VE* 23 (1993), 67–86.
25. The expression is taken from Darren Dochuk, 'Redeeming the City: Premillennialism, Piety and the Politics of Reform in Late-Nineteenth Century Toronto', *Historical Papers 2000: Canadian Society of Church History*, 53–72.

The patterns of evangelical social activism

Several noteworthy contours are apparent across the broad landscape of early twentieth-century evangelical activism. Fuelling effort at every level were individuals working more or less on their own who, by their words and deeds, sought not only to transform the lives of the people around them but to stir their organizations and communities to greater efforts in social ministry. While the distinction is far from clear cut, these were of two main types.

On the one hand were the men and women of action. A striking exemplar of this stance was F. B. Meyer, for over fifty years a Baptist minister in England and at times President of the Baptist Union and Secretary of the Free Church Council.[26] He engaged in a wide range of social, political and even commercial activities not as an alternative to the gospel but as a means of making it effective. In all that he did, the spiritual was the acknowledged priority; a renewed heart was the basis of social regeneration. As Superintendent of the American Board of Church and Labor from 1903 to 1913, the Presbyterian Charles Stelzle emerged as America's 'Apostle to labor' by campaigning relentlessly for the churches to embrace working people and to apply Jesus' principles of justice, love and service to every social problem. In 1910 he also founded the New York Labor Temple to minister to the social and intellectual as well as the religious needs of the thousands of working-class and immigrant people on the Lower East Side with clubs, health activities, films, choirs and public debates in addition to a Friday religious night.[27] The little-known British women whose philanthropic ministries were celebrated in *The Christian* (Miss Daniel, Miss Parks and Miss Weston for their soldiers' homes; Miss Brown and Miss Steer for their work with homeless and 'fallen' women; and Mrs Florence Wilkinson and Miss Charlotte Sharman for help to homeless children and orphans)[28] pointed to the contribution made to evangelical social ministry under the umbrella of 'women's work'.

On the other hand were those who, in addition to Rauschenbusch, led primarily by their thought and writings. In Scotland David Watson, minister

---

26. Ian M. Randall, *Spirituality and Social Change: The Contribution of F. B. Meyer (1847–1929)* (Carlisle: Paternoster Press, 2003).
27. Szasz, *Divided Mind of Protestant America*, 51–55.
28. *C* (13 Aug. 1908), 25; (17 Dec. 1908), 21–22; (13 May 1909), 23; (12 Aug. 1909), 17–18; (7 Oct. 1909), 17; (11 Nov. 1909), 21–22; (16 Dec. 1909), 37; (30 June 1910), 15; (10 Nov. 1910), 17; (24 Aug. 1911), 21; (5 Oct. 1911), 29; (9 Nov. 1911), 14; (25 Apr. 1912), 21; (16 May 1912), 16; (30 May 1912), 20; (17 Oct. 1912), 28; (11 Dec. 1913), 36; (7 May 1914), 22.

of St Clement's Church of Scotland, Glasgow, from 1886 to 1938, founder and President of the Scottish Christian Social Union, presented the case for the new social Christianity as integral to the church's mission to individuals, arguing in his many books and articles that the latter was far more likely to be effective if complemented by work for improved social conditions.[29] In the Dominions the Canadian Methodist Samuel Chown was another who advocated the systematic study of the social as well as the intellectual problems of the time as the basis of a choice between 'an un-social religion which cannot be Christianity' and 'a system of social salvation, without religious impact or influence'.[30] The Kansan Charles Sheldon wrote some twenty-five books to show that the traditional ethic of following the example and teaching of Jesus would improve social conditions. Far more substantial than generally supposed, early twentieth-century evangelical social commentary provided impetus to the ongoing application of the gospel to the conditions of contemporary society.

At the turn of the century welfare work also featured prominently in the home missions operations of the churches. Social service maintained its place alongside evangelism in the Salvation Army and its imitators. Alongside the denominations and quasi-denominations was a plethora of organizations and charitable agencies to help the sick, the poor and the disadvantaged. The bodies represented at the annual May meetings held in London to publicize the cause of evangelical and philanthropic work provide a fair sample. Alongside organizations such as the CMS were the London Medical Mission, the Anti-slavery and Aborigines Protection Society, the Society for the Suppression of the Opium Traffic, the Strangers' Home for Asiatics, the Commercial Travellers' Christian Association, the Whitechapel Working Lads Institute, the National Children's Home, the Aged Pilgrims' Friend Society and the Peace Society.[31] The non-denominational Young Men's and Young Women's Christian Associations combined evangelism with a variety of educational and service activities throughout the evangelical world. Similarly youth groups such as Christian Endeavour Societies and Epworth and Luther Leagues promoted evangelical social service activities among the young along a wide front. Seemingly wherever there was a need, evangelicals of the era developed a ministry or created an institution to alleviate that need's effects and remedy its causes.

---

29. Michael A. McCabe, '"Luther's Blunder": David Watson and Social Christianity in Early Twentieth-Century Scotland', *RSCHS* 30 (2000), 193–221.

30. Quoted in Christie and Gauvreau, *A Full-orbed Christianity*, 14–16.

31. 'May Meetings', *C* (4 Apr. 1912), 27.

In innumerable parishes and communities around the evangelical world social ministry was integral to the everyday life of local churches and their communities. Bethany Presbyterian Church in Philadelphia and Central Presbyterian Church in Atlanta are among the American churches known to have conducted extensive social ministries. In the 'Middlemarch world' of Coventry in England, at Queen's Park Baptist Church, a 'tradition of sensible philanthropy' was maintained with the church 'in direct touch with all the human needs of the city'.[32] Holy Trinity Anglican Church in Adelaide, always anxious to maintain its evangelical witness in a diocese dominated by Anglo-Catholics, included in its activities a branch of the Mothers' Union committed to the maintenance of marriage and the family from 1898, and the Band of Hope, the children's temperance meeting.[33] At the local level too the work of women in the service of others came into its own. Perhaps their many and various efforts best illustrate the taken-for-granted nature of evangelical social ministry.

The inherent tendency to social engagement in evangelicalism became particularly prominent under the special conditions of the mission field. While leaving no doubt that the primary purpose of evangelical missions was religious, the American missionary statesman Robert Wilder observed at the time that missionaries 'do interest themselves in the physical and moral condition of the people, and ... they do introduce changes of dress and industry and medical treatment, and that their work does spread enlightenment and make the people discontented with ignorance, injustice, tyranny and wrong'.[34] Many saw this as a matter of Christlike compassion and familial service, but contemporary missions analyst James Dennis added that missions

> bring the first principles of Christianity, in its application to the associate life
> of men, to bear at points where moral principle is at stake. They impinge upon
> social customs where they are in conflict with the ethical standards of God's Word.
> They seek to introduce new ideas where the old are incompatible with Christ's
> teaching.[35]

---

32. Clyde Binfield, *Pastors and People: The Biography of a Baptist Church, Queen's Road Coventry* (Coventry: Queen's Road Baptist Church, 1984), 105, 144.

33. Brian Dickey, *Holy Trinity Adelaide 1836–1988: The History of a City Church* (Adelaide: Trinity Church Trust, 1988).

34. Robert Wilder, *Missionary Principles and Practice* (New York: Fleming H. Revell, 1902), 29, 30.

35. James S. Dennis, *Christian Missions and Social Progress: A Sociological Study of Modern Missions*, 2 vols. (Edinburgh: Oliphant, Anderson & Ferrier, 1899), I, 25.

A turn-of-the-century count designed to illustrate the nineteenth-century achievement and present operations of missions revealed the results of these dynamics. The educational institutions established to promote enlightenment, practical skill and moral force included the foundation of 88 universities, 864 boarding and high schools and seminaries, 179 industrial training institutions and classes, 67 medical schools and schools for nurses, 121 kindergartens and 18,742 elementary or village day schools. Some 369 hospitals and 772 dispensaries had been established to provide relief for physical suffering and to counter the quackery of indigenous religions. The many philanthropic and reformatory institutions intended to alleviate other forms of social distress included orphanages; homes for the blind, lepers and widows; and asylums for the insane.[36] Work done for the emancipation of women through such institutions as the 'Zenana' missions was counted as one of the glories of the missionary movement. The early twentieth-century debate over the purpose of missions – evangelism or civilization – reflected the extent of the social dimension of evangelical missions.[37]

Wide support for social ministry largely accounts for the two new features on the landscape of *fin de siècle* evangelical social activism. Reflecting the contemporary trend in society towards bureaucratic organization, the first was increased planning and organization within denominations for greater efficiency and effectiveness in social ministry.[38] The Canadian churches showed the way. In 1902 the Methodists established a Department of Evangelism and Social Service. Four years later the Presbyterians followed with a Board of Social Services and Evangelism. Both organizations were intended to consolidate church efforts in the domain of social reform and to unite social service with evangelism with a view to ensuring that Christianity remained fully a part of a nation undergoing rapid transformation.[39] In America the Presbyterians created the Department of Church and Labor under Charles Stelzle in 1903, and later the Commission on Social Services, agencies that were widely imitated.[40] By 1910 all the major denominations had created agencies for social ministry. Indeed, so widespread was the tendency to systematic organization that the

---

36. James S. Dennis, *Centennial Survey of Foreign Missions* (New York: Fleming H. Revell, 1902), 67–120, 192–232, 265–267.

37. See 39 above.

38. Exemplified in Peter Shepherd, *The Making of a Modern Denomination: John Howard Shakespeare and the English Baptists 1898–1924* (Carlisle: Paternoster Press, 2001).

39. Christie and Gauvreau, *A Full-orbed Christianity*, 3, 21–22, 34–36.

40. Catalogued in Smith, *Search for Social Salvation*, 437–460.

Methodist H. K. Carroll observed wryly, 'It seems as though every phase of church activity must have some particular form of organization to look after its interests.'[41] Nevertheless, many evangelicals were glad to have the advantages of rational organization and unity in their social and philanthropic work.

Concern for using resources efficiently and maximizing social impact also activated the ecumenist tendency in evangelical social ministry. Among the reasons for facilitating cooperation among the Free Churches in Britain when they came together to form the Free Church Council in 1896 was the promotion of 'the application of the law of Christ in every relation of human life', including political and social problems.[42] After six years of negotiation, Canadian Methodists, Presbyterians and Congregationalists had devised a basis of union by the end of 1908. This point was reached, as Methodist N. W. Rowell explained, 'not by the spendthrift policy of competition, but . . . by the brotherly policy of cooperation'. He added as the rationale, 'It is only thus that the world will feel the impact of the combined strength and energy of the whole Church of Christ.'[43] The high point of pre-1914 efforts to achieve cooperation in Christian work was the foundation in 1908 of the Federal Council of Churches of Christ in America. While a voluntary association of Protestant Churches, it was 'distinctly evangelical in character', with the desire to 'secure a large combined influence for the Churches of Christ in all matters affecting the moral and social conditions of the people, so as to promote the application of the law of Christ in every relation of human life' prominent among its objects.[44] The Men and Religion Forward Movement, which evangelicals originated and led in 1911–12 and that placed reform of society alongside saving souls in its quest to build a Christian social order by winning back men to the churches, was a further sign of the willingness of American evangelicals to work alongside others in the cause of social Christianity.[45] Like their counterparts elsewhere, they had recognized the need for united

---

41. *EMC 1911*, 44.

42. E. K. H. Jordan, *Free Church Unity: History of the Free Church Council Movement 1896–1941* (London: Lutterworth Press, 1956), 53–54, with examples on 57, 75.

43. N. W. Rowell, 'Interdenominational Cooperation', *EMC 1911*, 296–297.

44. W. H. Roberts, 'Church Federation', *RPC 1909*, 400–401.

45. *Messages of the Men and Religion Movement*. Vol. 4: *Christian Unity/Missions* (New York: Association Press, 1912); Gail Bederman, '"The Women Have Had Charge of the Church Work Long Enough": The Men and Religion Forward Movement of 1911–1912 and the Masculinization of Middle-Class Protestantism', *AQ* 41.3 (1989), 432–465.

organization among the churches so that the work of Christianizing society could be done more effectively.

Aspects of evangelical social engagement

Of the specific issues around which early twentieth-century social concern took shape, the problems of urbanization remained fundamental. As cities became the primary demographic feature of the modern world, social difficulties abounded to challenge human ingenuity and moral character. The many aspects of city life causing concern included congested tenement housing and slums, poor sanitation, disease, high infant mortality rates, recurrent unemployment, sweat shops, exploitation of child and female labour, poverty, inadequate education and skills training, indifference to old workers and widows, vice and limited opportunities for worthwhile recreation. Modern cities, especially the wage-earning people who made up the bulk of their populations, presented a profound challenge to those who sought to apply the teachings of the gospel and their own calling to sacrificial service for their redemption.[46]

While individual conversion was still seen as the basic remedy, direct confrontation with the modern urban environment was accepted as a necessary adjunct. Social settlements, first established in the 1880s to Christianize their immediate environments and regarded in some quarters as the best form of urban ministry, were extended.[47] Methodists everywhere celebrated the success of central missions and halls as refuges for the abandoned, labour exchanges for the unemployed, centres for opposing debilitating social evils and as means for making life cleaner.[48] Some success was also claimed for the Pleasant Sunday Afternoon movement.[49] Evangelistic in purpose but intended to unite men in 'brotherhoods of mutual help', more than 2,000 such societies, with a membership of almost half a million working men, were formed in Britain in

---

46. E.g. Josiah Strong, *The Challenge of the City* (New York: Young People's Missionary Movement, 1907).

47. W. Schenk, 'The Settlement', *RPC 1909*, 345–350; George P. Eckman, 'Settlement Work', *EMC 1911*, 401–404.

48. Edward Boaden, 'Present Position of Methodism in the Eastern Section', *EMC 1901*, 47, 48; Simpson Johnson, 'Methodism in the Eastern Section in the Last Ten Years', *EMC 1911*, 71.

49. J. Y. Simpson, 'Aspects of Home Mission Work', *RPC 1909*, 350–355.

the early years of the twentieth century.[50] At the same time the Institutional
Church Movement began to spread from its beginnings in America.[51] A
network of organizations for men and women around a central church, it
served communities by providing 'companionship . . . training . . . culture . . .
everything that uplifts a man'. Initiatives of this order sustained a certain 'urban
optimism'. It was also evident in support for the garden city movement which
led to the creation of communities such as Letchworth (1903) and left a
permanent mark on town planning.[52] With cities having become centres of
religious activism, evangelicals had some justification for resisting criticism
(as did A. M. Fairbairn in 1899 on behalf of English Congregationalists)[53] that
they had not responded adequately to the new social conditions of the modern
industrial city.

   Responses to the cities were one sign that evangelicals were increasingly aware
of the difference between charitable relief, on the one hand, and authentic and
just remedies for social problems, on the other. They have often been accused
of social conservatism, accepting a status quo from which they benefited or
being too ensnared in their individualist soteriology to see beyond personal
responsibility to systemic causation. In fact, evangelical environmentalism, fed
largely by what they observed in the cities, caused many evangelicals to criticize
the prevailing order. An extensive critique of capitalism arose within the
movement as a result.[54] The target was rank materialism. It fostered immorality
by its passion for material luxury, and it sustained dishonesty and corruption in
the commercial world. Its operations pitted employers and workers against one
another, reduced the worker 'to the mere level of being a part of a machine' in

---

50. David Killingray, 'Hands Joined in Brotherhood: The Rise and Decline of a
    Movement for Faith and Social Change, 1875–2000', in Anthony Cross et al. (eds.),
    *Pathways and Patterns in History: Essays on Baptists, Evangelicals and the Modern World in
    Honour of David Bebbington* (London: Spurgeon's College; Didcot: Baptist Missional
    Society, 2015), 319–339.
51. Matthew Bowman, *The Urban Pulpit: New York City and the Fate of Liberal
    Evangelicalism* (New York: Oxford University Press, 2014), 112, 127–144.
52. David W. Bebbington, 'The City, the Countryside and the Social Gospel in Late
    Victorian Nonconformity', *SCH* 16 (1979), 415–426.
53. A. M. Fairbairn, 'Discussion Following Professor Taylor's Address', *ICC 1899*, 152.
54. E.g. Will Reason, 'The Bearing of New Testament Ethics in Family and Economic
    Relations', *ICC 1908*, 417–419; George Truett, 'The Coming of the Kingdom in
    America', *WBC 1911*, 424; S. D. Chown, 'Adaptation of the Church to the Needs
    of Modern Life', *EMC 1911*, 287.

the factory system, and tolerated recurrent unemployment. Competition could not be regarded as ethically sound so long as it failed to give workers a fair share of the wealth their labour created. Indeed there was something inherently wrong with a system that allowed great wealth to exist alongside desperate poverty. Monopoly of the land by small numbers of people and the exploitativeness of landlordism could not pass unchallenged. Much of what evangelicals experienced in the world around them did not align with the ethical values rooted in their faith.

Yet, with no proposal for social and economic reconstruction, evangelical critics of capitalism were far from being revolutionaries. Their remedy for the deficiencies of the capitalist system was the application of Christian principles and values to the current order.[55] An appreciation of the New Testament estimate of humanity would make exploitation and the unnecessary destruction of health and life unacceptable. Business would be at its best when it aimed chiefly to serve the community. Consecrated wealth would luxuriate in the joy of giving and acting to remedy poverty and misery. The higher standards that necessarily accompany a sense of personal responsibility to Christ would resolve tensions between capital and labour. Well aware that their prescriptions would be dismissed as naive and utopian, evangelicals nevertheless insisted that commercial life could be Christianized. Transformation of the capitalist order, not its replacement, was the solution they proffered.

Working people themselves had not of course waited for the Christianization of capitalism to remedy their situation. Given the materialistic aims and apparent subversiveness of the social order of the trade unions they had formed, opposition from within evangelicalism was perhaps inevitable.[56] At the same time their interest in the political, social and industrial as well as the moral and spiritual health of society caused other evangelicals to support trade unions. Some even saw in unionism their sphere of service. Thomas Burt, who rose to become President of the British Trades Union Congress in 1911, was one of many miners of Northumberland and Durham who were both active Methodists and

---

55. E.g. Charles J. Guthrie, 'Christian Morality in its application to Business', *RPC 1899*, 265–270; Charles Mills, 'The Bearing of New Testament Ethics on Social and Economic Relations', *ICC 1908*, 423–424; W. Hodson Smith, 'Our Social Duty as a People's Church', *EMC 1911*, 380; David F. Bonner, 'Christ and the Industrial Problem', *BS* 69.275 (1912), 492–512.

56. E.g. William C. Cochran, 'Labor Legislation', *BS* 57.225 (1900), 119–134; 226 (1900), 240–254; Ernest L. Bogart, 'The Steel Strike', *BS* 59.236 (1902), 108–128; 224 (1902), 294–304.

active trade unionists.[57] In Australia W. G. Spence, for more than a decade the Sunday School Superintendent of the Creswick Presbyterian Church in Victoria, became the greatest union organizer in Australian history. His own career was a leading example of his general teaching that evangelical Christianity and trade unionism aided and abetted one another.[58]

The advent of the labour movement meant that evangelicals had to decide to what extent socialism, its leading ideology, was compatible with their Christian outlook. That there were many socialisms by the turn of the century helps to explain the range of evangelical responses.[59] In various quarters socialism's doctrinaire environmentalism (the view that beliefs and values were created by the external environment of human behaviour), commitment to the collective ownership of property and social divisiveness were impugned.[60] It was further condemned as materialistic, atheistic, immoral and a diversion from the need for individual regeneration. Talk of the 'religion of socialism' also made it look like a dangerous substitute for Christianity, an impression given verisimilitude by the defection of some working men from the churches. The perception of socialism as a pretender moral force shaped this negative evaluation. It was a 'false prophet', incapable of bringing about individual moral reform. This opposition was mostly rhetorical, but it could be organized. In Britain a Nonconformist Anti-Socialistic Union was formed in 1909. In the following year it mutated into an Anti-Socialist Union of Churches. The major support came from English Anglican evangelicals among whom opposition to socialism was the norm.[61] A substantial part of the movement stood opposed to socialism as its major rival in the task of providing the moral basis of modern society.

Other evangelicals were more positive in their assessment. In socialism they recognized a force that had the capacity to realize the social application of the gospel. Generally, however, they argued that by itself it was not enough. Morally

---

57. Robert F. Wearmouth, *The Social and Political Influence of Methodism in the Twentieth Century* (London: Epworth Press, 1957), chs. 6–7.

58. Robert D. Linder, 'Australian Evangelicals in Politics in the Victorian Age: The Cases of J. D. Lang, W. G. Spence, and J. S. T. McGowen', *L* 13 (1992), 34–60.

59. E.g. Andrew Millar, 'Christianity and Socialism', *RPC 1904*, 116–120; Urquhart A. Forbes, 'Socialism', *LQR* 119 – 4th series (1908), VII, 52–68.

60. E.g. Will Reason, 'The Bearing of New Testament Ethics in Family and Economic Relations', *ICC 1908*, 411–420, esp. 415, 420; 'Disillusionment', *C* (25 Apr. 1907), 9; 'The Menace of Socialism', *C* (1 Aug. 1909), 9; James Lindsay, 'Philosophical Tests of Socialism', *BS* 67.265 (1910), 86–104.

61. Bebbington, *Evangelicalism in Modern Britain*, 215.

inadequate, it could not transform the individual into a social being. For that people needed Christ, so that Christianity was necessary to make socialism workable. Two Welshmen illustrate the different ways in which evangelicals supported socialism.[62] The Baptist T. Tudwal Evans of Newport, Monmouthshire, emphasized the overlap between the two creeds. Socialism was the means to hand to follow Jesus in working for the temporal as well as the spiritual salvation of humankind. Because of the principles embodied in his teaching, Jesus could be regarded as a socialist. John Morgan Jones, a Calvinistic Methodist of Merthyr Tydfil, differentiated between Christianity and socialism more sharply. Jesus was not a socialist; his teaching was spiritual and moral, not economic and political. But he did provide the spirit that would triumph over the environment and change it gradually. As a matter of practical piety Christianity and socialism should therefore be allowed to complement and reinforce one another. Such views were, as the English Baptist J. G. Greenhough observed about professed Christian Socialist and English Methodist J. E. Rattenbury, more Christian than socialist.[63] To effect a reconciliation the differences between the two movements were minimized.

Evangelicals and politics

Inevitably their aspirations for society brought evangelicals into contact with the state at a time when its nature in the English-speaking world was changing. In the early stages of the shift towards the welfare state the state was becoming larger and more interventionist. Recognizing its benefits, especially for the weak and underprivileged, evangelicals on the whole welcomed the development. Outwardly at least the particulars of national and political organization were of no great interest. For evangelicals the primary requirement was that the state be 'an instrument of righteousness'. While those who took an interest were generally content to assert the ideal, Walter Rauschenbusch controversially claimed that it had actually been realized.[64] Meaning that it was part of the organism by which the Spirit of Christ can do his work among humanity, and buoyed by the extension of progressive legislation to such matters as food production, sanitation and industry, he felt political life in early twentieth-century

---

62. Pope, *Building Jerusalem*, 49–54.
63. 'A Symposium on Socialism. What Is Its Relation to Christianity? What Ministers Say', *SC* (1 Apr. 1910), 400–401 (reproduced from the London *Christian Age*).
64. Evans, *Kingdom Is Always but Coming*, 231–236, 259–261, 321–322.

America had been Christianized. Few shared this optimistic assessment, but among evangelicals the new possibilities for social legislation and the more humanitarian spirit of the modern state attracted wide sympathy and support.[65]

In taking this line, politically minded *fin de siècle* evangelicals recognized that they were living in the age of 'the new democracy'.[66] In the polities of the English-speaking world, power was seen to be shifting from the rights of class and property to the rights of the people. While generally welcoming this development, evangelicals were mindful that the pluralism and the sometimes sordid realities of this new order made it unlikely that they would ever gain control of governments. Their task in this situation was to ensure that the state functioned Christianly.[67] Two responsibilities followed. The first was to form public opinion. Evangelical leaders were called to speak prophetically to identify issues and press for their resolution by enunciating ideals and probing consciences.[68] The other was for all their people to vote (although this was not yet an option for evangelical women everywhere) with a view to getting the right people elected to public office and the right causes addressed. The Congregational missionary scholar James Barton put the matter succinctly: 'If the Church's business is to preach the Gospel that makes new lives, it is the State's business, under the influence of Christian votes, to use its power to facilitate the making of new environments for these lives.'[69] Through public discussion and the ballot box early twentieth-century evangelicals recognized a capacity not only to oppose current abuses but to create and shape public issues for the Christianization of the social order. Adapting to the emerging political system, they assumed the mantle of the pressure group.

---

65. E.g. Samuel G. Smith, 'The Church and the Kingdom', *ICC 1908*, 179; J. T. Forbes, 'Baptist Polity and International Brotherhood', *WBC 1911*, 328; J. H. E., 'Studies in Social Christianity. The Basis for Christian Action', *HomR* 63.3 (Mar. 1912), 209–216, esp. 210–211.

66. E.g. R. F. Horton, 'The Christian and Public Life', *FCC* 13.154 (Oct. 1911), 211–212; James A. MacDonald, 'Christianity and Governments', *HomR* 64.1 (July 1912), 58–61 (60 for 'the new democracy').

67. E.g. 'Christ and Democracy', *C* (30 May 1907), 10; 'The Church and the Democracy', *C* (12 Oct. 1911), 9.

68. E.g. George E. Gates, 'The Minister as a Force in Civic Life', *HomR* 52.5 (Nov. 1906), 339–343; Josiah Strong, 'The Church and Reform', *HomR* 60.5 (Nov. 1910), 381–382.

69. James L. Barton, 'Will the Moral Leadership of the World Rest with Christianity?', *ICC 1908*, 152–153.

Of course many contemporary evangelicals were diffident about political involvement. They worried that it was a distraction from the spiritual life and that churches would be divided by political issues. Proponents of participation rejected these fears. Insisting their religion dealt with the whole of life, they dismissed the twin inferences that Christ's religion was not equal to the affairs of the world and that Christian holiness required withdrawal from everyday life. Their case for godly politics operated at several levels.[70] Pragmatically it was the only way to defend and promote Christian causes and, more generally, at least to minimize bad and unchristian legislation. In any case, some matters were unavoidably political because it was only through legislation that improvements could be achieved. Ideally securing good government was the responsibility of citizenship and, by overcoming injustices and doing right in the face of vested interests, a way of fulfilling the mission to serve the people. Theologically upholding the truths of the gospel amid the social and political realities of community life was one means by which the kingdoms of the world would become the kingdom of God. Seeing themselves without difficulty or reservation as the agents of the Almighty, politically minded evangelicals conceived of participation in politics as a way of getting God's will done on earth as it was in heaven.

Of the numerous areas of public life to which this aspiration applied, two were paramount. Provision of education had long been a matter of concern, but, as W. H. Whitsitt told delegates to the Baptist World Congress in 1905, early twentieth-century evangelicals were confronted by a new situation.[71] The need of mass education at the primary level meant that only the state commanded the resources to provide what was required. Attempts by various governments to meet this need caused widespread controversy. The British Government's Education Act of 1902 precipitated the greatest battle of the age, as English Nonconformists passionately resisted a system they believed used public money to favour the established Church of England.[72] Elsewhere in the religiously mixed communities of 'Greater Britain' and the United States where there were no established churches, evangelicals feared that education was becoming less religious as it became more public. When in 1904 Alexander MacEwan of Edinburgh insisted that, while religion is an essential part of education, it should

---

70. E.g. John Cuttell, 'The Christian in Politics', *FCC* 7.77 (May 1905), 133–134; J. H. E., 'Politics a Divine Ordinance', *HomR* 63.2 (Feb. 1912), 126–133.

71. W. H. Whitsitt, 'National Primary Education', *WBC 1905*, 39–43.

72. David W. Bebbington, *The Nonconformist Conscience: Chapel and Politics 1870–1914* (London: George Allen & Unwin, 1982), ch. 7.

not in a public system be denominational or under the control of church officials, he described the framework within which evangelicals endeavoured to resolve the situation.[73] Where it was not already the practice, the first requirement was to secure the reading of the Bible in primary schools as the basis of religion and/or morality. Disagreement among Protestants themselves, and opposition from Catholics and secularists, made this surprisingly difficult to achieve. What happened in New Zealand was not unusual. Despite a campaign of more than a quarter of a century in duration to achieve non-denominational Bible reading without comment by teachers, by 1914 the government had not been persuaded to alter the settlement of 1877, which had excluded religion from schools.[74] Education was one area in which evangelicals recognized they were losing ground in the modern state.

In the matter of temperance evangelicals fared better. With their Victorian forebears, many of them continued to believe that alcohol was the root cause of the vice and social distress seen in the cities and elsewhere. In addition to supporting temperance organizations and boycotting public houses and grocery stores implicated in the trade, they looked to remedial action by the state. Well aware of the power of the vested interest and of the unpopularity of their cause, some evangelicals advocated prohibition. Others, perhaps more pragmatic, were content with restrictionist measures such as local option, strict licensing, limited opening hours and Sunday closing as steps towards eventual abolition of the trade. These differences notwithstanding, the combined effects of agitation and use of the ballot achieved various improvements in the situation throughout the evangelical world.[75] In America in particular the Anti-Saloon League, a single issue and pioneering pressure group founded in 1893 and presenting itself as 'the Church in Action', achieved considerable success.[76] In 1913, after twenty years of operating at local and state level, it decided to mount a campaign for national prohibition. Buoyed by their progress, early twentieth-century evangelicals intensified their political campaign against the harmful effects of the liquor traffic.

---

73. Alex R. MacEwan, 'The Church and Public Education', *RPC 1904*, 167–174.

74. Ian Breward, *Godless Schools? A Study of Protestant Reactions to Secular Schools in New Zealand* (Christchurch: Presbyterian Bookroom, 1967).

75. See the various national entries in Jack S. Blocker, Jr., et al. (eds.), *Alcohol and Temperance in Modern History: An International Encyclopedia* (Santa Barbara: ABC-CLIO, 2003).

76. Jack S. Blocker, Jr., *American Temperance Movements: Cycles of Reform* (Boston: Twayne Publishers, 1989), ch. 4.

Because of the need for action in public matters affecting the position and prospects of Christianity in contemporary society, careers in politics at all levels of government were still regarded as normal and necessary for evangelicals. Edward Eaton, a Wisconsin Congregationalist, was among those who strongly maintained this standpoint: 'Every Christian should be in politics, he belongs there, *ex officio*, as a Christian man. *She* belongs there, whether a voter or not, in the exercise of an enlightened, self-devoting, purifying influence.'[77]

Local government was the primary sphere in which evangelicals worked out their political calling. The Scottish Congregationalist D. L. Ritchie gave the reason for this commitment: 'The best men in our churches devote themselves to civil duties, to purifying and keeping pure public life in order that they may help to lift up the population which is outside the churches.'[78] Other evangelicals aspired to representation at state and national levels. Of the 43 Labour representatives elected to the British Parliament in 1906, 7 are known to have had a conversion experience, 9 attended church regularly and 14 were preachers.[79] In New South Wales Methodists so dominated the parliamentary Labour Party in the 1890s (9 members out of 35) that it was denounced as composed of 'pulpit punchers and local preachers'.[80] When joined by 12 others with a similar Christian outlook, they made up 60% of its membership, so that the world's first parliamentary Labour Party was dominated by evangelicals.

Participation in politics created opportunities for community leadership, which evangelicals prized.[81] The first parliamentary Labour Party was headed by 'Honest' Jim McGowen, whose blending of faith and politics is evident in his being simultaneously Premier of New South Wales and Sunday School Superintendent of St Paul's Anglican Church in Redfern, Sydney.[82]

---

77. Edward D. Eaton, 'The Bearing of New Testament Ethics on Civic Relations', *ICC 1908*, 434–441, 437 for the quotations (emphasis in the original).
78. D. L. Ritchie, 'Discussion Following Professor Taylor's Address', *ICC 1899*, 153–154.
79. Kenneth D. Brown, 'Non-Conformity and the British Labour Movement: A Case Study', *JSH* 8.2 (1975), 113–120; David W. Bebbington, 'Baptist Members of Parliament in the Twentieth Century', *BQ* 31.6 (1986), 252–287.
80. Robert D. Linder, 'The Methodist Love Affair with the Australian Labor Party, 1891–1929', *L* 23, 24 (1997–8), 35–61 (quotations on 39, 47).
81. Edward Boaden, 'The Present Position of Methodism in the Eastern Section', *EMC 1901*, 49–50; 'Christian Mayors', *C* (27 Dec. 1906), 9.
82. Robert D. Linder, '"Honest Jim" McGowen (1855–1922) as a Christian in Politics', *L* 15 (1993), 44–59.

In America William Jennings Bryan, twice elected to the US House of
Representatives and three times Democratic candidate for the Presidency
(although never successfully), became Secretary of State from 1912 to 1915.
Known as the 'Great Commoner', his long and controversial career, in which
he often defended the weak against the strong and well organized, was
a colourful demonstration of Christian service through leadership in high
politics.[83]

The most distinguished evangelical in politics in this era was both motivated
by his faith and sought to express that faith politically. Woodrow Wilson, twenty-
eighth President of the United States from 1913 to 1921, the son of a Southern
Presbyterian home, who experienced conversion at the age of 17, saw himself
as a divinely called leader.[84] Even the apparent preoccupation with economic
issues in his early years was an expression of his commitment to realizing in
public life the underlying moral structures derived from his Presbyterian-
Calvinist formation. The same influence engendered a style that evinced
a sometimes unfortunate certainty that he was right and that his political
mission came from God. It could also accommodate a defence of segregation
that alienated American evangelicals such as fellow Presbyterian Reverend
Francis Grimké. His crusading idealism led Wilson to press upon the American
people a quest to convert material into moral force by showing humanity
'the paths of liberty and mutual serviceability'.[85] The events of the years
immediately ahead were to provide a wider stage onto which to cast this
moralized understanding of the meaning of American politics. As he did so,
in both strength and weakness, Wilson impressed the world as the leading
example of the evangelical conception of politics as a form of Christian life
and service.

The election of Wilson in 1912 represents the high point of evangelical
political and social influence in the pre-war years. Behind it was the contribution of evangelicals to the progressive era in America, indirectly through
their influence on the formation of the proponents of the movement, and
directly as their rhetoric and activity fed the value system that drove the
quest for greater congruence between individual moral standards and public

83. Michael Kazin, *A Godly Hero: The Life of William Jennings Bryan* (New York: Alfred
     A. Knopf, 2006).
84. Malcolm D. Magee, *What the World Should Be: Woodrow Wilson and the Crafting
     of a Faith-Based Foreign Policy* (Waco: Baylor University Press, 2008), ch. 1.
85. Richard V. Pierard and Robert D. Linder, *Civil Religion and the Presidency* (Grand
     Rapids: Academie Books, 1988), 152.

life.[86] In Canada progressivism had a more domestic focus, but evangelicals were in the forefront as the churches led the movement for social reform.[87] The importance of Nonconformity in contemporary British politics similarly points to the effect of evangelicals beyond their own communities. However, their ability to determine the government in 1906 but not its programmes in office foreshadowed the waning of evangelical social and political influence. *Fin de siècle* evangelicals themselves recognized that they did not have the same capacity to shape social perspectives and values as their fathers and grand-fathers. Perceptions of declining influence in the modern industrialized and bureaucratized society led to the belief that they were passing through a crisis of Christian civilization.[88]

Paralleling this sense of crisis was something of a reaction against social Christianity within the evangelical movement as the first decade of the new century drew to a close. Around 1910 statements about the priority of the spiritual became more insistent and prevalent, while direct criticism of social Christianity became more noticeable.[89] In Britain, with passions rising against the background of the General Elections of 1910 and Nonconformist leaders such as John Clifford and Sylvester Horne seen to be absent from their church posts, claims of neglect of spiritual work and the worldliness of politics gained credibility. Publication of the statistics revealing a decline in church attendance added to the sense of crisis.[90] In 1911 the Canadian Samuel Chown, who had spent the previous decade labouring in the cause of social Christianity, told his fellow Methodists, 'We recognize that the spiritual function of the Church is supreme.'[91] In America the end of the Men and Religion Forward Movement in 1912 sparked disapproval of the priorities and theological bases of social

---

86. David B. Danbom, *'The World of Hope': Progressives and the Struggle for an Ethical Public Life* (Philadelphia: Temple University Press, 1987), esp. chs. 2–3; and Robert M. Crunden, *Ministers of Reform: The Progressives' Achievement in American Civilization 1889–1920* (New York: Basic Books, 1982).

87. Christie and Gauvreau, *A Full-orbed Christianity*.

88. E.g. addresses by James L. Barton and Caspar W. Hiatt under the title 'Will the Moral Leadership of the World Rest with Christianity?', *ICC 1908*, 154–165; J. D. Jones, 'Is Church Life Necessary to Christian Civilization?', ibid. 166–174.

89. E.g. From the Presbyterian right in America, William B. Greene, 'The Church and the Social Question', *PTR* 10.3 (1912), 377–398.

90. Stephen Koss, *Nonconformity in Modern British Politics* (London: B. T. Batsford, 1975), 108–109, 115.

91. S. D. Chown, 'Discussion', *EMC 1911*, 63–64.

Christianity within the evangelical churches. Symptomatic of the change was the resignation in 1913 of Charles Stelzle, wrongly accused of having become preoccupied with social ministry, as Director of the Presbyterian Department of Church and Labor and adoption by the denomination of a theologically conservative 'United Declaration of Christian Faith and Social Service' in the following year.[92] Behind these developments was an emerging critique of social Christianity. Above all it was alleged that social reconstruction had superseded personal salvation in the ministry of the church, a standpoint which also maintained that the place of sin and evil in the world had been underestimated and the mission of Jesus misrepresented. With the primacy of conversionism over social activism being reasserted, a discernible shift to the right on the social question was taking place within the evangelical movement on the eve of the First World War.

Conclusion

Even so, in its social activism the evangelicalism of the *fin de siècle* years also ranks with the best eras in the history of the movement. As individuals and in innumerable organizations as well as their churches, in rhetoric and action across a wide range of interests and concerns, at home and on the mission field, the evangelicals of this period collectively were as strongly committed to social Christianity as their counterparts at other times. Quantitatively and qualitatively, the cities of the English-speaking world were sites of the greatest effort as evangelicals brought a growing understanding of moral environmentalism to bear on their thinking. They also addressed the underlying economic and social system and enunciated critiques of alternative approaches to improvement. At all levels of government evangelicals maintained high levels of involvement, including occupancy of the American presidency, in process of becoming the most powerful political office in the world. In the historiography of the period they have been overshadowed by newer secular and quasi-religious groups such as the progressive and the labour movements, and religious historians have given greater recognition to other Protestant groups. However, the quantity, breadth and energy of their commitment was not exceeded by other proponents of social Christianity and reached levels unsurpassed in the history of evangelicalism itself. While it is true that early twentieth-century evangelicals by themselves achieved no dramatic reforms of the order of the end of the slave trade, in an

92. Smith, *Search for Social Salvation*, 45–46, 364–370.

emerging welfare society there was less need for them to do so. Their achievement was to influence the public opinion to which democratic governments were obliged to respond. Judged by contemporary standards, evangelicals were full participants in the social gospel movement and made a worthy contribution towards the achievement of its objectives.

In doing so, *fin de siècle* evangelicals from across the full spectrum of theological opinion were seeking to maintain the pastoral effectiveness and social influence achieved in the previous generation. This shared commitment was due in part to anxiety about declining social influence, but it also flowed from the prior conviction that social ministry was part of their calling in response to biblical teaching and the example of Jesus. As in other aspects of the movement, seeking to maintain the relevance of the evangelical tradition to contemporary life gave rise to different approaches. Some of the evangelicals of these years were content to speak and act much as they had done before the effects of industrialization and urbanization became really pressing. But in varying degrees many others took the initiative and introduced new methods and strategies. Amid this diversity, responding to the social needs of the day again activated the ecumenist tendency in evangelicalism and gave rise to the cooperative effort secured by organizational unity. On the other hand, so substantial was commitment to service and reform that, by the end of the first decade of the twentieth century, it was being alleged that social ministry had become a distraction from the true work of the gospel. In this way the 'evangelical coalition', although holding together, was brought under further strain. But this reaction only highlighted the strength of evangelical social Christianity in the two decades before the outbreak of the Great War, when the evangelical gospel remained a social gospel.

6. 'MARCHING AS TO WAR'

The normal flow of evangelical life was interrupted when Britain declared war on Germany on 4 August 1914. Resistance to the German invasion of Belgium and France quickly gave rise to the 'western front' in northern France. An 'eastern front' also opened along the German–Russian border, while early in 1915 a British-led attack on the Turkish Empire in the Dardanelles took the war to the Middle East. Other imperial connections of the protagonists caused the war to become global in scope. 'Greater Britain' in particular rallied to the support of 'the mother country'. The mission fields of the nineteenth century were also affected, indirectly as men from these areas joined the British imperial forces, and directly as British and German colonial possessions were contested by the combatants. Having initially struggled to maintain its neutrality, the United States also entered the war early in 1917. From this point the entire evangelical movement was caught up in the conflict between the Allied and the Central Powers which, because of its un-precedented scope, its long duration, the scale of the violence and destruction in the fighting, and the involvement of civilian populations, is justifiably reckoned as one of the most important events in the making of the twentieth-century world.[1]

As an episode of this order, the war of 1914–18 was, with the Great Depression and Second World War, one of the three major world events whose disruptiveness affected early twentieth-century evangelicalism. Yet, in common with historians of Christianity in general, students of the evangelical tradition have shown little interest in the First World War.[2] In fact, as citizens of the warring countries with a long history of supporting their societies, evangelicals were quickly drawn into the war's events and processes. But the relation of evangelicals to the war remains to be established. How they responded to it, how they influenced it, and how they were affected by it became evident at three levels – first in their readiness to become involved spiritually as well as materially, and then in the conduct of evangelical servicemen 'under fire' at the front and also in the manner evangelicals fought 'the war within' at home.

Wars and rumours of wars

War was not a new experience for early twentieth-century evangelicals. In 1898 America went to war with Spain in a conflict fought in and over Spain's island colonies, Cuba and the Philippines. Evangelicals, like other American Christians, easily assimilated the war into the expansion and imperialism inherent in the belief in 'manifest destiny'. The justification of President (and serious Methodist) William McKinley's decision to take control of the Philippines, 'to educate the Filipinos, and uplift and civilize and christianize them',[3] chimed with their own sense of a call from God to evangelize the world through revivalist activity and foreign missions. In a manner also expressing typical evangelical ways of thinking, they went further and declared a holy crusade against benighted Spanish Catholicism that would open new fields of missionary endeavour in

---

1. David Reynolds, *The Long Shadow: The Legacies of the Great War in the Twentieth Century* (New York: W. W. Norton, 2014).

2. Except Robert D. Linder, *The Long Tragedy: Australian Evangelical Christians and the Great War, 1914–1918* (Adelaide: Openbook, 2000). For the historiography, Michael Snape, 'The Great War', in *CHC9*, 131–150. See now Philip Jenkins, *The Great and Holy War: How World War I Became a Religious Crusade* (New York: HarperCollins, 2014), for the religious history of the war.

3. Quoted in Martin E. Marty, *Modern American Religion*. Vol. 1: *The Irony of It All 1893–1919* (Chicago: University of Chicago Press, 1986), 309.

Asia. Scarcely imagining that America could be an oppressor, evangelicals upheld the Spanish–American war and its attendant imperialism as a legitimate out-working of America's divinely appointed world task.[4]

Beginning the next year, Britain and her leading colonies fought the Boers in the republics of the Transvaal and the Orange Free State in what is now known as the South African War (1899–1902). Although this was a war of imperial expansion, they did so for the most part enthusiastically supported by the majority of evangelicals. Blaming the recalcitrance and aggression of the Boers, the British authorities declared it a 'just' war, undertaken to increase the freedom of the natives, the 'Outlanders' and even (once they accepted the inevitable British victory) the Boers themselves. It is true that the war was denounced by a small number of Nonconformists, who argued that British territorial ambitions were unjust and that the independence of the Boer republics should be respected.[5] But this was an exception that proved an important rule. Generally the war was understood as an affirmation of the Christian character of the British Empire. For the 'neo-Britains' of Australia, New Zealand and Canada, it was also an investment in their future. As new nations, victory would ensure their prosperity and security as part of an order created by Providence to spread and protect Christian civilization. Even though the Boer War did not produce the easy victory that was expected, belief in the goodness of Britain and the Empire and their place in the purposes of God was largely unquestioned.[6]

The passions aroused by the turn-of-the-century conflicts soon blew over, but the clouds of war built up over the following decade.[7] Imperial rivalries, an arms race, the emergence of the alliance system in Europe and a series of international crises kept the question of war vividly alive. Evangelicals welcomed initiatives to find ways of placing international politics on a more peaceful footing and reduce the danger of conflict. They also regretted the arms race, not only for its effect on international relations, but also for the vast sums of

4. Augustus Cerillo, Jr., 'The Spanish–American War', in Ronald A. Wells (ed.), *The Wars of America: Christian Views* (Grand Rapids: Eerdmans, 1981), 91–125.

5. David W. Bebbington, *The Nonconformist Conscience: Chapel and Politics, 1870–1914* (London: George Allen & Unwin, 1982), 121–124.

6. Gordon L. Heath, *A War with a Silver Lining: Canadian Protestant Churches and the South African War, 1899–1902* (Montreal: McGill-Queen's University Press, 2009).

7. This and the next paragraph draw on Michael Hughes, *Conscience and Conflict: Methodism, Peace and War in the Twentieth Century* (Werrington: Epworth Press, 2008), ch. 2.

money that might have been better spent on more worthwhile causes. There was, further, some ambivalence about the British ententes with France (1904) and Russia (1907). While these arrangements were calculated to reduce the risk of war, they also ran the danger of entanglement in European power politics. Anglo-German relations similarly produced varying responses. Evangelicals at large entertained a natural sympathy for the home of the Reformation, while those on the left of the movement, especially in Scotland and America, felt an affinity with its tradition of theological learning. The corresponding wish for improved relations was more than offset by a call for tough action in the face of German expansionism, naval build-up and supposed provocations.

Evident in these developments in the two decades before 1914 was a pattern of thinking developed among evangelicals that held that waging war to oppose injustice and uphold moral causes was justified. This pattern took shape in a larger framework of imperial theology that interpreted the British Empire and the informal empire of America as parts of a providential order working to facilitate the spread of Protestant Christianity around the globe.[8] On both sides of the Atlantic, and throughout the 'neo-Britains' of Australia, New Zealand and Canada, evangelical spokesmen fervently enunciated this ideology, which required as a matter of responsibility before God that moral considerations come before *Realpolitik* in the conduct of foreign policy. The ethnocentric and patriotic sides of their thinking created a predisposition among evangelicals to see the moral dimension of British and American causes and to support wars fought for righteousness, Christian civilization and imperial defence.

Underneath this outlook was the militancy early twentieth-century evangelicals inherited from the Victorian era. This was reflected in the continuing popularity of hymns such as 'Onward, Christian Soldiers' and Sankey's 'Hold the Fort', written respectively under the influence of the Crimean War and the American Civil War.[9] The rhetoric and values of Christian militarism were still purveyed by the paramilitarism of church organizations such as the Salvation Army and the Boys' Brigade. Further, the revivalist campaigns and social reform movements at the turn of the century were tantamount to mobilization in the causes of mass conversion and social amelioration. Even the atonement furnished imagery which, in exalting sacrifice in the service of others, framed

---

8. John A. Moses, 'The British and German Churches and the Perception of War, 1908–1914', *WS* 5.1 (1987), 23–44.

9. John Wolffe, *God and Greater Britain: Religion and National Life in Britain and Ireland, 1843–1945* (London: Routledge, 1994), ch. 8.

the British Empire as a force for righteousness against oppression.[10] When war came in 1914, sacralization of the war effort was facilitated by evangelical patriotism, an already well-established militaristic mindset.

Justifying the war

Like most people, evangelicals were surprised when war was declared. Whatever shock they felt initially, it was soon overtaken by acceptance that this was a war that had to be fought. From the outset evangelicals condemned the German invasion of Belgium in defiance of guarantees of her neutrality as an affront to international order and the rule of law.[11] Germany's suggestions that the treaty with Belgium was a mere 'scrap of paper' and that 'necessity knows no law' were especially offensive to evangelicals. The power of a promise and the authority of God's Word in its written form were fundamental to their belief system. It was also necessary to protest against the assertion that 'God is on the side of the big battalions' that threatened a reversion to paganism, a reaction strengthened by news of German atrocities in Belgium. Evangelicals drew further assurance of the virtue of their cause from the conviction that action had been taken for the benefit of others without any consideration of Allied self-interest. Convinced that in every way the British Empire's motives for involvement were honourable and unselfish, evangelicals embraced war aims upholding the rule of law in international relations, saving the weak from the strong and protecting human freedom from German pretensions to world domination.[12]

In classifying the war as 'just', evangelical motivation was scarcely distinguishable from the justification of the war by the state. However, by quickly elevating it to the status of a 'holy war', evangelicals espoused a case for war more in line with their own characteristic thinking and purposes. Reflection on German motivation attributed nationalist aggression to half a century or

---

10. David W. Bebbington, 'Atonement, Sin, and Empire, 1880–1914', in Andrew Porter (ed.), *The Imperial Horizons of British Protestant Missions, 1880–1914* (Grand Rapids: Eerdmans, 2003), 14–31.

11. E.g. Andrew Wingate, 'The Empire and the War', *EC* (Sept.–Oct. 1914), 189–190; John Wood, 'Reflections on the War', ibid. 193–194; W. Y. Fullerton, 'The Mailed Hand and the Nailed Hand', *EC* (Nov.–Dec. 1914), 215–216.

12. E.g. Frank Ballard, *Britain Justified: The War from the Christian Standpoint* (London: Charles H. Kelley, 1914).

more of rationalist and materialist thinking.[13] This interpretation turned the war into a clash between Christianity and secularism, and as such both a reflection of the contest for Christian civilization that in recent years evangelicals had seen unfolding around them and also a blueprint for what would probably result if they lost the battle with similar forces at home. The involvement of Muslim Turkey on the side of the Central Powers added to the sense of the war as a 'crusade'. But, in a conflict between good and evil, the principal enemy was 'Satanic Prussianism'. 'God's war' had to be fought to rid the world of this malign force and to establish righteousness and Christian civilization.

This high-minded reasoning was augmented throughout 'Greater Britain' by deep religious and sentimental ties to Britain and the Empire.[14] Because of their identification of providence and empire, evangelicals in the 'neo-Britains' were easily swept along by the war fever of the day. This was not necessarily the same thing as the 'enthusiasm' that is often said to have characterized the popular response to the outbreak of war. It was more a sober commitment to the cause of Christian civilization, which the empire was thought to embody. If they found the prospect of war between Christian nations hard to fathom, evangelicals in Canada, Australia and New Zealand supported it because the principles involved made it a spiritual enterprise requiring the kind of service and sacrifice placed at the centre of their religion by the seminal influence of Christ. The situation was more complex in South Africa, where large numbers of Afrikaners, still smarting from their defeat in the war of 1899–1902, opposed participation in the conflict. But evangelicals among 'British loyalists' were no less committed than their counterparts elsewhere in the empire.

Defence of the war as a fight for justice and righteousness persisted in the evangelical community throughout the war. When war weariness and disillusionment set in following disastrous campaigns on the Somme and at Verdun in 1916, this reasoning was reiterated to maintain flagging spirits. However, a further note became prominent in evangelical war rhetoric around the same time in response to what after two years had plainly become a war

---

13. E.g. Dora M. Jones, 'Nietzsche, Germany and the War', *LQR* 123 (1915), 80–94; Elias Compton, 'German Philosophy and the War', *BRQ* 3.3 (1918), 331–351.

14. Graham Hucker, '"The Great Wave of Enthusiasm": New Zealand Reactions to the First World War in August 1914 – A Reassessment', *NZJH* 43.1 (2009), 59–75; Glen O'Brien, '"The Empire's Titanic Struggle": Victorian Methodism and the Great War', *AP* 10 (2012), 50–70.

of attrition. Whereas initially the German threat was abstract and distant, increasingly it was regarded as tangible and immediate. No doubt this was due to the durability of the Germans, the unexpected inability of the Allies actually to force a victory and the rising possibility that the Central Powers might win the war. If by this point the summons to holy war was perhaps wearing thin, it was now augmented by the need to fight in self-defence. According to one pundit, the issue had become 'the simple one of slavery under Germany or liberty above her'.[15] A more realistic appraisal of the situation meant that the war had to be fought to the end to overcome the threat to the existence of the Allies posed by German autocracy and militarism. This was an important shift in evangelical thinking. Right through to the end of the fighting in 1918, it appeared that Christian civilization had to be preserved rather than merely upheld.

The call to arms

In contrast with their European enemies, no part of the English-speaking world practised conscription for military service. As a result, the response to German mobilization required the rapid creation of citizen armies. Evangelicals were among those who answered the call to arms quickly and enthusiastically. While there is no way of ascertaining how many were evangelicals, the early enlistments clearly included large numbers of them. The policy of raising ethnic divisions facilitated an influx of Welsh Nonconformists and Ulster Protestants. In Scotland up to 90% of the sons of manses of military age volunteered.[16] Enlistments from evangelical churches in Australia numbered 'tens of thousands'.[17] Recruits seem to have flocked from the militaristic church youth organizations such as the non-denominational Boys' Brigade. Students in the universities and theological colleges also quickly joined up. If this early enthusiasm could not be maintained, evangelicals continued to feature prominently among the volunteers. The *Army and Religion* report, compiled in the later part of the war when the flow of volunteers had ebbed, was still able to note that the percentage of men 'with a vital church connection' was between 20 and 30%. While far from a majority, it was nevertheless a large number, a significant

---

15. 'The Hour of Great Danger', *C* (11 Apr. 1918), 8.
16. Stewart J. Brown, '"A Solemn Purification by Fire": Responses to the Great War in the Scottish Presbyterian Churches', *JEH* 45.1 (1994), 84.
17. Linder, *Long Tragedy*, 107–110.

proportion of whom would have been evangelicals.[18] Young evangelical men evinced a distinct willingness to offer their lives in the service of their country and its cause.

One reason for this eager response was the enthusiastic support for the war by evangelical leaders and clergy. As soon as war was declared, preachers and lay leaders mounted podiums of various kinds to put the case for the war, overcome Christian scruples about participation, and heap praise on those who enlisted. Some went further and became de facto recruiting sergeants. The British Baptist John Clifford admitted to it, while his friend, the Scottish journalist Sir William Robertson Nicoll, 'the intellectual leader of nonconformity', used the pages of the *British Weekly* to maximize the reach of his appeal to Nonconformists for voluntary recruitment.[19] Throughout 'Greater Britain' men such as the Anglican Archbishop of Sydney, J. C. Wright, energetically promoted the need under God to fight 'for King and country'. Accustomed to campaigning for righteousness, calling young men to arms fitted well with their activism, while strong support from the evangelical establishment and public exerted pressure on the young of their communities' men to join up.

While it is difficult to gauge the effect of this pressure, in many cases there would have been no need of it. Some young men were undoubtedly caught up in the enthusiasm of the moment, but many others acted under the influence of deeper causes. A strong sense of moral compulsion arising from an evangelical sensibility is reflected in the reasoning of the devout Presbyterian Owen Lewis, at the time a student at Melbourne University:

> It is hard to explain exactly what is impelling me to go but there is something allied to conscience which bids me go. I believe in a hereafter and if following the will of my conscience I enter it sooner than under ordinary circumstances I do not think anyone should regret it.

---

18. D. S. Cairns (ed.), *The Army and Religion: An Enquiry and Its Bearing upon the Religious Life of the Nation* (London: Macmillan, 1919), 189–192. The corresponding American report, The Committee on the War and the Religious Outlook, *Religion Among American Men As Revealed by a Study of Conditions in the Army* (New York: Association Press, 1920), 11, stated that up to 15% of the American Expeditionary Forces consisted of 'real Christians and active church members'. With Catholics excluded from the count, a large part of this group would have been evangelicals.

19. T. H. Darlow, *William Roberston Nicoll: Life and Letters* (London: Hodder & Stoughton, 1925), 236–242.

What comes to me a great deal is, that I am abiding here in comfort while others perhaps having people dependent on them are fighting my battles and giving their lives for me. Death must come to us all sooner or later and there is no way so noble of leaving than that in which you 'Lay down your life for your friends'.[20]

This sense of duty, framed by an evangelical understanding of self-sacrifice and death, was not uncommon. Thousands of other students volunteered for similar reasons.[21] It was akin to the thinking that for a generation had caused young men and women to commit their lives to missionary service through agencies such as the Student Volunteer Movement. For evangelicals, enlistment reflected the deep structures of their thinking and was almost second nature.

Of course, not all evangelicals were able to respond so readily to the call to arms. The peace churches – particularly the Quakers and Mennonites – maintained their traditional stance against war. Pentecostals too could be diffident.[22] Other churches that were ambivalent about the war took various positions. The Open Brethren, for example, generally upheld pacifism but allowed individual members to make up their own minds about participation. Seventh-Day Adventists worried that they would be in breach of the fourth and sixth commandments if they took part. Confronted by the prospect of conscription, New Zealand Adventists worked out a compromise whereby they could fill non-fighting positions in the military as 'conscientious co-operators' or 'patriotic non-combatants'.[23] While more mainstream churches tended to support the war, a significant number of evangelical churches and communities did not on the grounds that it was contrary to Christian beliefs and principles.

On the question of conscientious objection, evangelicals could hardly do other than support objection to military service on religious and moral grounds. Generally they urged respect for the scruples of conscientious

---

20. Reproduced in Brian Lewis, *Our War: Australia During World War I* (Carlton: Melbourne University Press, 1980), 127–133.
21. The recollection of Tissington Tatlow, *The Story of the Student Christian Movement of Great Britain and Ireland* (London: SCM Press, 1933), 512–515.
22. Roger Robins, 'A Chronology of Peace: Attitudes Towards War and Peace in the Assemblies of God: 1914–1918', *Pn* 6.1 (1984), 3–25.
23. Peter H. Ballis, 'Conscience and Compromise: New Zealand Adventists and Military Service During World War I', in Arthur J. Ferch (ed.), *Symposium on Adventist History in the South Pacific: 1885–1918* (Wahroonga, NSW: South Pacific Division of Seventh-Day Adventists, 1986), 40–52.

objectors when they were genuine and not merely an excuse for shirking.[24] While recognizing the difficulty of the task, evangelicals also spoke out against the harshness and injustices of unsympathetic administrators of the laws.[25] To a large extent this standpoint was an adequate response to the situation. Most objectors were prepared to contribute to the general well-being in some non-combative role as 'alternativists'. Less appreciated was the relatively small number of 'absolutists' who refused to contribute to the war effort in any way. It seemed unreasonable that they should have the benefit of the sacrifice of others at no cost to themselves. The rights of the state over its citizens in matters touching faithfulness to God and conscience – always a vexed issue for some evangelicals – was a matter of particular difficulty for evangelicals in a time of war.[26]

Supporting the war effort

Recruits for the services were not the only evangelicals to mobilize for war. The rapid appearance of volunteer citizen armies and the nature of modern warfare engendered conditions that at once stimulated and provided new outlets for the evangelical impulse to activism. With their plethora of existing agencies, evangelicals were well placed to respond to these opportunities. Rising to the hour of need was also well suited to the evangelical temper. As one observer noted when urging trust in God for the ordeal ahead, 'This will not mean any forgetfulness of the needs or claims of others, for those who rest most peacefully in the Lord will be most active in His service, seeking to do His will.'[27] In recognition of the urgency of the moment, a small 'army' of evangelicals devoted themselves to the task of supporting those who answered the call to arms.

Once mobilization was underway, the most obvious needs of the servicemen were material and physical. Established agencies such as the YMCA, and the Salvation and Church Armies swung into action. Their networks of soldiers'

24. Hughes, *Conscience and Conflict*, 57–70, 72; Martin Ceadel, *Pacifism in Britain 1914–1945: The Defining of a Faith* (Oxford: Clarendon Press, 1980), 31–46.
25. E.g. 'The Conscientious Objector', *C* (27 Jan. 1916), 9; (26 Oct. 1916), 11; (18 Oct. 1917), 7–8; 'Tribunals and Objectors', *C* (13 Apr. 1916), 10.
26. 'Christ and the State', *C* (29 Nov. 1917), 9; 'Loyalty to God and Duty to the State', *C* (10 Oct. 1918), 7–8.
27. 'Notes and Comments. Waiting Upon the Lord –', *C* (6 Aug. 1914), 9.

homes and institutes were rapidly expanded to reach all the major training centres and battle fronts. They also established canteens and huts near the lines to provide rest and refreshment for the men when they took a break from battle. They further provided hospitals and made their facilities available to caring for the wounded. Other agencies such as the Open Air Mission similarly adapted their operations to wartime demands. Local churches near the training camps opened their buildings to the soldiers as places of rest and recreation. Meeting the needs of the men provided alternative forms of service for those whose consciences did not allow them to take part in the fighting. The Princeton New Testament scholar J. Gresham Machen, for example, ran a YMCA canteen in France.[28] Others performed such roles as stretcher bearers and ambulance drivers. Although conceived as an alternative to combat, very often these other tasks and duties were no less dangerous than those faced by servicemen.

Important as these ministries were, the moral and spiritual needs of the men were paramount. Evangelicals were well aware of the temptations that accompanied military life. The various facilities they provided for servicemen were conceived in part as an alternative to the pubs and brothels by which soldiers were attracted. Evangelicals also spoke out against the moral dangers to which men in the camps were exposed. Amid the many urgent tasks of wartime, their criticisms were not always welcome to governments. While overwhelmingly in support of the war, evangelicals would not allow the special circumstances of the day to compromise their moral standards.

More positively, the war was regarded as an unparalleled opportunity for evangelism. Through the *fin de siècle* years men, especially working-class men, were felt to have eluded the best conversionist efforts of evangelicals. Now they were brought together in unprecedented numbers at a moment of the greatest solemnity. Recognition that many of these men would soon be dead added urgency to convenience. Again established agencies such as the Soldiers' Christian Association and the Open Air Mission swung into action alongside the YMCA and the Salvation Army. Other revivalists such as Gipsy Smith, John McNeil and Sherwood Eddy went to the front in the course of the war to preach the need for conversion. The situation also created a pressing need for distributing Bibles. Organizations such as the Pocket Testament League and the Scripture Gift Mission were given a great fillip.

Although they received less acclaim, evangelical women also answered the call to serve, a response hailed by its first chronicler as 'as important in its degree

---

28. Ned B. Stonehouse, *J. Gresham Machen: A Biographical Memoir*, 3rd ed. (Edinburgh: Banner of Truth Trust, 1987 [1954]), chs. 13–14.

as the actual taking up of arms'.[29] For a small number – such as the Misses Daniell, Perks and Wilson, all of whom already ran soldiers' homes in England – this was an extension of work undertaken years before. But for the great majority work in a national cause was a fresh departure. Apart from encouraging recruitment, women combined locally in their churches and nationally through the denominations to raise money and to provide war relief. Their many activities included supplying the troops with foodstuffs and garments such as socks, scarves, gloves and 'knitted helmets'. They also sent clothes and materials for use in hospitals where some served as nurses and a very small number as doctors. Apart from caring for the sick and wounded, and comforting the bereaved, as the war dragged on evangelical women were among those who stepped into work that relieved men for military service. Motivating this work was the patriotism they shared with their menfolk and recognition of an opportunity for women 'to show what they can do, very naturally and very properly'. These women also welcomed the chance to fulfil their calling as Christians by responding to the sacrifice of Christ with lives of sacrificial service.[30] Evangelical ideals of womanhood readily adapted to the demands of war.

America's entry to the war

The early years of the war were experienced differently by American evangelicals. While their country remained neutral, they closely followed the appalling spectacle of the leading Christian nations of Europe locked in bloody conflict.[31] As mere observers, they were left to ponder the moral and theological implications of war and to manage the impact on their missionary work. At the same time, prompted by deteriorating relations between the United States and Mexico, they considered the dilemmas posed by the argument for greater military preparedness in the interest of national security. The resignation in 1915 of William Jennings Bryan as Secretary of State in the Wilson Administration in protest against the President's 'active neutrality' highlighted the difficulties of America's position. In their general embrace of neutrality, evangelicals reflected the thinking of Americans at large. They were glad to be spared direct involvement in the fighting, and to be in a position to press

---

29. Mary Frances Billington, *The Roll-Call of Serving Women: A Record of Woman's Work for Combatants and Sufferers in the Great War* (London: Religious Tract Society, 1915), v.

30. Ibid. 218–220 (quotation on 218).

31. E.g. the regular section on 'Progress of the War in Europe' in the *Homiletic Review*.

Christian teaching on the subject of war on to the combatants and to suggest how peace might be restored.[32]

Whatever ambivalence American evangelicals might have felt, it quickly dissipated when their country joined the war on Good Friday, 1917. Evangelical churches and organizations sided with general community support for the war as resistance to Kaiserdom and a struggle for freedom.[33] Like their brethren throughout 'Greater Britain', they embraced the war as 'just', 'holy' and defensive. The Presbyterian James Vance caught this mood when he asserted, 'We must keep the flag and the cross together for they are both working for the same ends.'[34] In this spirit the missionary statesman Robert Speer agreed to act as chair of the Federal Council of Churches' (FCC) Inter-Church Committee on War Work. His leadership reflected evangelical support for the mechanisms necessary to conduct wartime ministry through the FCC. While this naturally involved provision of material support for servicemen, the Committee assigned primacy to meeting their spiritual needs. This endorsement of the war presented some difficulty for churches of German extraction, and the Mennonite Church of North America withdrew from the FCC. However, while there were some exceptions, for the great majority of evangelicals, conformity of the circumstances with the 'just war' theory of the Christian tradition was sufficient for them to heed the call to mobilize.

Interpreting the war

By the time America became embroiled three clear attitudes towards the war had emerged within evangelicalism. At one extreme was an outburst of jingoistic anti-Germanism as Christian commitment ran up against moral sensibilities, national feeling and mounting casualties. Typical of the 'jingoistic evangelicals' was the fiercely anti-establishment English Primitive Methodist A. T. Guttery who, following the outbreak of war, effected a *volte face* from extreme pacifism

---

32. E.g. D. Willard Lyon, *The Christian Equivalent of War* (London: Association Press, 1915), and the views expressed in the symposium 'The Clear and Urgent Duty of the Church in the Present World Crisis', *HomR* 73.1 (Jan. 1917), 20–25 and 28–30.

33. John F. Piper, Jr. (1987), *The American Churches in World War I* (Athens, OH: Ohio University Press, 1987).

34. Quoted in Ray H. Abrams, *Preachers Present Arms: The Role of the American Churches and Clergy in World Wars I and II, with Some Observations on the War in Vietnam* (Scottdale, PA, Herald Press, 1969 [1933]), 50.

to extreme bellicosity.[35] He used the pages of the *Primitive Methodist Leader* to express an unthinking patriotism that idealized young soldiers and identified their deaths with the sacrifice of Christ. In America the Congregationalist Newell Dwight Hillis similarly abandoned a pro-German outlook to lead the way in demonizing the German people by atrocity stories told all over the country as part of the Liberty Loan campaign.[36] An unfortunate outcome of this anti-German feeling was a turning on people of German descent in the English-speaking societies. Despite their protestations of loyalty, evangelicals joined in the abuse to which these people were subjected, and connived in their removal from positions of influence and even internment for the duration of the war. Evangelical faith was sometimes unequal to the emotional pressures released by the war.

At the other extreme were 'the peaceful evangelicals'.[37] These men and women felt unable to evade what they regarded as the clear teaching of Jesus. As a result they could not believe that it was right to fight at all. Some in this group were Christian pacifists. Others took less definite positions, but maintained that the war could not be reconciled with the Christian standpoint. In Australia such was the strength of their stand that 'peaceful evangelicals' led the protest against the war on moral grounds. Their *Manifesto from Protestant Ministers* in 1917 ranged the principles of Christianity and teachings of Christ against the civil religion that undergirded much of the imperial war effort.[38] B. Linden Webb's *Religious Significance of the War* was not only among the best arguments for biblical pacifism produced during the war; it also articulated the position held by the significant Methodist minority that opposed the war.[39] Characteristic evangelical thinking did not necessarily lead to enthusiasm for the war and enlistment.

Whether hesitant or enthusiastic, the great majority of evangelicals accepted the war as a righteous cause that could not be shirked. This was the standpoint of President Woodrow Wilson when he asked the American Congress for a declaration of war in 1917. Under provocation from Germany, he gave up the

35. Alan Wilkinson, *Dissent or Conform? War, Peace and the English Churches 1900–1945* (London: SCM Press, 1986), 29–32.

36. Abrams, *Preachers Present Arms*, ch. 6.

37. Robert D. Linder, 'The Peaceful Evangelicals: Refusing to Take up the Sword, 1914–1918', *L* 33–34 (2003), 5–65.

38. Two signatories were not evangelicals.

39. B. Linden Webb, *The Religious Significance of the War* (Sydney: Christian World, 1915). Hughes, *Conscience and Conflict*, 50–52.

'active neutrality' that had enabled him to work for peace to fight for a world order that secured freedom and justice for all peoples 'whether they be weak or strong'.[40] The Methodist James Hope Moulton, Professor of Hellenistic Greek at Manchester University and President of the Peace Society, was another torn between his ideals and the demands of the times.[41] A pacifist before the outbreak of the war, he wrestled with the issues posed by German conduct early in the war. If he could not endorse the war, he did acquiesce in it. Others who stood for due caution and moderation in their support maintained that it was important not to make God into a kind of tribal deity. They also counselled against making serving the empire into a kind of religion through a cult of imperial patriotism. Above all they warned against hatred of the German people and urged the need to maintain the primacy of the gospel in all things. The norm among evangelicals was a measured acceptance of the war and the resolution to do what they could to secure victory on both the home and foreign fronts.

The crystallization of these three positions helps to define Reuben Torrey's war. A man of his combative temperament might have been expected to support a war understood as the nemesis of the country that had led the way in developing the despised higher criticism of the Bible. Instead initially Torrey is to be numbered among the 'peaceful evangelicals', although he expressed his pacifism in paradoxically strident language. Before America's entry into the war he declaimed, 'the nation that is not quick to take umbrage nor "defend its honor" is not dishonored, but great and strong'. Against the advocates of 'preparedness' he argued that this was best achieved by prayer rather than by 'Germanizing the land' or building up a military system.[42] Once America was directly involved, Torrey's position shifted to a reluctant acceptance of the war. His preference was to concentrate on the spiritual issues it raised.[43] If ignoring the Bible was the fundamental cause of the war, its advocacy should be the priority of the

---

40. Malcolm D. Magee, *What the World Should Be: Woodrow Wilson and the Crafting of a Faith-Based Foreign Policy* (Waco: Baylor University Press, 2008), ch. 3 (quotation on 84).

41. James H. Moulton, 'Christianity and Defensive War', *LQR* 123 (1915), 32–45; [William F. Moulton], *James Hope Moulton, by His Brother* (London: Epworth Press, 1919).

42. R. A. Torrey, *The Voice of God in the Present Hour* (New York: Fleming H. Revell, 1917), quotations on 191, 228.

43. R. A. Torrey, *What the War Teaches or the Greatest Lessons of 1917*, in Joel A. Carpenter (ed.), *Conservative Call to Arms* (New York: Garland Publishing, 1988), 1–16.

day. In 1917 he published a new recension of *The Fundamentals* in which all the articles on biblical authority were brought together in the first volume. This position was further transformed when modernist professors at the University of Chicago launched an attack on premillennialism as unpatriotic and possibly even funded by German money. Torrey responded with a strong reiteration of premillennial teaching on the second coming seasoned with vigorous assertions of his belief in the war and assurances of a true patriotism. Indeed he sought to turn the tables by accusing the Chicago Divinity Professor Shailer Mathews of 'very effective pro-German propaganda' and insisting that God was teaching the Kaiser and the Germans 'a sorely needed lesson by the military might of America' and her allies.[44] The experience of war changed Torrey from a 'peaceful' to a 'patriotic' evangelical with decided jingoistic leanings. The war could be a crucible for evangelical sentiment.

Conclusion

Although war came unexpectedly in August 1914, evangelicals responded with alacrity. Their dispositions had been shaped by the militancy carried forward through the *fin de siècle* years from the Victorian era. From the outbreak of the conflict evangelicals readily and plentifully supported their governments in fighting their national cause against Germany and the Central Powers. Patriotism was fundamental to this combativeness, but was experienced in combination with their religion. For the evangelical tradition had already incorporated Britain and America into a providential scheme that blessed them as the principal bearers of Christian civilization in the contemporary world and characteristically upheld their national causes as righteous and beneficent. Earlier in the century there had been some dissent, but in 1914 the reprehensible conduct of Germany was such that opposition to the war was minimal, and more a matter of principle than circumstance when it did occur. In a pattern that was repeated when America joined the war in 1917, evangelicals enlisted and mobilized their material and spiritual resources to enable the war effort in the hope of achieving victory in what they regarded as a holy war for Christian civilization. That partici-pation in such a war involved great risk and cost was acceptable because the

---

44. R. A. Torrey, *Peanut Patriotism and Pure Patriotism: Our Duty to God and Our Country in This Time of Crisis* (Los Angeles: BIOLA, 1918); *Will Christ Come Again? An Exposure of the Foolishness and Falsehoods of Shailer Mathews* (Los Angeles: BIOLA, 1918), quotations from 23–25.

exaltation of sacrifice was also part of the synthesis between evangelicalism and patriotism. This support continued virtually unabated through the war years, even as the war descended into a grinding contest of attrition. Between 1914 and 1918, war provided a fresh outlet for evangelical militancy and activism; and the evangelical movement provided the English-speaking warring nations with the support of a significant component of their populations.

7. FAITH UNDER FIRE

In response to the call to arms in 1914, military camps sprang up all around the British Empire. Here men assembled in their thousands to form the new citizen armies and be prepared for combat. Camp life was followed by the experience of battle, at sea, increasingly in the air and, worst of all, in the trenches. In these settings the men encountered the worst of the modern world – the relentless toil of industrialized warfare, the spectacle of heavy casualties and the existential challenges of sustained institutionalized destruction. The great majority called on to face this ordeal had been swept into a new way of life – male dominated, authoritarian, highly structured and unforgiving – in which they had to find their place and prove themselves. As they made a complete break with home conditions and encountered the disintegrating influence of war, the men also faced deep questions about themselves. The war was a severe test to existing identities and world views, evangelicalism among them.[1]

Recent research shows how the once-common narrative of 'loss of faith' by First World War soldiers needs to be qualified by recognition of soldiers' religion. Recognized at the time by Donald Hankey, this religiosity functioned along a

---

1. The challenge of the war to the Christian world view is illustrated in Donald Black's evocative *Red Dust: An Australian Trooper in Palestine* (London: Jonathan Cape, 1931), 60–66, 94–100, 287.

spectrum ranging from an instinct for survival to a very considered reflection upon life in its spiritual dimension.[2] Although evangelicals were among those who experienced the war in the framework of active Christian belief, what this meant has not been established. It remains to identify the place of evangelicalism on the soldiers' 'spectrum of faith'.

Evangelicals as citizen soldiers

Although much of the evidence for the outlook and conduct of evangelicals at war is idealized and exaggerated,[3] it is possible to create a picture of evangelical attitudes and behaviour in the camps and at the front. Although the maintenance of religious life in the army was notoriously difficult, both in the camps and at the front men read their Bibles as a source of instruction and comfort. They also read other Christian classics such as John Bunyan's *Pilgrim's Progress*. They engaged in prayer, singly and in groups, privately and in public. Hymn singing, individually and collectively, relieved both monotony and hardship. Evangelical men respected the chaplains and participated in their services, and also organized their own informal gatherings, evincing in fellowship a Christian form of the renowned comradeship of the front. Amid so much suffering and death for the sake of others, the cross acquired a sharp salience in their thinking, particularly as crosses marking the graves of casualties proliferated across the landscape. Evangelicals shared their faith with others – by witnessing, distributing Christian literature, offering words of encouragement, and by abstaining from drinking and immoral conduct. As far as possible they saw to the physical and material needs of others (including occasionally those of the enemy) and showed

2. Donald Hankey, *A Student in Arms* (London: Andrew Melrose, 1916); Richard Schweitzer, *The Cross and the Trenches: Religious Faith and Doubt Among British and American Great War Soldiers* (Westport, CT: Praeger Publishers, 2003); Michael Snape, *God and the British Soldier: Religion and the British Army in the First and Second World Wars* (London: Routledge, 2005); Jonathan Ebel, *Faith in the Fight: Religion and the American Soldier in the Great War* (Princeton: Princeton University Press, 2010).

3. E.g. William E. Sellers, *With Our Fighting Men: The Story of Their Faith, Courage, Endurance in the Great War* (London: Religious Tract Society, n.d. [1915]); *With Our Heroes in Khaki: The Story of Christian Work with Our Soldiers and Sailors – And Some of Its Results* (London: Religious Tract Society, n.d. [1917]); Thomas Tiplady, *The Cross at the Front: Fragments from the Trenches* (New York: Fleming H. Revell, 1917); *The Soul of the Soldier: Sketches of Life at the Front* (London: Methuen, 1918).

consideration in various ways to the loved ones of the fallen. At many different levels of attainment and commitment evangelicals brought to the experience of modern warfare their characteristic biblicism, crucicentrism, conversionism and activism buttressed so far as the conditions of war permitted by typical devotional practices.[4]

But in this chaotic setting faith did not remain unchanged. For some it was strengthened and grew. A 'Hymn Lover' thought of the war as 'putting the theory to the test' and found that his faith was vindicated. After initial temptation to concealment, he summoned the courage to express it openly.[5] In the case of English wireless operator William B. Kitching the war called out a more conscious and hopeful faith: 'But now my eyes have been opened; oh how different things seem now and I thank God that he has opened them. If he will only give me the opportunity of returning I will profit by these hard-learnt lessons.' Written before his death in 1916, the diary of Salvation Army member Private A. E. Renshaw evinces a continuous sense of God's presence and his own spiritual progress. He also felt a growing conviction that the army was but a prelude to a higher form of service: 'I feel more every day that precious souls are dying for want of someone to speak to them and I in the good guidance of God am determined to be a fighter for God and a winner of souls.'[6] Despite the temptations to profligacy and despair, the spiritual effects of modern warfare for evangelicals included deeper conviction and sharper perception of God and his leading.

While the large-scale revivals expected among the troops at the beginning of the war never eventuated, faith was also acquired in the camps and at the front. With understandable hyperbole, chaplains and revivalists claimed large numbers of conversions among serving men. The Scottish chaplain William Ewing reported that many young soldiers came forward to become members of the United Free Church at Gallipoli in 1915.[7] Sherwood Eddy related how hundreds of men signed the pledge card of the war roll in YMCA meetings.[8]

---

4. These behaviours are evident in many sources such as 'Christians at the War. Testimonies from the Trenches', C (5 Aug. 1915), 12 and (19 Aug. 1915), 22; and 'The Christian Soldier on Service. A Batch of Letters', C (11 July 1918), 14.

5. 'Hymn Lover at the Front', C (3 Oct. 1918), 14. The other examples in this paragraph are from Schweitzer, Cross and the Trenches, 98–99, 103, 122–123, n. 108.

6. Quoted in ibid. 99.

7. Snape, God and the British Soldier, 165.

8. Sherwood Eddy, With Our Soldiers in France (New York: Association Press, 1917), 38–41.

These conversions took place in the two patterns already well known from pre-war revivalism. Active belief was renewed as lapsed believers were recalled to evangelical faith and life by the war. Men who had succumbed to the temptations of military life also repented and returned to lives of faithfulness. But faith was also genuinely acquired for the first time. The majority of conversions seem to have taken place in the training camps as men determined how they would approach the future in the new and unpredictable environment. If fewer in number, conversions also took place at the front itself. An officer in Palestine, for example, was led to Christ by a soldier from St George's Tabernacle, Glasgow, and exclaimed, 'What a difference!'[9] Similarly a letter from France reported, 'during the last few days nine have accepted the Lord Jesus Christ'.[10] There were also small revivals among the soldiers, particularly in the early war years.[11] The bulk of these conversions probably belong to the dynamics of 'emergency religion', the tendency to make a commitment when in danger and then relent once the danger has passed. Yet after battle men who were thankful to have survived sometimes embraced evangelical Christianity, and last-minute 'death bed' conversions were also reported from the dressing stations and hospitals. It also needs to be acknowledged that many who experienced genuine conversion were killed and left no imprint on the record. Claims of large numbers of conversions are difficult to verify, but they should not be dismissed.

How did faith function under fire? The dynamics of soldiers' overt religious belief described by Richard Schweitzer applies in its own way to evangelicals.[12] Before battle they drew on their faith to deal with their anxiety, especially if it was their first experience of combat. They read their Bibles and prayed – for courage, the ability to do their duty, survival and victory. This was when they were most open to the ministries of the chaplains, whether in the form of formal services or private conversations. The poem of G. H. Edwards Palmer on the eve of the Battle of Arras early in 1918 reflects the poignancy of Holy Communion at this time:

---

9. 'A Soldier's Letter to His Pastor. Work in Palestine', *C* (8 Nov. 1917), 22.

10. 'The Christian Soldier on Service. A Batch of Letters', *C* (11 July 1918), 14.

11. Neil Allison, 'Free Church Revivalism in the British Army During the First World War', in Michael Snape and Edward Madigan (eds.), *The Clergy in Khaki: New Perspectives on British Army Chaplaincy in the First World War* (Farnham: Ashgate, 2013), 41–55.

12. The next three paragraphs are based on Schweitzer, *Cross and the Trenches*, ch. 5.

Certain it is to those who live
    To speak of these past days with bated breath,
No service can again be like this one
    Wherein we took the Sacrament of Death,
Sharing, in measure, all he felt within
    Who bade his friends to so remember Him.[13]

During battle the demands of fighting and surviving made expression of faith almost impossible. This was mostly a time of passively trusting in Providence for survival and of falling back on well-established patterns of thought and practice. One sergeant major in a dugout expressed his trust in God by singing the familiar Keswick hymn

Hidden in the hollow of His blessed hand,
Never foe can follow, never traitor stand;
Stayed upon Jehovah, hearts are fully blest
Finding, as He promised, perfect peace and rest.[14]

At the first battle of Ypres in 1914 another evangelical soldier was upheld by reciting Psalm 23.[15] The fear of death was eased by the hope of heaven and immortality. Wounded men in apparently hopeless situations testified after their rescue to having had a deep sense of the peace of God in their helplessness. If to some extent these are stereotypical responses, they also bear the marks of instinctive reactions under duress. Evangelical soldiers prepared to die as they had lived.

After battle men turned to God for comfort and understanding of the death of comrades, and in thankfulness for their own survival. Confronted by this enigma, soldiers generally thought in terms of chance, whether as mere coincidence or as a force determining individual destinies. In contrast with this non-theistic sense of design, evangelicals spoke of their trust in God, placing their lives in his hands amid the violence and mayhem. The Englishman Murray Webb-Peploe, grandson of the prominent Keswick speaker H. W. Webb-Peploe, reflected the consolations of faith when he wrote to his mother, 'we cannot question the guiding hand of the Lord ... There is a reason for it all, while the dead are far better off with Him than they ever could

13. 'Communion on the Battlefield. Before the Attack on Arras', *C* (7 Feb. 1918), 6.
14. 'The Christian's "Dug-Out"', as quoted in *C* (27 May 1915), 9.
15. 'In Death's Dark Vale', *C* (3 June 1915), 8.

be down here.'[16] Evangelical servicemen still spoke of luck and chance, and could reflect the resignation common in their environment. Vinton Dearing, son of American Baptist missionaries, told his mother, 'I thoroughly believe that God has a way of working things out for the best, and though lots of us have to suffer in our own individual way, it is all for the best.'[17] Belief in God brought order and a sense of purpose to a chaotic experience where life could easily lose meaning.

Evangelicalism could also help to make good soldiers. The qualities soldiers admired – courage, unselfishness, straightforwardness, loyalty and humility – were among those fostered by evangelical Christianity.[18] Individuals lived up to these qualities in varying degrees, but it was suggested at the time that adding spiritual and moral discipline to the training provided by the military made for courage and endurance under fire. The majority of evangelicals went about their duty unnoticed but with quiet determination. Occasionally they were brought to the attention of the military authorities, as when in 1917 George Arthur Davies of the 14th Australian Field Ambulance, after the war a New South Wales state secretary of Christian Endeavour, earned a citation for 'consistently good work during the recent action near Polygon Wood', which included rescuing the wounded under heavy fire.[19] The American Alvin York won renown in October 1918 for an encounter in the Meuse-Argonne offensive in which he killed 25 Germans and captured a further 132. Although initially reluctant to engage in combat (he had petitioned unsuccessfully for conscientious objector status), York was sustained by the conviction that he was doing God's will and had his help.[20] A few evangelicals won great military distinction. In 1915 W. E. Sellers was pleased to salute Thomas Edward Rundle as the first Methodist to win the Victoria Cross in the war. Two years later he was able to add the names of Thomas Jones, Herbert Lewis and J. H. Flynn (who had been converted at the Somme).[21] Evangelicals were among those who emerged from the war as recognized heroes.

Many of the generals and officers who directed the Allied war effort were also religious. Their religiosity seems to have helped them to cope with the

---

16. Quoted in Schweitzer, *Cross and the Trenches*, 135 (with 139, n. 24).

17. Quoted in Ebel, *Faith in the Fight*, 58.

18. Committee on the War and the Religious Outlook, *Religion Among American Men As Revealed by a Study of Conditions in the Army* (New York: Association Press, 1920), 43–47.

19. I am grateful to my colleague Simon Davies for providing a copy of the citation.

20. Schweitzer, *Cross and the Trenches*, 101–102.

21. Sellers, *With Our Fighting Men*, 126–127; *With Our Heroes in Khaki*, 142–144.

burdens of leadership and maintain belief in the justice of their cause. As they recognized the role of morale in a war of attrition, it led also to an appreciation of the work of the chaplains and Christian service organizations such as the YMCA. Generally a broad Christianity emphasizing duty and service, this religiosity was largely a product of their education and the conformist nature of military culture.[22] What it meant to them personally is difficult to determine as religion was not a subject on which they readily disclosed their feelings.

Nevertheless, one in whom this religion was personally important and evangelical in character was no less a figure than the controversial Commander-in-Chief of the British Expeditionary Force, General Douglas Haig. The simple Presbyterian faith in which he had been raised, largely by his mother, bolstered his natural ambition and self-assurance with a strong Calvinistic sense of the benefits of hard work and the belief that he was the chosen instrument of God who was always with him.[23] These personal beliefs coincided with acceptance of the providential purpose of the British Empire, which raised his service as a soldier to the level of service of God. The Great War fitted easily into this framework as a just and holy conflict fought on behalf of a chosen race. At the front prayer and Bible reading were part of Haig's everyday life, and almost every Sunday he attended services where he encountered the reassuring teaching of the Free Church of Scotland minister George S. Duncan.[24] His Christian outlook helped explain the reverses and the horrors of the war as evidence of God's mystery and power. Yet his faith, admirable as a personal quality, also sustained the equanimity required while waiting for the divine purpose to work itself out as he repeatedly hurled his army against the German trenches at such a high cost in human life. At the same time Haig attributed his successes to God's benevolence. Seeing himself as a divine agent might have obscured Haig's judgement on some of the harsh realities of the war, but he did not succumb to the temptations to complacency and authoritarianism inherent in such a belief. While keenly sensitive to the suffering caused by the war, Haig was at the same time sustained in a stoical tolerance of the huge losses involved in his

---

22. Lawrence James, *Imperial Warrior: The Life and Times of Field-Marshal Viscount Allenby 1861–1936* (London: Weidenfeld & Nicolson, 1993), ch. 1.

23. Gerard J. de Groot, '"We Are Safe Whatever Happens" – Douglas Haig, the Reverend George Duncan, and the Conduct of War, 1916–1918', in Norman MacDougall (ed.), *Scotland and War AD 79–1918* (Edinburgh: John Donald Publishers, 1991), 193–211; Brian Bond and Nigel Cave (eds.), *Haig: A Re-appraisal 70 Years On* (Barnsley: Leo Cooper, 1999), esp. Nigel Cave, 'Haig and Religion', 240–260.

24. G. S. Duncan, *Douglas Haig As I Knew Him* (London: George Allen & Unwin, 1966).

military strategy. It was not only among the rank and file that evangelicalism influenced wartime thought and conduct.

Clergy and chaplains

Evangelical clergy also heeded the call to arms.[25] The widely accepted righteousness of the cause meant that military service was a way of fighting 'the good fight'. The Canadian H. J. Latimer reflected this line of thinking with disarming simplicity in offering his services to the Methodist Army and Navy Board: 'I want to be a good soldier of Jesus. I want to be of service wherever he invites me.'[26] The clergy also had their own reasons for wanting to serve. With so many of their men going off to fight, they experienced an understandable desire to be with them, the domestic demands of families and churches notwithstanding. In their willingness to identify with the experience of the men, it is not difficult to discern the desire to reconnect with the social group with whom they had lost touch during the *fin de siècle* years. Some clergy might have also felt the need to prove themselves as men in response to the allegation that the pulpit was 'a coward's castle'. Among the clergy the equation of nationalism and calling engendered their own version of Christian patriotism.

A military chaplaincy was the obvious role for the clergy, but not all took this option. While some believed that enlistment in the ranks was the way to be most effective, this was mainly because the number of chaplaincies was limited by quota. When they could not get one, disappointed and frustrated clergy simply joined up. A particularly poignant example is the emerging theologian Everard Digges La Touche, an Irishman who had settled in Australia because of ill health. In the early days of the war he enlisted as a private immediately his application to become a chaplain was rejected, 'as [according to his mother] he felt that he would get more in touch with the men by so doing and ... thought it was everyman's duty in such a crisis to fight for his country'. Discharged as medically unfit, La Touche joined up a second time after surgery had rectified the problem. Firing this determination was the fierce patriotism of the educated Irish

---

25. In addition to the works by Schweitzer and Snape already cited, the following section is based on Duff Crerar, *Padres in No Man's Land: Canadian Chaplains in the Great War* (Montreal: McGill-Queen's University Press, 1995); and Edward Madigan, *Faith Under Fire: Anglican Army Chaplains and the Great War* (Houndmills: Palgrave Macmillan, 2011).

26. Quoted in Crerar, *Padres in No Man's Land*, 85.

Protestant, which saw 'the Empire's cause to be just and therefore the cause of Christ'.[27] La Touche was killed on his first day in action. The Australian Methodist Robert Pittendrigh similarly enlisted in the Australian Infantry Force when he could not obtain a chaplaincy. He told friends that he had joined the army 'not only to serve his King as a soldier, but to serve his Divine Master by such testimony and service in the ranks as comradeship with men in camp and on the battlefield would afford opportunity'.[28]

Despite the limits on numbers, more and more evangelical clergy were able to become chaplains as the rise of the mass citizen armies of the Great War increased the demand for chaplaincy services. In the British army the number rose from the pre-war 117 to 3,475; in the American army, from 74 to 2,300.[29] Similar increases took place in the armies of 'Greater Britain'. Failure to differentiate between chaplains beyond their denominations makes it impossible to determine how many were evangelicals. As with the soldiers, however, the anecdotal evidence makes it clear that evangelicals were numerous. On this basis it has been suggested, for example, that they made up to 47% of those who came forward to serve in the Australian armed forces.[30] Between 1914 and 1918 war service as chaplains emerged as yet another new outlet for evangelical activism.

Because initially their role was undefined, and no training was provided, the chaplains faced many difficulties. They were expected to serve the needs of the military, but the military did not have a clear idea of what it needed. Many in the ranks saw no point in the clerical presence and mocked the chaplains. Yet, as they made their own way in the early years of the war, evangelicals (alongside the chaplains from other traditions) developed a wide-ranging role for themselves in response to the demands and conditions of service life.[31] In the training and marshalling camps and behind the lines at the front they sought to identify with the men by doing everything possible to minister to their spiritual and material needs. Naturally on Sundays the chaplains led religious services

---

27. Nigel Hubbard, *'Almost a Martyr's Fire': Everard Digges La Touche (1883–1915)* (Canberra: National Library of Australia, 1984), which is unpaginated.

28. Quoted in Robert D. Linder, *The Long Tragedy: Australian Evangelical Christians and the Great War, 1914–1918* (Adelaide: Openbook, 2000), 129.

29. Schweitzer, *Cross and the Trenches*, 63–64.

30. Linder, *Long Tragedy*, 125.

31. Frederic C. Spurr, *Some Chaplains in Khaki: An Account of the Work of the Chaplains of the United Navy and Army Board* (London: H. R. Allenson & The Kingsgate Press, n.d. [1916]), and Kenneth T. Henderson, *Khaki and Cassock* (Melbourne: Melville & Mullen, 1919), describe the role as it developed.

and church parades at which they preached for faith and righteous living. At other times they held informal services, Bible classes and prayer meetings. They prepared men for battle with prayer, Holy Communion and words of encouragement. Although in the early stages of the war they were not generally permitted to go into the lines themselves, increasingly the chaplains ventured into the trenches, and often assisted with picking up the wounded and the dead. Much of their time was also spent in the casualty-clearing stations and the hospitals. In diverse circumstances they ministered to the wounded and dying, and of course they conducted funerals and wrote to bereaved families supplementing official notification with details of the soldier's death. Maligned after the war as useless, shirking and even cowardly, the chaplains were not quarantined from the toil and horror of the war.[32]

Evangelical devotion and commitment also produced heroes worthy to set alongside their more renowned Roman Catholic counterparts. Among the Australians the most popular was the Salvation Army Captain 'Fighting Mac' McKenzie.[33] In the context of an extensive ministry among the troops, he distinguished himself by extraordinary feats of rescue, guided and protected by 'the Voice' that led him to the Salvation Army meeting at which he was converted. Awarded the Military Cross (MC) for his work at Gallipoli, and having been called home after wearing himself out in the service of his men, he was the subject of post-war adulation. Although wounded six times, the Anglican William E. Dexter continued the work of operating coffee stalls immediately behind the lines. Awarded the Distinguished Service Order (DSO) for his work at Gallipoli and the MC for gallantry under fire in France, Dexter finished the war as Australia's most decorated chaplain, an indication that clerical heroism did not always go unrecognized.[34]

For some chaplains the experience of war intensified or led to the discovery of their evangelicalism. The motivational role expected by the military was seen by some as a deflection from their true task of proclaiming Christ and preaching the cross. Cooperation with one another the more effectively to do their work brought out afresh the force of evangelical ecumenism. By 1917 Canadian Methodist chaplains recognized the futility of attempting to uphold Christian character by maintaining a wholesome moral environment amid the coarseness

---

32. Michael Snape, 'Church of England Army Chaplains in the First World War: Goodbye to *"Goodbye to All That"'*, *JEH* 62.2 (2011), 318–345.

33. Daniel Reynaud, *The Man the Anzacs Revered: William 'Fighting Mac' McKenzie Anzac Chaplain* (Warburton: Signs Publishing, 2015).

34. Linder, *Long Tragedy*, 130–135.

and brutality of the camps and the front. They concluded that the best way to maintain a Christian disposition among the men was by fostering personal relationship with God. H. E. Thomas acknowledged that the experience made 'an Evangelist of me where I never [had been] one before'.[35] This assessment of their situation also brought about some reconsideration of priorities among the same group. The traditional Methodist commandments against alcohol, card playing and dancing were felt to be out of place in their situation. Insistence on these puritanical standards was deemed more likely to lose than to win the men.

Chaplains with evangelical credentials also made a contribution at the leadership level. In addition to George Duncan, Anglican Bishop John Taylor Smith, already Chaplain-General to the British forces in 1914, continued in the role throughout the war.[36] The kind of leadership he sought to provide was reflected in his wide distribution of the Old Testament book of Proverbs and his *Soldier's Prayer*, which included the petition 'Help us to think wisely; to speak rightly; to resolve bravely; to act kindly; to live purely. Bless us in body and soul, and make us a blessing to our comrades.' In the chaotic early days of the war he introduced the 'Interdenominational Advisory Committee on Army Chaplaincy Service' to consider the steps to be taken for the welfare of the troops. He also sought the appointment of men of the highest calibre who would be up to the task of chaplaincy. Discerning the character of volunteers was the purpose of the controversial question 'What would you say to a man fatally wounded but conscious, and with only ten minutes to live?' Taylor Smith's approach was misunderstood by the increasingly skittish Anglo-Catholic party in the Church of England which lobbied successfully for the appointment of Bishop Llewellyn Gwynne as Assistant Chaplain-General with special responsibility for the troops in France. Gwynne emerged as a hero, and he has overshadowed Taylor Smith ever since.[37] But it is clear that the Chaplain-General was an efficient and fair-minded administrator who was unafraid to leave the safety of the War Office in London for the dangers of the front. His career illustrates both the opportunities and the complexities of evangelical chaplaincy service during the war.

---

35. David B. Marshall, 'Methodism Embattled: A Reconsideration of the Methodist Church and World War I', *CHR* 66.1 (1986), 54.

36. Maurice Whitlow, *J. Taylor Smith: Everybody's Bishop* (London: Lutterworth Press, 1938), ch. 9, with quotation on 97.

37. The criticism of Taylor Smith is a theme in John Bickersteth (ed.), *The Bickersteth Diaries* (London: Leo Cooper, 1995), 32–33, 81–82, 160–162, 203; and is continued in Alan Wilkinson, *The Church of England and the First World War* (London: SPCK, 1978).

Loss of faith

Identifying active evangelicalism in the services is not to deny that Christian belief was severely tested by the ordeal of war. Certainly military life, in and out of battle, was a notoriously unfavourable environment for the life of faith. Writing to his mother about the difficulties of leading a spiritual life in the army in 1915, the Englishman George Lacey observed that 'a soldier's life is very rough + tends to coarse + blunt the finer feelings'.[38] Openly maintaining the disciplines of Bible reading and prayer invited ridicule with such labels as 'Bible puncher', 'a man that's carrying the brick' or 'Mother's darling'. Hugh C. C. McCullough, later a missionary, who chose to maintain an 'open witness', described his treatment in his training camp as 'much more intense than that with which I faced my first baptism of fire in France'.[39] Worse still, proselytizing and standing apart from (if not standing against) common army vices such as overindulgence in alcohol, gambling and swearing could lead to ostracism. Self-proclaimed Christians who failed to live up to the moral standard to which they were held were branded as hypocrites. In this setting the story of the soldier willing to kneel for prayer at his bedside at the end of the first day in the barracks became a commonplace. Usually, as the story was told, this bold witness had a salutary effect. Tolerance for the practice was won, and others were encouraged to practise their faith openly. Yet it is clear that the atmosphere in the barracks was too much for some. Whether from tiredness or the desire to avoid opprobrium, devout soldiers often internalized their religion and avoided overt displays of piety, or gave it up altogether. Evangelical faith could be an early casualty of the war.

Faith was also lost because of what Richard Schweitzer calls 'the profanity of the front'.[40] The British soldier Robbie Roberts was unable to reconcile his military training with his Christian upbringing:

> I could not connect what the padre was lecturing us about with being taught the best way of getting a bayonet in and out. When I got to France I told myself 'I'm out here to do a job, and a bloody awful job, and I want nothing to do with Church – I'll live by my own religion.'[41]

---

38. Quoted in Schweitzer, *Cross and the Trenches*, 196.
39. Hugh C. C. McCullough, *The Call of the Sky* (London: Marshall, Morgan & Scott, 1935), 15–16, 22–23.
40. Schweitzer, *Cross and the Trenches*, 195.
41. Ibid. 205.

The Englishman W. H. A. Groom was another. Fresh from a three-month revival, when he arrived at the front Groom's crisis came during the Passchendaele campaign between June and November 1917 when he came across the body of a comrade killed while reading a letter, which finished with 'May God bless you':

> It was I suppose for me the moment of truth. I thought of the patriotic national churches all praying for victory. How could God choose? . . . I had had doubts before but I now saw clearly . . . that the Church's teaching of personal salvation, with all the emphasis on sin, forgiveness, confession, absolution was a selfish creed.[42]

Like Roberts, Groom moved to an idiosyncratic faith and never went to church again. The horror of the war could be fatal to traditional faith and institutional religion.

The perplexities and apparent hopelessness of their situation also caused soldiers to feel abandoned and to conclude either that there was no God or that he was uncaring and/or malevolent. In correspondence with his parents, Lieutenant Howard Bowser, whose former devoutness is evident in his scriptural language, asked, 'Is there a God? Pray for me that I may really know He lives . . . Of course He lives but why . . . I feel like crying as Jesus did, "My Lord, my God why has Thou forsaken us."'[43] Similarly the slaughter of men in spite of their prayers undermined belief in the efficacy of prayer.[44] One New Zealand private saw clearly that wartime conditions favoured a materialist explanation of life:

> On the battlefield material and physical force are so conspicuously predominant that it is easy to suppose that the side with the best equipment will win . . . Under such conditions the reality and power of God are difficult to realize and only the ear of a devout Christian can hear the still small voice above the roar of the cannon.[45]

While outright atheism was thought to be rare, some men gave up Christian belief altogether. According to the British soldier Stephen Graham, this response was summed up by the soldier who stated, 'War knocks all religion out of a

---

42. Ibid. 206.
43. Quoted in ibid. 216.
44. Ibid. 220.
45. Quoted in Michael Moynihan, *God on Our Side* (London: Secker & Warburg, 1983), 214.

man.'[46] Subversion of faith in God or orthodox Christianity was part (if not the whole) of the wartime experience.

As some of these examples indicate, the reaction was often more complex than a straightforward abandonment of Christian belief. Of the men from evangelical backgrounds, none described the impact of life in the trenches on the religious sensibility more powerfully than the war poet Wilfred Owen.[47] Although Owen had suffered doubt before the war, his Christianity was never far from his poetic sensibility. John Bunyan's *Pilgrim's Progress* supplemented the language of the Bible to describe the hell of the Somme: 'It is like the eternal place of gnashing teeth; the Slough of Despond could be contained in one of its crater-holes; the fires of Sodom and Gomorrah could not light a candle to it – to find the way to Babylon the fallen.' The strength of his disillusionment with the willingness of the Government and the church to sacrifice the young is evident in his parody of John 3:16: 'God so hated the world that He gave several million of English-begotten sons, that whosoever believeth in them should not perish, but have a comfortable life.' But while Owen lost the faith with which he entered the war, he did not lose faith. 'I am more Christian,' he told his devout mother, 'as I walk the unchristian ways of Christendom.' True Christianity was also to be found at the front: 'Christ is literally in no-man's land. There men often hear his voice: Greater love hath no man than this, that a man lay down his life – for a friend.' The result of these perceptions was chilling lines such as

> If you could hear, at every jolt, the blood
> Come gargling from the froth-corrupted lungs,
> Obscene as cancer, bitter as the cud
> Of vile, incurable sores on innocent tongues,
> My friend, you would not tell with such high zest
> To children ardent for some desperate glory,
> The old Lie: Dulce et Decorum est
> Pro patria mori.[48]

in which Owen described the suffering and condemned the hollowness of the patriotic exaltation of the war. He was killed a week before the Armistice; news reached his parents one hour after the war ended. Although Owen did not live

---

46. Quoted in Schweitzer, *Cross and the Trenches*, 227.
47. The paragraph is based on Arthur Orrmont, *Requiem for War: The Life of Wilfred Owen* (New York: Four Winds Press, 1972), quotations from 158, 146, 185, 111.
48. 'The War Poetry Website', www.warpoetry.co.uk/owen1.html.

to publish his poems in the manner intended, the timing of his death completed his indictment of traditional and institutional Christianity.

Having to endure the same hardships as the soldiers, the strength, sensibilities and faith of the chaplains were tested by the ordeal. Not all were able to cope. Alfred Plane, an Australian Methodist, returned home after less than a year's service because of shell shock.[49] Where they were expected to be cheerful and positive, some found they could not. They were dejected by a deepening sense of their inability to explain or alleviate the unbelievable suffering, or to help the men with their perplexities about their thoughts and actions. Captain E. M. Burwash, the son of prominent Canadian Methodist minister and educator Nathaniel Burwash, commented ruefully that 'the problem of suffering haunts the back of one's mind continually'.[50] This led to disillusionment with the way the war was being presented at home. To his fellow Canadian Methodist E. E. Graham depiction of the war as a Christian crusade was 'tommy rot'.[51] Chaplains could be wary too of the expectation that the brutality of the fighting would somehow produce a deepening of commitment to Christianity. As they looked within they also wavered. Another Canadian, S. D. Chown, once a champion of the war, acknowledged a rising sense of doubt and increasing difficulty in recognizing the presence and love of God.[52] The Anglican chaplain David Railton, son of notable Salvationist George Railton, with 'death and suffering all around', protested, 'I only believe in God in this war because I believe in Jesus Christ crucified.'[53] In the crucible of war the faith of evangelical chaplains was neither facile nor unqualified.

Survivors

The casualties of the First World War were appallingly high. The best available estimate indicates that there were 1,027,563 military deaths from the United Kingdom, Australia, Canada, New Zealand, South Africa and the United States between August 1914 and November 1918.[54] The number of evangelicals who

---

49. Linder, *Long Tragedy*, 138.

50. Quoted in Marshall, 'Methodism Embattled', 52.

51. Quoted in ibid. 53.

52. Ibid. 57–62.

53. Quoted in Moynihan, *God on Our Side*, 49–50.

54. Lance Janda, 'Casualties, Combatant and Non-Combatant', in Spencer C. Tucker (ed.), *The Encyclopedia of World War I*, 5 vols. (Santa Barbara: ABC-CLIO, 2005), I, 272–273.

died is yet another statistic that cannot be known. However, some idea of the impact on their communities can be gauged from the monuments to those who gave up their lives in the Great War set up in the churches of the English-speaking world. There is an indication of the qualitative dimension in the identities of some of the better-known of these men – such as the sensitive scholar James Hope Moulton and the emerging centre-right theologian Digges La Touche. The deaths of others still to make their mark – such as the Scotsman John Keith Forbes, a young Hebraist who managed to write notes for a commentary on Job while in the field, and the recently ordained Lionel F. Studd, nephew of the missionary hero C. T. Studd and said to be the first clergyman soldier killed in the war – robbed the movement of deep devotion, scholarly ability and energetic activism.[55] The evangelical community paid a high price for its support of the war.

Much has also been made of the deleterious effect on the religious outlook of the servicemen who survived the ordeal. But not all were disillusioned. Most were able to return to civilian life, affected by their experience to be sure, but able in due course to function again in post-war church and society. Among evangelicals one of these was Fred McLoughlin, who returned to his position as a bureaucrat in the Australian federal government and rose to become private secretary to Prime Ministers John Curtin (1941–5) and Ben Chifley (1945–6), while remaining an active Methodist layman.[56] The American Sherwood Eddy, a YMCA worker in 1916–17, was struck by the realization that the economic system was a war system. This moved him to join the social gospel with that of the individual to produce what he called 'the whole gospel'. Eddy's secretary, Kirby Page, who had travelled around the military camps with him, became an ardent pacifist.[57] In such cases the war produced a more critical and complex evangelical faith.

In still other cases the experience was the reverse of the stereotypical loss of faith. In 1917 near Ypres the Australian Baptist John Ridley decided to enter the ministry conceived of as an extension of his career as a soldier. The experience of war influenced his thought and language as an evangelist over the next fifty years.[58] This response to the war was by no means rare. Another Baptist,

---

55. Sellers, *With Our Heroes in Khaki*, 42–44; *With Our Fighting Men*, 124.

56. Linder, *Long Tragedy*, 47–49.

57. Rick L. Nutt, *The Whole Gospel for the Whole World: Sherwood Eddy and American Protestant Mission* (Macon, GA: Mercer University Press, 1997), 120, 124, 139.

58. John G. Ridley, *A Soldier's Testimony: Written for the Glory of God, the Honour of the Lord Jesus Christ, and the Help of Men, Especially Soldiers, and Veterans of the Great War*, 6th ed. (Melbourne: Marshall, Morgan & Scott, 1941).

the British soldier Hugh McCullough, came to a similar decision, and was joined
at Spurgeon's College by at least three other Great War veterans who had
similarly felt the call of the ministry.[59] As a member of the Church of England's
Service Candidate Committee, Edward Woods, later Bishop of Lichfield,
encountered hundreds of men who felt the same call. Early in 1919 he reported
how 'man after man has told . . . how he feels his life forfeit: that he has been
spared for a purpose, and that he cannot do other than give the remainder
of his days wholly to the service of God and the Kingdom'.[60] The experience of
war could leave men spiritually transformed with a profound sense of vocation.

The impact of the war on the surviving chaplains mirrored that of the men
in the ranks. Many were wounded, and all lived with the physical, psychological
and spiritual impacts of the war years. In addition to the standard difficulties
of resettlement, they also had to make the best of communities that were not
especially interested in their prophetic insights and wanted to resume normal
living as soon as possible.[61] Again the losses were potential as well as actual.
Large numbers of seminarians who went to war failed to resume their studies.
Many of the chaplains did not return to the ministry after the war, in their
disillusionment preferring social service and secular careers. But this preference
was not simply the result of loss of belief. Among evangelicals, the Australian
Kenneth Henderson, who had to be invalided out of the service in mid-1918
after two years' gruelling service on the western front, spent the years that
followed brooding on his experiences (which included the loss of two brothers)
and the theological problems raised by the war. Eventually he abandoned his
evangelical standpoint, left the ministry and withdrew from identification with
any church or religious group. Pursuing a career as a religious journalist, he
nevertheless insisted that he remained a servant of Christ.[62] Disaffection did
not necessarily lead to straightforward repudiation of traditional evangelical
faith and service.

If the war marred the faith and vocation of some evangelical clergy, it
renewed the commitment of others. Even a cursory survey of prominent
interwar clergy who had served as chaplains or Christian workers shows that
the war could be a time of spiritual chastening and deep reflection from which
they emerged with sharpened spiritual perceptions and an enlarged vision for
ministry. After eighteen months at the front, the Scot A. Herbert Gray returned

---

59. McCullough, *Call of the Sky*, 56–57.
60. Oliver Tomkins, *The Life of Edward Woods* (London: SCM Press, 1957), 45.
61. The best account is Crerar, *Padres in No Man's Land*, ch. 8.
62. Linder, *Long Tragedy*, 160–161.

to write the hymn of praise to Jesus with which he concluded *As Tommy Sees Us*.[63] Leslie Weatherhead, an English Methodist missionary in India, who joined the Indian army in 1917 and served as a chaplain through most of 1918, used this time in part to reconsider the relation of the people to the church and developed the approach he would follow when he returned to England.[64] The American J. Gresham Machen was affirmed in his belief that, amid the modern sense of self-satisfaction at having won the war, the only real hope for humanity was 'the gospel of grace'. *The Origin of Paul's Religion*, undertaken for the Sprunt Lectures in 1915 and both delivered and published in 1921, is a monument to his determination to fulfil his commitment as a minister.[65] Such men weathered the difficulties of demobilization, adjusted to home life and resumed their work. The encounter with the waste and tragedy of war was just as likely to bring about reaffirmation of confidence in the existence and goodness of God, and the call to service, as to lead to their denial.

Conclusion

In the strong belief that they were serving God's purpose, between 1914 and 1918 evangelicals took their religion to the theatres of war, where they served as soldiers and clergy in the new citizen armies. Whether as officers or rank and file, they occupied a place on the spectrum of 'soldiers' religion' among those for whom religion was a definite and positive commitment. As such, evangelical Christianity was not only a motivator in the face of what was viewed as un-conscionable German conduct: it also proved to be a sustaining influence amid drudgery and horror. In the settings of modern warfare, evangelicalism was a constancy that initially enabled men to adjust to the novel and difficult con-ditions of military life, and then, under fire, to face up to the ordeal of battle and its aftermath – sometimes with great distinction – and also to endure the protracted demands of a war of attrition. For better or worse, the evangelical outlook also had a bearing on the style and quality of leadership shown by the generals and other officers. While it might have facilitated acquiescence in the

63. A. Herbert Gray, *As Tommy Sees Us: A Book for Church Folk* (London: E. Arnold, 1918), ch. 13.

64. John Travell, *Doctor of Souls: A Biography of Dr Leslie Dixon Weatherhead* (Cambridge: Lutterworth Press, 1999), ch. 2.

65. Ned B. Stonehouse, *J. Gresham Machen: A Biographical Memoir*, 3rd ed. (Edinburgh: Banner of Truth Trust, 1987 [1954]), 257–311.

torment of trench warfare, it at least gave them a capacity to persist until, under Providence, circumstances improved (as they did in the last year of the war). Evangelical clergy, serving mostly as chaplains, were among those subject to the ire and ridicule of the troops, but were also among those who won gratitude and admiration for their willingness to identify with and provide to the utmost the spiritual and material needs of the men, and for their heroism. Even the army came in due course to recognize their contribution, especially in its effect on morale. From the top down, heightened evangelical activism expressed as commitment to military service shaped wartime thought and conduct of many men and was in this way one of the major enabling influences at the front.

At the same time the commitment of evangelicals to the war effort as a form of activism affected the evangelical tradition itself. For both soldiers and clergy, its adequacy as a world view was put to the test under the extreme conditions of protracted modern warfare. For some, evangelical Christianity as they had received it furnished a standard they could not live up to or a belief system that did not account for the spiritual and moral perplexities they encountered. For others its hold was strengthened as its efficacy was demonstrated under the most intimidating circumstances. As a result faith was lost and complicated, or confirmed and enhanced. Disaffection and transformation were thus both a part of the experience of evangelicals 'under fire'. In terms of the impact of the war on the outlook of its adherents, evangelicalism at least gained as much as it lost. The truly disruptive loss to the movement occurred in the form of massive casualties. And perhaps unavoidably the circumstances of the day intensified the activism of the *fin de siècle* evangelical social gospel now expressed as war service in many forms.

8. THE WAR WITHIN

From the standpoint of most English-speaking evangelicals, the Great War was fought 'over there', away from their home societies in various theatres in France, Eastern Europe, the Middle East and, to some extent, in Africa. Of the anglophone societies, only Britain sustained direct attacks on home soil. For the British this made manifest what was true for all, that in addition to the actual conflict there was another war to be fought on the home front. Outwardly this required support for the war effort of the Allies and adjustment to the effects of sustained warfare on their societies. Inwardly fighting the war at home called for resistance to debilitating malign spiritual and moral forces in their communities, churches and individuals including themselves. In the evangelical mind this 'war within' was at least as important as the overt warfare. Its objectives were to ensure their societies were both in a fit state to conduct the war and also worthy of victory. Daunting at one level, the task was also bracing. For it presented evangelicals with the possibility of exercising substantial influence in their communities. Making the most of this historic opportunity to recover their failing cultural authority became the challenge of fighting the war on the home front.

Maintaining spiritual direction

At the outset the British Government called for 'business as usual' as the best way of conducting the war on the home front. As large numbers of men joined up, with news of heavy casualties coming back from the theatres of war, and with women increasingly diverted into war work, the call quickly proved to be unrealistic. Although they had initially endorsed the call for 'business as usual', evangelical communities around the English-speaking world also soon felt the disturbing effects of the war, albeit in varying degrees.[1] In addition to contributing to the war effort along the lines recounted in chapter 6, they expressed support for their societies by adjusting to the new social conditions and making the best of their circumstances. The impact of the war on local evangelical churches and communities has been no more studied than that of the war as a whole, but their experiences appear to have varied widely. In the absence of so many men, some suffered falling membership and income. In other cases the sensitivities and needs of the time caused church life to thrive.[2] The determination to carry on was reflected in the widespread performance by women of many of the tasks normally reserved for men. Against a background of rising social tensions, evangelical churches held memorial services for the dead, welcomed wounded and maimed servicemen as they returned, and maintained their contribution to the war effort. In their steadfastness as communities of worship, service and sacrifice the churches sought to lead by example.

As it became clear that the war would not be over quickly, evangelical spokesmen also adapted to the emerging situation. In moving beyond initial patriotic excitement, they developed a more considered response that embraced the opportunity to shape attitudes and conduct by provision of distinct spiritual leadership. The Anglican Dean of Canterbury, Henry Wace, reminded his contemporaries of what this meant early in the war: 'It is the momentous and supreme office of promoting among men that apprehension and that love of righteousness which ought to be the controlling force of all their actions.'[3] Evangelicals should furnish this leadership for their nations at large, it followed, because, in their ability to see beyond the visible and the immediate, they as Christians could bring a perspective to events unavailable to others. Their leadership was also necessary for people in the Christian community for guidance on such ethical issues as forgiveness of the enemy, the proper response to atrocities, and the relationship between patriotism

---

1. '"Business As Usual": The Evangelistic Outlook', *C* (17 Sept. 1914), 8.
2. Robert D. Linder, *The Long Tragedy: Australian Evangelical Christians and the Great War, 1914–1918* (Adelaide: Openbook, 2000), ch. 7; S. D. Henry, 'Scottish Baptists and the First World War', *BQ* 31.2 (1985), 52–65, esp. 61–62.
3. Henry Wace, 'God's Call to the Nation', in *ICM 1915*, 12–23 (quotation on 20).

and piety. Together with many others in their various communities, Harry Fosdick in America and Patrick J. Murdoch (grandfather of the news magnate Rupert Murdoch) in Australia endeavoured to rise to the challenges of the time.[4]

As the magnitude of the struggle came into sharper focus, fundamental to this leadership was presentation of an interpretation of the war that affirmed its spiritual character and sustained the commitment of their communities. Whether construed as an answer to prayer for a time of divine visitation to break down spiritual indifference or more simply as an occasion for the salvation of the world, the war at home was consistently portrayed by evangelicals as providential, a time of *kairos* fraught with challenge proffering distinct advantages to a spiritually alert world alongside the obvious perils. Certainly the war seemed to expose the deleterious effects of the love of luxury and pleasure seeking they had routinely criticized in their societies during the *fin de siècle* years. The need for service and self-sacrifice brought out the value of self-denying and disciplined lives of the sort produced by Christian values and character. A common cause called for unity and cooperation in place of the industrial and class conflicts of pre-war days. Most importantly, the dangers to life of modern warfare enforced the unseen and eternal dimensions of human existence and thus called men and women to return to belief in God and Christian commitment. Far from endorsing their societies as they were in 1914, evangelicals identified the war with the cause of righteousness. Whereas at the front this entailed a crusade against German militarism, at home it required a campaign against secularism and indifference to religion.

A further requirement of the task of leading to victory in the war within was mobilization of the spiritual resources available in the life of faith. In the forefront was of course reading the Bible as *the* book for wartime. As a revelation of the unchanging God and 'the entire truth', it was the primary source for a true understanding of events and the proper response to them. It was also the 'Book of Comfort' for the many thousands who were in distress. Inevitably some parts were more salient than others. The Old Testament, with its accounts of the wars of Israel, was used extensively. More particularly, the Psalms stood out. It was not only that the Psalms illuminated wartime experience; the reciprocal was also true. In particular, the contrast between zeal for the Lord and personal vindictiveness brought into relief under the conditions of war

---

4. Harry E. Fosdick, *The Challenge of the Present Crisis* (New York: Association Press, 1918); Patrick J. Murdoch, *The Laughter and Tears of God and Other War Sermons* (Melbourne: Arbuckle, Waddell & Fawckner, 1915).

tended to resolve the age-old difficulty of the imprecatory psalms and duly sanctified anti-German sentiment.[5]

But no aspect of biblical teaching attracted more interest than prophecy. The cataclysmic scale of the conflict immediately suggested to premillennialists everywhere that the war was a preparation for the second coming. Specific events encouraged this kind of speculation. The Dardanelles campaign in 1915 shifted attention to the Middle East, where the fall of Jerusalem to Britain's General Allenby in 1917 seemed to presage the return of the Jews to Palestine, one of the cardinal signs of the end times. As premillennialism attracted more adherents, new writers joined with established teachers to elaborate what all this might mean. Many evangelicals were both excited and comforted during the war by the belief that the second coming was imminent.[6]

Freshened in their commitment by the pre-war debate on the subject, evangelicals believed that in prayer they had another great resource for fighting the war. In addition to encouraging private prayer, they supported days of intercession and organized public prayer meetings in centres all around the English-speaking world. Their advocacy was coupled with instruction about prayer's function. It was not a talisman, and evangelicals frequently repeated that God was not a tribal deity to be invoked in the national interest. Due circumspection also followed from the recollection that the enemy had access to the same resource. What to pray for was a further cause of concern. If it was in order to pray for victory, it was also necessary to pray for the enemy, although this aspect received less emphasis as the war dragged on. Asking for an end to the war came to seem more reasonable and pressing.

One thing for which evangelicals generally would not pray was the salvation of the dead.[7] At a time of great distress they were under pressure to do so. Anglo-Catholics, who readily drew on the Catholic tradition of prayers for the dead and doctrine of purgatory, appeared to be more pastorally sensitive. There was also some advocacy of the practice in their own publishing

---

5. W. S. Hooton, 'Imprecatory Psalms and the War', *C* (18 Nov. 1915), 12.

6. Ian Randall, *Spirituality and Social Change: The Contribution of F. B. Meyer (1847–1929)* (Carlisle: Paternoster Press, 2003), ch. 7; Matthew Sutton, *American Apocalypse: A History of Modern Evangelicalism* (Cambridge, Mass.: Belknap Press, 2014), ch. 2.

7. E.g. Professor J. Stalker, 'Shall We Pray for the Dead?', *C* (11 Jan. 1917), 7–9; W. H. Griffith Thomas, 'Prayers for the Dead', *LQR* 128 (1917), 255–271. For the setting, Michael Snape, 'Civilians, Soldiers and Perceptions of the Afterlife in Britain During the First World War', *SCH* 45 (2009), 371–403.

organs.[8] Some evangelicals wavered: two Scottish Presbyterian ministers, N. Maclean and J. R. P. Sclatir, both of whom worked with the YMCA, suggested that there ought to be a Protestant version of purgatory.[9] But evangelicals at large maintained that the Bible provided no warrant for the practice. The Anglican H. E. Fox, something of an archaeologist, supported biblical conviction with erudition by reporting that there was no evidence for the practice earlier than the sixth century.[10] In a very difficult situation evangelicals mostly matched encouragement of prayer with discouragement of its misuse.

Nor would evangelicals generally connive at the popular idea of 'salvation by sacrifice'. The avalanche of casualties among serving men coupled with the conviction that death in the service of the nation served a general purpose gave rise to the belief that it was redemptive. By this device, the meaning of Christ's death was transferred to those who had laid down their lives for their country. While they readily conceded that it illustrated the meaning of sacrifice, evangelicals would not allow that death on the battlefield was equivalent to conversion or regeneration.[11] The much-invoked text 'Greater love hath no man than this, that a man lay down his life for his friends' (John 15:13) was ruled out as not germane to the issue. Any suggestion that death in battle was salvific compromised the atonement. This meant in turn that it diverted people, and especially the men in the trenches, from the true basis of salvation. 'We render the truest service to the men when we refuse to send them upon a false track, and insist, rather, upon the foundation truths of personal religion.'[12] Although some did waver,[13] the pressures of wartime did not induce evangelicals at large to compromise their soteriology.

Ministry to the bereaved put evangelical spiritual leadership to a further test. All around the English-speaking world clergy and others – many of whom had suffered loss themselves – offered words of comfort as best they could privately

---

8. A. Plummer, 'The War and the Other World', *Ch* 30 (1916), 173–176, 258–262, 325–331, 377–383. Refuted by Andrew Given, 'Prayers for the Dead: A Reply', ibid. 588–594.

9. Stewart J. Brown, '"A Solemn Purification by Fire": Responses to the Great War in the Scottish Presbyterian Churches', *JEH* 45.1 (1994), 94.

10. H. E. Fox, 'Prayers for the Dead', *C* (25 Jan. 1917), 18.

11. W. S. Hooton, 'The New Dogmatism', *C* (8 June 1916), 7.

12. 'Notes and Comments. Nationality and Spirituality', *C* (18 Nov. 1915), 10.

13. David W. Bebbington, *Evangelicalism in Modern Britain: A History from the 1730s to the 1980s* (London: Unwin Hyman, 1989), 200.

and in public. Mostly they echoed the language of the high value of sacrifice in a noble cause current in the community. Some, such as the Calvinistic Free Presbyterians in Scotland, were sympathetic but insisted that it was a Christian duty to be strictly scriptural in maintaining that it would be a cruel delusion to say anything other than that unrepentant soldiers cut down in the service of their country would go to hell. Seeking no less to be faithful to the Bible and upholding the absolute uniqueness of the sacrifice of Christ, Handley Moule, Bishop of Durham, who had himself recently suffered the loss of his wife of thirty-four years, showed that compassion did not entail surrendering the evangelical position.[14] For those who died before they appeared to be ready, there could be confidence that God, whose mercy was limitless, would save 'to the uttermost', a condition that provided for last-minute acceptance of salvation 'in the twinkling of an eye'. Moule also proffered reassurance that the war dead were in the presence of Christ. Evangelicals who did not adjust their message to the popular demands of the age repeated traditional evangelical formulas about death and the afterlife with varying degrees of pastoral sensitivity and flexibility.

The theology of war

A specialized aspect of wartime leadership fell to the movement's theologians and teachers. The need for direction at this level was soon felt. At the end of August 1914 twenty-nine German theologians who had been involved in the missions movement fired the first shot in the theological war by appealing to 'the Evangelical Christians abroad' both for understanding of the motives that had led Germany to go to war and for condemnation of those who had forced it to take this dire step.[15] They alleged that Germany's actions were defensive, a necessary response to 'a wanton attack', that the British were guilty of unscrupulous acts against Germans living abroad, and that British actions discredited the cause of Christian missions. Following hard on the heels of

14. Handley Moule, *Christus Consolator: Words for Hearts in Trouble* (London: SPCK, 1915), quotations on 94, 95; *Christ and Sorrow: Thoughts for Stricken Hearts* (London: SPCK, 1916).
15. Charles E. Bailey, 'The British Protestant Theologians in the First World War: Germanophobia Unleashed', *HTR* 77.2 (1984), 195–221; John Moses, 'The British and German Churches and the Perception of War, 1908–1914', *WS* 5.1 (1987), 23–44.

news of atrocities in Belgium, the appeal was met with incredulity that these extraordinary claims could be made by men of such intellect and standing. When forty-two British church leaders – 'famous alike for their scholarship and piety' and including representatives from the evangelical churches – responded with an emphatic refutation of the German claims and assertion of support for the stand taken by the British Government, the evangelical community was reassured.[16] As *The Churchman* observed, 'as an answer to the allegations made, it could not be more convincing or decisive'.[17] By confirming that Germany was responsible for the war, the theologians justified the Allies' war effort and made a fundamental contribution to winning the war within.

Writers on the right wing of the evangelical movement attempted to build on this by drawing out the theological lessons of the war. One strand of their critique of Germany was a facile attribution of the unscrupulous ambition of German conduct to the development of higher biblical criticism in Germany during the nineteenth century. By this account the abandonment of a morality based on biblical authority created an opening for the nihilistic and militaristic philosophies that had flourished at the turn of the century. The resultant teachings of thinkers such as Nietzsche, Treitschke and Bernhardi were seen to account for the doctrines of Pan-Germanism and its underlying ethic of might makes right.[18] A more sophisticated interpretation looked to the effects on German behaviour of the decline of Christian doctrine in the previous half century.[19] Denial of the miraculous facts of Christianity had led to the abandonment of its doctrines and ethics. With their own situations in the forefront of their thinking, these writers used the downward moral spiral of Germany to warn English-speaking society of where the abandonment of evangelical Christianity would lead.

---

16. *To the Christian Scholars of Europe and America: A Reply from Oxford to the German Address to Evangelical Christians* (Oxford: Oxford University Press, 1914). The evangelicals were H. G. Grey, Principal of Wycliffe Hall, and W. B. Selbie, Principal of Mansfield College.

17. 'A Decisive Reply', *Ch* (28 Nov. 1914), 807–808. Cf. 'A Pathetic Appeal' and 'The Divine Verdict', *C* (17 Sept. 1914), 7; 'Anglo-German Friendship' and 'The Christian Attitude', *C* (8 Oct. 1914), 7.

18. E.g. J. Stuart Holden, 'The Real Inwardness of the Conflict', *EC* (Sept.–Oct. 1914), 185–186; W. Y. Fullerton, 'The Mailed Hand and the Nailed Hand', *EC* (Nov.–Dec. 1914), 215–216.

19. E.g. W. E. Chadwick, 'German Christianity (?) [*sic*] and the Great War', *Ch* 88.107 (Nov. 1914), 811–822.

Other writers from across the spectrum of evangelical opinion made their contribution by confronting the theological and ethical questions raised by the war.[20] The need for this kind of apologetics enabled the theologians to develop further positions they had already begun to occupy. A reaction against the optimism and values of the *fin de siècle* was already well underway before 1914, and the war could be interpreted as justification of this critique. In a wide-ranging exposition E. Griffith-Jones of the Yorkshire Independent College, for example, exposed the inadequacy of the rising materialism of the pre-war generation and promoted the Christian ethic of faith, hope and love as an alternative to the destructive militarism of the day and the only basis of lasting peace.[21] By demonstrating that the social order before 1914 was not based on the Christian ethic's values, such answers seemed both to refute the allegation that the war marked the failure of Christianity and also to attribute the conflict to the secularism of the modern world. Theological and ethical arguments highlighting society's need of Christianity were deployed as major weapons in the war within.

If the theological explanation of the war could be proffered with relative ease, the problems of theodicy were much more difficult. None responded to the challenge more trenchantly than P. T. Forsyth, the leading evangelical theologian of the day. To this pressing task he brought the characteristic crucicentric theology identified in chapter 4.[22] As the point of reference for everything in the creation, the cross of Christ revealed many things: the reasons for the war as a descent into a barbarism of which Germany was no more than a case study; the true significance of the war as a judgment on European civilization; the suffering of the war as but a sudden accumulation of what is typical in life; and the inability of philosophy and popular theologies to explain what was happening and furnish grounds for steadfastness. At such a time the cross in its manifold relations was the only adequate justification of God's ways. As the action of a holy God from outside history, it provided the goal of the world in advance,

---

20. A selection of works includes J. H. Oldham, *The World and the Gospel* (London: United Council for Missionary Education, 1916); Henry Wace, *The War and the Gospel* (London: Chas. J. Thynne, 1917); and W. Douglas Mackenzie, *Christian Ethics in the World War* (New York: Association Press, 1918).

21. E. Griffith-Jones, *The Challenge of Christianity to a World at War* (London: Duckworth, 1915).

22. Peter T. Forsyth, *The Justification of God: Lectures for War-Time on a Christian Theodicy* (London: Duckworth, 1916); *The Christian Ethic of War* (London: Longmans, Green, 1916).

and thus a guarantee of providence, assurance of purpose in all that was happening, a cure of the evil evinced by the war, a basis for the unity and peace of humankind, an ethical standard and power of moral regeneration and, above all, God's self-justification. As Forsyth well knew, this proposal was too radical or abstract for many, but it was what the world in its current situation needed to hear. To the secularists he insisted that the escape into religion was unavoidable: 'There is no final ethic, but a theological.' To Christians of other outlooks he was similarly unapologetic: 'no theodicy is possible, and no peace, except to an evangelical faith'.[23] Forsyth asked evangelicals to apply their faith and other Christians to embrace their evangelicalism. The war was the time for all to appropriate the cross of Christ in its full meaning.

After the war Karl Barth condemned the German theologians for their abandonment of 'the unconditional truths of the Gospel' in their national cause.[24] This was not generally true of the evangelical theological teachers of the English-speaking world. While it would have been easy for them to be critical of Germany, their strictures were directed primarily at their own societies. For them the war as *kairos* was the moment to articulate their message in protest against the religious and social dispositions that had so weakened the influence of evangelical Christianity on their societies during the *fin de siècle*. Not all were as strident as Forsyth. Yet they were all similarly critical of neglect of God and the resultant secularizing social changes that the war had brought to the surface. On these grounds they presented the war as the judgment of God. Recalling their societies to the truths and values of the gospel as a source of the strength required in the present and hope for a better future was their contribution to fighting the war within.

Evangelism in wartime

Definite leadership and sound theological guidance would be of no avail without adherence to the evangelical standpoint. It followed that the best evangelicals could do for their societies in wartime would be at least to maintain the conversionist activism so characteristic of the *fin de siècle* era. At the outset this was one aspect of the movement where 'business as usual' looked feasible and might be expected to meet the needs of the times. As people flocked to the

---

23. Forsyth, *The Justification of God*, 155–156, 159.
24. Stuart Mews, 'Neo-Orthodoxy, Liberalism and War: Karl Barth, P. T. Forsyth and John Oman 1914–18', *SCH* 14 (1977), 361–375.

churches in the early days, evangelicals observed that the uncertainties of wartime had in fact produced a not unexpected heightening of readiness to listen to the gospel appeal at home as well as at the front. They also discerned a new moral earnestness and reversal of the hedonistic patterns of behaviour they had recently found so disturbing, particularly as the effects of the war began to be felt. This receptivity was the leading aspect of the *kairos* of which they were eager to take full advantage. While church leaders considered how best to respond to the new situation, existing plans were implemented. The YMCA persisted with the Chapman–Alexander Mission to young men in London late in 1914, and the English Free Churches went ahead with their 'Come to Church' campaign early in the following year.[25] Because the circumstances appeared so favourable, hopes ran high that the outbreak of war would bring about the long-awaited revival.

In fact, between 1914 and 1918, while there was no weakening of commitment to evangelism in principle, evangelicals were unable to sustain pre-war levels of conversionist activism. With men and resources diverted to the war effort, local evangelistic activity continued, but on a greatly reduced scale. Perhaps more tellingly, international revivalism was suspended as impractical. Only in neutral America during the early war years was revivalist work continued along pre-1914 lines. Here Billy Sunday reached the zenith of his career with great campaigns in Philadelphia in 1915 and New York City in 1917.[26] These caught the imagination of the wider evangelical world and for a time maintained the hope of wartime revival, although nobody else wanted such a controversial figure in their own backyard. With the early spiritual responsiveness of the people quickly fading and hedonism returning to alarming levels, the war years proved to be a time of disappointment in evangelism.

While the full significance of this development did not emerge until after 1918, contemporary evangelicals worried that a serious declension was taking place. Their alarm was reflected in controversy over allegedly unseemly activities in YMCA facilities and squandering of crucial evangelistic opportunities.[27] More broadly this prompted reflection on the apparent indifference or hardening

---

25. 'The Come to Church Campaign', *FCC* 17 (1915), 7–8, 32, 41–42.

26. Lyle W. Dorsett, *Billy Sunday and the Redemption of Urban America* (Grand Rapids: Eerdmans, 1991), ch. 5.

27. 'The YMCA and the Camps. Important Letter from M. J. W. Fegan', *C* (7 Jan. 1915), 20, with correspondence from readers in the next four issues; 'The YMCA – Whither?', *C* (16 Mar. 1916), 7–8; C. Howard Hopkins, *History of the Y.M.C.A. in North America* (New York: Association Press, 1951), 497–519.

towards Christianity in society and on the likely causes. The analysis involved some recrimination for inaction or peddling an anaemic gospel by the churches. Consideration of the place of evangelism in the contemporary church led to proposals for new evangelistic methods such as 'vocational evangelism' and debate about the old, especially in relation to the role of the revivalist.[28] The situation also encouraged reflection on revival and how it was fostered.[29] In this respect history tendered cause for hope: periods of war and despair in the past had often been followed by revival. Concern to make Christianity the missionary force in society that it ought to be coincided with a deterioration in the military situation. As the war dragged on, evangelicals felt an increasingly urgent need to lead their nations back to God.

Only in England and Wales was there an organized attempt to do so. In September 1916, the Church of England launched the National Mission of Repentance and Hope.[30] This was not an evangelical initiative, but evangelicals were involved throughout. However, their involvement was not enough to prevent the undertaking being criticized as 'Pelagian' and a contradiction of their theology of grace. Non-Anglicans complained about their exclusion. This, together with manifest confusion about the method and the message, was enough to make the Mission neither 'national' nor (in the eyes of some) a 'mission'. At least the evangelicals in the Church of England had a clear sense of what it might achieve.[31] Personal repentance was the beginning and condition of national repentance. Of course this was not the outcome. While there were acknowledged benefits in some places, the decline in Christian profession and practice the Mission set out to address was not reversed. Instead its effect was to confirm the secularizing drift it had been expected the war would correct, and to justify abandonment of the hope of a wartime revival.

---

28. E.g. 'He Gave Some . . . Evangelists. The Outlook for Gospel Work', *C* (15 Apr. 1915), 11; 'The Greatest Opportunity', *C* (8 June 1916), 7; P. Whitwell Wilson, 'Why Not an Intensive Mission?', *C* (21 June 1917), 12.

29. E.g. H. Elvet Lewis, 'Studies in Revival', *MBC 1915*, 93–153; Cyril C. B. Bardsley and T. Guy Rogers (eds.), *Studies in Revival* (London: Longmans, Green, 1915).

30. David M. Thompson, 'War, the Nation, and the Kingdom of God: The Origins of the National Mission of Repentance and Hope', *SCH* 20 (1983), 337–350. Keith Robbins, *England, Ireland, Scotland, Wales: The Christian Church 1900–2000* (Oxford: Oxford University Press, 2008), 133–135.

31. Commentary on the National Mission from an evangelical standpoint is available in *The Churchman* 30 (1916) and 31 (1917).

Missionary effort was also adversely affected by the war. On the field missions had quickly to adapt to new and unexpected conditions for which they were unprepared.[32] Because of their imperial connections, parts of Africa became the scene of combat, and mission hospitals and colleges were used for military purposes. Here and in other British territories German missions were shut down or subjected to restrictions with losses to social and philanthropic as well as evangelistic work. Similarly in the Turkish domains of the Middle East, English-speaking missions were brought to a virtual standstill. While American numbers were not affected, overall the size of the missionary force decreased as missionaries and ancillary staff were diverted into military service. Financial support was more or less maintained, but the international flow of money was hampered by wartime conditions. Perhaps most damaging for missions was the discrediting effect in the host countries of the war in Europe between so-called 'Christian nations'.

A similar impact was felt in the homelands. Missionary recruitment in Great Britain and Ireland suffered immediately and dramatically as students preferred military to missionary service.[33] This effect was exacerbated in the course of the war as its human and financial costs increased. According to one estimate, by 1917 casualties were such that the number of missionary candidates had been halved. Funds that would have gone into missions were diverted to the war. The effects were psychological as well as material as something of a 'generation gap' opened between the established missionary leaders and the rising generation. The older men quickly adapted to the war as a crusade reflecting *fin de siècle* missionary values that would secure the conditions for an authentic Christian internationalism. Although initially they had supported the war, increasingly the younger men were less sanguine about what the war would achieve and less accepting of the failings of their own churches and societies.[34] Some began to doubt whether Christianity in its present state was worth giving to the rest of the world. Most agreed on the need to concentrate attention on properly Christianizing their own civilization. The pre-war missionary impulse

---

32. The annual reports (usually prepared by J. H. Oldham) in the fledgling *International Review of Missions*, and summed up in G. A. Gollock, 'A Survey of the Effect of the War upon Missions: The Church in the Mission Field', *IRM* 9 (1920), 19–36.

33. Nathan D. Showalter, *The End of a Crusade: The Student Volunteer Movement for Foreign Missions and the Great War* (Lanham, MD: Scarecrow Press, 1998), ch. 4.

34. E.g. J. Lovell Murray, *The Call of a World Task in War Time*, rev. ed. (New York: Association Press, 1918).

weakened as a result of the realization that evangelism and Christian reformism
were needed as much at home as abroad.

No evangelical leader felt the disruptive effect of the war more than John
Mott.[35] Initially, both as a neutral and as the recognized leader of three world
organizations (the YMCA, the WSCF and the Edinburgh 1910 Continuation
Committee), he tried to hold the two sides together, and sought to preserve the
supranational solidarity of the missionary movement. However, his closeness
to President Wilson and participation in a diplomatic mission to Mexico in 1916
led to his impartiality being questioned by the Germans. It was seriously compromised when he immediately placed himself and the resources of the YMCA
at the disposal of President Wilson on America's entry into the war, and then
participated in the diplomatic mission to Russia led by Wilson's personal
representative Elihu Root, the aim of which was to keep the new Provisional
Government in the conflict on the side of the Allies. Mott took these steps in
the belief that the Allied cause was a truly Christian undertaking, but they led
to repudiation of his leadership of international organizations by the Germans.
This loss of confidence in his leadership was a setback to his hope of fostering
international comity in the cause of missions and ultimately the creation of a
Christian world order.

Activism on the home front

As with conversionism, the war imparted fresh impetus to the evangelical social
engagement of the *fin de siècle* years. In addition to creating new outlets in
providing support for the military, it not only engendered additional grounds
for pursuing well-established social causes but also gave them additional salience
as conditions of victory in the war with the Central Powers. Accordingly evangelicals launched a direct attack on some old enemies.

The most emotive public issue for evangelicals during the war was alcohol.
In 1915 the British Minister for Munitions David Lloyd George declared, 'We
are fighting Germany, Austria and the drink; and, as far as I can see, the greatest
of these three deadly foes is drink.'[36] Advocates of temperance were quick to
seize the opportunity to step up their campaign. The British Baptist Arthur

---

35. Richard V. Pierard, 'John R. Mott and the Rift in the Ecumenical Movement
    During World War I', *JES* 23.4 (1986), 601–620.
36. Quoted in J. S. Blocker et al. (eds.), *Alcohol and Temperance in Modern History:
    An International Encyclopedia*, 2 vols. (Santa Barbara: ABC-CLIO, 2003), I, 372.

Mee, for example, founded the Strength of Britain Movement, which petitioned the Government for the introduction of prohibition for the duration of the war and one year afterwards.[37] The war furnished new arguments for the prohibitionist cause: loss of industrial efficiency; waste of resources that would be better allocated to food production; and the pernicious practice of 'treating' servicemen. As the war dragged on and the impact of food shortages and casualties was felt, support for the campaign grew. It was now argued that continuation of the trade in alcohol prolonged the war, jeopardized the lives of men at the front and betrayed them by not protecting the homes they were fighting to defend. The increasingly hysterical tone of the campaign was evident in the allegation that the men of the trade were traitors whose misguided priorities threatened defeat in the war. By 1917 victory over 'the drink evil' at home was raised to the same level of importance as military defeat of the enemy: 'It is idle to talk of conquering Germany if we cannot kill the demon at our own hearthstone.'[38]

Despite this apparent despair, the agitation was not without effect. Under pressure in 1915 the British Government created the Central Control Board, which imposed restrictions on the production and sale of beer. Evangelicals also thought they had won a great moral victory in the same year when King George V promised to abstain from alcohol until the end of the war. Between 1915 and 1917 the Canadian provinces passed prohibition measures that were strengthened in 1918 when the Federal Government, notwithstanding the resistance of Quebec's Catholics, enacted national prohibition for the duration of the war and one year after. In 1916 four Australian states introduced six o'clock closing of pubs and New Zealand followed in the next year. When America entered the war, Congress passed the Lever Act limiting beer production as a war measure and moved to introduce national prohibition. The effects of these measures, which 'by the scientific method' of experimentation would show the benefits of restriction,[39] were welcomed as important successes in this other war and encouraged hope for final victory in the future.

That the evangelical concern was for the future well-being of society as well as present survival is evident in the ongoing protest against the profanation of

---

37. Arthur Mee and J. Stuart Holden, *Defeat or Victory? The Strength of Britain Book* (Christchurch: L. M. Isitt, published for the Auckland Branch NZ Alliance and the Auckland Sunday School Union, n.d. [1917]), testifies to the geographical reach of the campaign.
38. 'Shipping and Drink', *C* (4 Jan. 1917), 9.
39. 'America and Prohibition', *C* (7 Mar. 1918), 9.

the Sabbath.[40] From early in the war evangelicals were quick to speak out against relaxation of the standards that made for the observance of a proper Christian Sunday. They reluctantly acknowledged that the exigencies of food and wartime production required that some exceptions be allowed. In general they maintained that Sunday as a day of rest was a divine provision that enabled working people to maintain health and well-being. But they were also mindful of the symbolic value of Sunday as an index of the spiritual state of society. Relaxation of standards was a clear sign that a major cultural change was taking place. Once the ground was lost to increasing secularism, they recognized, it would not be regained. For this reason evangelicals resisted the encroachments of newspapers, sports and popular entertainments on Sunday as a matter of national concern.

Evangelicals also engaged with the manpower issues generated by the war, which they tended to view as reflecting the standard of citizenship required to win the war. For the Americans, who relied on the draft from the beginning of their involvement, this was never really a problem. But for Britain and the allies of the empire the need for fresh recruits was unrelenting, especially when the early enthusiasm for enlistment waned. When the need became critical, the British Government resorted to compulsion early in 1916. Despite uneasiness about militarism and the excessive power of the state – the very things against which they were fighting – evangelicals generally supported conscription, maintaining as a matter of fairness that all who benefited from the war should carry their share of the burden. Similar responses were evident when conscription was introduced in Canada and New Zealand, although in the latter the issue was complicated by a racial factor when the Maoris refused to comply.[41] The situation was more complex in Australia.[42] When the government put the matter to a referendum in 1916 and again in 1917, evangelicals were strongly divided. The leaders of the evangelical churches were mostly in favour of conscription, but opinion among the clergy at large and church members was mixed, with a majority possibly opposed. Like their counterparts elsewhere, proponents felt it was a matter of duty in the hour of public need. Opponents maintained that conscription was contrary to Christian teaching and confused the religion of Christianity with the religion of the state. There was no consensus among Australian evangelicals on the question of public duty in wartime.

---

40. E.g. 'Hands off the Lord's Day', *C* (22 Mar. 1917), 7–8.

41. Allan Davidson, *Christianity in Aotearoa: A History of Church and Society in New Zealand*, 3rd ed. (Wellington: Education for Ministry, 2004), 99.

42. Linder, *Long Tragedy*, ch. 6.

Finally, the war injected fresh life into the inveterate anti-Catholicism of the evangelical movement in Britain and the Empire. While the loyalty of Catholic servicemen was unquestioned, hostility towards the papacy intensified. Old suspicions flared up and new animosities appeared, especially regarding the failure of the Pope to condemn German wartime atrocities. Above all, evangelicals alleged that the Vatican was scheming to benefit from the war. During its last two years their outlook became avowedly political as they used by now standard methods for influencing public opinion and government policy. In 1917 the Protestant Alliance lobbied the British Prime Minister to put a stop to Catholic proselytization of troops at the front.[43] Later in the year evangelicals rejected the pretensions of Pope Benedict XV to be an even-handed mediator between the warring parties and denounced his attempt to broker a peace as too shallow to be of use.[44] Around the same time the Irish-born Catholic Archbishop of Melbourne, Daniel Mannix, was publicly condemned for disloyalty to the Allies' cause and for weakening the war effort. Similarly the recall of the world to Catholicism and the claim to be the champion of labour and social reform in the Archbishop of Westminster's Lenten Pastoral in 1918 was ridiculed as a disclosure of Catholicism's true ambitions.[45] As the final victory in the war proved frustratingly difficult to achieve, the Pope was finally added to the list of the enemies that had to be defeated, while the prospect of his having a seat at the peace conference was utterly unacceptable. With increasing anxiety, evangelicals moved politically to prevent a dangerous rival from strengthening its political position and increasing its international influence.

Peace

Almost from the outbreak of fighting in 1914 evangelicals looked forward to peace and deliberated about what it should be like.[46] Both inclinations deepened as the war moved towards its conclusion. While wanting an end to the war as soon as possible, evangelicals opposed peace for its own sake and held out for 'a righteous and lasting settlement' worthy of the sacrifices that had been made

---

43. 'Roman Catholic Attempts to Proselytize the British Soldiers at the Front',
     C (22 Feb. 1917), 23.
44. 'The Vatican and Peace', C (23 Aug. 1917), 9; 'The Pope and Peace', C (30 Aug.
     1917), 7–8.
45. 'Cardinal Bourne's Arrogance. The Roman Catholic Lenten Pastoral', C (21 Feb. 1918), 9.
46. E.g. W. B. Selbie, 'The Churches, the War and the Future', ConsQ 3.9 (1915), 54–65.

to achieve victory. To ensure that such a catastrophe never happened again, peace would require primarily the unconditional surrender and disarmament of Germany, the removal of the Kaiser and the end of Prussianism. While there were some noteworthy exceptions, relatively few evangelicals harboured any desire to destroy Germany. With its capacity to wage war curbed, it should be left to develop in every legitimate way and contribute to the world's well-being. From about mid-1917 the evangelical peace ideal also incorporated the principle of collective security, the proposal for a League of Nations and eventually President Wilson's 'Fourteen Points'. By delivering justice and putting an end to the unchristian idea of world domination, these conditions would produce a morally defensible end to 'the Lord's War'.

When the war finally ended on 11 November 1918, evangelical responses were mixed. Of course evangelicals were relieved that at last the conflict and slaughter were over. They were also satisfied that, in the defeat and discrediting of German militarism and autocracy, their war aims had been achieved. Seeing the ideals for which they had fought upheld added a strong sense of vindication.[47] Their thanksgiving was enhanced by the wide acknowledgement in the general public that the victory was recognizably due to Almighty God. These enthusiasms were offset by broad acceptance that the world would not go back to where it had been in 1914. Revolutionary stirrings in Europe, particularly in Russia and Germany, left no doubt that the world was in a state of flux, and there was no telling where the present circumstances would lead. Apprehension about the future strengthened the determination to build a social order of a standard commensurate with the human and financial cost of the war. After four years of 'total war', rejoicing was tempered by the responsibilities of peace and apprehension about the future.

As the war ended, evangelicals were inclined to take stock of how they had fared. Having moved beyond the idealism of the early war years, they were able to see that they had passed through a time of testing and exposure.[48] On one

---

47. E.g. W. P. Wilks, 'The Churches and the Present War', *RE* 15.2 (1918), 157–171; John B. Harford and Frederick C. MacDonald, *Handley Carr Glyn Moule, Bishop of Durham: A Biography* (London: Hodder & Stoughton, n.d. [1922]), ch. 8.

48. From a large literature, this and the next paragraph are based on Samuel Chadwick, 'God's Judgment Through War', *C* (25 July 1918), 19; Frederic Spurr, 'Four Years of War', *C* (1 Aug. 1918), 7–8; 'Our Day of Judgment', *HomR* 77.1 (Jan. 1919), 31–32; Harry E. Fosdick, *The Church's Message to the Nation* (New York: Association Press, 1919); A. Herbert Gray, *As Tommy Sees Us: A Book for Church Folk* (London: E. Arnold, 1918); Robert Speer, *The Gospel and the New World* (New York: Fleming H. Revell, 1919).

side of the ledger, the war was tallied as a 'day of salvation'. With the consequences of human failure and sin laid bare, evangelical conceptions of repentance, righteousness, service and fellowship appeared to have acquired new meaning and salience. Indeed, these beliefs and ideals seemed to be just what the post-war world needed, moving one evangelical to observe, 'the church faces the greatest and supreme opportunity of its long history'.[49] At the same time it was clear to evangelicals that their churches had been less influential in the response to the war than they would have liked. While glad to have had the contribution of chaplains and other Christians in the various service organizations, governments had been unwilling to entrust the churches with their natural task of maintaining the morale of the troops because of their divisions and inefficiency. Unresponsiveness of the people to their message brought out the continuing loss of influence and capacity to lead their societies morally and spiritually, while exposure of the soldiers' misunderstanding of the Christian gospel revealed the ineffectiveness of their teaching prior to the outbreak of war. Above all there was a greater willingness among evangelicals by the end of 1918 to face up to their fair share of the responsibility for the war and its atrocities – in their inability to curb the nationalistic foreign policies of their governments and the public opinion that supported them. Because the war brought home the failure and weakness of the *fin de siècle* churches, it had been God's 'day of judgment' on themselves as much as on their societies and Germany.

Amid this mixed response, perhaps inevitably the war left a deep mark on the evangelical temper as an abiding militarism. It was widely felt that the same heroic qualities shown by wartime volunteers were now needed for Christian service. The thinking with which John Ridley determined to become a preacher was mentioned in chapter 7. A 'call to battle' helped to galvanize the SCM as it contemplated the end of the war and work for a better world.[50] According to the Vicar of Islington, to make the most of the new era it was necessary to 'have men ready to go over the parapet, to join in the mad enterprise, the hopeless cause'.[51] The endlessly quoted observation of Curtis Lee Laws, editor of the *Watchman-Examiner* – that the anti-modernist faction in the Northern Baptist

---

49. Samuel Zane Batten, 'The Churches and the War', *RE* 15.2 (1918), 172–196 (quotation on 195).

50. Tissington Tatlow, *The Story of the Student Christian Movement of Great Britain and Ireland* (London: SCM Press, 1933), chs. 32–33.

51. C. J. Proctor, *ICM 1918. After the War – 'Renewal'* (London: Record Newspaper Office, 1918), 8–9.

Convention in America was ready 'to do battle royal for the Fundamentals' –
reflects how they conceived of their task.[52] Although different in content and
objective, these sentiments expressed constructive ideas about what needed to
be done. But this militaristic thinking also had an ugly side. It surfaced in its
imperial dimension when in 1917 an Australian Presbyterian minister endorsed
the suggestion of a Canadian friend that the way to deal with wartime pleasure
seeking by attending the races would be to fly over Randwick racecourse
in Sydney and wake up the crowd by dropping bombs.[53] For better or worse,
the war affected the way evangelicals looked at the world and how to operate
within it.

Conclusion

In conducting their war on the home front, evangelicals waged the moral and
spiritual battles necessary to win the war within so that their communities would
be fit and able to achieve victory in the conflict with the Central Powers. To this
end they endeavoured to provide the theological and ethical leadership necessary
to generate the spiritual force that would sustain commitment to the war effort
and ensure it was unhampered by serious shortcomings of perspective and
character. In doing so, although totally supportive of their societies, they were
far from quiescent in the prevailing social condition, both admonishing
and seeking to improve it to achieve alignment with the providential order and
worthiness of its blessing. If they did not win the war within manifestly and
decisively, evangelicals nevertheless had a 'good war' to the extent that their
leadership and influence had had some bearing on the motivation and social
arrangements of their societies. Most importantly, the war seemed to have
created a setting in which the world might turn again to evangelical Christianity
as the moral and spiritual basis of the new world order. Evangelicals faced the
post-war years with this hope.

While seeming to confer these benefits, the war also had powerful disruptive
effects. Outwardly its demands affected social and church life, and the impact
of death and maiming had to be faced within the evangelical community no
less than in the wider society. The war proved to be unfavourable to organized

---

52. Quoted in George M. Marsden, *Fundamentalism and American Culture: The Shaping of
Twentieth-Century Evangelicalism 1870–1925*, rev. ed. (Oxford: Oxford University Press,
2006), 159.

53. Linder, *Long Tragedy*, 151.

conversionist activity, so that there was marked declension from the high point
of the first decade of the century. The prospects for mass conversion also
turned out to be illusory and hopes for wartime revival gradually receded. Evangelicals spoke their prophetic word, but with no appreciable effect. Apart from
a brief moment early in the war, society remained troublingly hedonistic, and
the extent of misunderstanding of evangelical teaching and alienation from
society's religious culture was exposed by the attitudes of the troops. It became
necessary too to defend their fundamental message about sin and salvation and
communion with God, not only from unbelievers, but also from the advocates
of different Christian traditions and popular wishfulness. Although important
advances were made in the area of temperance reform, similar progress was
not achieved in other areas of political and social concern. Moreover, the
movement was not the same at the end of 1918 as it had been four years earlier.
The exigencies of wartime had brought activism to the fore, a priority the
circumstances of the reconstruction era just beginning seemed also to require.
If at the beginning of the war there had been something of an equilibrium
between the forces that constituted evangelicalism, this was no longer the case.
The legacy of the war to evangelicalism was heightened activism and significantly weakened conversionism.

PART 3: EVANGELICALISM AT THE CROSSROADS
(1919 – C. 1940)

9. MODERNISM, LIBERAL EVANGELICALISM AND FUNDAMENTALISM

At the beginning of 1919 the War had evidently ended on a good note for the anglophone powers. Victory looked like a triumph of the military forces of the British Empire and America and brought the prospect of peace and a straight-forward restoration of civilization. Within a year the outlook was very different. The Treaty of Versailles, based more on national revenge than President Wilson's idealistic Fourteen Points, jeopardized the peace by imposing punitive terms of compliance on Germany. By refusing to ratify it, the American Congress gravely weakened the push for collective security and a new era of international cooperation through the League of Nations. Events in Russia, coupled with widespread industrial unrest and the 'Red Scare' in the West, made the spectre of world revolution seem very real. Severe recession between 1920 and 1922 also made the victory in the Great War feel hollow. In the tension between high-minded idealism and hard-nosed pragmatism, these developments set the tone for the era to follow as governments attempted to secure their war aims at the same time as restoring order and stability in the highly complex task of post-war reconstruction.[1]

Like their governments, evangelicals also wanted to win the peace. As reconstruction became the focus for their post-war aspirations, they gave a great deal

---

1. Adam Tooze, *The Deluge: The Great War and the Remaking of Global Order, 1916–1931* (London: Allen Lane, 2014).

of thought to how the church (as they understood it) might capitalize on the end of the War.[2] It was clear enough that they stood on the cusp of a turning point in history defined by 'its desire to forget those things which are behind – the horrors and suffering and bloodshed of warfare, the violence and destruction that have marked it – and to reach forth unto those things that are before, the new era with its new prospects and possibilities and relationships that will stand the strain of human striving'.[3] In a manner reflecting the high idealism of the era, evangelicals were supremely confident that, in the 'redemptive agency' of Christ, they were the bearers of the principle and power 'to remake men, remould society, and re-establish the world in righteousness and peace'.[4] With the War having shown what the world would be like without vital Christianity, it followed that their task and responsibility was to lead the restoration of Christian civilization by bringing 'the redemptive agency of Christ' to bear on post-war society. The prospect of success held out the hope that evangelicalism's loss of cultural authority would be reversed.

Early optimism was soon checked by the turn of events. Domestic turmoil suggested that locally individual self-seeking had displaced the wartime commitment to the common cause, while the menacing international setting indicated that the fundamental problems of the world order had not been solved by four years of conflict. The uncertainty produced by these unexpected developments tempered the idealism of evangelicals with a sense of the hard realities of their situation. But the effect was to accentuate their sense of the importance of the gospel (and themselves as its representatives) to the post-war world. H. M. Gooch, Secretary of the Evangelical Alliance in Britain, stated the basic conviction of many of his contemporaries: 'Only the facts and fellowship of the Gospel of Christ can enable men and nations to use the Peace worthily, to substitute self-denial and heart devotion to the common good for selfishness and surrender to low ideals.'[5] In circumstances much less favourable than expected, the great task was to convince the world that the peace ideal required the gospel to become a reality.

---

2. E.g. *ICM 1919. Evangelicals and the Reports of the Archbishop's Committees: Evangelisation, Teaching, Worship* (London, 1919); Robert Speer, *The New Opportunity of the Church* (New York: Macmillan, 1919).

3. William Jobson, 'The New Age and Its Demand', *CWP* 95 (22 Jan. 1919), 41–42 (quotation on 41).

4. W. Williams, 'Divine Reconstruction', *CWP* 95 (26 Feb. 1919), 101–102 (quotation on 102).

5. 'Peace and Its Issues', *EC* (July–Aug. 1919), 85.

What evangelicals wanted to do for the world in the all-important task of reconstruction was only one side of the crisis. The post-war situation raised the question of whether they would be equal to their historic opportunity. As they reflected on their predicament, contemporary evangelicals saw that their churches needed to be effective in order to be authoritative. Speculation about what this required was brought into focus by the *Army and Religion Report*, which found a perception that 'the churches are out of touch with reality'. The exposition of this finding included claims that the churches had lost contact with modern thought, lacked 'independent life or a spiritual message' and showed 'want of sympathy with workers' efforts for social reform'.[6] Above all, they were weakened by disunity arising from differences no longer widely understood or deemed to matter. With the future of evangelicalism apparently at stake, rectifying these deficiencies to demonstrate realism and efficacy emerged as the condition of the success of the evangelical reconstruction project. Anxiety that the movement would be unable to make good its place in the post-war world had been expressed even before the end of the fighting by the English Baptist J. H. Shakespeare when he declared in 1918 that the churches, because of their divisions, were at a crossroads.[7] The idea that its deficiencies had brought evangelicalism to a crossroads echoed down the post-war years.[8]

The post-First World War era did not turn out as evangelicals expected in 1918–19. For a time the menacing political and economic environment improved as prosperity returned in the mid-1920s almost everywhere except in Britain, and arrangements for a lasting peace seemed to have been secured by the early success of the League of Nations (despite America's failure to participate) and conclusion of the Locarno and Kellogg–Briand Pacts of 1925 and 1928 that set up systems of international collective security. However, evangelicals did not share in the optimism of 'the roaring twenties' as developments in popular and secular culture made alarmingly clear that society had not returned to Christianity as the basis of civilization. While the masses were drawn to the pleasures of the new leisure, thinkers such as Bertrand Russell, Julian Huxley

---

6. D. S. Cairns (ed.), *The Army and Religion: An Enquiry and Its Bearing upon the Religious Life of the Nation* (London: Macmillan, 1919), esp. the summary on 187.

7. J. H. Shakespeare, *The Churches at the Cross Roads* (London: Williams & Norgate, 1918).

8. E.g. E. Y. Mullins, *Christianity at the Cross Roads* (New York: George H. Doran, 1924); L. Elliott-Binns, 'Evangelicalism and the Twentieth Century', in G. L. H. Harvey (ed.), *The Church and the Twentieth Century* (London: Macmillan, 1936), 347–390, esp. 354–355.

and H. L. Mencken subjected Christianity to a sardonic critique. Perceived ineffectiveness in this encounter with an increasingly secular order gave rise to a malaise in evangelicalism which has been, in its American context, represented as 'the religious depression' of 1925–35.[9] The gloom and low morale of the later 1920s were compounded by the onset of the Great Depression at the end of the decade, the emergence of the totalitarian state – overtly godless in Russia, neo-pagan in Germany and in league with Catholicism in Italy – and the drift to the war that eventually broke out in 1939. The attempts of evangelicals to engage with this unreceptive and increasingly threatening environment with a view to reversing the loss of cultural authority provide the framework for the evangelical experience in what turned out to be the interwar decades.

Modernism and liberal evangelicalism

As evangelicals moved into the post-war era, the presumption of the role they claimed in the reconstruction project was their belief system and teaching. The importance of doctrine for the times was enunciated by the English Methodist J. Scott Lidgett: 'Doctrine is, or should be, the dwelling place of ideals, and should supply the principles by which reconstruction is guided.' This function was inherent in the nature of doctrines: 'They reveal the nature and constitution of the universe. They are prophetic of its future.' It also arose from their effect: 'when formed and accepted, [doctrines] have a power of their own. They become part of the mental outlook, and mould the temper with which men handle the institutions to which they belong.'[10] The prevalence of this view of the function of doctrine is signified by publication of the standpoint of the left-wing theologian Scott Lidgett in the pages of the right-wing newspaper *The Christian*. On the basis of such thinking, in 1919 evangelicals at large sought to supply the theological basis of a restored Christian civilization as the new world order.

At the same time the consequences of failure to bring doctrine into contact with the whole of modern thought and life were well understood. In no other

---

9. R. T. Handy, 'The American Religious Depression, 1925–1935', *CH* 29 (Mar. 1960), 3–16.

10. J. Scott Lidgett, 'Christian Doctrine Restated: For Times of Reconstruction', *C* (27 Mar. 1919), 13; (10 Apr. 1919), 10; (8 May 1919), 12; (22 May 1919), 13; (5 June 1919), 20; (19 June 1919), 14; (3 July 1919), 12; (17 July 1919), 12; (31 July 1919), 11. Quotations from (27 Mar.), 13 and (31 July), 11.

area of the evangelical tradition did the conditions of effectiveness in the post-war world identified by T. B. Kilpatrick of Knox College, Toronto, apply more than in theology:

> It is a safe prediction that, if the Church were to withdraw from any sphere of its world enterprise, or refuse the adventures that await it in unoccupied fields, it would be devitalized, and lose the energy it was seeking to conserve. The wider is the Church's outlook, the bolder its policy, the more heroic its endeavour, the greater will be its influence in the world, and the greater its portion in the riches of Christ.[11]

However, theology was the first point at which the key difficulty of the era was faced as evangelicals sought to establish their place in the rebuilding of the spiritual and moral bases of their communities. The divisions of diversity meant that there was no longer broad agreement about evangelical teaching. In the years that followed, various attempts to supply the theology needed by the age not only failed to achieve the ultimate objective of a restored Christian civilization. They also further diversified evangelicalism and deepened its divisions.

Within Protestantism, the primary intellectual rival to the pretensions of evangelicals to determine the normative Christianity of the post-war world came from theological modernism.[12] Its optimism checked but uncurbed, modernism emerged from the War surprisingly robust and confident. Its writers – the best of whom were New Zealand expatriate H. D. A. Major and the American Shailer Mathews – attempted to set the theological agenda by putting the case for a Christianity ostensibly in step with the modern world. Journals (such as *The Modern Churchman* and *The Christian Century*) and conferences (most notably that of the Churchmen's Union)[13] presented the reconciliation of theology with the latest discoveries of science and the modern mind not only as a method of unfettered enquiry but also as a claim to cultural centrality. Although it had been developing for half a century, in the years just after the War theological modernism reached the high point of its ambition and influence. Along with resurgent Catholicism, it was frequently identified by contemporary evangelicals as one of the two leading challenges of the era.

---

11. T. B. Kilpatrick, 'The Church of the Twentieth Century', *ConsQ* 7.27 (Sept. 1919), 432–433.

12. Kathryn Lofton, 'The Methodology of the Modernists: Process in American Protestantism', *CH* 75.2 (2006), 374–402.

13. From 1928 the Modern Churchmen's Union.

Apart from its perceived theological defects, modernism posed two problems for interwar evangelicals. One was its success. Increasingly modernists achieved positions of power and exercised wide influence both in the traditional churches and on the mission field. The modernist programme for reform could also make evangelicalism seem well behind the times and quaint in its persistent super-naturalism. In attempting to incorporate the immense achievements of contemporary science and learning into the Christian synthesis, it raised in the sharpest way the challenge of how to be orthodox without being reactionary. Opposition looked like rejection of the common mind of modern humanity. As they faced the modernist–reactionary dichotomy alongside other conservative Christians, evangelicals appeared to be on the wrong side. Ecclesiastical and intellectual conditions in the post-war world seemed to block the evangelical recovery of cultural authority.

A second problem was the vigorous proselytizing of the modernists. Typically they presented the move from traditional faith to the new truth as a conversion experience and set about making converts.[14] Apologists for evangelicalism – most notably the American J. Gresham Machen – wrestled with modernism more or less successfully.[15] Despite the efforts of such apologists, modernists emerged within the evangelical churches. The corrosive effects of their presence were strikingly evident in the career of the Congregationalist C. J. Cadoux, Professor of New Testament at the Yorkshire United Independent College at Bradford (1919–33) and Mackennal Professor of Church History at Mansfield College, Oxford (1933–47). As his studies progressed through the 1920s, his restatement of Christian belief in terms of modern knowledge led his Principal at Bradford to warn that he was close to throwing over 'the Evangelical faith'. Cadoux's defence of his quest for intellectual truth in *The Case for Evangelical Modernism* drew considerable criticism for its negativity.[16] The responses to Cadoux represented the strained reception of modernism within the evangelical movement. Through the interwar years modernism remained an object of criticism – no longer Christianity, as Gresham Machen maintained, but a new religion – and yet a challenge to evangelical belief.

––––––––––––––––

14. Robert D. Linder, 'Apostle to the Australians: The Rev. Dr Samuel Angus in Australia, 1915–1943', in Geoffrey R. Treloar (ed.), *The Furtherance of Religious Beliefs: Essays on the History of Theological Education in Australia* (Sydney: Centre for the Study of Australian Christianity and the Evangelical History Association of Australia, 1997), 156–179.

15. J. Gresham Machen, *Christianity and Liberalism* (New York: Macmillan, 1923).

16. Cecil J. Cadoux, *The Case for Evangelical Modernism: A Study of the Relation Between Christian Faith and Traditional Theology* (London: Hodder & Stoughton, 1938).

If Cadoux was perhaps an extreme case, he reflected an important development in interwar evangelicalism. Impossible to ignore, the challenge of modernism drew out the liberal evangelicals much more definitely. In numerous addresses and sermons they declared the legitimacy of theological restatement in the light of current thought and culture.[17] The warrant for doing so was provided by the understanding of divine revelation as progressive in the sense that new intellectual discoveries merely brought to light what had already been given in the teaching and person of Christ. On this basis biblical scholarship could be embraced, the nature of the atonement reinterpreted as only Christ's moral example, and new developments in church life welcomed without loss of commitment to the gospel and evangelical activism. Determined to steer a course between stagnant orthodoxy and irresponsible modernism, such a standpoint enabled liberal evangelicals to be critical of the language and categories of evangelicalism as outmoded while claiming to retain the essentials of orthodoxy and remain in alignment with the tradition. In doing so they offered the movement an option that was at once historically grounded and also held out the promise of adapting evangelicalism to modern life.[18]

This 'coming out' was clearest organizationally among British Methodists and Anglicans. The first post-war stirrings along these lines occurred when the Methodist Fellowship of the Kingdom was formed in 1919 out of a group that had taken shape over the previous decade.[19] Its manifesto declared its continuity with historic evangelicalism along with the desire to adapt to the present. Although its priorities were spiritual experience and evangelism, its interest in finding new ways appropriate to the age also had a theological component. The enlightened scholarship it needed to inform its other endeavours was provided by men of the order of R. Newton Flew of Wesley House, Cambridge.[20]

More overtly theological were the Anglicans of the Group Brotherhood Movement who formed the Anglican Evangelical Group Movement (AEGM) in 1923. They similarly proclaimed continuity with the fundamental spiritual truths of evangelicalism, but also recognized the need for their presentation in

---

17. E.g. J. D. Jones, 'The Doctrine of Development', *ICC 1920*, 59–66.

18. Vernon F. Storr, *Spiritual Liberty: A Study of Liberal Evangelicalism* (London: SCM Press, 1934), is the classic statement of interwar liberal evangelicalism.

19. Ian M. Randall, *Evangelical Experiences: A Study in the Spirituality of English Evangelicalism 1918–1939* (Carlisle: Paternoster Press, 1999), ch. 5.

20. Gordon S. Wakefield, *Robert Newton Flew, 1886–1962* (London: Epworth Press, 1971), ch. 5.

modern language and thought forms.[21] The desire for a restatement of the faith in reasonable terms reflected some sympathy with modernism. Yet clear differentiation from other well-organized groups in the Church of England – notably the Modern Churchmen's Union and the Anglo-Catholic English Church Union – was required lest the evangelical voice go unheard in determining the issues of the day. Although undertaken reluctantly, going public proved to be successful. Membership rapidly increased from 222 in 1921 to 1,500 by 1939, and the Group's influence reached such a level that one observer at least regarded the liberal evangelicals (with some hyperbole) as 'the most important party in the Church'.[22] The formation of groups in Australia, Canada and the United States testified to a shared aspiration throughout the Anglican Communion. In some dioceses the liberal evangelical standpoint had come to predominate by the 1930s.[23]

The activities of other less formally organized groups and networks also established a liberal presence throughout the evangelical movement. Many of those who had felt the broadening impulse before the War spoke into the post-war scene through the pages of Peake's *Commentary on the Bible* to 'put before the reader in a simple form, without technicalities, the generally accepted results of Biblical Criticism, Interpretation, History, and Theology'.[24] They were joined by others who wanted to demonstrate the complementarity of divine revelation and human discovery in science, philosophy and literature. A succession of Presbyterian theologians including H. R. Mackintosh and John and Donald Baillie continued to work at the relation between faith and culture in

---

21. T. Guy Rogers (ed.), *Liberal Evangelicalism: An Interpretation by Members of the Church of England* (London: Hodder & Stoughton, 1923), v–viii, 27, 28, 76–79, 287–288, 293–295; *Liberal Evangelicalism: Pamphlets*, 2 vols. (London: Hodder & Stoughton, n.d. [1923]).

22. The anonymous author of *The Looking-Glass of Lambeth* (1928), quoted on 68 of Martin Wellings, 'The Anglican Evangelical Group Movement', in Andrew Atherstone and John Maiden (eds.), *Evangelicalism and the Church of England in the Twentieth Century: Reform, Resistance and Renewal* (Woodbridge: Boydell Press, 2014), 68–88.

23. William H. Katerberg, *Modernity and the Dilemma of North American Anglican Identities, 1880–1950* (Montreal: McGill-Queen's University Press, 2001), 136, 149; D. Hilliard, 'Intellectual Life in the Diocese of Melbourne', in Brian Porter (ed.), *Melbourne Anglicans: The Diocese of Melbourne 1847–1997* (Melbourne: Mitre Books, 1997), 27–48, esp. 35–38.

24. A. S. Peake (ed.), *A Commentary on the Bible* (London: Thomas Nelson, 1919), xi for the quotations.

the manner of George Adam Smith and James Denney before the War, while the American gadfly Harry E. Fosdick and others reared in the milieu of the YMCA and Student Volunteer Movement (SVM) propounded increasingly liberal evangelical views.[25] Proponents of this standpoint created new organs such as *The Congregational Quarterly* and *The Canadian Journal of Religious Thought* for the exploration of the relation between Christianity and culture. Such networks reflected the approach to theology within evangelicalism in the era of reconstruction as a progressive discipline well capable of improvement by restating the received tradition. While it is impossible to say how numerous they were, liberal evangelicals were a pervasive presence confronting the interwar movement with the case for an open and progressive faith.

In developing their standpoint the liberal evangelicals emerged as the best-known representatives of evangelicalism in an age of transition.[26] Their pathway was never straightforward. Without always understanding the nuances of liberal evangelical thinking, other evangelicals simply dismissed the claim to continuity with the evangelical tradition and classified them as modernists. Certainly their theology was widely condemned as vague and confused, 'more liberal than evangelical'.[27] Peake's *Commentary* was a particular flashpoint in the early 1920s as evangelicals still wrestled with the problem of how much of the higher criticism they could accept.[28] The attitudes of other evangelicals reflected deeper issues within liberal evangelicalism itself. Among Anglicans, some of whom were members of both the AEGM and the Modern Churchmen's Union, the

25. Alec C. Cheyne, 'The Baillie Brothers: A Biographical Introduction', in David Fergusson (ed.), *Christ, Church and Society: Essays on John Baillie and Donald Baillie* (Edinburgh: T. & T. Clark, 1993), 3–37; Matthew Bowman, *The Urban Pulpit: New York City and the Fate of Liberal Evangelicalism* (New York: Oxford University Press, 2014), ch. 8; Heather A. Warren, *Theologians of a New World Order: Reinhold Niebuhr and the Christian Realists 1920–1948* (New York: Oxford University Press, 1997).

26. A. E. Snashall, 'A Reasonable Evangelicalism', *CQ* 8.2 (1930), 137–151; numerous addresses in *ICC 1930*; *The Liberal Evangelical*, the periodical of the AEGM; and the Methodist *LQHR*.

27. Wellings, 'Anglican Evangelical Group Movement', 81.

28. E.g. W. H. Fitchett, *Where the Higher Criticism Fails* (London: Epworth Press, 1922); Robert D. Linder, 'William Henry Fitchett (1841–1928): Forgotten Methodist "Tall Poppy"', in Geoffrey R. Treloar and Robert D. Linder (eds.), *Making History for God: Essays on Evangelicalism, Revival and Mission in Honour of Stuart Piggin* (Sydney: Robert Menzies College, 2004), 197–238, esp. 214–221.

boundary between liberal evangelicalism and modernism was blurred.[29] With the limits of accommodation unclear, the primary difficulty was remaining genuinely connected to evangelicalism and its overt supernaturalism. Closely related was the question of coherence. How much could be surrendered before liberalism ceased to be viable as an expression of evangelicalism? The confusion was highlighted by the case of E. W. Barnes, a distinguished mathematician and a Fellow of the Royal Society and, from 1924, the Anglican Bishop of Birmingham. Although regarded by many as an egregious modernist, Barnes himself never repudiated his identification with the liberal evangelicals.[30] The relationship of interwar liberal evangelicals to modernity and modernism was never entirely clear.

   In spite of these difficulties, liberal evangelicalism was important for the evangelical movement as a whole. For those who had felt the broadening impulse before the War, it provided a less reductive alternative to modernism. At a time when evangelicals were on the defensive along a number of fronts, it offered a means of engagement with contemporary life and thought and with other Christians in an age of ecumenical advance. In its recognition of the need to adapt to changing times and conditions it was a creative force. In America liberalism contributed to the revival of evangelicalism within the Episcopal Church.[31] Individual evangelicals found liberalism an attractive option in several ways. Perhaps its star recruit was Vernon Faithfull Storr, Canon of Westminster Abbey and an established theologian, who was drawn by the prospect of freedom to develop a progressive theology.[32] The English Congregationalist D. R. Davies, once 'an out and out modernist', found in liberal evangelicalism a channel for a return to orthodox faith and the ministry after ten years of working directly on social and political problems in the wake of the General Strike of 1926.[33] To the American Episcopalian Carl Grammer, who had renounced the evangelicalism of his upbringing, it furnished a basis for reconnecting with the

---

29. The boundary is negotiated in M. G. Glazebrook, 'An Eirenicon to Evangelicals', *MC* 11.7 (Oct. 1921), 373–377; and C. W. Emmet, 'Relations Between Evangelicals and Broad Churchmen', ibid. 389–396.

30. John Barnes, *Ahead of His Age: Bishop Barnes of Birmingham* (London: Collins, 1979), 132–134, 175–176, 186–187, 296.

31. E. Clowes Chorley, *Men and Movements in the American Episcopal Church* (New York: Charles Scribner's Sons, 1946), ch. 15.

32. G. H. Harris, *Vernon Faithfull Storr: A Memoir* (London: SPCK, 1943), esp. ch. 7.

33. D. R. Davies, *In Search of Myself: The Autobiography of D. R. Davies* (London: Geoffrey Bles, 1961), esp. 64–65; *On to Orthodoxy* (London: Hodder & Stoughton, 1939).

movement.[34] For up-and-coming men it could be a framework for remaining within evangelicalism as modern men. Leaders of the next generation who had been nurtured amid the freedom of liberalism included several thinkers later respected by almost all evangelicals, such as missionary statesman Max Warren and historian Stephen Neill.[35] In an age of transition liberal evangelicals maintained a subculture that allowed 'cognitive bargaining' between tradition and culture and in turn kept many within the movement.

Fundamentalism

Not all evangelicals wanted to negotiate with modern thought. At the other end of the evangelical spectrum fundamentalism emerged after the War as a parallel response to the modern outlook. It functioned as an aggressive habit of mind constituted by a cluster of theological perspectives and social attitudes ostensibly opposed to modernism.[36] One contemporary, while recognizing that the term was difficult to define, nevertheless pinpointed the essentially antithetic nature of fundamentalism as

> the opposite of rationalism, liberalism and modernism. It means orthodoxy as opposed to heterodoxy, the support of the common evangelical articles of the Christian faith as against the religious vagaries of the times. It looks to the Scriptures as its source of belief, not to human reason.[37]

Whereas liberal evangelicals sought a synthesis between tradition and modernity, fundamentalists were intent on controlling modernity by subordinating it to the evangelical tradition as they construed it.

Theologically fundamentalists adhered to traditional Protestant beliefs seen to be under attack from modernists. These normally included a high view of biblical authority, a hermeneutic of stressing factual history, the reality of miracles, the virgin birth and expectation of the second coming in a premillennial framework. Apart from the estimate of the Bible, none of these elements was

---

34. Katerberg, *Modernity*, ch. 8.

35. Max Warren, *Crowded Canvas: Some Experiences of a Life-Time* (London: Hodder & Stoughton, 1974); Stephen Neill, *God's Apprentice: The Autobiography of Stephen Neill*, ed. E. M. Jackson (London: Hodder & Stoughton, 1991).

36. Harriet Harris, *Fundamentalism and Evangelicals* (Oxford: Clarendon Press, 1998).

37. Anon., 'The Review', *BR* 8 (1923), 590.

necessarily part of the fundamentalist belief system or unique to it, but all were prevalent. Nor were they new, all having been a part of the pre-war fundamentalist impulse. Presented as apostolic Christianity, 'the faith once delivered to the saints', in fact this set of beliefs was an expression of the revivalist evangelicalism that had taken shape across the course of the previous century. While for liberal evangelicals the boundary with modernism became increasingly porous, for fundamentalists it was raised as a bulwark against those who would draw them into apostasy.

The novel element that mobilized these theological ideas was social. Whereas other evangelicals joined with their contemporaries in adjusting to 'normalcy' after 1918, fundamentalists remained at war. In the era of reconstruction the fundamentalist belief system was held up as the proper basis of the political and social order. As the proponents of a counterfeit Christianity, modernists were the primary obstacle to the realization of this aspiration. Fundamentalists were none too discriminating in their definitions of modernism. To the extent that other Protestants (other evangelicals included) were not with them, they were against them. In this concerted opposition to the abandonment of received orthodoxies, fundamentalism was new. It crystallized as an ideology of opposition, directed as much against contemporary tendencies within evangelicalism itself as other expressions of Christianity and modern society at large.

Fundamentalism emerged as a definite movement of significance in America.[38] In May 1919 a gathering of 6,000 people in Philadelphia formed the World's Christian Fundamentals Association to contend for the faith against what it called 'the Great Apostasy' of modernism.[39] Never a particularly strong organization in itself, its creation signalled the commencement of battle. The fighting was most intense in the mainline denominations, where the 'modernist compromisers' were seen to have gained control. Among Northern Baptists and Presbyterians in particular the contest for the denomination raged until the mid-1920s when it became clear that the fundamentalists had been defeated by a combination of liberals and moderates who were repelled by the intolerance of the militants. In the meantime fundamentalist zealots had taken the struggle to the South and into non-mainstream and smaller churches. In these locations

---

38. In a large literature George Marsden, *Fundamentalism and American Culture: The Shaping of Twentieth-Century Evangelicalism 1870–1925*, rev. ed. (Oxford: Oxford University Press, 2006), pt. 3, remains foundational.

39. Joel A. Carpenter (ed.), *God Hath Spoken: Twenty-Five Addresses Delivered at the World Conference on Christian Fundamentals May 25–June 1, 1919* (New York: Garland Publishing, 1988).

it became a well-established conservative Protestant subculture, but, stigmatized by a series of embarrassing events, especially the trial of John T. Scopes for teaching evolution in a Tennessee high school, and the murder trial of Texas Baptist J. Frank Norris, fundamentalism came to be viewed widely as out of date and obscurantist. By 1930 it was clear that America at large had rejected the fundamentalist version of a restored Christian civilization. But it was equally clear that fundamentalism was established as a divisive and, as it turned out, a permanent force in American evangelicalism.

Despite the widely shared premillennialism (which ought to have made them indifferent to society), American fundamentalists were motivated by a perception that the whole of Christian civilization was at risk in the post-war world.[40] They decried theological modernism as a threat to the Christianity at the heart of the American way of life. If it were to triumph, the moral basis of society would collapse. This fear was compounded by a corresponding anxiety that the future of world Christianity was also at stake. America's role as leader in the evangelization of the world before the War turned on the character of its Christianity. This was why concern for what was happening on the mission field was so much a part of the rhetoric of the period. Circumstances immediately after the War – the 'Red Scare' and the flood of immigrants – maintained a sense of threat posed by 'the other' from outside and kept alive the combative spirit. The connection made between theological modernism and Bolshevism reflected fundamentalists' need to lead the crusade in defence of American culture.

In other parts of the evangelical world fundamentalism also crystallized out of the pre-war fundamentalist impulse. In neighbouring Canada leaders such as Roland Bingham, Oswald Smith, P. W. Philpott and especially T. T. Shields stood at the head of scattered (but never coordinated) fundamentalist activities.[41] While they interacted extensively with American fundamentalists, theirs was no mere reflex response to developments south of the border. Important as they were individually in their own immediate circles, the impact of these fundamentalists on Canadian Protestantism was limited. America was more receptive, so that Canadian fundamentalists tended to look south for alternative power bases and for large followings. This southern orientation reflected their weakness.

---

40. George Marsden, 'Fundamentalism as an American Phenomenon', *CH* 46.2 (1977), 215–232.

41. David Elliott, 'Knowing No Borders: Canadian Contributions to American Fundamentalism', in George A. Rawlyk and Mark A. Noll (eds.), *Amazing Grace: Evangelicalism in Australia, Britain, Canada and the United States* (Grand Rapids: Baker Books, 1993), 349–374.

Canadian Christians generally, less troubled about the future, did not share their concerns. Although fundamentalism was a presence in Canadian evangelicalism, it was not a significant cultural force.

The Canadian rather than the American experience was more representative of the place of fundamentalism in the evangelical world at large. In Britain and 'Greater Britain', driven by their concern for the menace of modernism, fundamentalist spokesmen rapidly emerged after the War and created institutions for the propagation of their standpoint. Bible demonstrations and protest meetings were held. Organizations and conventions for biblical defence were established. Periodicals carried the fundamentalist critique of modernism and its implications. Aggression was shown both towards opponents and more charitably minded evangelicals. But non-American fundamentalists were generally more moderate and less self-assured. While their impact was by no means negligible, none of these organizations became large, and they produced no mass movement. Away from North America organized fundamentalism remained weak.

The importance of local political and cultural frameworks for the impact of fundamentalism is confirmed by contemporaneous developments in Northern Ireland.[42] Partition in 1921–2 set Ulster apart as a Protestant state with a large Roman Catholic minority committed to joining this part of the island to the Catholic majority in the new Irish Republic. In a situation where Protestant identity was seen by many as a condition of survival, the clear-sighted world view of fundamentalism was attractive. From the circumstances of the 1920s and 1930s many Protestants, neither republican Irish nor fully British, saw in 'closed evangelicalism' their source of identity that reaffirmed their existence as a group, justified their social control and enabled them to cope with the stress of embattlement. In turn rigorous biblical orthodoxy was necessary to keep the Reformed church true to its standards, now seen as a pre-condition of the survival of the community. As in the United States, the issue of national destiny engendered the salience and influence of fundamentalism. It remained integral to the 'closed evangelicalism' at the centre of the conflict with the Roman Catholic minority for much of the remainder of the twentieth century.

The pervasiveness of fundamentalism indicates that it was to some extent inherent in evangelicalism. Certainly by 1919, as chapter 4 has shown, the fundamentalist impulse was well established throughout the evangelical world. Because

---

42. Patrick Mitchell, *Evangelicalism and National Identity in Ulster, 1921–1998* (Oxford: Oxford University Press, 2003).

of its biblicism, it was inevitable that naturalistic approaches that undermined the oracular status of the Bible would be opposed. But the circumstances of the post-war world induced a sense of crisis. The rising challenge of modernism was of course basic. After years of fighting in the cause of righteousness, it made sense to continue the struggle, particularly in view of the perception that modernism was an expression of the German frame of mind. New hostile forces on the contemporary scene, particularly the advent of an aggressively anti-religious regime in the Soviet Union, gave added impetus. Catholicism, in both its Roman and Anglican forms, also appeared to be making substantial progress. The resultant sense that apostolic Christianity was endangered and worth fighting for in the emerging world order imparted a new combative edge to a pre-existing outlook within evangelicalism. Fundamentalist demagogues emerged to provide leadership to and organization of these fears. Disruptive forces, from within Christianity and from the world without, acted on the fundamentalist impulse to produce a disposition to fight, and even suffer, for evangelical truth.

Yet fundamentalists presented a far from homogeneous bloc. Apart from larger international differences, there were national variations within Britain.[43] The British experience also brings out distinctive denominational features and permutations.[44] C. Allyn Russell's study of American fundamentalist leaders shows further that fundamentalism produced pronounced individualisms that limited the coherence of, and cooperation within, the movement.[45] To take three of his cases only, the Texas Baptist J. Frank Norris was a 'violent fundamentalist'; the Presbyterian J. Gresham Machen of Princeton, a 'scholarly fundamentalist'; and the Baptist pastor and evangelist J. C. Massee, a 'moderate fundamentalist'. This was an important reason for fundamentalism itself being prone to the separatist tendency in evangelicalism. Certainly there were deep conflicts among fundamentalists, such as the dispute in the late 1920s over J. M. MacInnis's *Peter the Fisherman Philosopher*, which seemed to doubt the atonement, and the dispensational–covenantal

---

43. Essays by Andrew Holmes, Kenneth Roxburgh and David Ceri Jones in David Bebbington and David Ceri Jones (eds.), *Evangelicalism and Fundamentalism in the United Kingdom During the Twentieth Century* (Oxford: Oxford University Press, 2013), 253–306.

44. Essays by Andrew Atherstone, Martin Wellings, David Bebbington and Tim Grass in ibid. 55–131.

45. C. Allyn Russell, *Voices of Fundamentalism: Seven Biographical Studies* (Philadelphia: Westminster Press, 1976).

rift in America ten years later.[46] Although fundamentalism occurred everywhere throughout the evangelical world, it was not experienced in the same way.

Immediate consequences

The coexistence within evangelicalism of a definite fundamentalist right wing and an equally distinct liberal left wing had three immediate consequences. The first was the addition of the word 'fundamentalism' to the vocabulary of the evangelical movement. As is well known, just after the War William Bell Riley and the Baptist Curtis Lee Laws appropriated the term from the pre-1914 discourse of basic Christian beliefs. It was rapidly taken up and soon became pejorative, as in Harry Fosdick's 1922 sermon 'Shall the Fundamentalists Win?'[47] Reactions to Fosdick made it a rallying point, a banner for true belief under which men and women were prepared to gather. The events of 1925–6 (especially the Scopes Trial) established the label's identification with back-wardness and obscurantism.[48] As such it was deprecated by other evangelicals, who increasingly did not wish to be known as fundamentalists. Generally it referred to an extreme position within evangelicalism. It was a term of derision for some, of honour for others. Some were happy to be called funda-mentalists; for others it became an incubus to cast off. Emotive and divisive, in its various connotations and the different responses it evoked, 'funda-mentalism' became one of the markers of the diversity and tensions of interwar evangelicalism.[49]

Second, the evangelical movement was subjected to a powerful polarizing force. With both wings of the movement vigorous, dismissive of the other (with varying degrees of charity) and proselytizing, evangelicals were under pressure to take sides. Sometimes they were pulled in different directions. The career of the English-Canadian W. H. Griffith Thomas illustrates how shifts in outlook

---

46. Daniel W. Draney, *When Streams Diverge: John Murdoch MacInnis and the Origins of Protestant Fundamentalism in Los Angeles* (Milton Keynes: Paternoster Press, 2008); R. Todd Mangum, *The Dispensational–Covenantal Rift: The Fissuring of American Evangelical Theology from 1936 to 1944* (Milton Keynes: Paternoster Press, 2007).
47. Reproduced in Barry Hankins (ed.), *Evangelicalism and Fundamentalism: A Documentary Reader* (New York: New York University Press, 2008), 52–58.
48. Barry Hankins, "The (Worst) Year of the Evangelical: 1926 and the Demise of American Fundamentalism', *FH* 43.1 (2011), 1–14.
49. E.g. Percy Austin, *Letters to a Fundamentalist* (London: SCM Press, 1930).

and position could occur.[50] As principal of Wycliffe Hall in Oxford and editor of *The Churchman* before the War, he showed some affinity with the rising liberal evangelical Group Movement. Following his move to the centrist Wycliffe College in Toronto in 1910, he was disappointed at not being allowed to teach theology and not being appointed Principal as he had been led to expect. Eventually he moved south of the border, where he became involved with the newly established dispensationalist Dallas Theological Seminary. The encounter with extreme, sectarian fundamentalism in Texas turned him back to less militant views just prior to his death. Temperament and personal setbacks played a part in these changes, but the tensions of the interwar years caused some evangelical identities to fluctuate.

A third consequence was the widening and complication of the evangelical centre. Evangelicals at large recognized the two extreme positions that had developed around them and resiled from both. Many conservatives preferred peace and cooperation to controversy and disputation. Nor would they necessarily dismiss biblical criticism out of hand or embrace premillennialism. These evangelicals wanted to retain 'the fundamentals' without becoming fundamentalists. Representative of this right-of-centre stance were the 'interdenominational evangelicals' identified by Michael Hamilton and the English Anglican Fellowship of Evangelical Churchmen, which produced the volume *Evangelicalism* to represent the views of those who were not attracted to modernism or 'central churchmanship' (a label appropriated by the liberal evangelicals).[51] Another shade of opinion, while open to the possibilities of intellectual adaptation, felt that accommodation was going too far and leaving out essentials. These evangelicals wanted to be liberal without becoming liberals. The Southern Baptist E. Y. Mullins, who argued that the Bible should be put to critical and scientific tests so that it could retain its influence in the modern world, was a distinguished

---

50. Katerberg, *Modernity*, ch. 5. Another documented example is the American Midwestern Baptist Chester Tulga (1896–1976). See Kenneth W. Rhodes (2001), 'Ambivalent Fundamentalist: The Life and Ministry of Rev. Chester E. Tulga', PhD thesis, University of Akron, 2001.

51. Michael Hamilton, 'The Interdenominational Evangelicalism of D. L. Moody and the Problem of Fundamentalism', in Darren Dochuk et al. (eds.), *American Evangelicalism: George Marsden and the State of American Religious History* (Notre Dame: University of Notre Dame Press, 2014), 230–280; J. Russell Howden (ed.), *Evangelicalism: By Members of the Fellowship of Evangelical Churchmen* (London: Thynne, n.d. [1925]); David W. Bebbington, *Evangelicalism in Modern Britain: A History from the 1730s to the 1980s* (London: Unwin Hyman, 1989), 222–223.

example of this left-of-centre position.[52] While scholarship on this period has dwelt on the left and right wings of the movement, probably the great majority of evangelicals were to be located at some point on this wide and varied centre.[53]

The increasing differentiation of evangelicalism evident in these three effects made the interwar years an era of unprecedented argument and controversy. In relation to science, the period was marked by fundamentalist hostility to evolution, but this was an extreme expression of a larger declension on the centre-right of the movement from the *fin de siècle* accommodation with Darwinian thought.[54] At the other end of the spectrum liberal evangelicals, led by men with highly creditable scientific credentials, such as Bishop Barnes of Birmingham and Charles Raven (from 1932 Regius Professor of Divinity at Cambridge University), took the opposite view and advocated the reconciliation of Christianity and science on the basis of a natural theology that saw progressive evolutionism as the means of God's activity in the world. Attitudes to science among centrist evangelicals were mixed. Reservation was sustained by the exhibition of the worst side of science and technology during the Great War. Through the 1920s and 1930s the materialism of modern life was also often sheeted home to science. Yet centrist thinkers such as E. Y. Mullins continued to work at the harmonization of Christianity and science on the condition of a proper delimiting of their respective spheres of understanding.[55] Attitudes towards science among interwar evangelicals were uneven but remained generally uneasy.

However, attitudes to science were overshadowed by the more basic issue of biblical authority. Its numerous aspects – the Bible's status as the Word of God, the manner and extent of its inspiration, how it should be read and interpreted, and the place and legitimacy of critical scholarship – were all at times matters of intense debate. In this environment the question of inerrancy was

---

52. William E. Ellis, *'A Man of Books and a Man of the People': E. Y. Mullins and the Crisis of Moderate Southern Baptist Leadership* (Macon, GA: Mercer University Press, 2003).

53. Douglas Jacobsen and William V. Trollinger, Jr. (eds.), *Re-forming the Center: American Protestantism, 1900 to the Present* (Grand Rapids: Eerdmans, 1998), is a welcome attempt to explore this middle ground.

54. Peter Bowler, *Reconciling Science and Religion: The Debate in Early-Twentieth-Century Britain* (Chicago: University of Chicago Press, 2001), esp. chs. 8–9; David N. Livingstone, *Darwin's Forgotten Defenders: The Encounter Between Evangelical Theology and Evolutionary Thought* (Grand Rapids: Eerdmans, 1987), ch. 5.

55. Mullins, *Christianity at the Cross Roads*, chs. 4–5.

particularly contested, with fundamentalists insisting on the absence of error as the *sine qua non* of its authority, while for this purpose centrists and the left preferred to highlight the Bible's uniqueness as divinely inspired. Following the First World War the broad evangelical consensus on the Bible, already under strain at the turn of the century, unravelled and produced the crisis of evangelical biblicism.[56]

The primary result of this division on the biblical question was a new level of acrimony and suspicion as a solvent of the more traditional eirenicism and cooperation of the movement. This was largely the effect of the fundamentalists who, while they saw themselves as champions of the truth, also saw themselves as victims.[57] In maintaining their position they were not averse to criticizing other evangelicals as apostates and dismissing charity in argument as 'Laodiceanism', an expression of their characteristic militancy. Aggression provoked defensiveness and mockery of those perceived as narrow-minded heresy hunters. One example will suffice. The English Baptist liberal evangelical T. R. Glover was controversially elected Vice President of the Baptist Union in 1923. Then, and in the succeeding years, Glover was the target of much abuse and criticism. He could give back as good as he got.[58] In the divided world of post-First World War evangelicalism much of the goodwill once characteristic of the movement was dissipated.

This new atmosphere went well beyond attitude and style as the interwar years became an era of open conflict and division. Fundamentalists and those they influenced were not prepared to acquiesce in disagreement. With scriptural injunctions to separate in mind, for them it was necessary to take action. The Bible Churchman's Missionary Society split from the CMS in 1922 in the name of biblical fidelity and set the scene for other post-war rifts.[59] Similarly the withdrawal of Presbyterian J. Gresham Machen and his allies from Princeton Seminary in 1929 to form Westminster Seminary (which itself suffered division in 1937), and then his efforts to set up a new Presbyterian denomination in the

56. Geoffrey R. Treloar, 'The Word Disputed: The Crisis of Evangelical Biblicism in the 1920s and 1930s', *L* 2.7 (2014), 105–122.

57. David W. Bebbington, 'Martyrs for the Truth: Fundamentalists in Britain', *SCH* 30 (1993), 417–451; 'Baptists and Fundamentalism in Interwar Britain', in Bebbington and Ceri Jones, *Evangelicalism and Fundamentalism*, 95–114.

58. H. G. Wood, *Terrot Reaveley Glover: A Biography* (Cambridge: Cambridge University Press, 1953), esp. 8.

59. David W. Bebbington, 'Missionary Controversy and the Polarising Tendency in Twentieth-Century British Protestantism', *Anvil* 13.2 (1996), 141–157.

mid-1930s, reflected the tensions within the mainline churches in America.[60] Splits at the local level were highlighted by what happened in 1921 at the Jarvis Street Baptist Church in Toronto (where the controversial T. T. Shields was the minister) when some 350 liberal-minded members left to form their own congregation. This was followed six years later by a larger schism when the Baptist Convention of Ontario and Quebec divided.[61] From 1941 Carl McIntire perpetuated this separatism by establishing the American Council of Churches to keep evangelicals out of the Federal Council of Churches and even the more inclusive National Association of Evangelicals. Around the evangelical world, and across the denominations, the separatist tendency in evangelicalism strengthened as differentiation of outlooks led to disintegration and outright schism through the interwar decades.

Fragmentation did not need to take the form of open conflict and schism. Less bellicose but equally determined fundamentalists simply withdrew from the mainstream of Protestant church life and developed alternative structures and institutions. This development was clearest in America, where fundamentalists tended to go to ground after the Scopes Trial and defeat in the counsels of the major denominations. Their retreat was no surrender. Away from the scrutiny of the traditional churches, fundamentalists built up their own cultural and institutional networks, which grew in strength through the 1930s while mainstream American Protestantism struggled with the large public issues of the day.[62] Elsewhere men such as Joseph Kemp in New Zealand and Oswald Smith in Toronto built up their own organizations, which operated as independent entities. This approach in fact minimized the conflict, but it also made the evangelical movement less integrated and cohesive than it had been before the War.

These developments brought the disruptiveness of diversification into the open. The effect was a significant change in the character of interwar evangelicalism. Before the War activism had been dominant in the cluster of forces and attitudes that constituted the evangelical movement. Between the wars the quest for an evangelicalism capable of commanding cultural authority brought the biblicist-crucicentric axis to greater prominence. As chapter 12 will note, one result was a challenge to the legacy of social activism left by the War.

---

60. D. G. Hart, *Defending the Faith: J. Gresham Machen and the Crisis of Conservative Protestantism in Modern America* (Grand Rapids: Baker Books, 1995).

61. Paul Wilson, 'Central Canadian Baptists and the Role of Cultural Factors in the Fundamentalist–Modernist Schism of 1927', *BHH* (winter–spring 2001), 61–81.

62. Joel A. Carpenter, *Revive Us Again: The Reawakening of American Fundamentalism* (New York: Oxford University Press, 1997).

Another was that the movement became more inward looking and interested in doctrinal conformity. A by product of this reorientation was a new propensity for stating doctrinal standards and setting tests for adherence. The newly formed Advent Testimony Movement and the Baptist Bible Union were among the organizations to provide a statement of faith. In 1928 the nascent Inter-Varsity Fellowship published a doctrinal statement and asked for subscription from members. This was far from unprecedented in Christian, or even evangelical, history but its rising incidence signalled the arrival of a new concern to establish and maintain doctrinal boundaries that entrenched the divisions within contemporary evangelicalism.

While a development of the highest importance, the breakdown of coherence and its consequences should not be overstated. For there was certainly resistance to it. More eirenic evangelicals, mainly in the centre, appalled by the conflict, emphasized the grounds for unity and cooperation. The English Baptist Graham Scroggie, for example, an increasingly influential teacher in the Keswick movement, whose public persona was not without a polemical side, took the view that 'anyone who fairly interprets and wholeheartedly accepts the Apostles' Creed is loyal to the evangelical faith'. On the central question of the day he affirmed that it was 'enough that evangelicals agree on the fact of the unique and inclusive inspiration of the Scriptures, leaving theories to the enlightened judgement of the individual'. As subsequent chapters will show, there were also countercurrents. Committed to 'comprehensiveness within the truth', the Evangelical Alliance worked against rising disunity.[63] The Oxford Group Movement emerged as a force in the late 1920s with a stress on the essence of faith and non-denominational cooperation. The evangelical churches continued to meet for international congresses through the interwar years. At these meetings the biblical question barely rated a mention. Some evangelicals were participants in the ecumenical movement, while the international missionary movement (although much less homogeneously evangelical in the 1930s than previously) remained a rallying point. And evangelicals were almost as one in resisting the progress of Catholicism in its Roman and Anglican forms. If the ecumenist tendency in evangelicalism had been unable to contain separatism, it remained a significant force within the movement.

Similarly evangelicals from across the spectrum of opinion got on with the task of rebutting the modernist reformulation of Christian belief. J. Gresham

---

63. Ian Randall and David Hilborn, *One Body in Christ: The History and Significance of the Evangelical Alliance* (Carlisle: Evangelical Alliance and Paternoster Press, 2001), ch. 8, esp. 198–200.

Machen furnished a defence of the virgin birth, while at Princeton in the wake of his departure Geerhardus Vos developed an understanding of 'biblical theology' that incorporated themes of development with a strong affirmation of supernatural Christianity. On the left, older writers such as Alfred Garvie and J. Scott Lidgett himself began the work of reconstructing evangelical theology envisaged in 1919, and younger men such as the Baillie brothers carried it forward.[64] Almost as a last testament, the veteran H. R. Mackintosh wrote a history of modern theology justifying the task by bringing out its tendency to minimize the supernatural and the awfulness of sin and the 'contrast' rather than the 'likeness to the faith of Prophets and Apostles'.[65] Especially noteworthy in this development was the swing to the right in English Congregationalism where the so-called 'new Genevans' recalled their denomination to orthodoxy against the modernist blandishments of the likes of C. J. Cadoux and the so-called 'Blackheathens'.[66] By 1940 the movement had at its disposal a steady flow of literature seeking to overcome the divisions of the day by restating the gospel of the evangelical tradition in modern language.

Further relief from the problem of modernism resulted from selective appreciation of the thought of Karl Barth and the 'theology of crisis' in the evangelical community from around 1930.[67] On both sides of the Atlantic evangelicals in the Reformed tradition, who were accustomed to dogmatics and prophetic preaching, together with those who had been influenced by P. T. Forsyth, welcomed the restored emphasis on the transcendence of God and the utter reliance of humanity on divine provision for revelation and salvation. The scope of Barth's enterprise and the radical character of his thought left much to puzzle and irritate – especially at the fundamentalist right and liberal left ends of the movement – but a theology that presented God as an objective reality and stressed freedom from prevailing culture seemed to some, mainly centrist, evangelicals to give them something to say in the face of advancing secularism. Similarly there was some appreciation within evangelicalism for

---

64. Alfred E. Garvie, *The Christian Faith: A Sketch of a Constructive Theology* (London: Duckworth, 1936); J. Scott Lidgett, *God, Christ and the Church* (London: Hodder & Stoughton, 1927).

65. In the Croall Lectures of 1933, published as H. R. Mackintosh, *Types of Modern Theology* (London: Fontana, 1964 [1937]).

66. E.g. Nathaniel Micklem, *What Is the Faith?* (London: Hodder & Stoughton, 1936).

67. D. Densil Morgan, *Barth Reception in Britain* (London: T. & T. Clark, 2012); Philip R. Thorne, *Evangelicalism and Karl Barth: His Reception and Influence in North American Evangelical Theology* (Allison Park: Pickwick Publications, 1995).

the Christian Realism developed in America around Reinhold Niebuhr.[68] Like Barthianism, Christian Realism seemed to confirm the soundness of basic evangelical teaching about the sovereignty of God, the function of the Bible and humanity's need of forgiveness. These developments coincided with the gathering storm clouds of war, which also seemed to validate the basic evangelical theological categories of evil and sin and humanity's need of redemption. At the end of the interwar era evangelicals were able confidently to reaffirm their theology as a defensible basis of reverent belief in God and faithful life in the modern world.[69]

Embarrassment of evangelicalism

A final effect was the embarrassment of evangelicalism. This was a reaction against the intellectual barrenness ascribed primarily to fundamentalism but also by extension to the evangelical movement as a whole. Already a spur to liberal evangelicalism, by 1930 it was being felt keenly in the centre, and there was even some sheepishness among evangelicals on the right not bound by dispensationalist and typological systems of biblical interpretation.[70] In the vanguard of this response to lack of intellectual credibility was the English Brethren surgeon Arthur Rendle Short, who from about 1930 declared that the intellectual tide was turning in favour of biblical Christianity.[71] Developments in science, criticism and especially archaeology supported the intellectual honesty of faith in the Bible. By the middle of the decade he was supported by others from a Brethren background – Douglas Johnson of the Inter-Varsity Fellowship (IVF), W. J. Martin of the University of Liverpool, and the businessman John Laing – in looking for ways to promote theological advance at an academic

68. Warren, *Theologians of a New World Order*; Mark T. Edwards, *The Right of the Protestant Left: God's Totalitarianism* (New York: Palgrave Macmillan, 2012).

69. Exhibited by J. S. Whale in radio talks such as his *Facing the Facts* (London: Hodder & Stoughton, 1940). Cf. '"Spiritual Rearmament." The Oxford Conference of Evangelical Churchmen, 1939', *Ch* 4.2 new series (Apr.–June 1939), 61–108.

70. 'Are Evangelicals Unscholarly?', *C* (20 Nov. 1930), 3–4; 'The Sanctification of the Intellect', *C* (23 May 1935); P. W. Evans, '"God Hath Spoken": Dr Zwemer's Challenge to Evolution', *C* (24 Oct. 1935), 3–4.

71. Arthur Rendle Short, *The Bible and Modern Research* (London: Marshall, Morgan & Scott, n.d. [1930–1]). The date is assigned tentatively from the review in *The Christian* (17 Dec. 1931), 8.

level.[72] They were joined by the Welsh Calvinistic Methodist D. M. Lloyd-Jones whose move to London in 1938 strengthened the commitment to specialist scholarship. Across the decade more conservative British evangelicals joined with those on the left in evincing increasing openness to the benefits of scholarship and learning for biblical understanding, preaching, apologetics and the enunciation of sound doctrine.

The first institutional expression of this intention to remedy the reproach of evangelical anti-intellectualism was the commencement in Scotland in 1929 of the *Evangelical Quarterly* under the editorship of J. R. Mackay and Donald MacLean of the Free Church College in Edinburgh. Intended for 'the Exposition and Defence of the Reformed Faith regarded as the historic Christian Faith in its purest form',[73] its pages afforded a forum and point of identity for a large number of evangelical scholars from throughout the evangelical world who shared Rendle Short's confidence over a wide range of biblical and theological subjects. The IVF also moved to provide for the intellectual needs of students, publishing instructional and apologetical booklets from the first,[74] founding the Theological Students' Foundation in 1933, providing systematic biblical study through *Search the Scriptures* from 1934, and then by setting up the Biblical Research Committee in 1938. These two developments converged in 1942 when the *Evangelical Quarterly* was taken over by the IVF. In the meantime a similar group of people moved to set up an interdenominational theological college and a first-class biblical research centre.[75] The outcome was the foundation of the London Bible College in 1943 and Tyndale House in Cambridge in 1944. In providing for the strengthening of scholarship through both theological education and research, British centre-right evangelicals created instruments not only to counter allegations of obscurantism but also to shape evangelical thinking up to the highest academic standards across the denominations for the years to come.

---

72. Roger Shuff, *Searching for the True Church: Brethren and Evangelicals in Mid-Twentieth-Century England* (Carlisle: Paternoster Press, 2005), ch. 4.

73. 'Editorial', *EvQ* 1 (1929), 1.

74. E.g. Sir Ambrose Fleming, *The Christian Faith in Relation to Modern Thought*, Inter-Varsity Booklet 4 (London: The Inter-Varsity Fellowship of Evangelical Unions, 1929); *The Veracity of Holy Scripture*, Inter-Varsity Booklet 5 (London: The Inter-Varsity Fellowship of Evangelical Unions, 1930). Later came the *Current Notes and Abstracts on Science and Theology*, edited by R. E. D. Clark and Alan Stibbs.

75. Ian Randall, *Educating Evangelicalism: The Origins, Development and Impact of London Bible College* (Carlisle: Paternoster Press, 2000); T. A. Noble, *Tyndale House and Fellowship: The First Sixty Years* (Leicester: Inter-Varsity Press, 2006).

By the end of the 1930s a parallel development had begun in the United States where a cohort of young scholars nurtured in fundamentalism was forming around the hope of reviving the intellectual heritage of evangelicalism.[76] At Wheaton College the philosopher Gordon H. Clark inspired a group of young men, which included Edward J. Carnell and Carl Henry, to pursue careers of committed Christian scholarship founded on the most creditable academic credentials.[77] Around the same time a group of young 'new evangelicals', the most significant of whom was Harold Ockenga, Pastor of the Park Street Church in Boston, obtained the qualifications from major secular universities necessary for credibility in the wider cultural community. Acknowledging their roots in fundamentalism, these men rejected its disengagement from the wider culture and set out to lead 'a new reformation' that would restore the intellectual standing of evangelical Christianity.

Construction of an institutional framework for the realization of an evangelical scholarly renaissance was also commenced.[78] The promotion of scholarship readily found a place on the agenda of the National Association of Evangelicals when it was established in 1942. The opening of Fuller Seminary in 1947 provided a base from which, in the words of its foundation President, Harold Ockenga, evangelical scholars could lead 'the revival of Christian thought and life' needed to 'rebuild the foundations of society'.[79] It was an aspiration made possible by the determination in the later 1930s to gather the people and the resources to counter the modernist takeover of contemporary Protestantism and the fundamentalist denigration of scholarship.

The call to the classicist F. F. Bruce in 1938 to assist the IVF Biblical Research Committee demonstrated at once the difficulty to be overcome in realizing these aspirations and the importance of the strategy of American evangelicals to obtain culturally relevant qualifications. With no suitably qualified New Testament scholar on the ground in Britain, he was the best man available. However, in spite of his lack of training, Bruce produced the scholarly biblical

---

76. George M. Marsden, *Reforming Fundamentalism: Fuller Seminary and the New Evangelicalism* (Grand Rapids: Eerdmans, 1987), 45–46.

77. Both would become leaders at Fuller Theological Seminary after its founding in 1947, for which, see the next paragraph.

78. This and the following paragraphs are based on Carpenter, *Revive Us Again*, esp. chs. 8–12; Garth M. Rosell, *The Surprising Work of God: Harold John Ockenga, Billy Graham, and the Rebirth of Evangelicalism* (Grand Rapids: Baker Academic, 2008), esp. chs. 3, 7–8.

79. Quoted by Carpenter, *Revive Us Again*, 195.

work for which his sponsors hoped.[80] Having delivered the first annual Tyndale
New Testament Lecture in 1942, in the next year he published *Are the New
Testament Documents Reliable?* as the first of a succession of works demonstrating
for the coming generation the benefits of a wider range of methods for the
study of the Bible. The *New Bible Handbook* published in 1947 with contributions
from twenty-three others apart from the editors was a sign of a slowly rising
tide of evangelical biblical scholarship.[81] On a wider front, the early books of
Carl Henry and Ed Carnell challenged sectarian anti-intellectualism within evangelicalism and announced a willingness to engage with the wider church and the
world.[82] The small flow of scholarly literature in the later 1940s was the early
fruits of the undertaking in the previous decade to engage with modern culture
in a bid to regain the cultural authority of evangelicalism.

While moves to reverse the embarrassment of evangelicalism were welcome
to many, they also extended the rancour of the interwar years and reflected the
tensions of an age of transition in which evangelicals grappled with their place
in the modern world. This became clear in relation to F. F. Bruce. He regarded
his burgeoning career as a biblical scholar as of a piece with his public stance
as an evangelical Christian. But, in spite of his open identification with the
Brethren, Bruce was suspected of really being a conservative liberal masquer-
ading as an evangelical.[83] The 'new evangelicals' in America had similarly to cope
with criticism of their agenda and aspersions on their character from those
further to the right.[84] The critics were at least correct in their perception that
the advocates of scholarship and learning had trafficked with liberalism. In
finding a way to participate in the scholarly world, the evangelical centre-right
had embraced something of the agenda of the liberal evangelicals. By the
mid-1940s the evangelical movement suffered the tensions of being pushed to
the right by anxiety over biblical orthodoxy, while also being pulled to the left

---

80. F. F. Bruce, *In Retrospect: Remembrance of Things Past* (London: Pickering & Inglis,
    1980), chs. 16–18; Tim Grass, *F. F. Bruce: A Life* (Milton Keynes: Paternoster Press,
    2011), ch. 4.
81. G. T. Manley (ed.), *The New Bible Handbook* (London: Inter-Varsity Christian
    Fellowship, 1947).
82. E.g. Carl Henry, *Remaking the Modern Mind* (Grand Rapids: Eerdmans, 1946);
    E. J. Carnell, *An Introduction to Christian Apologetics: A Philosophic Defense of the
    Trinitarian–Theistic Faith* (Grand Rapids: Eerdmans, 1948).
83. Peter Oakes, 'F. F. Bruce and the Development of Evangelical Biblical Scholarship',
    BJRULM 86.3 (2004), 99–124.
84. Rosell, *Surprising Work of God*, 199–200.

by the increasing acceptability of modern biblical scholarship, something for which liberal evangelicals had long contended.

Recognition of the need for the intellectual recovery by the centre-right also provided the setting for the emergence of the Irish-Australian Thomas Chatterton Hammond in international evangelicalism.[85] Converted as a teenager through the ministry of the local YMCA, he began to practise his evangelical faith amid the sectarian violence of late nineteenth-century Cork. After working as an itinerant evangelist for the Irish Church Missions for several years, he prepared for ordination in the Church of Ireland at Trinity College, Dublin, from which he graduated in 1903 with the gold medal in Philosophy. For some fifteen years he maintained a vigorous Protestant witness in the parish of St Kevin's, Dublin, first as curate and then from 1910 as the rector. In this setting he also developed a theological position that, in its opposition to the 'new theology' and insistence on the availability of objective truth in the biblical revelation, is best described as 'empirical realism'.[86]

After the War, Hammond was appointed Superintendent of the Irish Church Missions, a work prosecuted under the difficult conditions produced by the Irish war of independence and civil war, and then the Roman Catholic hegemony of the Irish Free State. On visits to England to raise support for the Missions, Hammond came into contact with the British evangelical mainstream through attendance at the Keswick Convention and the Islington Clerical Conference. In these circles he made a mark as a doughty Protestant opposed to Roman Catholicism and revision of the Anglican Book of Common Prayer, and as a theologian of force and energy. Aligning himself with the recently formed Fellowship of Evangelical Churchmen, in 1925 he exhibited the apologetic value of his empirical realism in a defence of biblical authority in their programmatic volume *Evangelicalism*.[87] Recognizing his clearly articulated orthodoxy, Hammond's English connections soon drew him into the work of the nascent IVF, for which he drafted its doctrinal statement.

85. Warren Nelson, *T. C. Hammond: His Life and Legacy in Ireland and Australia* (Edinburgh: Banner of Truth Trust, 1994).

86. For Hammond's theology, see John McIntosh, 'Anglican Evangelicalism in Sydney 1897–1953: The Thought and Influence of Three Moore College Principals – Nathaniel Jones, D. J. Davies and T. C. Hammond', PhD thesis, University of New South Wales, 2014.

87. T. C. Hammond, 'The Fiat of Authority', in J. Russell Howden (ed.), *Evangelicalism: By Members of the Fellowship of Evangelical Churchmen* (London: Thynne, n.d. [1925]), 156–206.

Hammond's soundness on the biblical question and vigorous Protestantism appealed to the Trustees of Moore College in Sydney. When the Principalship became vacant in 1935, they pressed the Archbishop, Howard Mowll, veteran of the CICCU controversy at Cambridge in 1910–12 mentioned in chapter 4, to appoint Hammond. Arriving in Sydney early in 1936, his fortunes took a dramatic turn for the better. From being part of a despised minority and not even well accepted in his own denomination, Hammond became the right-hand man of the Archbishop at the head of the largest denomination in the community. Together they succeeded where others in the evangelical world had failed by driving the liberals out of the diocese, and laid the foundations for the conservative evangelical culture that came to dominate Sydney Anglicanism.[88]

As a writer and theologian Hammond came into his own in Australia. Over the next seven years he published three substantial works of theology for the IVF, which consolidated the centrist evangelical position. As he had prepared to leave for his new post, Hammond had completed *In Understanding Be Men*. A handbook of Christian doctrine for non-theological students, it purported to be an introductory statement of what evangelicals believed. It was followed two years later by *Perfect Freedom*. Directed to the same audience, it asserted the need for and demonstrated the possibility of a Christian ethics. The sequence was capped in 1943 by *Reasoning Faith*, a work of apologetics for the theological as well as the general student in response to the main currents in Western culture. While the impact of these works might have been muffled by the Second World War, their effect was twofold. For the present, Hammond's work provided a measure of reassurance that evangelicalism could mount an effective intellectual response to its ideological rivals. Directed in the first instance to students with the contemporary crisis of Western civilization in mind, Hammond's mature writing was also an exhortation to the rising generation to use their minds to exhibit the cultural salience of evangelical Christianity as a counter to the course being taken by the modern West.[89]

---

88. Geoffrey R. Treloar, 'T. C. Hammond the Controversialist', *AHSDSJ* 51.1 (June 2006), 20–35.

89. Thomas C. Hammond, *'In Understanding Be Men': A Synopsis of Christian Doctrine for Non-Theological Students* (London: Inter-Varsity Fellowship, 1936); *Perfect Freedom: An Introduction to Christian Ethics* (London: Inter-Varsity Fellowship, 1938); *Reasoning Faith: An Introduction to Christian Apologetics* (London: Inter-Varsity Fellowship, 1943); *Fading Light: The Tragedy of Spiritual Decline in Germany* (London: Marshall, Morgan & Scott, n.d. [1940]).

Conclusion

At the beginning of the post-war era evangelicals ventured to think their theology could furnish the spiritual and ethical basis of the new world order. In making this claim for social influence, they felt the rivalry of modernism that similarly sought to furnish the normative Christianity for the reconstructed world. Three main responses emerged among evangelicals as definite alternatives were enunciated on the left and right wings of the movement, leaving a broad centre to work out its position somewhere between them. Liberal evangelicals, a pervasive presence, endeavoured to assimilate modern culture while remaining attached to the evangelical tradition. Fundamentalists, also a pervasive presence but a force only in America and Northern Ireland, opposed those aspects of modern culture that seemed to require modification of received evangelical teaching. The modernizing evangelicals of the centre came under pressure to choose between these alternatives as they negotiated with modern culture to maintain the credibility of evangelicalism in contemporary society. Increasingly in the 1930s they moved away from fundamentalism and sought the intellectual respectability necessary for influence in the modern world. This trend over-lapped with theological restatement on the centre-left of the movement intended to provide a modern expression of evangelical Christianity in the language of the day. Validated by the advent of Neo-orthodoxy and Christian Realism in theology at large and by a deteriorating world situation, these develop-ments initiated something of an intellectual recovery in evangelicalism that gathered momentum in the 1940s, the distractions of the Second World War notwithstanding.

Although it had this positive side, the coexistence of these positions had several effects that limited the effectiveness of evangelicalism in the post-war world. Importantly the emergence of different standpoints furthered the diversification of the movement and brought the 'divisiveness of diversity' to a head in actual conflict and division. While conflict did not characterize the entire movement, different ways of resisting modernism and providing a normative Christianity for the contemporary world created the wariness between evangelicals themselves reflected in the increasing use of doctrinal statements on the centre-right of the movement. Accentuated doctrinalism also altered the balance between the components of the evangelical synthesis as the biblicist-crucicentric axis became more forceful. This development not only made the evangelical movement more inward looking than it had been previously, but, by further weakening the capacity of its ecumenism to contain the separatist tendency in evangelicalism, it was also counterproductive in the quest for cultural authority. Evangelical theology was already too diverse in 1919 for the hopes evangelicals entertained for their belief system to be realistic. But further differentiation and contestation meant that the movement fell well short of that clear and coherent connection with contemporary life felt to be necessary for evangelical Christianity to guide the post-war world with its ideals and principles. The weakness of the theological component vitiated the evangelical reconstruction project from the outset.

10. REMEMBERING THE REFORMATION

No less important than theology for the place of evangelicalism in the new world order was the life of faith. With the world seeking to rebuild, and confident that evangelicalism had proved itself during the War, evangelicals recognized that their approach to Christianity could present Christ as the supreme source of healing and of life at a deeply troubled time in history, supply the 'spiritual susceptibility' of the day with an effective religion, provide moral and spiritual vision as an alternative to 'the political and moral delusions of the time', and bring the spiritual principle of the Church to bear on human relationships, society and the wider world.[1] This outlook carried forward into the post-war years the assumption underneath the evangelical expectation of social influence – that the formation of Christian character would generate public benefit. Without underestimating the difficulty of their position, evangelicals ventured on the post-war era in the belief that they could furnish the way of life that would restore Christian civilization and prevent any repetition of war.

As with theology, the vision of the function of the life of faith in the post-war world also brought evangelicalism to the crossroads. Again, according to the

---

1. 'Facing the New Year', 'Christ and the Present Hour', 'I Will Overturn', '—To Your Faith, Patience', C (2 Jan. 1919), 7–8; (30 Jan. 1919), 7–8; (6 Feb. 1919), 9–10; (22 May 1919), 9–10.

conditions specified by T. B. Kilpatrick of Toronto, presenting the life of faith for the new world order was the key to effectiveness. 'The Church of the twentieth century', he maintained, 'will have power over the lives of men in proportion as it counsels and exhibits a positive reference of all, even the most practical, things to God, a direct dealing of every soul with God, a continual practice of His presence and a daily communion with Him.'[2] With this went the need for evangelicals to legitimate the life of faith's reality and efficacy by their own practice. As one of them observed, the spiritual principle leading to regenerate and sacrificial lives must be realized first in themselves and their churches to justify the claim of evangelical Christianity to be the basis of the world's way of life.[3] If their theology was the presumed basis of the evangelical vision of the new world order, the life of faith would be the condition of its success.

The legacy of the War

The first and inescapable demand upon the life of faith in the post-war world was adjustment to the return of peace. A many-sided task, it necessarily began with reintegration of the soldiers and chaplains into community and church life with acknowledgement of the difficulty and counsel about how to settle back into the normal mundane way of life.[4] Women relinquishing war work were advised to find outlets for the skills they had acquired unexpectedly. Adjustment called too for the promotion of the spiritual health and well-being of their communities. A fundamental condition was forgiveness of the enemy, the difficulty of doing so notwithstanding. Its most pressing side was reckoning with the enormous cost in human life and the abiding effects of loss on the living. A wave of teaching about death and immortality washed over the evangelical landscape in the immediate post-war years as laymen and clergy struggled to console the grieving.[5] The call for patience and confidence in the faithfulness

---

2. T. B. Kilpatrick, 'The Church of the Twentieth Century', *ConsQ* 7.27 (Sept. 1919), 413.

3. Thomas Yates, 'The Recovery of the Spiritual Principle of the Church as a Condition of Spiritual Revival', *ICC 1920*, 70–73.

4. E.g. 'Letters of Quartus', in *The Christian* in the first half of 1919; 'Talks with the Demobilized' in 1919 and 1920.

5. E.g. J. Edgar Park, 'The Triumph of Love Over Death', *RCW* 38.1 (Apr. 1919), 223–225; Harris Kirk, 'The Resurrection Body', ibid. 225–233.

of God amid their perplexities showed the resources of the evangelical tradition
were stretched in the aftermath of the War.[6]

These spiritual and emotional needs were one reason for evangelicals readily
embracing the vogue for commemoration as it expanded through the post-war
years. After the wartime experience of prayers for the dead, this was a matter
on which evangelicals tended to be wary. Generally they taught that the best
commemoration was a life worthy of the sacrifice of the dead. However,
participation in formal ceremonies and the construction of suitable monuments
were accepted as legitimate activities. Evangelicals immediately recognized the
importance of Armistice Day (11 November) as a day of sacred remembrance
and the Tomb of the Unknown Soldier in London received their approbation.[7]
Even as attitudes towards the War became more ambivalent around 1930, they
preserved its image as an occasion for heroic sacrifice in the service of high
ideals. No evangelical gave more to the remembrance of this unique episode
than the Australian Methodist John Treloar, who laboured incessantly for twenty
years to secure the opening in 1940 of the Australian War Memorial in Canberra,
of which he became the foundation director.[8] For Treloar and other evangelicals,
remembrance honoured the sacrifice of the war dead and fostered spiritually
and morally responsible living.

It was no less important to protect their communities from false commemoration. Accordingly evangelicals condemned the upsurge of spiritualism in the
early post-war years. With grief such a widespread experience and mourning a
large-scale organized activity, the consolation, reassurance and guidance for the
living in knowing what happens in and after death greatly increased the appeal
of an already well-established phenomenon.[9] Its influence was nurtured by
celebrity figures – such as Arthur Conan Doyle and Sir Oliver Lodge – who
travelled widely to speak on its behalf. Some Christians, mindful of their own
belief in the spirit world and moved by the extent of grief around them, showed
a modicum of sympathy. But evangelicals at large were opposed to spiritualism
and attacked it as reprehensible necromancy perpetrated by fraudulent
mediums.[10] On the grounds that it had no message of redemption and only a

6. E.g. '— To Your Faith, Patience', *C* (22 May 1919), 9–10.
7. 'The "Unknown Warrior"', *C* (4 Nov. 1920), 3.
8. Michael McKernan, *Here Is Their Spirit: A History of the Australian War Memorial 1917–1990* (St Lucia: University of Queensland Press, 1991).
9. Jennifer Hazelgrove, 'Spiritualism After the Great War', *TCBH* 10.4 (1999), 404–430.
10. E.g. Jane T. Stoddart, *The Case Against Spiritualism* (London: Hodder & Stoughton, 1919).

meagre view of the continuity of life after death, they also opposed the tendency of spiritualism to function as an alternative religion to Christianity. Evangelicals insisted that, as with prayers for the dead, spiritualism held out false grounds for hope and was an unworthy rival of Christianity.

Apart from mass bereavement, the continuation of physical and mental suffering in the aftermath of the War was a further challenge for contemporary evangelicals. Many became interested in divine healing as faith healers such as the Australian-born Anglican James Hickson attracted large crowds to public meetings all around the English-speaking world.[11] Prominent evangelicals on both the left and the right of the movement maintained cures either did not last or were not really cures but the result of auto-suggestion or hypnotism. They worried too that healing overshadowed preaching for repentance and shattered faith by disappointing false hopes. Despite this critique, evangelicals were drawn to the faith healers by the same factors that attracted the wider community. They were similarly confronted by the needs of the suffering bodies and minds of wounded and injured returned servicemen. The influenza pandemic of 1918 and its ongoing effects exposed the limitations of modern knowledge and technology by seeming to place whole populations beyond medical help. But the manifestation of divine power in physical cures also served the post-war evangelical agenda by showing that God is active in the world and that the gospel is practical.

The need for healing of the mind in the post-war setting also favoured incorporation of the 'new psychology' into the life of faith.[12] Cures for shell shock and other war-related nervous conditions by psychotherapy suggested the advent of a new remedy for mental disorders suffered by civilians. At the same time evangelicals were cautious. In its explanations of human behaviour the reductive tendency of psychology was suspected of dismissing sin and minimizing moral responsibility, and its various remedies were suspected of offering cheap grace.[13] Undeterred by the opposition, progressive evangelical

---

11. A. Fay Farley, 'A Spiritual Healing Mission Remembered: James Moore Hickson's Christian Healing Mission at Palmerston North, New Zealand, 1923', *JRH* 34.1 (2010), 1–19; James Opp, *The Lord for the Body: Religion, Medicine, and Protestant Faith Healing in Canada, 1880–1930* (Montreal-Kingston: McGill-Queen's University Press, 2005), chs. 6–7.

12. Stephanie Muravchik, *American Protestantism in the Age of Psychology* (Cambridge: Cambridge: University Press, 2011), ch. 1.

13. E.g. J. C. M. Conn, *The Menace of the New Psychology* (London: Inter-Varsity Fellowship, 1939).

ministers explored ways of introducing psychological perspectives and techniques – including to some extent psychoanalysis – to their pastoral practice.[14]
As a result, systematic counselling of individuals started to become a significant
function of the ministry. Psychology also provided a new perspective on writing
and preaching that could now be conceived as a kind of group counselling.
Inevitably in the early stages of a new approach, enthusiasts were hampered by
a lack of training and professional experience. None acquired the requisite
training and specialized knowledge to better effect than the English Methodist
Leslie Weatherhead.[15] In private counselling, preaching and teaching, and in a
succession of books beginning with *Psychology in Service of the Soul* (1929), he
showed the way in coupling evangelical theology with psychology. To the one
he brought his Christian convictions, while to the other he introduced the
explanations of and remedies for human anxieties and neuroses. Although a
target for a good deal of criticism, for Weatherhead and his followers there was
no doubt that psychology provided a new means of making Christianity real
and effective for the people of their generation.

Spirituality for the post-war world[16]

Apart from the adjustments required to serve the peculiar needs of the post-war
world, evangelicals in 1919 expected that the life of faith would continue along
much the same lines as before the War. Aided by new publishing and marketing
strategies, their writers poured out ever-increasing volumes of material to feed
the spiritual demand of the day.[17] The perennial aspiration of nurturing lives
of commitment to Christ and faithful service was shared across the movement.
However, the need for an efficacious spirituality for the new world order drove
the development of different approaches to show what crystallizing theological
positions meant in experience and practice.

---

14. Dean R. Rapp, 'The Reception of Freudianism by British Methodists During
    the "Psychoanalytic Craze" of the 1920s', *FH* 25.2 (1993), 23–46.
15. John Travell, *Doctor of Souls: A Biography of Leslie Dixon Weatherhead* (Cambridge:
    Lutterworth Press, 1999).
16. The remainder of the chapter draws heavily on Ian M. Randall, *Evangelical Experiences: A
    Study in the Spirituality of English Evangelicalism 1918–1939* (Carlisle: Paternoster Press, 1999).
17. Matthew S. Hedstrom, *The Rise of Liberal Religion: Book Culture and American
    Spirituality in the Twentieth Century* (New York: Oxford University Press, 2013),
    the purview of which is broader than the title suggests.

Modern evangelicals urged the deepened spiritual life available in the appli-cation of freedom, their leading principle. Harry Fosdick, increasingly suspect to many evangelicals but now probably the leading devotional writer of the era, showed the way. His conception of 'adventurous religion' involved a venture-some life grounded in a personal relationship with Christ and experimental pursuit of the way of life he taught as an alternative to finished systems of belief and action.[18] Liberal evangelicals such as Fosdick and others maintained that only such an open-ended and unstructured religion would furnish an effective Christianity for a society intent on building a new and better world informed by the ideals arising from the War years.[19] Sounding a note that was to be heard frequently during the interwar years, they expected that it would lead to a new Reformation – understood as the recovery of 'liberty and movement in religion . . . throwing out its frozen forms, restoring spontaneity and creativeness again and so replacing static rigidity, which is death, by free-dom and progress, which is life'.[20]

Against this approach anti-modern evangelicals advocated a spirituality based on fidelity to received truth. These evangelicals asserted the priority of know-ledge and theology whose function included both informing and regulating experience. J. Gresham Machen elaborated this alternative as part of his rebuttal of modernism.[21] He argued for dependence on the revelation of the biblical writings, and for adherence to theological propositions and confessional standards. A new life free from the power of sin follows from compliance with facts that are permanently and objectively true. Change and progress in this scheme would be due to better understanding of the Bible and closer approxi-mation to its teachings, and to more sensitive consciences and more obedient wills. Gresham Machen spoke for other, mainly centre-right, evangelicals ranging from fundamentalists, Strict Baptists and Brethren to conservative members of major evangelical churches who in varying degrees worked with a similar conception of truth. This perspective also looked for a new Reformation. It would come from facing up to the historical and doctrinal facts of the gospel of Christ, as in the sixteenth century.

---

18. H. E. Fosdick, *Adventurous Religion and Other Essays* (London: SCM Press, 1926).
19. E.g. T. Guy Rogers (ed.), *The Inner Life: Essays in Liberal Evangelicalism Second Series by Members of the Church of England* (London: Hodder & Stoughton, 1925); E. Stanley Jones, *Victorious Living* (London: Hodder & Stoughton, 1936).
20. Fosdick, *Adventurous Religion*, 304.
21. E.g. J. Gresham Machen, *What Is Faith?* (London: Hodder & Stoughton, 1925).

The emergence of alternative approaches to the life of faith left many evangelicals caught between them. Dismayed by contemporary controversy, they were wary of excessive intellectualism but no less desirous of vital spiritual experience. Even at Keswick, the major influence on interwar evangelical spirituality as a centre-right force for orthodoxy and stability, the teaching was refashioned – largely at the hands of Graham Scroggie – by bringing the more subjective aspects of its piety under the control of biblical teaching without descending into fundamentalist excess.[22] Rather than charting a middle course, other evangelicals simply modelled a moderate, eirenic evangelicalism. From Hobart and Melbourne the Baptist Frank Boreham sent out into the world each year volumes of sermons and essays reflecting on spiritual experience, his character of John Broadbanks functioning as the archetype of this kind of centrist evangelical.[23] A similar approach was propagated by the Biblical Seminary in New York by its direct teaching and its journal *The Biblical Review.*[24] Over the interwar years centrists developed less theologically prescriptive and subjective approaches, content to allow encounter with the biblical text to produce Christian lives that they hoped would be attractive to the world and acceptable to other evangelicals.

Apart from developing theological positions, behind this deepening diversification in approaches to the life of faith was a perennial tension in evangelicalism now accentuated by the need of a manifestly efficacious spirituality. 'Adventurous religion' represented a fresh upsurge of the experiential component of the evangelical tradition. It was the force behind the pursuit of a renewed spiritual life relevant to the post-war world called the 'quest' by the Fellowship of the Kingdom in interwar Methodism. Among Methodists more generally it engendered a defence of the primacy of experience in their heritage. Amid the economic and social difficulties of the Depression they offered this heritage as the means of a better order of things in the world.[25] However, the striking representative of the trend to experientialism was Frank Buchman's Oxford

---

22. Randall, *Evangelical Experiences*, ch. 2.
23. Frank W. Boreham, *My Pilgrimage: An Autobiography* (London: Epworth Press, 1940); T. Howard Crago, *The Story of F. W. Boreham* (London: Marshall, Morgan & Scott, 1961).
24. Steven M. Nolt, '"Avoid Provoking the Spirit of Controversy": The Irenic Legacy of the Biblical Seminary in New York', in Douglas Jacobsen and William V. Trollinger (eds.), *Re-forming the Center: American Protestantism, 1900 to the Present* (Grand Rapids: Eerdmans, 1998), 318–340.
25. Addresses on 'Personal Religion', *EMC 1931*, 81–106, 311–341.

Group Movement that emerged between the wars. Primarily conversionist in intent, it is treated in detail in chapter 11, but it also brought to the movement a distinctive approach to the life of faith. Buchmanism explicitly exalted experience over doctrine, a feature underlined by its extensive use of personal testimony. Although an evangelistic strategy, 'life changing' required a way of life characterized by the four absolutes of honesty, purity, unselfishness and love. Consistent with engagement with the world and many of its enjoyments, the Oxford Group Movement was the most prominent case of evangelicals seeking realism in the post-war world by emphasizing vitality and fulfilment as the answer to widespread low morale and the persistent sense of world crisis.

By contrast rational spirituality was an expression of the doctrinalist impulse in the tradition that reflected that side of post-war life which looked for certitude and assurance. Favoured by the centre-right, it appealed to those groups that emphasized theological and ecclesiological integrity in day-to-day practice and organization. Outwardly proponents of this outlook such as the fundamentalist John Roach Straton in New York in the 1920s pitted biblically based morality against the hedonism of contemporary culture and its underlying humanism. Within evangelicalism the doctrinalist priority reinforced the revival of Calvinism of which it was in part an expression. What this meant practically was developed in a series of conferences in the 1930s, especially the fourth held in Edinburgh in 1938, which was devoted to 'the Reformed Faith and its Ethical Consequences'.[26] Around the same time the nascent IVF promoted the Reformed perspective as the normative account of the life of faith.[27] Other effects included bolstering the view of sanctification as the outcome of life-long struggle and encouragement of the expository preaching taken to a new level when Martyn Lloyd-Jones joined G. Campbell Morgan at Westminster Chapel in London in 1938. By 1940 the doctrinalist approach to the Christian life had been powerfully reaffirmed as an alternative to the liberal claim that freedom was the pathway to the new Reformation.[28]

---

26. J. H. S. Burleigh et al. (eds.), *The Fourth Calvinistic Congress Held in Edinburgh 6th to 11th July 1938* (Edinburgh: Congress Executive, 1938).

27. W. S. Hooton, *Problems of Faith and Conduct* (London: Inter-Varsity Fellowship, 1937); Donald M. Maclean, *The Revival of the Reformed Faith* (London: Inter-Varsity Fellowship, 1938).

28. E.g. Addresses on 'Reformation Principles in their Modern Application', in *RPC 1925*, 238–286; G. H. C. MacGregor, 'The Church: Its Nature, Authority and Evangel', *RPC 1937*, 48–60; Stuart C. Parker, 'The Worship of the Reformed Church: The Word and Sacraments', in ibid. 60–73.

The differences resulting from this tension emerged through the 1920s. Organizationally they became evident in the conferences for the promotion of the 'higher Christian life' which retained their prominent place in interwar evangelicalism. During these years the Keswick movement continued to spread, with new conferences established as far afield as Upwey in Melbourne and Niagara near Toronto. Moreover, catering for the centre-right, it became the defining influence on evangelical spirituality within the movement as a whole. In England at least there was a reaction as liberal evangelicals set up their own conferences, the Methodists at Swanwick in 1920 and the Anglicans at Cromer eight years later. Meeting in small study groups was also a hallmark of liberal evangelicalism. Such groups as the Theological Discussion Group in America from 1928 and the Moot in Britain from the late 1930s (both of which interacted with people of other outlooks such as T. S. Eliot and Reinhold Niebuhr) became important sites for considering how evangelicals should approach contemporary life.[29]

The differences in belief and practice among interwar evangelicals were especially telling in relation to the signature doctrine of the atonement. Substitutionary atonement certainly remained the mainstream view. Liberal evangelicals continued to affirm the power of the cross, but more through representative and moral influence interpretations than reliance on the vicarious sacrifice of Christ as the basis of salvation and life. Other evangelicals adapted the cross to their own priorities and preferences. Adherents to the Oxford Group Movement emphasized personal experience: it was not a theory of the cross in which they believed but an experience of it. In the holiness tradition it was the means of sanctification as well as of justification. Among Pentecostals it was widely held that healing is available in the atonement. By the time he produced his summary of evangelical Christianity in 1936, the right-of-centre T. C. Hammond was able to allow exemplary and representative aspects of the atonement while insisting absolutely on substitution as the heart of evangelical belief and devotion.[30] How to appropriate the cross was central to the contemporary discussion of what it meant to be an evangelical and how to secure the effectiveness of evangelical Christianity in the post-war world.

That heightened experientialism and doctrinalism drew out the tension in the evangelical movement between separatism and ecumenism was a profound

---

29. Mark Edwards, *The Right of the Protestant Left: God's Totalitarianism* (New York: Palgrave Macmillan, 2012); Keith Clements (ed.), *The Moot Papers: Faith, Freedom and Society 1938–1944* (London: T. & T. Clark, 2010).

30. Thomas C. Hammond, *'In Understanding Be Men': A Synopsis of Christian Doctrine for Non-Theological Students* (London: Inter-Varsity Fellowship, 1936), 148–162.

disappointment to many. In an appeal to the historical tendency for a broadly shared approach to the spiritual life to correct the separatist impulse in evangelicalism, it was maintained by some evangelicals that the life of faith could remedy the theological tensions and conflicts of the time. Their ecumenism did not prevail against those who countered that the importance of truth and the integrity of evangelicalism were the priority. The effect was to consolidate theological differences by carrying them down into the everyday life of the movement. With the failure of ecumenism to contain separatism, the life of faith became a further site for the contemporary disruption of evangelicalism. To the extent that this favoured the centre-right, it contributed to the upsurge of the biblicist-crucicentric axis in interwar evangelicalism.

The Holy Spirit, Pentecostalism and Aimee Semple McPherson

Another area of belief and practice where the differences among evangelicals affected their post-war agenda was the doctrine of the Holy Spirit, at the time held by many to be the key to the realism needed for effectiveness in the post-war world. However, within a wide consensus about its importance, there was disagreement about its meaning and application. Although still marginal to evangelicalism, Pentecostals pressed on to the whole movement the direct supernatural action of the Spirit on believers as the norm. Adherents of Buchmanism, widely known as 'Groupers', also claimed that the Holy Spirit continued to act supernaturally and was encountered in everyday life in the exercise of his gifts (except tongues). Conservative Methodists and holiness churches too insisted on filling with the Spirit as a 'second blessing' as the condition of full salvation. But reference to direct activity of the Spirit as the source of active holiness and spiritual effectiveness was not uniform on the centre-right. Interwar Keswick came to de-emphasize climactic experiences of the Spirit in favour of a notion of continual infilling through submission to the lordship of Christ. Among liberals the Holy Spirit was similarly decentred. They preferred to interpret the pervasive work of the Spirit as the presupposition of life in Christ in all of its dimensions. Both approaches were part of a trend to normalize the action of the Spirit in the life of faith.[31]

This normalizing trend was further evident in differences about both how fullness of the Spirit was obtained and also the baptism of the Holy Spirit.

---

31. Rogers, 'Introduction', *Inner Life*, viii–ix; Charles R. Erdman, *The Spirit of Christ: Devotional Studies in the Doctrine of the Holy Spirit* (Chicago: Moody Press, 1926).

Traditional Wesleyans such as Samuel Chadwick maintained received teaching about Spirit baptism as the way to fullness of spiritual life and even instantaneous sanctification after conversion. In contrast Keswick reversed the nineteenth-century pneumatological trend by rejecting baptism of the Spirit as a special or second blessing and insisting that it was received by faith at conversion.[32] Filling with the Spirit came with increasing acceptance of the lordship of Christ. Groupers similarly moderated the doctrine by holding that no special experience was required; gifts of the Holy Spirit were simply part of normal living. More stridently, some fundamentalists also opposed theologies of the Spirit as unscriptural. Pentecostals differentiated themselves from all these positions. For them baptism of the Spirit as an experience subsequent to conversion was one of the key elements of the gospel necessary for receiving the spiritual gifts, including tongues speaking. But they differed about whether tongues speaking was an essential initial evidence of Spirit baptism and whether it was for sanctification as well as power. Even Pentecostals could not agree among themselves about the baptism of the Holy Spirit.

Continuation of this debate in part reflected the steady if numerically unspectacular expansion of Pentecostalism during the interwar decades. Following the return of peace, membership increased (especially during the Depression years), new leaders emerged, and the features of other evangelical churches were replicated as Pentecostals wrote constitutions and statements of belief, established churches, opened Bible colleges, began new periodicals and staged annual conventions. These developments were part of the larger social process sociologists call 'routinization of charisma' that took place as Pentecostalism moved into its second generation and the realities of living in the world had to be taken more seriously. Notwithstanding concern that institutionalization expressed a turning away from reliance on charismatic gifts, a definite Pentecostal movement took shape within interwar evangelicalism as the new churches and denominations expanded nationally and internationally.[33]

This institutionalization was not simply a matter of settling down. Pentecostal leaders, especially in Britain, sought acceptance within the evangelical movement at large. However, their efforts were generally fruitless. Five to six million

---

32. E.g. Graham Scroggie, *Baptism with the Spirit: What Is It?* (London: Pickering & Inglis, n.d.).

33. James Robinson, *Pentecostal Origins: Early Pentecostalism in Ireland in the Context of the British Isles* (Milton Keynes: Paternoster Press, 2005), chs. 7–8; Edith Blumhofer, *The Assemblies of God: A Chapter in the Story of American Pentecostalism*, 2 vols. (Springfield: Gospel Publishing House, 1989), vol. 1, esp. ch. 11.

Pentecostals worldwide were thought to have been ejected from evangelical churches. The powerful anti-Pentecostal rhetoric of the Irish revivalist W. P. Nicholson, sometimes called 'the rude evangelist', was an extreme expression of a widely felt antipathy. While Pentecostal leaders might deny that tongues speaking defined their movement, this remained the primary cause of offence. Critics condemned tongues as demonic manifestations and pagan practices, while *The Life of Faith* asserted that 'corybantic exhibitions' were 'subversive of genuine spirituality'.[34] More generally, Pentecostal teaching was condemned as unscriptural. From within the holiness tradition there was doubt about whether unsanctified people could have received the baptism of the Holy Spirit, while the preoccupation with power was said to reveal spiritual immaturity. Pentecostals themselves could also be provocative by making claims to extraordinary spiritual power coupled with allegations of languor and rigidity in other churches. For all of its interest in effectiveness in the contemporary world, interwar evangelicalism was unable to absorb Pentecostal enthusiasm and practice.

For some, one reason for this continued opposition was the spectacular and controversial career of Aimee Semple McPherson. The product of a holiness background combining Methodist and Salvation Army elements, she received the baptism of the Holy Spirit in 1907. In the following year she married the Pentecostal evangelist Robert Semple with whom, intent on missionary service in China, she travelled to Hong Kong in 1910. When her husband died suddenly, she returned to America where she married Harold McPherson (who divorced her in 1921) and embarked on a career as an itinerant Pentecostal preacher and faith-healer in the eastern states. Her rise to national prominence began in 1918 when she drove across the country – perhaps the first woman to do so – and set up her ministry in Los Angeles, which she used as a base for preaching tours up and down the west coast and into the Midwest. Also crossing the country eight times between 1918 and 1923, her ability to attract large crowds earned her recognition as 'the female Billy Sunday'. In 1923 she opened the capacious Angelus Temple, the site of her pageant-like services, and the first of a complex of buildings that was to include a prayer tower that operated twenty-four hours a day, a state-of-the-art radio station and a Bible college. Four years later she founded the International Church of the Foursquare Gospel whose network of churches and missions spread around the world. Within this organizational framework during the years down to her death in 1944 she attracted the

---

34. Quoted in David W. Bebbington, 'Evangelism and Spirituality in Twentieth-Century Protestant Nonconformity', in Alan P. F. Sell and Anthony R. Cross (eds.), *Protestant Nonconformity in the Twentieth Century* (Carlisle: Paternoster Press, 2003), 196.

enormous following that made her the most successful Pentecostal leader of the day. In the first age of show-business celebrities she also sought and obtained celebrity status for herself.[35]

In some respects McPherson's rise was favoured by circumstances such as a shortage of revivalist preachers following the War. Yet underlying her success was a combination of genuine charisma and shrewdness that enabled her to augment her natural appeal by taking advantage of new cultural and strategic opportunities. These qualities are evident in the move to Los Angeles, the mythic birthplace of Pentecostalism, a tourist hub and the centre of the emerging film industry. She thought on a large scale, deliberately 'fishing for whales rather than minnows' by reaching out to the expanding middle class while retaining the support of Pentecostalism's traditional constituency among the lowest socio-economic band of American society. Ever the pragmatist with a keen eye for what would work, she was adept at fundraising, a skilled exponent of the media and alert to the capacity of the latest communication technologies to promote herself and her message. Her use of spectacle and emphasis on spiritual vitality catered to the culture shaped by the post-war craze for leisure and entertainment. Withdrawal from the Assemblies of God and establishment of her own denomination enabled her to sidestep internal Pentecostal conflicts and retain control of her church. Avoiding tongues speaking in her services and preferring 'evangelical' and 'undenominational' as descriptors for her church minimized the stigma attached to 'Pentecostal' and facilitated solidarity with other centre-right evangelicals. Similarly her own oft-repeated story and limited theological writing drew out continuity with the revivalist tradition and led to identification of her cause with the well-being and success of America.[36] McPherson's innovativeness was not held in check by the 'routinization of charisma'.

But she was always controversial. For some critics it was enough that she was a woman preacher, an offence she compounded by encouraging other women also to preach. Theologically she was denounced as a fundamentalist – naive, superficial and unsound. As a divorcee and single mother who provided support for unmarried mothers, she was accused of subverting marriage. Her affront to contemporary gender norms was aggravated by the inescapable sexuality of her

---

35. The most recent biographies are Chas. H. Barfoot, *Aimee Semple McPherson and the Making of Modern Pentecostalism 1890–1926* (London: Equinox Publishing, 2011); Mathew Sutton, *Aimee Semple McPherson and the Resurrection of Christian America* (Cambridge, MA: Harvard University Press, 2007).

36. E.g. Aimee Semple McPherson, *This Is That: Personal Experiences, Sermons and Writings of Aimee Semple McPherson, Evangelist* (Los Angeles: Bridal Call Publishing House, 1919).

presence and presentation. In this respect she was accused of vulgar showman-
ship, wanton advertising and profligacy. To the list of vitiating flaws was added
shameless self-promotion and manipulation of the media. She was thought to
be in sympathy with the Ku Klux Klan and her good character never quite
recovered from the suspicions aroused by her brief but mysterious disappear-
ance (and alleged kidnapping) from Venice Beach near Santa Monica in 1926.
Although she went to great lengths to establish family-like identity with as many
people as possible, Aimee McPherson was not 'everybody's sister'.[37]

Although never free from criticism, McPherson had done much to redeem
her reputation by the time she died unexpectedly in 1944. With the Second
World War raging, her assertion of the importance of the 'old-time religion' for
the survival of Christian civilization was at its height. This message, which
retained its resonance after her death, was an important component of her
legacy to Pentecostalism and evangelicalism at large. Importantly she had been
among those Pentecostals who affirmed the place of Pentecostalism in evangelicalism and hoped to renew the larger movement by their enthusiasm and
emphasis on the gifts of the Spirit. Other significant Pentecostal leaders such
as the British Assemblies of God teacher and writer Donald Gee emerged
during the interwar years, but none raised the public standing of Pentecostalism
like Aimee McPherson and, with it, the traditional evangelical message of
salvation by faith in Christ. Her creative use of modern communication technologies, entertainment and spectacle aligned this conservative form of
Christianity with the culture of the modern world. By strongly reasserting
activism, social as well as conversionist, she found numerous ways to reconnect
Christianity with society, while by deprecating conflict with other broadly like-
minded evangelicals she countered the debilitating disintegration of the
movement with an injection of ecumenism from an unexpected quarter. Perhaps
only Frank Buchman did as much to realize evangelicals' post-war agenda of
commending Christianity to contemporary society by demonstrating its realism
and efficacy.

Eschatology

It was not only different styles and specific doctrinal constructions that added
to the divisions of diversity in interwar evangelicalism. The quest for

---

37. Edith Blumhofer, *Aimee Semple McPherson: Everybody's Sister* (Grand Rapids:
Eerdmans, 1993).

effectiveness in the post-war world also led to different priorities in the praxis of the main segments of the movement.

The emphasis of the centre-right was on the premillennial return of Christ, now brought arguably to its highest point of influence on English-speaking evangelicalism. As noted in chapter 8, the War transformed the standing of premillennialism. The unrest of the months immediately after the War and the survival of the communist regime in Russia consolidated the sense that these were the end times. By 1920 biblical prophecy was established as the lens through which to interpret the political and social developments of the day for an increasing number of evangelicals. Particularly for historicist premillennialists – those who looked for the fulfilment of biblical prophecy in the events of human history against the futurists who expected this fulfilment to occur just before the second coming – the effect was to embark on the post-war era full of confidence with incentive to spread their message. As a result new adventist organizations sprang up to foster speculation about the meaning of these developments. The aim of *The Advent Witness*, the monthly magazine of the English Advent Preparation and Testimony Movement founded in 1917 'to herald the coming again of the Lord Jesus Christ, and earnestly contend for the faith once delivered to the saints', reflected the aspirations of these organizations.[38] As they carried out this intention, these centre-right evangelicals lodged their claim for the relevance and authority of evangelicalism by interpreting contemporary events in prophetic terms.

During the 1920s and 1930s, several factors combined to make the premillennial message more and more compelling. Memory of the War undermined confidence both in human capacity to build a better future and also in evolution as the basis of the idea of progress. Economic and social conditions belied the optimism at the root of postmillennial thinking. Elements of popular culture – especially the cinema and contemporary dance styles – pointed to moral degeneracy reminiscent of the times of Noah and Sodom. Economic collapse during the Great Depression heralded the failure of capitalism, while the statism of the New Deal marked out President Franklin Roosevelt as a forerunner of the Antichrist. The advent of a new Roman Empire under the rule of Benito Mussolini

---

38. From the cover of the magazine. The other periodical tracked for this aspect of evangelicalism from the many that might have been selected is *The Dawn: An Evangelical Magazine*, commenced in 1924 by David M. Panton, pastor of Surrey Chapel, Norwich, in England. A wide survey of Adventist periodicals underpins Matthew Sutton, *American Apocalypse: A History of Modern Evangelicalism* (Cambridge, MA: Belknap Press, 2014), esp. chs. 5–8.

combined with the spectre of Russian communism to suggest the alignment of political forces to be expected at the end of the age. Events in Europe threatening war seemed to bring Armageddon nearer. Buoyed by the hope of the second coming, adventists claimed to be the true optimists of the day. As evidence for its imminence mounted, for these evangelicals the life of faith during the interwar decades was largely about preparing for the second coming.

Adventism also gained impetus from the adherence of celebrities, the most notable of whom was the suffragette Christabel Pankhurst.[39] Convinced by reading H. Grattan Guinness's *The Approaching End of the Age Viewed in the Light of History, Prophecy and Science* (1878), in 1918 she gave up work for women's suffrage and devoted herself to the propagation of adventist thinking. Over the following twenty years she wrote and campaigned to persuade others – particularly the influential – that world events indicated that Christ would soon come again and this would resolve the world's problems. Pankhurst further commended her outlook by criticizing modernism as passé, and by emphasizing her conformity with basic doctrines such as the atonement and biblical authority. Her orthodoxy and ongoing interpretation of current events as evidence of the fulfilment of biblical prophecy combined with her change of life direction to commend her apocalyptic brand of evangelical Christianity as the message for the times.

Although collectively a rising force, adventists were far from a united bloc. While agreeing that humanity was living in the end times and that the parousia would come soon, there was much difference over what would actually happen. The main disagreement arose over the tribulation, with one wing claiming that the 'rapture' would precede, while another claimed the church would have to endure, the time of suffering. A smaller group believed there would be a 'partial rapture', in which particularly 'watchful' believers would be rescued before the great tribulation. These differences were not dissimilar from those arising over the baptism of the Holy Spirit. Within a broad consensus, particularly in relation to their more esoteric beliefs, high expectation and excitement caused premillennial evangelicals to differ over the details.

As influential as they became, the adventists failed to take the whole evangelical movement with them. From the beginning of the post-war era other evangelicals resisted the premillennial expectation.[40] Through the years that followed, premillennialists were the target of dismissive criticism and some

---

39. Timothy Larsen, *Christabel Pankhurst: Fundamentalism and Feminism in Coalition* (Woodbridge: Boydell Press, 2002).

40. E.g. James H. Snowden, *The Coming of the Lord: Will It Be Premillennial?* (New York: Macmillan, 1919).

ridicule from centre-left evangelicals.[41] By the time T. C. Hammond sought to codify the evangelical position in the mid 1950s, he entered a strong caution in relation to eschatology:

> Holy Scripture is the only utterly reliable guide, and even here, since God has seen fit to give us but brief statements on certain matters, care in the interpretation of isolated texts is clearly necessary. Much harm has been done by well-meaning but incautious zealots, who have allowed their enthusiasm to run riot in wild and dogmatic assertions upon points where dogmatism is impossible. Still more harm has been done by those who have seized upon certain isolated texts, and woven around them doctrines which are inconsistent with the rest of Scripture.

What purported to be the standard evangelical position deprecated speculation about both the timing and the events of the second coming in favour of concentration on the present with the eschatological hope as 'one of our chief incentives to holy living and diligence in Christian service'.[42]

Ecumenism and ecclesiology

If eschatology was the preoccupation of the centre-right during the interwar years, ecumenism came to occupy a similar place in the outlook of centre-left evangelicals. Initially, however, unity among the churches was regarded as a condition of post-war effectiveness right across the movement. One reason was the expectation that servicemen would be deeply disappointed if they returned from the experience of camaraderie in the armed services to find no progress had been made towards overcoming ostensibly outdated denominational differences. More generally evangelicals had little doubt that the modern world would not listen to a divided church. Nor could the churches hope to lead in the restoration of genuine peace if their own divisions were not overcome. Indeed, for these evangelicals the war had been a parable, for it showed that only cooperation under one leader in a common cause leads to victory. With so much at stake, evangelicals quickly evinced a willingness to consider ways of

---

41. E.g. 'Comment and Outlook. Professor Peake on Millenarianism', *HomR* 87.3 (Mar. 1924), 202; C. H. Titterton, 'The Second Advent', in J. Russell Howden (ed.), *Evangelicalism: By Members of the Fellowship of Evangelical Churchmen* (London: Thynne, n.d. [1925]), 306–325.

42. Hammond, *'In Understanding Be Men'*, 231, 232.

coming together. In 1919 English Anglicans met with Free Churchmen who indicated a preparedness to consider a modified form of episcopacy. The same year American evangelicals joined in the ill-fated Interchurch World Movement before its crash. The call for unity issued by the Anglicans' Lambeth Conference in 1920 was also widely welcomed. Within evangelicalism as it emerged from the War there was a strong push to promote unity among the churches in a bid for credibility and greater social impact.[43]

During the 1920s, however, the push for unity became a characteristic of the centre-left. This was partly because, as fundamentalism became better organized and increasingly strident, it also became more sectarian. Other centre-right evangelicals were guarded, as Anglicans clarified their expectations by insisting on episcopal ordination. Even so, in a manner reflecting the idealism of the era, large numbers of centre-left evangelicals remained committed to ecumenicalism, which was extensively discussed throughout the interwar years.[44] Generally they were modest in their aspirations. Organic union of all Christians was thought to be unrealistic and not necessarily desirable. But intercommunion, sharing of pulpits and open cooperation in matters of shared interest were considered achievable and perhaps sufficient.

On the basis of this outlook ecumenically minded evangelicals were prepared to work for greater institutional unity where it was feasible. At the denominational level in Britain Scottish Presbyterians came together to form the reconstituted Church of Scotland in 1929 and three years later Methodist union was achieved when the United Methodists and the Primitve Methodists joined with the Wesleyan Methodists. Interdenominationally these ecumenical evangelicals participated in parachurch and interchurch organizations such as the American Federal Council of Churches, of which the centrist missionary statesman Robert Speer was elected President in 1920, the year in which the rising liberal evangelical Samuel McCrae Cavert was appointed as a secretary.[45]

---

43. *Towards Reunion: Being Contributions to Mutual Understanding by Church of England and Free Church Writers* (London: Macmillan, 1919); Charles E. Harvey, 'John D. Rockefeller, Jr., and the Interchurch World Movement of 1919–1920: A Different Angle on the Ecumenical Movement', *CH* 51.2 (1982), 198–209.

44. The development of ecumenicalism in contemporary evangelicalism can be followed through the interwar decades in *Evangelical Christendom*, the periodical of the Evangelical Alliance, especially in the regular 'Reunion Notes' section.

45. John F. Piper, Jr., *Robert E. Speer: Prophet of the American Church* (Louisville, KY: Geneva Press, 2000), chs. 9–10; William J. Schmidt, *Architect of Unity: A Biography of Samuel McCrae Cavert* (New York: Friendship Press, 1978), chs. 3–4.

However, the greatest ecumenical achievement of the era was the creation of the United Church of Canada in 1925 by a union of Presbyterians, Methodists and Congregationalists, most of them centrist evangelicals. Of course it was stoutly resisted by many, especially by a large minority of Presbyterians who clung to the heritage of Scotland and the Westminster Confession. But for the United Church's many evangelical supporters the push for union was sustained by the hope of a genuinely Christian society achieved through the removal of obstacles to belief and effective action.[46]

A small number of leftist evangelicals also recognized in the incipient ecumenical movement the means of achieving their hope of restoring Christianity to its place in the moral and spiritual life of Western civilization. In Britain they included the liberal evangelical Anglican Edward S. Woods, student leader Tissington Tatlow and the Scots Donald and John Baillie. In America centre-left evangelicals William Adams Brown and J. Ross Stevenson and several of the group of rising leaders who had been nurtured in the YMCA, SVM and WSCF, such as Henry Van Dusen and Francis Miller, were of a similar outlook.[47] These people hastened to align themselves with the Faith and Order and Life and Work Movements as they emerged in the 1920s to consider points of difference and agreement between the churches and to secure common endeavour in applying Christian principles to social and international problems.[48] Both organizations were broader than evangelicalism, but centre-left evangelicals participated largely because they provided structures through which to pursue on the largest scale possible the reconstruction project of the resacralization of their world.

In the following decade the support of the evangelical centre-left for the ecumenical movement strengthened as the leaders of the International Missionary Council (IMC) became involved. Joseph Oldham took the lead in organizing the important Life and Work Conference at Oxford in 1937, which set out to ascertain the Christian message in the world of dictatorships and crumbling democracies. He in turn drew in John Mott, who played a leading

46. Phyllis D. Airhart, *A Church with the Soul of a Nation: Making and Remaking the United Church of Canada* (Montreal: McGill-Queen's University Press, 2014), chs. 1–4.

47. Mark T. Edwards, 'Can Christianity Save Civilisation? Liberal Protestant Anti-Secularism in Interwar America', *JRH* 39.1 (Mar. 2015), 51–67.

48. Tissington Tatlow, 'The World Conference on Faith and Order', and Nils Karlström, 'Movements for International Friendship and Life and Work, 1925–1948', in Ruth Rouse and Stephen C. Neill (eds.), *A History of the Ecumenical Movement 1517–1948*, 3rd ed. (Geneva: World Council of Churches, 1986), 405–441, 545–596.

role in the conference in Oxford and another at Edinburgh later in the year that brought the World Council of Churches to the verge of formation.[49] Evangelicals have not generally been credited with significant influence on this major development in world Christianity, but they clearly played a prominent part motivated by the realization that, although the fundamental obstacle to the achievement of the evangelical hope for a Christian world was rampant secularism, the problem was as much in the church as in the world.

One effect of the rising emphasis on Christian unity was to focus evangelical attention on its doctrine of the church.[50] Many evangelicals came to appreciate the benefits of evangelical ecclesiology and ventured to think it provided a realistic and theologically sound basis for all the churches to come together. Paradoxically the conflicts within evangelicalism also concentrated attention on the nature of the church at the same time as challenging denominational sensibilities. Within the tradition of orthodox dissent, the revival of Calvinism encouraged a leaning towards a higher ecclesiology as the proponents of the revival thought about the meaning of the gospel for the church. The sufferings of the European churches, in the wake of the peace settlements of the 1920s and then because of the rise of totalitarian regimes, further pressed the question of connection between the churches and their mutual obligations. In parts of the movement at least, the circumstances of the post-war years strengthened the corporate tendency in evangelical thinking.

Anti-Catholicism and the Reformation anniversaries

As ever, the limit to evangelical ecumenism was set by Catholicism. For several reasons, the anti-Catholic sentiment noted in chapter 3 as characteristic of the evangelical tradition actually intensified during the interwar years. It was true that the bravery of Catholics in the trenches had mitigated animosity towards Catholicism, but this was offset by suspicion of the ambitions of the Vatican in the peace negotiations. Through the 1920s a new wave of anti-Catholicism was prompted by the success of Anglo-Catholicism and the Malines Conversations between 1921 and 1925, which explored possible reunion of the Churches of England and Rome. Evangelicals, urged on by pressure groups such as the

---

49. Keith Clements, *Faith on the Frontier: A Life of J. H. Oldham* (Edinburgh: T. & T. Clark, 1999), pt. 4.

50. E.g. P. Carnegie Simpson, *The Evangelical Church Catholic* (London: Hodder & Stoughton, 1934).

militant Protestant Truth Society and the more respectable Evangelical Alliance, participated in the sectarianism that remained a significant feature of English-speaking societies. Fundamentalism and the tendency of adventists to equate the Pope with the Antichrist further energized anti-Catholic feeling. The 1928 presidential election, in which the Roman Catholic Al Smith ran for the presidency as the Democratic candidate, aroused the Protestant feeling of America. The intersection of political, cultural and theological influences was such that seemingly the one thing on which interwar evangelicals could agree was the need to oppose the Church of Rome.[51]

One anti-Catholic outburst with surprisingly wide resonance was the 1927–8 Prayer Book controversy in Britain.[52] By the mid-1920s Anglo-Catholics in the Church of England had attained sufficient strength to warrant a move for Prayer Book reform to accommodate their aspirations and practices. When the bishops submitted proposals to Parliament for an alternative Prayer Book, it was met with strong opposition from various Protestant groups, including evangelical Anglicans led by the redoubtable E. A. Knox, the retired Bishop of Manchester, who felt the revision went too far in a Catholic direction. They were supported not only by evangelicals in the Anglican communion, but also by other evangelicals throughout 'Greater Britain'. For it was widely felt that Catholicization of the Church of England would undermine the Reformation and the Protestantism that was part of the English-speaking inheritance.

For all the relief it gave when Parliament rejected the alternative Prayer Book, anti-Catholicism did not abate. It was stirred up again in 1933 by the centenary of the Oxford Movement, which was marked throughout the English-speaking world by Anglo-Catholic celebrations and evangelical protests.[53] The high mass at White City in London in July attended by some 50,000 people was a cause of deep offence and alarm. Anglican evangelicals in particular resented Anglo-Catholic calumnies against the condition of the church before 1833 and rejected claims that the Tractarians completed the Evangelical Revival. They responded by producing their own interpretation of the history of the Oxford Movement and alternative accounts of key

---

51. John Wolffe, 'A Comparative Historical Categorisation of Anti-Catholicism', *JRH* 39.2 (2015), 182–202.

52. John Maiden, *National Religion and the Prayer Book Controversy, 1927–1928* (Woodbridge: Boydell Press, 2009).

53. Andrew Atherstone, 'Evangelicals and the Oxford Movement Centenary', *JRH* 37.1 (2013), 98–117.

aspects of church life.[54] In this warfare of words T. C. Hammond was representative in declaring the Evangelical Revival had brought a new power of vital
religion while, in all that it stood for, the Oxford Movement was regressive.[55]
Non-Anglican evangelicals were also offended by the Anglo-Catholic celebrations, and they denounced the Oxford Movement as un-English, law breaking
and anti-Protestant. Some liberal evangelicals were mildly conciliatory, but most
remained implacable towards the Oxford Movement's manifest Romanizing.

The underlying theological objections to Catholicism were continually brought
to the surface through the interwar years by a succession of Reformation anniversaries. Beginning with the quatercentenary of Luther's ninety-five theses in
1917 and including the third centenary of the settlement of America by the
Pilgrim Fathers, evangelicals were recalled to their roots as they remembered
the landmark events of 'the long sixteenth century'.[56] These culminated in the
mid-1930s with the four hundredth anniversary of the English Reformation, a
celebration throughout the English-speaking world of independence from Rome.
Its high point was the commemoration of the publication of the English Bible
and of the martyrdom of its translator, William Tyndale, in 1937–8. Celebrating
the contribution to civilization of the intersection of their Protestantism and
biblicism coincided with stirrings noted elsewhere in the evangelical movement
towards the end of the 1930s. Morale recovered as the great events of their past
reminded evangelicals of who they were and what they had given to the world.

Although anti-Catholicism was pervasive in evangelicalism, it did not thwart
a taste for more elaborate worship. All around the English-speaking world evangelicals adopted practices that once would have been regarded as unequivocally
'Romish'. Adaptation to higher expressions of churchmanship was easiest
among Anglicans with their tradition of liturgy. The ideal of freedom among
the liberals, together with acceptance of the need for renewal, opened the way
for innovation in the use of music, vestments, crosses and up-to-date language
that brought colour, dignity and reality to worship. However, the impact of
Catholic ideas and practices was not confined to the Anglican evangelical left.

---

54. E.g. E. A. Knox, *The Tractarian Movement, 1833–1845* (London: Putnam, 1933); Charles S.
     Carter and G. E. A. Weeks (eds.), *The Protestant Dictionary: Containing Articles on the History,
     Doctrines and Practices of the Christian Church*, new ed. (London: Harrison Trust, 1933).
55. Thomas C. Hammond, *The Evangelical Revival and the Oxford Movement* (London:
     Church Book Room, n.d. [1933]) [= *Ch* 47.2 (Apr. 1933), 79–86]).
56. A term historians use as shorthand for the period incorporating the antecedents of
     the major developments of the sixteenth century before 1501 and the immediate
     consequences after 1600.

Centrists of various hues and denominations also showed enthusiasm for liturgies, vestments, symbols, candles and robed choirs. Even among those who had traditionally preferred spontaneity and freedom from structure, set readings, prayers and praise gained a foothold in the interest of greater substance in worship and openness to the whole Christian tradition. Inevitably innovation and experimentation aroused opposition, again right across the spectrum of opinion. In response it was claimed that a middle way in worship was being created between 'tawdry pseudo-Romanism' and 'arid ugly Protestantism'. As ideas and practices were drawn from a broader ecclesiological deposit, the question whether evangelicals could craft patterns of worship that were more Catholic while remaining evangelical bred further tension within the movement.

The dilemma was sharpest in relation to the celebration of Holy Communion. While typically evangelicals held to a symbolic understanding of the sacraments, both Catholic and Puritan sources pointed towards a higher sacramentalism. Among Anglicans there were certainly limits, such as public devotion before the reserved sacrament, but Anglo-Catholic influence certainly promoted more advanced thinking and practice about Eucharistic worship, with some Anglican evangelicals even adopting the more priestly eastward position.[57] Methodist thinking was similarly pushed towards greater sacramentalism by the Swanwick Convention and the Methodist Sacramental Fellowship, created in 1935. Those who were independent of the Anglican tradition did not simply follow Anglican patterns. Reformed and Puritan influences also suggested higher views of the sacraments to them. On all sides there was a growing appreciation of a 'real presence of the Lord in the Holy Communion',[58] although there was some difference about what this meant, together with a desire to live a more sacramental life. By 1940 memories of the Reformation had not prevented higher views of the sacraments gaining a strong following in evangelicalism.

Conclusion

Evangelicals embarked upon the post-war years in the belief that their task was both to present the life of faith for the new world order and to demonstrate

---

57. Apart from Randall, *Evangelical Experiences*, see Christopher J. Cocksworth, *Evangelical Eucharistic Thought in the Church of England* (Cambridge: Cambridge University Press, 1993), ch. 6.

58. An expression of the British Methodist Gordon James, quoted in Randall, *Evangelical Experiences*, 131.

such a life's value and effectiveness by their own conduct. Their efforts to show the realism and efficacy of evangelical Christianity entailed ensuring that the life of faith accommodated the particular spiritual and emotional needs of a world recovering from four years of war. More broadly, evangelicals also sought in various ways to develop a spirituality attuned to the dispositions and needs of the post-war world. Their efforts took as a primary reference point the Reformation of the sixteenth century, which was especially salient in the era of the anniversaries of its leading events. The hope of 'a new Reformation' did not preclude taking what was valuable from the contemporary upsurge of Catholicism, providing that evangelical principles were not compromised or opposition to the Church of Rome weakened. Other variations on the common task of promoting the life of faith included the characteristic approaches of Pentecostalism, adventism and ecumenicalism. Taken together, the efforts of interwar evangelicals to provide a way of life for their world engendered what the leading historian of contemporary evangelical experience judges to have been an age of heightened spirituality.[59]

Despite this achievement, the impact of the life of faith on the post-war world was limited by its diversity. Within a broad framework of shared aspiration, interwar evangelicals had developed spiritualities that applied their own emphases and priorities and reflected attitudes held in common with other contemporaries. Those whose outlook was shaped more by the biblicist-crucicentric axis within the evangelical synthesis tended to favour compliance with the requirements of doctrine as the best way to address the spiritual needs of contemporary society, while those more influenced by the idealism of the era tended rather to look to the possibilities of experience. The effect of this tension between experientialism and doctrinalism was not only to deepen the diversification of evangelicalism, but also to vitiate the credentials of evangelicals as representatives of a way of life that would restore Christian civilization and ensure that the Great War would be 'the war to end war'. At a time when they had to reckon with modernists and aggressive Anglo-Catholics, their divisions also precluded rebuilding to previous levels their influence within Protestantism as well as English-speaking society at large.

---

59. Ibid. 269.

11. EVANGELISM AND MISSIONS IN THE MODERN WORLD

The great task of post-war reconstruction also presented a challenge to the conversionist impulse in evangelicalism. For the re-establishment of Christian civilization as envisaged by evangelicals in 1919 required wide adherence to Christianity. Towards the end of the War, the elder statesman of the movement, Bishop Handley Moule of Durham, restated a familiar conversionist rationale at the annual Islington Clerical Meeting: 'society for its health and hope depends vitally, incalculably, on the diffusion all through it of souls, of lives which express souls, which are true, in the new birth and being of grace, to God'.[1] At the next Islington Clerical Meeting after Moule spoke, the convenor indicated what the circumstances required: 'we must seek an Evangelistic fervour which is satisfied with nothing less than securing definite results in manifest conversions, a force strong enough to emulate the impact of the Early Church on the world when it turned it upside down'.[2] Still thinking in military terms, post-war evangelicals set out to win their homelands for Christ and to send 'a mighty expeditionary

---

1. Handley Moule, 'The Means of Renewal', in *ICM 1918. After the War – Renewal* (London: 'Record' Newspaper Office, 1918), 29–30.
2. C. J. Procter, 'Introductory', in *ICM 1919. Evangelicals and the Reports of the Archbishops' Committees* (London: 'Record' Newspaper Office, 1919), 11.

force' to the mission field.[3] They hoped for nothing less than a new awakening at home and the extension of Christianity on the mission field that would create the following necessary for the emergence of a Christian world order.

In this respect too there was a strong sense that evangelicalism was at the crossroads. Because evangelism is the perennial task of the church, the post-war moment was an opportunity for the movement to show its authenticity as an expression of New Testament Christianity: 'we must have a greater confidence about the things of faith . . . The Church is most like her Master when she speaks with authority.'[4] The need was all the greater because the peace had not brought the anticipated benefits:

> the disappointment has meant a deeper conviction that it is in the heart of man that all evil has its roots. It is with the heart of man that the Gospel has to do, to save him from his radical recalcitrance from God. It is a doctrine of individual regeneration. To-day it is largely recognized that not by any social scheme or political plan or balance of power shall we find an issue from the present disordered and unhappy conditions which afflict humanity.[5]

The analysis of T. B. Kilpatrick of Knox College, Toronto, again spelt out the cost of the Church not proclaiming its message: 'if this passion withers and the evangelical note is lost, the Church will lose its place and power. Its moral influence will be seriously diminished; and it will fail even in those social and philanthropic activities, for the sake of which it has surrendered its distinctively evangelical quality.'[6] Its conversionism would be a second condition of realizing the evangelical reconstruction project and demonstrating the legitimacy of evangelicalism.

Evangelism in the era of reconstruction[7]

With the usual imperative to evangelism bolstered by the peculiar need of the post-war world, evangelicals began the era hopefully. At first their confidence

---

3. Robert E. Speer, 'Why We Must Enlarge Our Missionary Obedience', *RCW* 38.8 (Aug. 1919), 548–554.

4. Oliver Russell, 'The Evangelical Programme', *RPC 1921*, 260–265 (quotation on 265).

5. Ibid. 261.

6. T. B. Kilpatrick, 'The Church of the Twentieth Century', *ConsQ* 7.27 (Sept. 1919), 400–432 (quotation on 415–416).

7. This chapter is informed by David W. Bebbington, 'Evangelism and Spirituality in Twentieth-Century Protestant Nonconformity', in Alan P. F. Sell

seemed to be justified by large church attendances following the Armistice and conclusion of the peace settlement, and by a certain receptiveness to Christianity fostered by the desire to return to normality. A shift in popular culture seemed also to favour evangelicals' prospects. Exposure by the War of the naivety of belief in inevitable progress and of the depths to which unredeemed human conduct could sink furnished a good environment in which to maintain that only 'the new birth' could turn the disposition of the human heart towards the lives of self-sacrifice and service required by civilization.[8]

However, this early optimism was soon tempered as the realities of the post-war world came into focus.[9] Against the background of widespread political and industrial unrest, reports of the low state of religion in the army administered a shock, and the return of men from the front did not produce the anticipated outburst of religious enthusiasm. The effect of people wanting to return to normality also quickly fell away, to be replaced by a marked indifference to religion. With declining adherence, already apparent before the War, seeming to have worsened, the evangelistic task appeared at once more difficult and urgent than it had seemed early in 1919. The War and its immediate aftermath led evangelicals to reaffirm the importance of evangelism in their communities.

The importance of evangelism for the reconstruction project engendered appeals for reactivation of traditional evangelistic methods.[10] 'Personal work' as advocated by Torrey and Alexander remained fundamental, and a 'League for Personal Evangelism' was established in England to foster proselytization by individuals.[11] Public preaching too was of the first importance. As late as 1935, the Australian Hugh Paton of the recently formed Open Air Campaigners was urging the use of loudspeakers to make preaching in public places effective. A more comprehensive distribution of Christian literature was also urged. Because the people were not coming to the churches, taking the gospel to the people emerged as the priority in post-war evangelism.

An unreceptive culture also stimulated experimentation with new methods. In Britain a Cinema Mission movement was established to capitalize on the

and Anthony R. Cross (eds.), *Protestant Nonconformity in the Twentieth Century* (Carlisle: Paternoster Press, 2003), 184–215.

8. 'The Witness of the Church', *C* (3 Mar. 1921), 1–3; 'Notes and Comments. The Moral Element', *C* (12 May 1921), 3.

9. E.g. 'Looking Back. An Eventful Year', *C* (25 Dec. 1919), 1–3.

10. G. B. F. Hallock, *The Evangelistic Cyclopedia: A New Century Handbook of Evangelism* (New York: George H. Doran, 1922).

11. 'Questing Discipleship. An Urgent Call to Duty', *C* (7 July 1921), 1–3.

great popularity of the medium of film.[12] Also in Britain halls were often built instead of churches in the new council housing estates because they allowed leisure and entertainment activities that would have been opposed in traditional church buildings.[13] Basic to the success of the fundamentalist entrepreneurs of the era were the independent tabernacle-like churches they created. Paul Rader and Oswald Smith, founders of the Chicago Gospel Tabernacle in 1922 and the Cosmopolitan Tabernacle (later renamed the People's Church) in Toronto in 1928, were the trendsetters.[14] Beyond the reach of denominational control, they were free to advertise to maximize their audiences and to use such means as slide shows, films and free concerts to take advantage of the contemporary vogue for entertainment. Despite some criticism, their methods were copied far and wide.[15] As in previous eras, the conversionist tradition was modified so that people could hear the gospel.

The most significant innovation of the day, however, was the use of radio. After its beginning in January 1921, religious broadcasting caught on rapidly among evangelicals as reservations about 'worldliness' and the possible impact on church attendance gave way to recognition of the advent of a powerful new medium for preaching the word. It was difficult to grasp the opportunity in Britain where the BBC required that religious broadcasting be nationally uplifting and non-partisan.[16] Elsewhere increasing government regulation gave rise to a broadcasting environment in which public and commercial stations operated alongside one another. With access to free public air time difficult to achieve, would-be broadcasters with a definite evangelistic message mostly had to purchase air-time on commercial stations. By forcing them to improve their formats to build commercially viable audiences, the commercial imperative was a hidden benefit. Certainly such evangelical entrepreneurs as Walter Maier of 'The Lutheran Hour' (which in time was to become the largest radio broadcast of its kind in the world)

---

12. 'Work and Workers. The Cinema and the Church', *C* (22 Apr. 1920), 10; 'Work and Workers. Can the Cinema Help the Church?', *C* (24 June 1920), 10.

13. Callum G. Brown, *Religion and Society in Twentieth-Century Britain* (Harlow: Pearson Education, 2006), 141.

14. Kevin Kee, *Revivalists: Marketing the Gospel in English Canada, 1884–1957* (Montreal: McGill-Queen's University Press, 2006), ch. 2.

15. Jane Simpson, 'Joseph W. Kemp: Prime Interpreter of American Fundamentalism in New Zealand in the 1920s', in Douglas Pratt (ed.), *'Rescue the Perishing': Comparative Perspectives on Evangelism and Revivalism* (Auckland: College Communications, 1989), 23–41.

16. Kenneth M. Wolfe, *The Churches and the British Broadcasting Corporation 1922–1956: The Politics of Broadcast Religion* (London: SCM Press, 1984), pt. 1.

were undeterred.[17] The enthusiasm of evangelicals for radio marked the advent of 'the electronic church' and created a means of reaching many whose adherence did not necessarily translate into regular church attendance.[18]

As ever in the history of evangelicalism, reservations about what was being attempted and the standard criticism that not enough was being done were expressed during the early post-war years. At the same time a degree of satisfaction with what had been accomplished was registered. One contemporary survey, which intended to give 'some idea of the magnitude, the variety, and the supreme importance of the field', found that 'the aftermath of war has been a period of singular evangelistic activity, the spirit of love and service finding expression along widely different lines'.[19] Its extensive coverage included the Salvation and Church Armies, the Settlement and Brotherhood Movements, the Children's Special Service Mission, the YMCA and the Religious Tract Society. These organizations were markedly different in aim, character and method, but were seen to be united in 'consciousness that they embody essentially the same Christian ideal, manifest the same spirit of purposive service, and contemplate the same ultimate goal of a renewed humanity, living in real harmony with God and happy fellowship man with man'.[20] Other commentators also noticed a commitment to evangelism as the hope of civilization.[21] With many historic agencies still operating effectively as part of the evangelical order, and with new personalities and technologies having come on to the scene, confidence in the power of the gospel and hopes for its effectiveness in the post-war world were the norm in the early 1920s.

Evangelism during the 'religious depression'

By the mid-1920s this optimism had ebbed. The obvious reason was that the multitude turning back to Christianity anticipated in the immediate aftermath of the War had not eventuated. Nor had the great revival reckoned at the beginning

---

17. L. Eskridge, 'Maier, Walter Arthur', in *BDE*, 405–407.
18. Tona J. Hangen, *Redeeming the Dial: Radio, Religion, and Popular Culture in America* (Chapel Hill: University of North Carolina Press, 2002); Quentin J. Schultze, 'Evangelical Radio and the Rise of the Electronic Church', *JBEM* 32.3 (1988), 289–306.
19. [David P. Thomson and Hubert L. Simpson], *Modern Evangelistic Movements. Edited by Two University Men* (New York: George H. Doran, 1924), quotation on 18.
20. Ibid. 19.
21. E.g. William Younger, 'The Recent Emphasis on Evangelism', *EMC 1921*, 29–31; A. Douglas Brown, 'Evangelism', *WBC 1923*, 206–210.

of the interwar era as the necessary condition of the return to peace, prosperity and progress occurred.[22] Coupled with disappointed expectations was an awareness that the contemporary mood in society was now actually unfavourable. Evangelicals observed that belief in God was being displaced by a materialist outlook that was preoccupied with pleasure and entertainment. They also lamented that their language about sin and salvation was no longer understood. As they felt the loss of their influence, talk of drift from religion and the churches and of the loss of Christian standards in society became common among them.[23]

To their assessment of the times they added analysis of their own short-comings. Some said the churches were cold and lifeless. If this was an extreme judgement, more reasonable was the common charge that they lacked faith in their mission and in the gospel message. Allegedly the churches were more concerned with their own organization and activities than with reaching people outside. Or they were accused of promoting social programmes rather than engaging in serious evangelism. Although there were notable exceptions, the loss of evangelistic drive feared by Kilpatrick in 1919 seemed to have occurred within a few years of the end of the War.[24]

Another sign of loss of commitment to conversionism was the failure of mass revivalism to revive after the hiatus of the War years. Gipsy Smith and Billy Sunday were the leading pre-war evangelists who continued to ply their trade, but both were in the twilight of long careers. New evangelists also arose, among them W. P. Nicholson in Northern Ireland, Jack Troup in England and John Ridley in Australia. But there were fewer of them, and none made a mark comparable with the leading figures of former ages.[25] Large-scale international revivalism had also fallen away. Chapman died in 1918, Alexander followed in 1920 and Torrey was preoccupied with the fundamentalist cause until his death in 1928. In the decade after the War no one arose to take their place. Indeed there was much less demand for such services as the case against mass revivalism strengthened. It was said to be more about the aggrandizement and enrichment of the revivalist than revival. In any case, cost–benefit analysis suggested revival meetings were not worth the expense. Although its techniques were taken up

----

22. E.g. 'Revival and Reconstruction', *C* (7 July 1921), 3; '1921 – A Review', *C* (29 Dec. 1921), 1–3.
23. E.g. 'Practical Atheism', *C* (25 July 1935), 3–4; L. Fletcher, 'Shall Revival Come Again?', *EC* (Jan.–Feb. 1938), 1–2.
24. Kilpatrick, 'Church of the Twentieth Century', 415–416.
25. The lists of 'Evangelists at Work' in *The Christian* became shorter as the decade progressed.

by Pentecostals, in the 1920s revivalism was no longer the prominent feature on the evangelical landscape that it had been before 1914.

The failure of revivalism to revive reflected the eclipse of that evangelical ecumenism that had underpinned the great evangelistic enterprise of the *fin de siècle* era. In this aspect of the movement evangelicals also faced the irony that their shared desire to seize the post-war moment had given rise to different approaches that both weakened their evangelistic impact and discredited the integrity of the church.[26]

Liberal evangelicals responded to calls for a 'new evangelism'. While claiming continuity with historic evangelicalism, they wanted to dispense with the dogmas and traditions of former times in favour of 'vital Christianity' understood as 'the real Jesus' made accessible by scholarship and presented in relation to the needs and circumstances of the day. As one proponent stated:

> The evangelism of our time must appeal to the head as well as the heart; while refusing
> in any way to cheapen or to compromise all that Christ is and stands for, it nevertheless
> can and should set forth His significance and His claims with sanity and complete
> sincerity, with reality and entire relevance to the actual conditions of life to-day.[27]

The priorities of liberal evangelicals contributed to the progress of the religious education movement between the wars and countered the low estimate of human nature in Neo-orthodoxy and Christian Realism. While retaining the need for personal relationship with Christ, their message – more in the nature of apologetics and nurture than an appeal for conversion – also widened beyond concern for individual redemption to an aspiration for the salvation of whole communities.[28]

'Anti-modern' evangelicals felt no need to update or modify the 'old evangelism' in the light of culture.[29] For them it was still a matter of discharging the

---

26. This diversity is evident in D. P. Thomson (ed.), *The Modern Evangelistic Address* (New York: George H. Doran, 1925).

27. E. S. Woods, 'The Presentation of the Gospel at Home', in T. Guy Rogers (ed.), *Liberal Evangelicalism: An Interpretation by Members of the Church of England* (London: Hodder & Stoughton, 1923), 251–271 (267 for the quotation).

28. E.g. [D. P. Thomson and Hubert L. Simpson (eds.)], *Evangelism in the Modern World. Edited by Two University Men* (Glasgow: Thomson & Cowan, 1923), esp. Essays I, II, IX and X.

29. E.g. George Campbell Morgan, 'The Biblical Authority for Evangelism'; George Eayrs, 'Secrets of Whitefield and the Wesleys in the Evangelism of the Eighteenth Century', in E. Aldom French (ed.), *Evangelism: A Reinterpretation* (London: Epworth Press, 1921), 29–45, 120–152.

responsibility of declaring the Bible's message of God's desire and provision of redemption for human inadequacy and failure. Its basis remained the cross, which put an end to sin and its effects. These evangelicals insisted that the gospel is the condition of social progress:

> It is at that point that socialism breaks down when it leaves God and the regeneration of man out of its calculations. No League of Nations can maintain order in a world such as this, apart from the finding of a new spirit on the part of men.[30]

While it would benefit society, it must therefore be primarily personal and individual. The failure of civilization during the War and the inefficacy of alternatives meant that it was still the supreme need of individuals, society and the human race.

The development of alternative approaches to evangelism again caught centrist evangelicals between the two. Their dilemma is illustrated by the situation faced by the Presbyterian R. C. Gillie in his London context:

> I have ... a number of conservative evangelicals, and also ... a number of progressive thinkers. I am sometimes asked how I manage between these two constituencies, and my answer is always, 'By starting with the fundamental facts of human experience, and bringing in modern conceptions, not as subversions of the old, but as new interpretations of old experience.' My purpose is to conciliate, or rather to mediate. I want to try and secure that the 'broad' people shall be broad enough to include their 'narrow' brethren, and that the 'narrow' people shall learn to be sufficiently broad to believe in one spiritual experience of 'broad' people.[31]

Gillie's strategy typified the approach of the centrists, who welcomed new ideas and methods provided they did not suggest 'the substitution for old truths of modern conceptions of the Gospel'.[32]

These developments set the tone for the 1930s. Against the background of the 'Great Depression', evangelistic activity continued at various levels, but, apart from the significant exceptions to be considered below, apparently

---

30. Campbell Morgan, 'Biblical Authority for Evangelism', in ibid. 41.
31. E. Herman, 'Is the Church Holding Her Own. Interview with Rev. R. C. Gillie ... President-Elect of the National Free Church Council', *HomR* 81.1 (1921), 9–14 (12–13 for the quotation).
32. 'Books Worth Reading. *Evangelism in the Modern World*. By various writers', *EC* (Nov.–Dec. 1923), 180.

with no great expectation and to little effect.[33] The Depression encouraged the hope of a great spiritual revival to compensate for material decline (as apparently in the past); but none eventuated, except in distant East Africa.[34] In the eyes of the critics the churches had not taken advantage of the opportunities of the post-war moment for the 'furtherance of the Christian cause' and some observers acknowledged the failure of the reconstruction project.[35]

At one level the despondency of interwar evangelicals was unwarranted. Despite the perceptions, the available statistics show religious adherence held steady during the interwar years. In Britain, Protestant church membership recovered after the War and achieved new peaks in the mid-1920s. Only in the later 1930s was there a small fall.[36] Similarly in America in the 1920s religious adherence remained strong.[37] Again during the Depression decade, although the traditional, mainly white, denominations had stopped growing, there were no significant changes in church membership apart from a slight decline towards the end.[38] Similar patterns were evident in the 'neo-Britains' of Australia, New Zealand and Canada, where a broad Christian social framework could still be assumed.[39] And some evangelical churches actually expanded during the interwar years. This was the case with the Brethren in Britain. In America, Southern Baptists, minority (more sectarian) and immigrant churches also tended to grow. On the other hand, church membership was not the same thing as church attendance. Moreover, adherence was often regionally uneven. In these terms England, for example, was less 'religious' than Wales and

33. Rev. Herbert Lockyer, 'The Church and Its Mission', *C* (23 Mar. 1933), 22; 'A Year of Evangelization', *C* (3 Jan. 1935), 3–4.

34. Richard McMaster, *A Gentle Wind of God: The Influence of the East African Revival* (Scottdale, PA: Herald Press, 2006).

35. E.g. 'Needs of the Hour. Statement by Parliamentary Lay Preachers', *C* (1 Jan. 1931), 29; Henry W. Tiffey, 'The Church and the Cataclysm', *C* (22 June 1933), 19.

36. Robert Currie, Alan Gilbert and Lee Horsley, *Churches and Churchgoers: Patterns of Church Growth in the British Isles Since 1700* (Oxford: Clarendon Press, 1977), 25, 30.

37. H. C. Weber, *Evangelism: A Graphic Survey* (New York: Macmillan, 1929).

38. Samuel Kincheloe, *Research Memorandum on Religion in the Depression. Bulletin 33* (New York: Social Science Research Council, 1937).

39. Ian Breward, *A History of the Churches in Australasia* (Oxford: Clarendon Press, 2001), 247–250; Nancy Christie and Michael Gauvreau, *Christian Churches and Their Peoples, 1840–1965: A Social History of Religion in Canada* (Toronto: University of Toronto Press, 2010), ch. 4.

Scotland.[40] Whatever the figures and their meaning, the situation fell well short of the major Christian impact on society envisaged in 1919–20. For evangelicals generally a diffused 'culture Protestantism' was not authentic Christianity, and it was not enough merely to hold their own numerically. If they were not advancing, they were failing. Against this general background of decline from pre-war levels of enthusiasm and activity, some evangelicals took steps to restore the conversionist tradition of the movement.

Frank Buchman and the Oxford Group Movement

Frank Buchman, founder and leader of the Oxford Group Movement, was one evangelist who sought to return to earlier levels of evangelistic effectiveness.[41] An American Lutheran, he had decided at the Northfield Conference in 1901 that winning people for Christ would be his life's work. Seven years later an encounter with Jessie Penn-Lewis at Keswick led to recognition of the priority of Christian living over doctrinal correctness and a decision to live by the cross, 'the central experience of Christianity'.[42] From F. B. Meyer he learned the importance both of 'personal work' and reserving time at the beginning of each day to listen for God's guidance. Holding together and directing these aspirations was Moody's belief in the power of the consecrated individual and John Mott's ideal of 'the evangelisation of the world in this generation'.[43] In work with the YMCA at Pennsylvania State University and on the mission field in Asia he worked out his ideas on personal evangelism, which he taught for a brief period at Hartford Seminary. Buchman's roots were deep in *fin de siècle* evangelicalism, whose revivalist energy he carried forward into the middle decades of the twentieth century.

But Buchman also brought change. In seeking to bring about real conversion experiences, he and his teams differentiated themselves increasingly from the received pattern of revivalism, in method and somewhat in message. In the belief that there would be a leverage effect, they targeted leaders, a priority

40. S. J. D. Green, *The Passing of Protestant England: Secularisation and Social Change c. 1920–1960* (Cambridge: Cambridge University Press, 2011), 32–34.

41. Garth Lean, *Frank Buchman: A Life* (London: Constable, 1985); Daniel Sack, *Moral Re-Armament: The Reinventions of an American Religious Movement* (New York: Palgrave Macmillan, 2009).

42. Lean, *Frank Buchman*, 32.

43. Ibid. 81–82.

EVANGELISM AND MISSIONS IN THE MODERN WORLD 237

that led to a general concentration on society's 'up and outs'. Convinced that something less organized and more relational was needed, Buchman rejected large meetings in favour of individual evangelism through which it was possible to get at the root motives and desires of men and women. The preferred collective experience was the house party, an informal gathering over a weekend at a private home or country inn. Storytelling and sharing replaced the sermon as the means of conveying the message. To meet the post-war desire for reality and excitement, Buchman promoted adventurous and 'life-changing' Christian living through a personal experience of God. Adherents were supported through a network of cells that provided vital fellowship and intimate community. The elements were by no means novel, but by the time it became known as the Oxford Group Movement in 1928, Buchman's synthesis had forged a new path in evangelical outreach.[44]

From the first the vision of the movement was global. Inspired by Mott, Buchman felt that his calling was to raise a force of God-directed people and set out to transform the world. Believing that countries no less than individuals could become God-directed, he urged others to think in terms of nations and even continents. In the 1930s, as his focus moved from students to adults and their concerns, this aspiration seemed attainable. The strategy was still to concentrate on leaders, and through them to influence communities and whole societies. As its goals expanded, the movement's style changed. House parties were enlarged, traditional evangelical rallies were held, city-wide campaigns and even national assemblies were conducted. Its communication techniques became those of the mass movement – generation of its own literature and use of newspapers, radio and film. This shift culminated in 'New Enlistment Camps' in 1937 and 1938. Promoting conversion under the guise of 'life changing' as the basis of world transformation, Buchman and his teams travelled the globe.

Inevitably for one so confrontational in method, Buchman attracted criticism and encountered opposition. With varying degrees of justification, he was said to be self-important, extravagant, elitist, moralistic, prone to oversimplification, and dismissive of the views and efforts of others.[45] The similarities of his methods with those of the Nazis led to allegations that Buchman was a fascist. If this was unfair, a more serious criticism was that he lacked doctrinal substance. In fact, doctrinal minimalism was one reason for Buchman's success. It had

---

44. His ideas are presented in Frank N. D. Buchman, *Remaking the World: Selections from the Speeches of Dr Frank N. D. Buchman* (London: Heinemann, 1942).

45. E.g. Marjorie Harrison, *Saints Run Mad: A Criticism of the 'Oxford' Group Movement* (London: John Lane, 1934).

particular appeal to the evangelical left, where the need for doctrinal renegoti-
ation was most keenly felt. More broadly the practical emphasis and the reality
of changed lives had wide appeal. Buchman's optimism and emphasis on
spiritual adventure offered an alternative to the demoralization left over from
the War and stirred up by the Depression. His informality and independence
from established structures retained spiritual belief as an option for those who
found the churches lifeless and bound by convention. In the 1930s Buchman's
vision of a total Christianity was an answer to the appeal of fascism on the right
and communism on the left. While it deliberately posed as an alternative to
contemporary movements, it is clear in retrospect that in these matters the
Oxford Group Movement offered an expression of evangelicalism closely in
step with the times.[46]

Towards the end of the interwar era the Movement began its metamorphosis
into Moral Rearmament. As it did so, although retaining many of its features, it
was no longer distinctly evangelical. But, in becoming a minor mass movement,
it had made its mark. While the individual remained its primary target, in the
1930s hundreds, and sometimes thousands, attended the house parties and
(occasional) other meetings. Prominent people such as the head of Queen's
College, Oxford, B. H. Streeter, came out among its supporters. The Movement
also achieved the kind of social and political influence to which it aspired.
Among its achievements in this respect are said to be the moral basis for the
Norwegian resistance movement in the Second World War.[47] Whatever its
limitations, the Oxford Group Movement was the most successful conversionist
force in interwar evangelicalism, while Buchman was the outstanding international evangelist. No evangelical did more to realize the aspirations of the
movement for the post-war world.

Youth and student movements: SCM, IVF

Another response to the malaise in evangelism was a change in evangelistic
priorities. In the post-war years the focal point of concern shifted from men,
especially working-class men, towards youth. Of course the interest in the young
was not new. But the War brought a fresh consciousness of the capacities and

------

46. David W. Bebbington, 'The Oxford Group Movement', *SCH* 23 (1986), 495–507.
47. Anders Jarlert (1995), *The Oxford Group, Group Revivalism, and the Churches of Northern
    Europe, 1930–1945, with Special Reference to Scandinavia and Germany* (Lund: Lund
    University Press, 1995).

likely social impacts of young people. Their diminished numbers because of wartime losses and disaffection from Christianity meant that the churches now had less of the 'splendid enthusiasm and power of sacrifice' characteristic of youth, and also of 'the larger vision of life' of the War generation.[48] By the 1930s awareness of the absence of those who would have been in the prime of middle life sustained the sense of their importance. The feminization of Christianity and the relative absence of men from the churches remained a concern during the interwar years, but, with an eye on the future, recruiting youth became a leading evangelistic objective.

This priority was evident in the careers of dedicated individuals at various points around the evangelical world. Between 1930 and 1946, the Reverend William Orange conducted an influential ministry of Bible teaching and spiritual witness to the members of the Crusaders Union at Canterbury Boys' High School and the students of the Canterbury University College in Christchurch, New Zealand. Henrietta Mears developed an extensive work in Sunday schools from 1928 as Director of Christian Education at Hollywood Presbyterian Church and co-founder of Gospel Light Publications. From 1932 Eric Nash – better known as 'Bash' – as a travelling secretary and missioner of the Children's Special Service Mission maintained a camp ministry to evangelize the boys of English Public Schools.[49] Such efforts engendered numerous conversions and inspired many to take up the work of Christian ministry and witness. Among those so influenced were John Stott of later evangelical renown, Bill Bright, founder of Campus Crusade for Christ, and the noted Australian historian of the early Christian world, Edwin Judge.

The group attracting the greatest specific attention was university students. What had already been accomplished with them was evident in the operations of the World's Student Christian Federation, now a quarter of a century old.[50] However, as the new world order took shape, evangelicals recognized not only the need to evangelize the next generation of students amid an intense questioning of Christianity, but also their unique needs and interests as the post-war

---

48. 'Notes. The Oncoming Generation', *EC* (May–June 1923), 82.

49. Stuart Lange, *A Rising Tide: Evangelical Christianity in New Zealand 1930–65* (Dunedin: Otago University Press, 2013), ch. 3; Ethel M. Baldwin and David V. Benson, *Henrietta Mears and How She Did It!* (Glendale: Regal Books, 1967); John Eddison (ed.), *'Bash': A Study in Spiritual Power* (Basingstoke: Marshalls, 1983).

50. Philip Potter and Thomas Wieser, *Seeking and Serving the Truth: The First Hundred Years of the World Student Christian Federation* (Geneva: WCC Publications, 1997), esp. chs. 4–5.

cohort. Alongside this pastoral motive was an awareness of their deep strategic importance. Students would become the bearers of Christian civilization as the ministers, leaders and scholars of the future.[51]

Amid these developments the Student Christian Movement (SCM) remained the mainstay of Christian student work in Britain and 'Greater Britain'. In the rhetoric of the period it tended to be written off by the evangelical right as having rapidly descended into an intolerable modernism. In fact, the interwar SCM under the leadership of Tissington Tatlow and Robert Mackie followed a liberal evangelical agenda.[52] While it sought to be faithful to the Bible, it was receptive to biblical scholarship as a pathway to deeper spiritual understanding. Both at home and abroad the social application of the gospel loomed large in SCM thinking, which also welcomed the prospect of interdenominational cooperation brought by contemporary ecumenicalism. In 1929 it declared the only condition of membership was the 'desire to understand the Christian faith and to live the Christian life'.[53] There was enough in this standpoint to cause alarm for more conservative evangelicals who discerned doctrinal laxity and even apostasy. As tensions grew, the SCM sought to clarify its position by reaffirming the connection with the WSCF and its aim 'To lead students to accept the Christian faith in God . . . according to the Scriptures, and to live as true disciples of Jesus Christ'.

For all of the SCM's attempts at reassurance, the wider fissiparity of the era was reflected at the level of student work in the establishment of the Inter-Varsity Fellowship (IVF) in Britain in 1928.[54] The SCM had been unacceptable since 1910 to conservative evangelicals, who responded by setting up alternative evangelical unions in the British universities in the immediate post-war years. Suggested by the conferences of these unions held annually from 1919, the formation of the IVF as a rival organization was due in part to the drive of

---

51. E.g. William F. Quillian, 'How May Christ Be Brought to the Student World', *EMC 1931*, 383–386; R. P. Wilder, 'College and University Work as a Preparation for Christian Leadership', *RPC 1925*, 377–381.

52. Robin Boyd, *The Witness of the Student Christian Movement: 'Church Ahead of the Church'* (Geneva: WCC Publications, 2007).

53. From the 'Aims and Basis' of 1919. See Tissington Tatlow, *The Story of the Student Christian Movement of Great Britain and Ireland* (London: SCM Press, 1933), 628.

54. The standard accounts are Donald Coggan (ed.), *Christ and the Colleges: A History of the Inter-Varsity Fellowship of Evangelical Unions* (London: Inter-Varsity Fellowship, 1934); Douglas Johnson, *Contending for the Faith: A History of the Evangelical Movement in the Universities and Colleges* (Leicester: Inter-Varsity Press, 1979).

the founders to assert their identity as distinctly *evangelical* unions. Underlying this, as the constitution maintained, was the commitment 'to stimulate personal faith and to further evangelistic work among students'. The drawing power of the centre-right evangelicalism represented by the IVF was reflected in a decade of steady growth and development in the decade before the return of war. By 1940 it had extended its reach to all but one university in Britain and had groups in technical and teachers' colleges as well.

From its inception the IVF (like the SCM) developed internationally. At its first meeting a call from Canada resulted in the despatch of Howard Guinness to establish evangelical groups in the Canadian universities. Following the formation of the IVF of Canada in September 1929, Guinness continued on to fresh fields in Australia and New Zealand where, during 1930–1 and again in 1933–4, he achieved similar results.[55] The IVF was taken to the United States by one of those influenced by Guinness. During the mid-1930s the Australian Stacey Woods established a reputation as an energetic and able student leader as General Secretary of the Canadian IVF.[56] Readily responding to overtures from American student groups, in the late 1930s Woods built up a grass-roots student movement on campuses in the United States, initially under the direction of the Canadian Board but then, from 1941, under an American counterpart.[57]

One reason for the growth of the IVF was its reaffirmation of the trans-denominational character of evangelicalism evident in welcoming students and workers from varying denominational backgrounds. It also furnished in student work a more conservative alternative to the SCM by its insistence on traditional spiritual goals, a high view of biblical authority and substitutionary atonement. This appealed to students such as the Canadian Melvin Donald who, in their university days, looked for familiar teaching and piety.[58] Yet, of the two student organizations, the SCM remained the stronger. Some students such as the future evangelist and ecumenist Lesslie Newbigin (1909–98) preferred the SCM. In any case, although there was occasional conflict, relations between the IVF and

---

55. Howard Guinness, *Journey Among Students* (Sydney: Anglican Information Office, 1978).

56. A. Donald MacLeod, *C. Stacey Woods and the Evangelical Rediscovery of the University* (Downers Grove: IVP Academic, 2007).

57. C. Stacey Woods, *The Growth of a Work of God: The Story of the Early Days of the Inter-Varsity Christian Fellowship of the United States of America As Told by Its First General Secretary* (Downers Grove: InterVarsity Press, 1978).

58. John G. Stackhouse, Jr., *Canadian Evangelicalism in the Twentieth Century: An Introduction to Its Character* (Toronto: University of Toronto Press, 1993), 89.

SCM were not always as strained as partisan accounts suggest.[59] In some places there was open and cordial cooperation between the two groups. Nor was the gap between them unbridgeable. The young F. F. Bruce joined both groups, and this was not uncommon. As in the wider movement, a middling position existed in student work as the two organizations coexisted. In both its expansion and outlook, however, the nascent IVF gave satisfaction to the evangelical right. This provided encouragement to strong leaders such as Woods and the Englishman Douglas Johnson to build a network of full-time workers and many more volunteers to work on campuses all around the evangelical world. Perhaps their greatest achievement was to counter the sense among evangelicals of the 1930s that the golden age of student work was in the past and the increasingly secular universities were no longer likely recruiting grounds for the gospel.

Revival of revivalism

A third response to the depressed condition of evangelism a decade or so after the Great War was a new literature recalling evangelicalism to its evangelistic heritage. From around 1930 a steady flow of books and a new periodical took up the cause of evangelism.[60] Marked by varying degrees of urgency, the writers evinced several important themes. All protested against neglect of evangelism by the contemporary churches. Appalled by the blandishments of materialism and humanistic culture, they also declared the era to be one of great need. The obstacles they identified repeated familiar criticisms and recommendations: the churches were self-absorbed; outdated, counterproductive methods should be avoided; there was a need for able, passionate and dedicated preachers to bring a definite message with a call for decisions. Whatever the perspective, there was broad agreement on the method: the cross of Christ needed again to be lifted up in the midst of society. Its example of sacrifice would motivate the churches; its message of redemption would provide the solution to humanity's need. At the same time there was an unmistakable narrowing of vision.

---

59. E.g. Lange, *Rising Tide*, pt. 1, esp. ch. 4.
60. Lionel B. Fletcher, *Effective Evangelism* (London: Religious Tract Society, 1932);
    Conquering Evangelism (London: Marshall, Morgan & Scott, 1946); J. Ernest
    Rattenbury, *Evangelism: Its Shame and Glory* (London: Epworth Press, 1932);
    F. C. White, *Evangelism Today* (London: Marshall, Morgan & Scott, n.d.). The
    periodical was *Evangelism: A Monthly Bulletin of Evangelistic Work in the Church
    of England*, begun in 1935.

Motivation was now in the main a pietistic intention to obey the command of Christ or an impassioned call to save a denomination. If it had not quite disappeared, the hope of building a Christian civilization by widespread conversion was much less prominent than ten years previously.

The literature heralded steps to revive mass evangelism on an international scale. In the forefront of this development was the World Evangelisation Trust which in 1932 appointed the Australian Methodist Lionel Fletcher as 'Empire Evangelist'.[61] A veteran of the 1909 Chapman–Alexander mission in Adelaide, he had subsequently held successful pastorates in Wales (1916–22) and New Zealand (1924–32). Determined to overcome the contemporary aversion to evangelism, he approached the task with passionate commitment: 'We must make the campaigns audacious in their aims, and in their extent – we must simply attack Christendom, and demand an answer to our question . . . What will you do with Jesus?'[62] Based in London, Fletcher led evangelistic campaigns through the 1930s in Britain, South Africa, Australia and New Zealand, covering in all more than 300,000 miles by land, sea and now air. He supplemented public campaigning by explaining and commending evangelism by writing and an extensive personal correspondence. Continuing in the role until 1941, and preaching a message of repentance from sin as the basis of conversion, Fletcher was a reminder of what had been achieved in international evangelism before the War. Historian of revivals and revivalism J. Edwin Orr rated Fletcher, said to be responsible for 250,000 conversions, the outstanding evangelist of the interwar period.[63]

The view that only revival could restore Christianity to its proper place in society was pursued on a global scale by Edwin Orr himself.[64] Well aware from his Belfast background of the part played by revivals in church and national renewal, as a 20-year-old he was appalled that great numbers were not being added to the churches and Christianity was not shaping society. Determined to do something about it, Orr took three steps. One was to set up the Revival Fellowship, an organization intended to put the work for revival on a systematic basis. Second, in 1933, he set out personally to exhort the churches worldwide

61. C. W. Malcolm, *Twelve Hours in the Day: The Life and Work of Rev. Lionel B. Fletcher* (London: Marshall, Morgan & Scott, 1956).

62. Ibid. 118.

63. J. Edwin Orr, 'A Call for the Re-Study of Revival and Revivalism', 51, at www.jedwinorr.com/resources/pdf/Orr_Revival_and_Revivalism.pdf.

64. A. J. Appasamy, *Write the Vision: Edwin Orr's Thirty Years of Adventurous Service* (London: Marshall, Morgan & Scott, 1964).

to pray for and expect revival, and to demonstrate the power of God to bring it about by relying on him for leading and provision. After pursuing this mission throughout Britain, for two years from early in 1935 Orr circled the world, visiting forty-eight countries and territories in Europe, the Middle East, North America, New Zealand, Australia and Southern Africa. Third, Orr published narrative reports as he went with a view to providing verifiable accounts of God's redemptive activity in the world and encouraging eagerness for revival.[65]

Edwin Orr's activities connected with other revivalist cells around the world. Of these perhaps the most important was the New England Fellowship (NEF) created in 1931 by the real-estate businessman J. Elwin Wright.[66] Open to evangelicals of all stripes, Wright's enterprise brought hope at a low point in America and soon achieved a wide following in the New England region. His efforts in the late 1930s to reproduce on a national scale the cooperation enjoyed by the NEF led to the establishment of the National Association of Evangelicals (NAE) in 1942. Among the instruments created was a Secretariat for Evangelism to 'formulate plans for the promotion of . . . co-operative evangelistic efforts' in the hope of bringing about the revival that would sweep America and the world.[67]

At the same time as the NAE was taking shape radio began to realize its potential as an evangelistic agency. By 1932, with radio established as the country's primary leisure activity, over 400 evangelical radio programmes on 80 different stations were available in America. Use of radio by fundamentalist evangelists reached its high point with Charles E. Fuller's 'Old Fashioned Revival Hour'.[68] Heard nationwide, by 1940 it reached an estimated audience of 20 million listeners. This was an achievement that did much to restore the legitimacy of revivalist Christianity in the eyes of the American people following the setbacks of the 1920s. While the conversionist impact of such programming

---

65. Summarized in J. Edwin Orr, *Such Things Happen: 100,000 Miles Around the Globe* (London: Marshall, Morgan & Scott, n.d. [1937]).

66. Elizabeth Evans, *The Wright Vision: The Story of the New England Fellowship* (Lanham, Md.: Fellowship Press, 1991); Joel Carpenter, *Revive Us Again: The Reawakening of American Fundamentalism* (New York: Oxford University Press, 1997), ch. 8.

67. James D. Murch, *Cooperation Without Compromise: A History of the National Association of Evangelicals* (Grand Rapids: Eerdmans, 1956), ch. 9, with the quotation (the words of Harold J. Ockenga) on 112.

68. Phillip Goff, '"We Have Heard the Joyful Sound": Charles E. Fuller's Radio Broadcast and the Rise of Modern Evangelicalism', *RAC* 9.1 (1999), 67–95.

cannot be measured exactly, some 500,000 conversions are attributed to it. Evangelical radio even appeared to hold out hope of winning back Western civilization to the Christian message evangelicals believed had made it great.

The prospects for evangelism were also bolstered by the convergence of the changing theological setting and the menacing ideological climate in the later 1930s. Neo-orthodoxy's boldness as a self-consciously public theology seemed to address the urgency of the world situation as the likelihood of war increased. As one pundit observed, 'It brings life to the individual soul, and supplies the tired preacher with a burning evangelical message.'[69] At the same time developments on the world stage were almost literally brought home by the World Union of Freethinkers Conference – otherwise known as the 'Godless Conference' – held in London in the fateful September of 1938.[70] The statement made in 1937 by the Presbyterian Churches holding the Reformed Faith was typical of the response of contemporary evangelicals as they confronted the spectre of atheistic totalitarianism:

> We believe that God's purpose of grace extends to the whole world, and that the Church is His instrument for bringing the Gospel to all men. Alien creeds are being proclaimed which aim at converting the whole world: atheism has become militant and missionary; nationalism is claiming to be the supreme rule of faith and life . . . The supreme need is for men and women whose life has been renewed and consecrated. By the world's distress the urgency of the missionary command is intensified that in the name of Christ His followers should go into all the world and preach the Gospel.[71]

Such sentiments recalled the outlook of evangelicals early in 1919 as they confronted the task of reconstruction. While the prospect of the renewal of hostilities twenty years later was a reminder of earlier failure, it also bolstered the faith of evangelicals in the surpassing value of their message for civilization. After a period of disappointment, circumstances once more seemed to be holding out

---

69. Allan J. MacDonald, 'Professor Karl Barth and the Theology of Crisis', *Ch* 46.3 (1932), 201.

70. Ben Edwards, 'The Godless Congress of 1938: Christian Fears About Communism in Great Britain', *JRH* 37.1 (2013), 1–19.

71. 'Pronouncement on Matters of Faith and Life', *RPC 1937*, 221. Cf. papers under the rubric 'Civil and Religious Freedom, World Peace (and related topics)', *WBC 1939*, 186–225; and the papers read at the Oxford Conference of Evangelical Churchmen in 1939 on the general subject of 'spiritual rearmament' in *Ch* 4.2, NS (Apr.–June 1939).

the prospect of a reversal of evangelicals' loss of cultural authority by their preaching for conversion, differences over aims and methods notwithstanding.

Missions between the wars

As with evangelism at home, enthusiasm for missions was part of the evangelical scheme for reconstruction. From this standpoint the inescapably transformative effect of the gospel in the new world order would raise social standards and ideals of social service and international harmony in the countries that constituted the mission field. With missions in mind, the Southern Baptist J. F. Love averred in 1920, 'the world may now get a new start if the right forces can be applied to the moral impulses and powers of men'.[72] This aspiration presupposed the continuation of the pre-war Anglo-American enterprise and turned on the simple hope that missions would pick up from where they had been obliged to leave off because of the War. Discerning eyes soon perceived that this expectation was unrealistic and that the place of missions in the new world order required reconsideration. As a result missions – their motive, message, methods and objectives – became a subject for lively debate within evangelicalism through the interwar years.[73]

At least three forces interacted during the 1920s to destabilize the pre-war evangelical conception of missions. One was the new vision of Christian internationalism in which missions were seen as a key part of the emerging world order with a leading role to play in promoting understanding, friendship and cooperation across national and racial boundaries as a basis for peace.[74] This style of thinking that viewed missions as achieving the ostensible aims of the War was consistent with the traditional evangelical conception, but also enlarged it. Second, the War had changed the conditions under which the missionary enterprise was conducted. On the mission field itself the 'War of Christendom' had discredited the sending nations of the West, while the Wilsonian principle of self-determination nurtured a nationalism that condemned Christianity as a

---

72. J. F. Love, 'Baptist Missions in the New World Order', *RE* 17.3 (1920), 251–266 (quotation on 265).

73. This section draws on Robert Wright, *A World Mission: Canadian Protestantism and the Quest for a New International Order, 1918–1939* (Montreal: McGill-Queen's University Press, 1991).

74. Dana Robert, 'The First Globalization: The Internationalization of the Protestant Missionary Movement Between the World Wars', *IBMR* 26.2 (2002), 50–66.

foreign religion. In the sending societies interest shifted from 'foreign' to 'world' mission, a change signalled by the virtual collapse of the Student Volunteer Movement (SVM) from the mid-1920s and replacement of the pre-war watchword ('the evangelization of the world in this generation') with 'world Christianization' as a slogan more in keeping with the enthusiasms and pre-occupations of the reconstruction era.[75] Third, implementation of the decisions of Edinburgh 1910, particularly the establishment of the International Missionary Council (IMC) in 1921, brought the new Protestant ecumenicalism to bear on missions. The paradigm it fostered promoted reconsideration of relations between the older churches of the West and the younger churches of Africa and Asia, attitudes towards the non-Christian religions and the cultural impact of missions. These issues were faced squarely in 1928 at the Jerusalem Council, which acknowledged the advent of a new era of plurality in missions by endorsing indigenization of local mission churches and measured cooper-ation with the historic religions of the East to resist materialism and secularization. The involvement of evangelicals in these decisions indicated that the evangelical missionary consensus was breaking down.

A demand for the modernization of missions took shape alongside these developments. Begun even before the end of the War,[76] it was carried through the 1920s by calls for a realistic restatement of the missionary appeal, proper professional training for intending missionaries based on up-to-date cultural and scientific knowledge, surrender of the cultural pretensions of Western missionaries and reformulation of the missionary message to concentrate on Christ as the unique revelation of God. Pressure for modernization culmin-ated in the Laymen's Foreign Missions Inquiry, which, initiated and funded by industrial magnate J. D. Rockefeller, ran for two years (1930–2) under the chair-manship of the Harvard Philosophy professor W. E. Hocking. It resulted in a report that abandoned the normativeness of Christianity and necessity of explicit evangelization. In their place it advocated collaboration with non-Christian religions in the cause of developing a universal religion as an alternative to secularism. Widely read, the Hocking Report and its construction of mission as a contribution to religious universalism and social and political enablement was generally dismissed as 'another gospel' and 'not . . . of the evangelical faith

75. Michael Parker, *The Kingdom of Character: The Student Volunteer Movement for Foreign Missions (1886–1926)* (Lanham, MD: American Society of Missiology and University Press of America, 1998), chs. 8–9.

76. E.g. J. Lovell Murray, *The Call of a World Task in War Time*, rev. ed. (New York: Association Press, 1918).

or of the New Testament'.[77] Confronted by a new conception of 'salvation', evangelicals generally at this point thought the reconsideration of missionary motivation had gone too far.

Evangelical responses to these developments in missionary thinking ran along the same lines evident elsewhere in the contemporary movement.[78] Evangelicals on the left were able to reach varying degrees of accommodation with the new perspective. Adaptation was represented outstandingly on the home front by the Scottish Presbyterian J. H. Oldham who, as a layman, emerged between the wars as one of the key leaders of Protestant missions; and, on the field, by the American Methodist E. Stanley Jones who, primarily in relation to an Indian setting, showed the way in trying to find an expression of Christianity that separated Christ from Western culture.[79] While as ever in reconciling progressive thinking with the evangelical tradition the challenge was to determine how far they could go with radical modernist theorists, liberal evangelicals retained the ultimate propriety of seeking to convert non-Westerners to Christianity.

In direct contrast right-wing evangelicals resisted pressure to modernize their missionary endeavours. From the first Pentecostals made the mission field a primary sphere of their operations, preaching a 'full gospel' of individual salvation, physical healing, personal holiness and baptism of the Spirit with great urgency in view of the impending return of Christ, a priority that was to have spectacular results in Asia, Africa and Latin America after 1945.[80] Similarly the 'faith' missions and other very conservative missionary societies spurned any broadening of the missionary task as a reprehensible declension from the biblical mandate.[81] Responding to specific texts and the missionary message of the Bible as a whole, these evangelicals maintained wholehearted commitment to missions

---

77. Alexander McLeish, 'Re-Thinking Missions', *WD* 11.2 (Apr. 1933), 164–166.

78. James A. Patterson, 'The Loss of a Protestant Missionary Consensus: Foreign Missions and the Fundamentalist–Modernist Conflict', in Joel A. Carpenter and Wilbert Shenk (eds.), *Earthen Vessels: American Evangelicals and Foreign Missions, 1880–1980* (Grand Rapids: Eerdmans, 1990), 73–91.

79. Keith W. Clements, *Faith on the Frontier: A Life of J. H. Oldham* (Edinburgh: T. & T. Clark, 1999); Paul A. J. Martin, *Missionary of the Indian Road: The Theology of Stanley Jones* (Bangalore: Theological Book Trust, 1996).

80. Allan Anderson, *Spreading Fires: The Missionary Nature of Early Pentecostalism* (London: SCM Press, 2007).

81. Joel A. Carpenter, 'Propagating the Faith Once Delivered: The Fundamentalist Missionary Enterprise, 1920–1945', in Carpenter and Shenk, *Earthen Vessels*, 92–132.

as uncompromising evangelism throughout the interwar years and denied divine revelation in any significant sense to other religions.

Centrist evangelicals likewise remained committed to the traditional claims of evangelical Christianity, but evinced a willingness to follow the leadership of the IMC and to make adjustments in the light of new missiological insights.[82] This partial modernization of missions lamented the false antithesis between evangelism and social service and allowed the legitimacy of the indigenization of mission churches and the incorporation of local cultural traditions into non-Western Christianity. It could even stretch to a measure of cooperation with non-Christian religions in the struggle with irreligion and materialism. Such semi-progressive views appealed because, not only were they consistent with the traditional evangelical conception of missions, but they could also strengthen the gospel message by removing cultural barriers to its acceptance. Easily the largest segment of the movement, centrists combined their certainty about the primacy of evangelism in missions with a deep interest in what would make it effective.

Although the pre-war missionary consensus among evangelicals had broken down by the mid-1930s, because of their common commitment to the superiority of Christianity they were generally gratified by the return of a more aggressively evangelistic vision of missions towards the end of the interwar era. In addition to the reaction to the Hocking Report, this was caused by the financial austerity required by the Depression that focused attention on the true purposes of mission. Militant nationalism and communism in Asia as well as Europe also emphasized the world's need of the regenerative and unifying power of Christianity. Evangelicals received a further boost from *The Christian Message in a Non-Christian World* written in preparation for the IMC's council at Madras late in 1938 by the Dutch missiologist Hendrik Kraemer.[83] A reflection of Neo-orthodoxy, his concept of 'biblical realism' answered the relativism of the day by both affirming the uniqueness of the revelation of God in Christ and asserting its corollary that non-Christian religions should be confronted and converted. At Madras missions, promoted as the only force that could establish a genuinely universal brotherhood, were conceived of as part of a strong Christian witness in the face of totalitarianism. Within a year it had become obvious that this witness had been insufficient to prevent a new outbreak of war, but it did mean that in missions, as in other areas of evangelicalism, the interwar era came to an end with a resurgence of evangelical aims and hopes.[84]

---

82. E.g. Kenneth S. Latourette, *Missions Tomorrow* (New York: Harper & Brothers, 1936).

83. H. Kraemer, *The Christian Message in a Non-Christian World* (London: IMC, 1938).

84. E.g. W. O. Carver, 'Madras', *RE* 36.2 (1939), 214–218.

These developments in missions provided the setting for much of the later career of John Mott.[85] As he was chairman of the IMC in its first twenty years, missions now became the focal point of his life and work. With characteristic organizational flair, he prosecuted the ecumenical agenda of indigenization and empowerment of local churches, cooperation of Christians of different denominations and outlooks, and opposition to the injustices of colonialism. As part of this undertaking he promoted the Jerusalem Council of 1928 as 'the first truly representative global assembly of Christians in the long history of the Church' and a strong forward movement of the Christian forces of the world in the face of materialism, nationalism, pan-Islamism and communism.[86] Ten years later Mott organized the Tambaram Missionary Conference, in his own estimation the greatest of his three world mission conferences, and, against the background of rising international tensions, 'a unifying event in the life of the whole church'.[87] Mott's expansive evangelicalism, which did not escape criticism, enabled him to influence the World Council of Churches 'in process of formation' in the later 1930s, a contribution that led eventually to his being made Honorary President of the organization in 1948 and to the award of the Nobel Peace Prize in 1946.[88] Although his centre-left activism took Mott in directions of which other evangelicals disapproved, he insisted to the end that evangelism was his vocation. In all that this meant and led to John Mott was the most significant evangelical leader of his era.

Conclusion

In 1919 as evangelicals addressed the post-war world they recognized the importance of evangelism at home and abroad for the reconstruction project. Initially reaffirmation of conversionism by post-war evangelicals sustained the use of traditional evangelistic methods and encouraged innovation. But the effects of the War combined with unfavourable cultural and structural change

---

85. John R. Mott, *Five Decades and a Forward View* (London: Harper & Brothers, 1939), chs. 3–6; William R. Hogg, *Ecumenical Foundations: A History of the International Missionary Council and Its Nineteenth-Century Background* (New York: Harper & Brothers, 1952), chs. 6–7, with quotations on 244, 301.

86. Ibid. 244.

87. Ibid. 301.

88. C. Howard Hopkins, *John R. Mott 1865–1955: A Biography* (Grand Rapids: Eerdmans, 1979), 685–689, 695–698.

to make the work of outreach in English-speaking societies much harder than expected. This dampened the early enthusiasm for evangelism and explains in part the failure of contemporary evangelicals to restore the drive and organ-ization of the early twentieth-century evangelistic campaigns. In missions too, early post-war expectations proved to be misplaced and, as zeal for foreign work weakened, had to be adjusted to the new conditions. However, the declension in the commitment of evangelicals to evangelism as the means of extending their influence in the world seems to have bottomed around 1930. By that point a reaction had already begun. Through the Oxford Group Movement Frank Buchman developed pre-1914 conversionism in new and unexpected ways. The IVF represented a fresh focus on student recruitment as a way of renewing Christian leadership and missionary endeavour. The response to evangelistic weakness built through the 1930s by means of the activities of revivalists such as Lionel Fletcher and Charles Fuller together with the less public initiatives of other highly motivated individuals. These undertakings were upheld by a renewed sense against the background of totalitarianism in Europe that the message of evangelical Christianity answered the questions and satisfied the hopes of the interwar generation. Similarly in the missionary movement confidence in the Christian message and the need to take it to the world revived in the later 1930s. Evangelicals shared in the apprehensions of their con-temporaries as the spectre of war again cast its shadow over the world, but finished the interwar period with a renewed sense of the importance for the world of the conversionist dimension of their tradition.

While confidence in the evangelical message had been restored by 1940, through the interwar years it had not been the same energizing and binding force as in previous eras. The conversionist-activist axis in the evangelical synthesis weakened as zeal for evangelism at home and abroad declined and as disagree-ment between the main divisions in the movement about recruitment marred the evangelistic endeavour that did take place. The tensions of the era were also evident in responses to Frank Buchman and the rivalries in the student movement. Differences about the purposes and methods of missions also caused the pre-war missionary consensus to break down. Again such differences discredited evan-gelicalism and hampered the efforts of evangelicals to secure conversion on a large scale. The differences of diversity were one of the main reasons for the years that followed the end of the 'Great War' not being one of the great eras in the history of evangelical conversionism, and for failure to realize the hope that a combination of evangelism, revival and vigorous missionary activity would achieve the levels of adherence required to enable a Christian civilization.

12. A GREAT REVERSAL?

Among evangelicals generally there was no question that the work of post-war reconstruction would also involve social and political engagement. While they readily acknowledged that the great political and social issues of the day were primarily the responsibility of governments, they also insisted that there be a Christian voice on such questions for the attainment and operation of a truly Christian civilization. The sanguineness of contemporary evangelicals is evident in the comment of Archibald Jamieson of the United Free Church of Scotland: 'Whenever you use that word "Christian" you affirm a truth that is without boundaries, social or national, and of universal application, and therefore it is that no society of men is better fitted to give the new direction of thought than the Christian Church.'[1] This was not taken to mean that evangelicals should provide a programme for the reconstruction of society. But it did entail the responsibility to furnish the moral principles and power the world needed supported by actions both remedial and constructive in character. Again the important analysis of T. B. Kilpatrick of Toronto indicated that the standing of the Church in the world was at stake:

---

1. Archibald Jamieson, 'The Individual and Society', *CWP* (23 Apr. 1919), 108–110 (quotation on 109).

the Church cannot surrender the function which belongs to it as representative and instrument of the right royal rule of God, or cease to interpret and apply the principles of His righteous sovereignty to the various situations and problems with which men in society are confronted. To do so would incur the contempt even of men who did not believe in God and were not prepared to bow to His will.[2]

As with the life of faith, the capacity of evangelicals to present a picture of a social order spiritualized and Christianized would be the desideratum of success. Thinking of this order guided evangelicals as they set out to provide the post-war world with spiritual and moral leadership on the social and political questions of the day commended by the example of their own actions and corporate life.

The role evangelicals claimed for themselves in the reconstruction of the post-war world runs counter to one of the shibboleths of evangelical historiography. During the interwar years there is said to have been a 'great reversal', a distinct loss of interest in social service and political reform among evangelicals in favour of self-centred church concerns and activities.[3] This interpretation originated with the 'new' fundamentalists in America just after the Second World War as they distinguished themselves from the 'old' fundamentalists whom they hoped to supersede. Their view was not without good grounds, for there were certainly interwar evangelicals, such as Billy Sunday and the English Anglican E. L. Langston, who mounted theological objections to social ministry alongside evangelistic and pastoral ministry.[4] For it to be correct, however, explicit rejection of social ministry and significantly reduced social engagement would have to have been the characteristic position of the interwar evangelical movement as a whole. Some allowance would also have to be made for an understandable reaction against the prominence of social ministry during the War. Further, the interpretation involves the improbable surrender of the cultural authority to which post-war evangelicals aspired. It has already been shown in chapter 5 that, while a tendency to retreat from social engagement was present within the

2. T. B. Kilpatrick, 'The Church of the Twentieth Century', *ConsQ* 7.27 (Sept. 1919), 407–408, 419–425.
3. David Moberg, *The Great Reversal: Evangelism and Social Concern*, rev. ed. (Philadelphia: J. B. Lippincott, 1977).
4. See David W. Bebbington, 'The Decline and Resurgence of Evangelical Social Concern 1918–1980', in John Wolffe (ed.), *Evangelical Faith and Public Zeal: Evangelicals and Society in Britain 1780–1980* (London: SPCK, 1995), 175–197, esp. 177–179; Matthew A. Sutton, *American Apocalypse: A History of Modern Evangelicalism* (Cambridge, MA: Belknap Press, 2014), 33–34, 39–42, 293–295.

movement, it had not gone very far before the War. Did this change after 1918? Was there in fact a 'great reversal' during the interwar decades?[5]

Peace, the League of Nations and disarmament[6]

In the years immediately after 1918 evangelicals took a distinct interest in the formation of the new world order.[7] Continued reflection on their recent experience sustained the determination to ensure that the return to peace served their Christianizing agenda. No evangelical of note entertained any doubt about the justice or the necessity of their involvement in the War. Equally everybody was glad of the fact of victory and the opportunity to build a Christian society. While transition to a principled and worthwhile peace required reiteration of the evangelical case for the War, the successful outcome imposed a responsibility to achieve their war aims, harvest the fruits of victory and realize the divine purpose. Getting the most out of the War was a strong undercurrent in evangelical attitudes to the world in the years that followed.

Framing this interest in world affairs among evangelicals was their version of the Christian internationalism that developed during the post-war years.[8]

---

5. The need for a more wide-ranging and nuanced account of interwar evangelical social activism is also suggested by David Bebbington's qualifications in his review of the British evidence in 'The Decline and Resurgence of Evangelical Social Concern' and by the ambiguities in the premillennialist position pinpointed in Sutton's revisionist account of 'radical evangelicalism' in *American Apocalypse*, esp. 34–39. For Baptists as a case study, see Geoffrey R. Treloar, 'Baptists and the World 1900–1940: A "Great Reversal"?', in David Bebbington and Martin Sutherland (eds.), *Interfaces: Baptists and Others* (Milton Keynes: Paternoster Press, 2013), 177–198.

6. This section owes much to Robert Wright, *A World Mission: Canadian Protestantism and the Quest for a New International Order, 1918–1939* (Montreal: McGill-Queen's University Press, 1991).

7. See e.g. the session on 'Christ and the Peace of the World', *EMC 1921*, 208–229; the report on 'Congregationalism and International Relations', *ICC 1920*, 354–373; W. A. Curtis, 'Christianity a Force in National Life and International Relations', *RPC 1921*, 104–110; and Arthur J. Brown, 'The World Message of the Church', ibid. 315–320.

8. E.g. Basil Mathews, 'Introduction', in Basil Mathews (ed.), *World Brotherhood* (London: Hodder & Stoughton, 1919); Sherwood Eddy, *Everybody's World* (New York: Association Press, 1920).

Generally understood as a consciousness of international relations as a domain for the application of Christian principles, its immediate aim was goodwill and understanding between the nations. Christian internationalism also held that only Christianity provided the basis for a lasting peace, because it alone furnished an outlook sufficiently large and compelling to displace selfish nationalism. In addition to the evangelism at home and abroad noted in chapter 11, its specific responsibilities included promotion of peace and cooperation between nations and the Christianization of international relations. The spur to activism both conversionist and social was pinpointed by one contemporary editorialist writing from a standpoint well to the right on the evangelical spectrum of opinion: 'The keen Christian will take a deep interest in every world movement in order that he may discover how to take advantage of it for the highest ends.'[9] Of course Christian internationalism was not universally embraced within interwar evangelicalism. Many on the centre-right of the movement opposed entanglement in world affairs by overt social and political action. However, others on the centre-left wanted to discover what could actually be achieved by applying Christian principles to the mechanisms of international relations and gave extensive support for agencies promoting better international relations and turning them to Christian ends.[10]

The immediate concern was the peace settlement that would formally end the War. With barely an exception holding Germany responsible, evangelicals in the early months of 1919 looked forward to arrangements that would be just and righteous but not vengeful. When the Treaty of Versailles was promulgated in June, they were generally satisfied with terms judged to be harsh but consistent with Christian standards.[11] At the same time they were concerned that the Germans had not embraced the principle of 'war guilt'. Nevertheless they hoped that in time the settlement would provide a basis for reconciliation and harmony. By the end of the year they had realized that, with militarism uncurbed, the Great War might not have been 'the war to end all wars'.[12] In these circumstances

9. 'Editorial. World Movements of Moment', *WD* 6.4 (Oct. 1928), 319–327 (quotation on 327).

10. For the involvement of Theodore Woods, Alfred Garvie and Joseph Oldham, see Kenneth C. Barnes, *Nazism, Liberalism and Christianity: Protestant Social Thought in Germany and Great Britain 1925–1937* (Lexington: University Press of Kentucky, 1991), 41–42, 52–55, 104–106.

11. G. H. Morrison, 'Peace', *C* (10 July 1919), 7–8; 'Notes and Comments. The Peace Treaty. The Vindication', ibid. 8.

12. 'Looking Back. An Eventful Year', *C* (25 Dec. 1919), 1–3.

evangelicals saw that the Treaty was a mere beginning and recognized that their role would be to provide the spiritual force necessary to make peace real.[13]

Among the consequences was support for the League of Nations. Evangelicals generally welcomed the League as the instrument of peace required by the new world order. If they did not go so far as the Federal Council of Churches in America and declare the League 'the political expression of the kingdom of God on earth',[14] from their standpoint it was hailed as an instrument of God's eirenic purpose, even a fulfilment of prophecy. Many American evangelicals joined the campaign for the ratification of the Treaty of Versailles that brought the League into existence, and they shared in the wider disappointment when opponents – supported by evangelicals on the right (mostly fundamentalists) – kept America out of the League.[15] Even apart from this crippling defect, evangelicals acknowledged the difficulty of making such an organization (and its underlying ideals) effective. Recognizing that only a Christian underpinning of public opinion could make it work, they undertook (as with the Treaty of Versailles) to create the moral conditions for its effectiveness.[16] The responsibility to evangelize and advocate the Christian standpoint followed, but also the obligation to pray for the League and to lobby and work for its success. Over the next fifteen years or so, as the League came under increasing pressure evangelicals maintained their belief in the ideal embodied by the League and hoped for its success.

As the difficulties of maintaining the peace grew through the 1920s and into the 1930s, evangelicals also evinced an interest in the peace movement. Many recognized the maintenance of peace as the great moral challenge of the era and accepted the corresponding obligation to promote universal brotherhood and international accord.[17] The actions they were prepared to take included passing resolutions at the congresses of the evangelical churches calling on their people and governments to make the maintenance of peace their first aim and

---

13. 'Peace and Its Issues', *EC* (July–Aug. 1919), 85.

14. Martin E. Marty, *Modern American Religion*. Vol. 2: *The Noise of Conflict 1919–1941* (Chicago: University of Chicago Press, 1991), 230.

15. Markku Ruotsila, *The Origins of Christian Anti-Internationalism: Conservative Evangelicals and the League of Nations* (Washington, DC: Georgetown University Press, 2008).

16. E.g. 'Report of Commission No. 1. Nationalism', *WBC 1934*, 34–35, 38.

17. E.g. 'Findings of the Council. International Peace', *RPC 1929*, 297–298; J. Y. Simpson, 'International Peace', ibid. 302–306; Henry Alford Porter and J. H. MacDonald, 'Militarism', *WBC 1928*, 244–249, 266–269; 'Wider Human Relationships', *EMC 1931*, 219–251, 401–429.

to counter everything likely to lead to war.[18] Evangelicals also supported disarmament, a process by which nations agreed to limit arms production, even if only in their own economic and strategic self-interest. Fearful of the prospect of 'the next war', evangelicals followed the series of disarmament conferences through the period.[19] At the same time they were aware of the limits on what such meetings could achieve.[20] Only transformation of the human heart by Christ provided any hope of lasting peace, a conviction that maintained their sense of responsibility to speak into the post-war situation. The belief that the churches still possessed considerable influence encouraged some evangelicals (such as English Congregationalist John Henry Jowett before his death in 1923) to think they should be doing more.[21]

Some evangelicals also aligned themselves with the pacifist movement, ever present but resurgent in the 1920s as what has been called 'pacificism', an anti-war view which allowed that resort to war may sometimes be necessary.[22] Existing opponents such as the Australian Methodist Norman Makin for the most part continued their stand. British Nonconformists too retained a broad commitment to the peace movement in the post-war years.[23] Those who maintained their stand were joined by new adherents such as the Americans Sherwood Eddy and Harry Fosdick as they reflected on the general Christian endorsement of the War. At the end of the 1920s, as the reaction against the War set in, Anglican clergy who joined the pacifist ranks included the liberal evangelical Cambridge Divinity professor Charles Raven, while in the early 1930s Methodists such as Henry Carter and Donald Soper also came out in support. However, the opposition to war was not confined to the evangelical left. It also

18. E.g. 'Minutes', *WBC 1923*, xxx; 'A Plea for Peace', ibid. 212–213; 'Public Meeting on International Peace and Resolution', *RPC 1925*, 314–330.

19. E.g. 'Editorial Comment. The Washington Conference', *HomR* 83.2 (Feb. 1922), 113–114; 'The Naval Conference', *EC* (Jan.–Feb. 1930), 43–44.

20. 'Editorial. An Uneasy Disarmament', *WD* 5.1 (Dec. 1926), 3–5; 'Notes and Comments. Navies', *C* (17 Feb. 1927), 3.

21. 'Outlook and Comment. Dr Jowett On Peace Through the Churches', *HomR* 84.5 (Nov. 1922), 370. Cf. D. M. Panton, 'The Outlawry of War', *EC* (Sept.–Oct. 1928), 148–150.

22. Martin Ceadel, *Pacifism in Britain 1914–1945: The Defining of a Faith* (Oxford: Clarendon Press, 1980).

23. Keith Robbins, 'Protestant Nonconformists and the Peace Question', in Alan P. F. Sell and Anthony R. Cross (eds.), *Protestant Nonconformity in the Twentieth Century* (Carlisle: Paternoster Press, 2003), 216–239.

became a part of the culture of traditionally evangelical student and youth groups such as the YMCA and Christian Endeavour as they grappled with the part young people might play in rebuilding the post-war world.[24] While not an evangelical cause as such, pacifism was an aspect of the wider evangelical opposition to war during the interwar decades.

Both cause and consequence of the heightened sense of the importance of their world setting among interwar evangelicals was their concern about the advent of an anti-Christian state in Russia as a result of the revolutions of 1917. From the first the regime of Lenin and the Bolsheviks was regarded as a direct threat to Christianity. This antipathy deepened in the course of the 1920s in response to the anti-religious policies of the Soviet government and attacks on missions in China as part of its experiment in spreading communism. Local communist movements, occasional 'red scares' in North America and the expansionism of communist ideology that upheld the ideal of the worldwide overthrow of capitalism added to the sense of menace. At one level evangelicals responded by organizing relief funds to help the starving and oppressed Russian people, and by supporting evangelistic missions to Russia. At another level, apart from some relief that the hold of the Russian Orthodox Church was at least being weakened, they sustained a critique that characterized Russia and communism as the most serious challenge Christianity had yet faced.[25] When they could do little else, evangelicals prayed for their Russian brothers and sisters.

Evangelicals also took note of events in Western Europe. Apart from students of prophecy, they were not greatly interested in the government of Benito Mussolini following the fascist seizure of power in 1922.[26] This changed in 1929 when the Lateran Agreement ended the historic standoff between the church and the Italian state and released the Pope from his situation as 'the prisoner of the Vatican'.[27] Evangelical worries were due to what was called 'ecclesiastical Bolshevism', the enhancement of the world political power of the papacy. For a time in the early 1920s evangelicals were also concerned about

24. Patricia Appelbaum, *Kingdom to Commune: Protestant Pacifist Culture Between World War I and the Vietnam Era* (Chapel Hill: University of North Carolina Press, 2009), ch. 1.

25. E.g. A. W. Gough, 'Bolshevism and Christianity', *EC* (Jan.–Feb. 1920), 16–17; 'Bolshevism and the Church in Russia', *HomR* 84.5 (Nov. 1922), 370–371; Nicholas Arseniew, 'Bolshevism and Christianity', *WD* 7.3 (July 1929), 274–282.

26. 'Notes and Comments. The Fascisti', *C* (9 Nov. 1922), 3.

27. E.g. 'The Pope, Mussolini and Great Britain', *EC* (Mar.–Apr. 1929), 41–42; J. W. Poynter, 'The Vatican-and-Italy Arrangement', ibid. 51–53; 'Reunion Notes', ibid. 57–58.

Germany's resistance to fulfilling the terms of the Treaty of Versailles.[28] Later
in the decade signs of moral and religious recovery were welcomed as evidence
of 'a complete change of mind'.[29] While wariness persisted, by the end of the
1920s Germany had been practically forgiven for the War.

Temperance, race and leisure

The determination of evangelicals to take part in the work of reconstruction
in 1919 indicated their continuing desire to influence the life of their own
societies at the beginning of the post-war period.[30] It also renewed the debate
about the propriety of doing so and added to the tensions of the period.
Conservative evangelical Anglicans in England were among those who condemned more liberal-minded evangelicals for having abandoned the true gospel,
and fundamentalists tended to eschew the social gospel – although they
engaged in various social ministries and political battles according to their
own priorities and understanding.[31] By contrast there were some, especially on
the left, for whom the social application of the gospel was all-important, the
American Sherwood Eddy and the Englishman Guy Rogers among them, while
in Canada the fusion of evangelism and social service in the ideal of 'social
evangelism' was the characteristic post-war standpoint.[32] As ever, the large
majority of evangelicals continued to assert in varying degrees the primacy of
the gospel while insisting on its relevance to the needs of contemporary society.

---

28. 'The War Criminals. Justice Not Revenge', *C* (12 Feb. 1920), 3.
29. 'Comment and Outlook. The Change in Spiritual Values in Germany', *HomR* 87.4
    (Apr. 1924), 283.
30. From various perspectives within the evangelical movement, David J. Davies, *The
    Church and the Plain Man* (Sydney: Angus & Robertson, 1919); Robert Speer, *The New
    Opportunity of the Church* (New York: Macmillan, 1919).
31. Bebbington, 'Decline and Resurgence', 177; Daryl G. Hart, *That Old-Time Religion
    in Modern America: Evangelical Protestantism in the Twentieth Century* (Chicago: Ivan
    R. Dee, 2002), chs. 2–3.
32. Rick L. Nutt, *The Whole Gospel for the Whole World: Sherwood Eddy and American
    Protestant Mission* (Macon, GA: Mercer University Press, 1997), ch. 5; T. Guy Rogers,
    A Rebel at Heart: The Autobiography of a Nonconforming Churchman (London:
    Longmans, Green , 1956), esp. chs. 9, 12; Daryl Baswick, 'Social Evangelism, the
    Canadian Churches, and the Forward Movement, 1919–1920', *OH* 89.4 (1997),
    303–319.

Ambivalence about the pretensions of the social gospel was frequently expressed, but outright rejection of social Christianity was unusual.[33] The reasons in its favour were mixed: the teachings of Jesus plainly had a social application; that application made it easier for people to hear the gospel; and social relevance made the gospel credible. While in practice it might have been difficult to strike the right balance, evangelicals typically retained in-principle commitment to social Christianity, often citing the tradition of Wilberforce and Shaftesbury in justification.[34]

The period opened with a great triumph. In 1919, to the great joy of the evangelical community around the world, the American Congress passed the Eighteenth Amendment and the Volstead Act to outlaw the manufacture and sale of intoxicating liquor in the entire country.[35] Spokesmen quickly rebutted charges that the prohibition legislation was hasty, ineffective and unpopular as a restriction on individual self-determination. Over the next few years they celebrated as vindication of a campaign of almost a century its considerable achievements – dramatic reductions in alcohol-related arrests and deaths, distilleries and breweries put to more productive uses that employed more men, the rescue of thousands of women and children from poverty, and, in some quarters, increased church membership. Feeling justified in taking a stand in the public interest, the evangelical churches claimed credit for the benefits prohibition conferred on civilization.

Success in America engendered a sense of responsibility to seek the same benefits in other countries.[36] In 1919 the largely evangelical World League Against Alcoholism was formed. For almost fifteen years it supported prohibition campaigns wherever they were conducted. Success was almost achieved in New Zealand where the vote in a referendum of 1919 fell just 3,000 votes

---

33. The debate was reviewed in Robert M. Kerr, 'The Gospel: Individual or Social?', *BS* 83.331 (1926), 257–297.

34. The survey that follows draws on Nancy Christie and Michael Gauvreau, *A Full-orbed Christianity: The Protestant Churches and Social Welfare in Canada 1900–1940* (Montreal: McGill-Queen's University Press, 1996); Paul T. Phillips, *A Kingdom on Earth: Anglo-American Social Christianity, 1880–1940* (University Park, PA: Pennsylvania State University Press, 1996).

35. Barry Hankins, *Jesus and Gin: Evangelicalism, the Roaring Twenties and Today's Culture Wars* (New York: Palgrave Macmillan, 2010), ch. 2.

36. See the various national entries in Jack S. Blocker, Jr., et al. (eds.), *Alcohol and Temperance in Modern History: An International Encyclopedia*, 2 vols. (Santa Barbara: ABC-CLIO, 2003).

short of the required 60%. Here and in Australia and Britain pressure for prohibition achieved no more than the perpetuation of wartime restrictions on opening hours. A different outcome emerged in Canada, where wartime prohibition was replaced in the 1920s by state control. While these were significant restrictions on the trade in alcohol, and to that extent a reward for considerable evangelical effort, nowhere else was the American achievement of the National Prohibition Act reproduced.

In any case, Prohibition in America could not be sustained. The campaign against it began almost immediately and was continued through the 1920s. Prohibition turned out to be almost unenforceable, and organized crime flourished in its defiance. Community support weakened as attitudes to alcohol changed and the inequities of the prohibition legislation became evident. The economic benefits of the alcohol industry also became clear in the early 1930s as the Depression took hold. Opposition was led by several pressure groups, not least the Women's Organization for National Prohibition Reform, organized in 1929 to counter the widespread notion nurtured by the Woman's Christian Temperance Union that women supported bans on alcohol. Victory of the anti-prohibition Democratic Party in the 1932 presidential election led to the repeal of the Eighteenth Amendment in the following year.

The defeat of Prohibition was a major setback for evangelicals active in the cause in America and beyond. It had in any case been somewhat counterproductive, in that it encouraged perceptions of organized Christianity as joyless moralistic legalism, and thereby furthered the loss of public influence evangelicals were seeking to curb. Putting the best face they could on the defeat, from this point they turned to moral suasion as the primary means of combating the drink evil. If the interwar era had begun with a great victory, it ended in a significant setback for evangelical social reformism and claims for cultural authority.

While temperance was the leading social issue for interwar evangelicals, a matter of rising concern was race. Again this was not new, but it came to prominence after 1918 as 'the most vital question' of the era because the War had shown the interdependence of the world and its peoples, and discredited the pretensions of the white races to superiority.[37] Struggles for independence for some ethnic groups and for equal rights by others made it clear that resolution of race issues was also fundamental to maintaining world peace. In this climate of opinion the ideals of national self-determination and trusteeship confronted evangelicals with the implications of their own creed.

------

37. F. C. Spurr, 'Racialism', *BWC 1928*, 270–272 (quotation on 270).

In response several prominent evangelicals made notable statements on the issue.[38] At a time when there was little Christian thinking and theology on race, they enunciated the ideal of racial equality and harmony from which followed an obligation to end everything in racial relations out of accord with the ideal. They also affirmed the reality of racial difference and its place in the providential order as the means of a life-enriching diversity. Racial prejudice and inequality were shown to be acquired rather than innate, and therefore correctible as matters of social organization and morality. The practical steps that might be taken included exercising personal influence, supporting study and research on racial questions, encouragement of interracial cooperation, promotion of a right public opinion on racial issues and, as ever, proclamation of the gospel. For all of its weaknesses and divisions, the Church, as 'the World Community created by the Spirit of Christ', was exalted as a model of 'the commonwealth of man' that transcends differences of race, wealth, culture and status.[39] By indicating how progress towards this ideal was achievable, interwar evangelicals aspired to lead society on the racial question.

The laudable ideals evangelicals promoted globally were often undermined at the national and local levels where the racial assumptions of the age were more difficult to disturb. In Australia and New Zealand conviction of white supremacy perpetuated the racism that marginalized the Aborigines and the Maoris. Arrangements such as the 'White Australia Policy' were justified (by T. C. Hammond, among others) in the name of preserving the British, and therefore the Christian, heritage that safeguarded evangelical witness in the Pacific region.[40] In America evangelicals joined in the protest against the 1924 Immigration Act that barred Japanese from entering the country, but largely acquiesced in the widespread confinement of African-American Christians to segregated churches. The violence of the resurgent Ku Klux Klan against black people in the 1920s in the name of '100 Percent Americanism' and the persistence of lynchings highlighted the sharp contours of the racial problem in spite of efforts to combat intolerance and inequality. During the 1920s and 1930s the English-speaking churches in South Africa – which, despite a significant black

---

38. Basil Mathews, *The Clash of Colour: A Study in the Problem of Race* (London; Edinburgh House Press, 1924); J. H. Oldham, *Christianity and the Race Problem* (London: SCM Press, 1924).

39. Mathews, *Clash of Colour*, 170.

40. Ian Breward, *A History of the Churches in Australasia* (Oxford: Clarendon Press, 2001), 320–322.

membership in missionary churches, had supported the racially discriminating constitution of South Africa in 1909 – tended to side with the Dutch Reformed Church and Afrikaner nationalism in the rising advocacy of the segregation that led to apartheid after the Second World War.[41] While they continued to assert and press for Christ as the solution to the world's race problems, interwar evangelicals made only limited progress towards living up to their own ethical standards, much less persuading society to change its thinking and practice.[42]

They were even less inclined to challenge contemporary gender conventions. Although the objects of much criticism, the careers of Aimee McPherson and Christabel Pankhurst pointed to the leadership roles achievable by women in interwar evangelicalism. There were many others in an assortment of roles. Ruth Paxson wrote a three-volume systematic theology. The Canadian Agnes Scott Kent and the English Jane Stoddart were journalists for the *Evangelical Christian* and the *British Weekly* respectively. In Britain and Australia Monica Farrell maintained a preaching ministry counteracting Roman Catholic teaching. Ruth Rouse and other women emerged as leaders of the student movement. To the extent that they were exceptional, a feminist agenda was implicit in the careers of all these women. But it was not taken up. Gender was not a pressing social issue for interwar evangelicals.

Part of the explanation for this lack of interest was acquiescence in women's work as a complement to that of men in the service of the gospel. While the great majority of evangelical women were fully occupied in caring for their families, voluntary church work was vast and various, and it enabled women to move backwards and forwards across the boundary between the public and the private. Moreover, the times provided new causes around which to defend the home and the family – bad films, increasing divorce rates, immodest behavior and sex education. Women's work was in fact a matter of great interest to the church conferences of the era and it encompassed an ever-increasing range of activities. If the sense of subordination to roles dominated by males was difficult to avoid, these discussions brought out both the extent and the indispensability of women's work and its complementarity with that

----

41. J. R. Cochrane, 'Christianity During a Period of "National Consolidation"', in J. W. Hofmeyr and G. J. Pillay (eds.), *A History of Christianity in South Africa Volume I* (Pretoria: HAUM Tertiary, 1994), 200–245.

42. J. Raymond Henderson, 'Negro Baptist History', *WBC 1939*, 266–268, and Gordon B. Hancock, 'The Colour Challenge', ibid. 266–272; J. Pius Barber, 'The Colour Bar in the Light of the New Testament', *WBC 1947*, 62–64.

of men. Directly and indirectly women contributed substantially to evangelical social ministry.[43]

The evangelical analysis of the times as preoccupied with pleasure and entertainment sustained concern with popular leisure as a third significant strand in evangelical social engagement between the wars. The new leisure had numerous dimensions – cinema and the radio, organized and professional sport, the motor car, new forms of racing, and the gambling that went with it.[44] In responding to these developments it was easy for evangelicals to seem guilty of the obscurantism, reaction and dullness of which they were frequently accused. In fact, they often understood the causes of leisure-mindedness realistically as due to unemployment, rising real wages, and arrangements for holidays with pay. They further acknowledged the legitimacy of recreation and amusement, and appreciated some of the benefits. Although evangelical attitudes towards the new leisure were not uniform, the concern about its moral and spiritual implications was pervasive. The more enlightened understood that mere taboos were likely to be unhelpful. Guidance by teaching principles of sensible conduct offered the best approach, while the churches continued seeking due regulation of leisure facilities through their resolutions and pronouncements.[45] Reaffirming and teaching the moral principles of Christ were paramount. Without them, evangelicals argued, the continued progress of human society would be jeopardized. Even among conservatives there was no thought of abandoning society at large in this respect.

The principal focal point of concern about the impact of the new leisure was its effect on Sabbath observance. Evangelicals generally retained a high view of the Sabbath as a day set apart for physical and spiritual renewal on which the moral and spiritual power of both the church and the wider society depended.[46] In varying degrees the need for relief from the strictures of the Puritan and high-Victorian Sunday was conceded, but the relaxation of standards during the War and subsequent 'passion for recreation and amusements' were lamented.

---

43. Anne O'Brien, *God's Willing Workers: Women and Religion in Australia* (Sydney: University of New South Wales Press, 2005), pts. 2, 3.

44. E.g. Wilfrid R. Wilkinson, 'Gambling, Amusements in General, and Sunday Recreation', *EMC 1921*, 374–378; addresses on 'The Christian Social Order', *EMC 1931*, 375–400.

45. E.g. 'Manifesto and Appeal on Public Questions in Religion and Morals', *RPC 1933*, 236–240.

46. E.g. *RPC 1921*, 350–355; *EMC 1921*, 374–378; [Newman Watts], *Why Sunday? By a London Journalist* (London: Lutterworth Press, 1932).

Opposed to the rising tendency to see Sunday as a day for sport, motoring and social pleasures, during the interwar years evangelicals rose to Sunday's defence. Eric Liddell's refusal to compete on Sunday at the 1924 Olympic Games highlighted the issue.

Predictably there were differences of opinion on how to go about it. In some quarters Sabbath defence was regarded as a matter for the churches only. By emphasizing the opportunities for private devotion, public worship and acts of 'service', they needed to present Sunday as a source of joy and personal replenishment. In other quarters Sabbath defence was a matter for public action. Without agreeing on what was required, the churches passed resolutions against disregard of the Lord's Day as a time for worship and rest, while they were joined by organizations such as the Lord's Day Observance Society in bringing pressure to bear on authorities at different levels for legal protections. Restrictions on cinema opening, Sunday trading and use of public spaces for pleasure-seeking activities provided some success. Yet, in the face of changing public attitudes, it became increasingly difficult to maintain the stand. As with temperance, Sabbath defence was a matter in which evangelicals won some battles but continued to lose ground in the overall campaign.

Industrial capitalism, economics and the Depression

Concern with contemporary patterns of behaviour was accompanied by some reflection on the underlying structures of society. Material and industrial conditions in the first post-war decade occasioned much comment about the economic system. Although a few advocated socialism, on the whole evangelicals accepted industrial capitalism, but expressed misgivings about the unequal distribution of wealth, chronic unemployment and class divisions that seemed to be a part of the system.[47] While some statements on the subject were facile and uninformed, they were not so naive as was sometimes alleged. Evangelical spokesmen often evinced a good understanding of the history, complexities and prospects of industrial capitalism. Yet their analyses and remedies were mainly moral in character. They urged Christianization of the system, a prescription that ranged from vague sentimentalism to realistic

---

47. E.g. 'The Church and Modern Industrial Problems', *EMC 1921*, 386–404;
R. J. Drummond, 'The Principles of Christ As Applied to Industrial and Social Problems', *RPC 1921*, 167–173; J. C. Carlile, 'Christianity and Industrial Relations', *WBC 1923*, 61–66; J. Morgan Jones, 'The New Social Outlook', *RPC 1925*, 381–390.

advocacy of an ideal requiring hard-headed thought and experimentation to find its practical applications. To the criticism that they did not understand the complexities and hard realities of the business world, they replied that Christianization was the only remedy that would work. Developments in Britain in the 1920s such as the Industrial Christian Fellowship and the Conference on Politics, Economics and Citizenship (COPEC) – neither of which was an evangelical initiative but nevertheless sustained the hope of a Christianized system – attracted some support.[48] While their main proposal for improvement was not embraced, interwar evangelicals, far from being uninterested, maintained their commentary on and criticism of the contemporary economic system.[49]

The moral appreciation of industrial capitalism was in line with the attitudes evangelicals had traditionally taken towards economics.[50] However, in the moderate Wesleyan Sir Josiah Stamp, Chairman of the London, Midlands and Scottish Railway and subsequently Governor of the Bank of England, interwar evangelicalism could boast a hard-nosed economist of genuine distinction, who was prepared to write about the relation of Christianity and economics. Sharply critical of amateurism in economic pronouncements by church people and concerned to raise the standard of economic thinking in the churches, he often rebutted cherished evangelical ideas. In *Christian Ethics as an Economic Factor* (1926) he argued that a great deal of poverty and adverse economic circumstances were not caused by moral factors. He was particularly severe on theories of social credit, which did attract a following in some evangelical quarters. Their claim that banking practices deprived money of its true purchasing power was dismissed as crackpot. Favouring neither capitalism nor socialism, in place of all these contemporary ideas Stamp posited 'godly pragmatism', the rational determination of which of the available options would actually work. Economics was thus presented to the churches as a tool for 'better thinking, cleansed from wishful delusion by the scientific method', to complement their work for social

---

48. 'Labour and Religion. Industrial Christian Fellowship', *C* (9 Dec. 1920), 44; Edward Shillito, *Christian Citizenship: The Story of C.O.P.E.C.* (London: Longmans, Green, 1925).

49. James N. Britton, 'Industrialism', *WBC 1928*, 236–244; U. M. McGuire, 'Industrialism', *WBC 1928*, 261–266; E. E. Kresge, 'The Social Mission of the Church', *RPC 1929*, 123–132.

50. Boyd Hilton, *The Age of Atonement: The Influence of Evangelicalism on Social and Economic Thought, 1795–1865* (Oxford: Clarendon Press, 1988); Malcolm Anderson, 'Economic Science in Evangelical Social Thought: A Missing Dimension of the English Christian Social Movement', *L* 15 (1993), 21–43.

improvement by raising character through conversion and their teaching and pastoral ministries.[51]

Through the interwar years evangelical ranks also included substantial business people who were prepared to make the most of the prevailing economic system. Somewhat surprisingly given their emphasis on separation from the world, Brethren engaged in business enjoyed particular success. Prominent British Brethren businessmen of this era included Sir John Laing and A. H. Boulton, and the petrol engine manufacturer, Percival W. Petter. Such men argued that business, like all aspects of life, was under the lordship of Christ, provided a sphere for witnessing to their faith and in any case generated the resources to support various ministries.[52] The American industrialist R. G. Le Torneau, whose businesses grew and prospered in the 1920s and 1930s, also came from a Brethren background.[53] Having taken God as his 'partner', he gave 90% of his salary and company profits to evangelical causes. The coterie of businessmen that took shape around C. H. Nash in interwar Melbourne similarly did not question the economic order in which they functioned so successfully. They accepted that their profits and organizational skills, which helped establish the Melbourne Gospel Crusade, the Upwey Convention, the Melbourne Bible Institute and Campaigners for Christ, were given by God for the support of his causes.[54] For these evangelicals business and evangelism were different sides of the same calling. They brought their Christian values and standards to the world of business, and brought their business strategies and practices to their Christian stewardship. The general tendency among them was to believe that individuals, not systems, were redeemed.

Apart from the inequalities and inequities produced by capitalism, the structural issue by which interwar evangelicals were most deeply troubled was

---

51. E.g. Josiah Stamp, *Motive and Method in a Christian Order* (London: Epworth Press, 1936), with quotation on 189; *Christianity and Economics* (London: Macmillan, 1939).

52. Tim Grass, *Gathering to His Name: The Story of Open Brethren in Britain and Ireland* (Milton Keynes: Paternoster Press, 2006), ch. 15. The thinking of contemporary Nonconformist businessmen was consistent with these attitudes. See David Jeremy, 'Twentieth-Century Protestant Nonconformists in the World of Business', in Alan P. F. Sell and Anthony R. Cross (eds.), *Protestant Nonconformity in the Twentieth Century* (Carlisle: Paternoster Press, 2003), 264–312.

53. Sarah R. Hammond, '"God Is My Partner": An Evangelical Business Man Confronts Depression and War', *CH* 80.3 (2011), 498–519.

54. Darrell Paproth, *Failure Is Not Final: A Life of C. H. Nash* (Sydney: Centre for the Study of Australian Christianity, 1997), chs. 9–10.

industrial relations. A wave of industrial unrest in 1919 and 1920 set the tone for the era.[55] That capital and labour were pitted against one another was widely recognized as part of the industrial scene requiring correction. The conflict was given added urgency by its larger ideological implications: workers' movements were easily identified with Bolshevism or Catholicism. The evangelical diagnosis was again largely moral: there was too much self-centredness on both sides of the industrial divide. The situation required an ethic based on cooperation in the service of the national community. This frequently expressed ideal made little impact as strikes recurred through the 1920s. While there was no lack of sympathy for workers' demands for fair wages and safe working conditions, evangelicals tended to side with capital and the establishment. They deplored the use of force and the subversion of democracy underlying strike action. It was often difficult too for local ministers whose communities included representatives of both sides of the conflict. Evangelicals were glad, for example, when the worst strike of the era, the General Strike in Britain in 1926, was beaten but still worried (in varying degrees admittedly) about the plight of the workers.[56] No more than others did evangelicals succeed in finding answers to the pressing industrial questions of the day, but they remained anxious through the 1920s about a matter that threatened the peace and stability of their communities.

The 'Great Depression' of the 1930s was the second of the geopolitical catastrophes to impact evangelicalism in the first half of the twentieth century. Its onset brought a decade of high levels of unemployment and attendant deprivation to people of the English-speaking world. Although a social calamity of the first order, evangelicals unsurprisingly showed little interest in it as an economic phenomenon. Their understandings were largely an extension of their economic thinking in the 1920s. The causes and the basic remedies were primarily moral, and 'reckless speculation' was now added to the list of ethical defects inherent in industrial capitalism. This was no great failing on their part. Where financiers and statesmen were baffled, it was unlikely that religious thinkers would fare any better. The few who ventured into economic analysis could be surprisingly hard-hitting in their critique. Allowing the profit motive to go unchecked and the tendency to treat people as a mere factor in the

---

55. Robert M. Miller, *American Protestantism and Social Issues 1919–1939* (Chapel Hill: University of North Carolina Press, 1958), pt. 3, provides a full account of the strikes of this period.

56. Stewart J. Brown, '"A Victory for God": The Scottish Presbyterian Churches and the General Strike of 1926', *JEH* 42.4 (1991), 596–617.

production process were incompatible with the teaching of Christ. Advocacy of some reconstruction of the economic order – with due measures of social planning and social control – to reflect more adequately the social teaching of Jesus supplemented more traditional calls for inner spiritual and moral reform.[57]

In reacting to mass unemployment and its consequences, evangelicals at large were on surer ground.[58] Although their experiences of the Depression varied widely, responses ran along two main lines. Many supported government intervention, both to relieve the suffering and to reform social structures to reverse the causes or at least ameliorate the effects. Measures commanding support from evangelicals included unemployment relief, proposals for new industries, retraining the unemployed and public works. Such measures were of course the sinews of the New Deal in America, and were roundly opposed by some as the elements of state socialism. Against the activist state, conservatives upheld the efficacy of individual initiative in a self-regulating marketplace.[59] While the Depression produced the by now characteristically diversified response from evangelicals, few were indifferent to the major social and economic issue of the day, even if they framed it in religious and moral terms.

But whatever their outlook on the role of the state, evangelicals themselves were more or less at one in contributing directly to the relief of the suffering. Individuals and churches all around the evangelical world provided food, clothing and shelter to the needy, while the resources of organizations such as the Salvation and Church Armies were stretched to the limit as they provided material aid at an unprecedented level. More forward-looking schemes sought to limit the psychological damage of chronic unemployment in an effort to prevent the unemployed becoming unemployable. These included recreational facilities, instruction centres and labour exchanges. The human effects of the Depression produced some outstanding individual contributions, none more so than those of the Sydney Anglican evangelical R. B. S. Hammond, whose

---

57. E.g. Gilbert Jackson, *An Economist's Confession of Faith* (Toronto: Macmillan, 1935); papers on 'The Christian Social Order', *EMC 1931*, 191–203, 389–400; Rolvix Harlen, 'Economics and the Mind of Christ. Report of Commission No. 5', *WBC 1934*, 57–62, with discussion at 68–70.

58. E.g. The special articles on the churches and the unemployed in *C* (26 Jan. 1933), 3, 17, 19, 23, 26; S. E. Keeble, 'What the Churches Are Doing: Social Activities', in Percy Dearmer (ed.), *Christianity and the Crisis* (London: Victor Gollancz, 1933), 286–305.

59. Sarah R. Hammond, '"God's Business Men": Entrepreneurial Evangelicals in Depression and War', PhD thesis, Yale University, 2010.

many schemes to help the unemployed culminated in the purchase out of his own pocket of the land on which Pioneer Village – subsequently the outer Sydney suburb of Hammondville – was established to provide housing on a rent-purchase basis for destitute families.[60] Without necessarily understanding what they were dealing with, and often with limited resources, evangelicals shared in the sense of crisis and acted to alleviate the hardship caused by the Depression.

Politics

Reconstruction, the new Christian internationalism and the domestic problems confronting the English-speaking societies provided the setting for the political interest and engagement of interwar evangelicals. The Wilson presidency marked the high point of the direct influence (for better or worse) of evangelical Christianity on international and American domestic affairs. Presidents Harding (a Baptist), Coolidge (a Congregationalist) and Hoover (a Quaker) who followed him all had a definite Christian strand in their make-up, but it was not overtly evangelical. The Roosevelt presidency marked a further shift, from Protestantism to a pluralism that championed religious freedom for all and upheld faith but no specific faiths. Like the American presidents, the outlook of the British prime ministers of the era was tinctured with Christianity, but, with the possible exception of Stanley Baldwin, whose 'democratic Protestantism' was described as 'comfortable with a low church and evangelical frame of mind',[61] it was not evangelical in character. Changing political conditions and the rise of new issues also confirmed the end of the influence exerted at the highest levels of government by Nonconformity in the early 1900s. From the beginning of the 1920s the evangelical outlook was decidedly less of a presence at the centres of world power than it had been in the opening decades of the century.

Of course this did not mean that evangelicals themselves had lost interest in politics. Where data is available, it is evident that they still regarded political careers as a legitimate outlet of Christian service. Although the overall trend was towards decline in the number of representatives from a peak in the 1920s, practising Baptists were a significant presence in the interwar British

---

60. Meredith Lake, *Faith in Action: Hammondcare* (Sydney: University of New South Wales Press, 2013).

61. Stuart Ball, 'Baldwin, Stanley', in *ODNB*, consulted online, 13 Sept. 2012, 10.

Parliament.[62] In 1929, according to the Methodist Secretary of the Labour Party, Arthur Henderson, the British parliamentary Labour Party still drew much of its energy from radical Nonconformity, an observation that was true also of local government. This was mainly through individuals who, having been formed in the churches and chapels, expressed their faith by involvement in public life. A. V. Alexander spoke for these Free Churchmen in 1931 when he explained, 'The basic reason as to why we are politicians is this, that we are going sincerely to labour for the improvement of the conditions of those for whom Christ died.'[63]

This same sentiment had its effect away from Britain. The Christian Socialist J. K. Archer (1865–1949) was both a leading Baptist minister and also at different times Mayor of Christchurch and President and Vice President of the New Zealand Labour Party.[64] In Alberta, Canada, William 'Bible Bill' Aberhart formed his own political party, the Social Credit Party, and swept to power in the 1935 provincial election.[65] If Archer was a decidedly leftist evangelical, theologically Aberhart was as decidedly from the right. Both men used their time in office to improve the material life of the people in their constituencies. Interwar evangelicals of all outlooks continued to find in politics the means of pursuing the moral interest inculcated by their faith and church life.

The specific political issue that most exercised interwar evangelicals was the nature and increasing power of the state. Because of their underlying conviction that what was morally good for themselves was good for society, they looked to the state to embody their ideals in national policy. At the same time (as the next section will show) they were made keenly aware of the extent to which interference in their lives by the state could be taken by the totalitarian regimes in Europe. With their governments acting to respond to the problems of the Depression, the danger seemed to be coming nearer to home. Evangelicals as usual responded in a variety of ways. As the English-speaking societies were

---

62. David W. Bebbington, 'Baptist Members of Parliament in the Twentieth Century', *BQ* 31.6 (1986), 252–287; 'Baptist Members of Parliament: A Supplementary Note', *BQ* 42.2, pt. 2 (2007), 148–161; 'Baptists and Politics Since 1914', in K. W. Clements (ed.), *Baptists in the Twentieth Century* (London: Baptist Historical Society, 1983), 76–95.

63. Peter Catterall, 'Morality and Politics: The Free Churches and the Labour Party Between the Wars', *HJ* 36.3 (1993), 667–685, with quotation on 681.

64. M. P. Sutherland, 'Pulpit or Podium? J. K. Archer and the Dilemma of Christian Politics in New Zealand', *NZJBR* 1 (1996), 26–46.

65. George Rawlyk, 'Politics, Religion, and the Canadian Experience: A Preliminary Probe', in Mark A. Noll (ed.), *Religion and American Politics: From the Colonial Period to the 1980s* (New York: Oxford University Press, 1990), 269–270.

confronted by the question of socialism, some were persuaded that this was the answer. Others, regarding democracy as the provision of providence, were alarmed by the prospect of socialism. Still others were uncommitted to any particular form of government. They asked only that it be controlled by Christian principles. Amid these differences of opinion on the nature and role of the state, there was wide consensus on the right of the individual to complete religious autonomy.[66] At a time when they felt there was cause for concern evangelicals strongly asserted the political conditions necessary for the maintenance of their own religious position.

It is evident that interwar evangelicals retained an interest in the social and moral patterns of their societies and continued to press for the practical realization of their ideals. Still an influence that could not be ignored, the evangelical churches and communities achieved no great successes in the interwar years comparable with the social triumphs of previous eras. The reason they gave to themselves was the self-indulgence of contemporary society and increasing secularization. In taking this line evangelicals had picked up on the tension between the new individualism of the era and the communitarian standards they represented. But other factors were also at work. Matters that evangelicals had once made their own were now the business of the state, which, bound to hold together an increasingly pluralist constituency, could not easily concede their demands. But even from within Protestant Christianity evangelicals were no longer the dominant voice. In particular new prophets – most notably William Temple in Britain and Reinhold Niebuhr in America – had arisen from outside their ranks with a more appealing Christian interpretation of society. That evangelicals were overshadowed by others should not be taken to mean their activism was in eclipse. In fact, throughout the interwar period they held to a broad understanding of what society should be like and continued working towards achievement of their vision of the future. As they did so, developments on the international scene from the early 1930s created new uncertainties and fresh problems to address.

Communism, Nazism, the Jews and the return of war

In the mid-1930s, the demands of the Depression notwithstanding, the attention of evangelicals swung dramatically back to world affairs.[67] Initially the focal

---

66. *EC* (May–June 1938), 101–102; (Sept.–Oct. 1938), 164–165.

67. The international concerns of evangelicals are readily accessible in the pages of the journal of the right-of-centre Evangelical Alliance, *Evangelical Christendom*.

point of this renewed attention to the international stage was again the Soviet Union. This was largely because the Depression brought the failings of Western capitalism into deep relief at the very time that Stalin's first Five Year Plan was achieving spectacular and unexpected success. As the 1930s unfolded, the standing of the Soviet Union improved further by the comparison with the fascist regimes of Western Europe. While the evangelical right remained implacable in its opposition to communism, there was some reassessment on the left where it was allowed that communist social and economic aspirations were similar to those of Christianity. If in this there was some moderation of the demonization of the Soviet Union as the enemy, the stature of communism as the leading ideological rival to Christianity crystallized for all evangelicals. As a missionary movement similarly claiming the total allegiance of the individual and society, it was advancing in countries – principally China and India – where Christian missions were also at work. In the struggle between Christianity and communism nothing less than the future of the world appeared to be at stake.[68]

However, the focus of evangelical interest in the wider world soon shifted back to Germany where the advent of Hitler's government in 1933 began a 'revolution' that sought to 'nazify' every aspect of German life. From the first there was suspicion among evangelicals about what this might mean. But there was also some sympathy for a movement so strongly opposed to communism. This dissipated as the menace of Hitler's dictatorship came into sharper focus. The extension of *Gleichschaltung* (coordination) to the churches was a spectacle that gripped the Protestant world, particularly as it was taking place in the home of the Reformation.[69] Evangelicals viewed the Confessing Church, formed in 1934 to resist the nazification of the church, as an heroic defence of Christian freedom in the face of fierce political repression. At a deeper level they were horrified by the state's assertion of its authority over the church, a development that portended loss of religious freedom elsewhere and direct conflict between church and state. With Karl Barth to remind them that outspoken criticism of the regime was not necessarily the best response, evangelicals reacted to the plight of German Christians by calling for Christian renewal in their own communities in order to confront Nazism with a better alternative. They also grew in their resolve to preserve democratic institutions, for only in a free society

---

68. The classic statement is E. Stanley Jones, *Christ and Communism* (London: Hodder & Stoughton, 1935).

69. Tom Lawson, 'The Anglican Understanding of Nazism 1933–1945: Placing the Church of England's Response to the Holocaust in Context', *TCBH* 14.2 (2003), 112–137.

could there be true religious freedom. In taking a stand for their distinctive beliefs, evangelicals believed they were acting on behalf not only of German Christians but of Christian civilization at large.[70]

Anti-semitic policies of the Nazis also stirred up the Jewish question for evangelicals. Their well-established interest in the Jews had recently increased as a product of the concern with race in general, and because of their eschatological significance for premillennialists.[71] But this rising interest was not enough to overcome the deep anti-semitism in some quarters of the evangelical movement, and a more general ambivalence felt in others. As news of the persecution of the Jews came through, some evangelicals were highly critical of what they now knew was occurring, while others sought at least to rationalize Nazi policies until the fraudulence of their bases was exposed. Also hard to die was the suspicion that both the Depression and communism were the result of a Jewish international conspiracy. Towards the end of the 1930s a small number of evangelical churchmen campaigned for intakes of Jewish refugees in the Western democracies to be increased. These efforts met with only very limited success. High levels of unemployment coupled with the perceived need to preserve the Anglo-Saxon character of the English-speaking societies militated against significant impact. In any case, support from within the evangelical community was not concerted. The Jews were not a cause to galvanize evangelicals.

As they contemplated the world of the later 1930s evangelicals acknowledged that, contrary to their hopes for the post-war order, much of the civilized world was in the grip of the new ideology of totalitarianism. Although the nature of their regimes differed, Germany, Italy and Russia were grouped as countries in which the authority of the state was exalted as requiring the supreme loyalty. Naturally evangelicals condemned the anti-Christian stance of the totalitarian regimes, whether as sponsors of atheism or of some quasi-religious alternative. However, in facing up to these regimes, their basic criticism was the denial of their citizens' freedom to form their own opinions about life and morals, without which undivided loyalty to Christ was impossible.[72] Coming on top of the great

---

70. T. C. Hammond, *Fading Light: The Tragedy of Spiritual Decline in Germany* (London: Marshall, Morgan & Scott, n.d. [1940]).

71. William R. Glass, 'Fundamentalism's Prophetic Vision of the Jews: The 1930s', *JSS* 47.1 (1985), 63–76.

72. E.g. R. C. Gillie, 'The Church's Witness for Freedom: In Relation to the State', *RPC 1937*, 104–113; A. G. Pite, 'The Responsibility of the Church to the World: Anti-Christian', *Ch* 2.3, NS (July 1937), 149–153; M. E. Aubrey, 'Christianity and the Totalitarian State', *WBC 1939*, 198–202.

Reformation anniversaries, this opposition to totalitarianism caused evangelicals to define who they were in relation to the state by reaffirming the duty to adhere to their own Christian beliefs and principles as their highest loyalty. Ironically, as several evangelical spokesmen pointed out, the comprehensive claims of totalitarianism now set the benchmark for the level of commitment required by evangelical Christianity. The much-vaunted economic and material success of the totalitarian regimes also raised the need to ensure that democracy was worth saving by abolishing slums, overcoming unemployment and closing extremes of wealth and poverty, all further incentives to social reform.

As the situation in Europe deteriorated in the later 1930s, evangelicals were appalled by the prospect of a return to war. They followed events closely, condemning the aggression of the fascist dictators, leading public agitation for the maintenance of peace, and applauding Neville Chamberlain's efforts to preserve it. After the Munich Agreement in September 1938 they again led public prayers of thanksgiving for the apparent deliverance from war and put forward the Christian formula for the maintenance of peace.[73] As the clouds of war continued to gather, what could be done to maintain the peace remained a major concern.[74] Work for the eradication of the conditions leading to war, advocacy of disarmament, influencing public opinion, development of cooperation between the churches and promotion of a peace mentality were included on the list of actions calculated to achieve this end. Even as they were being reiterated, the point at which they might have been effective was long past. As the peace continued to break down through 1939, evangelicals generally came to accept the necessity of war in the interest of creating a true peace based on justice.

Although they continued to believe right up until the last minute that it might be averted, the likelihood of war was a deep disappointment to the internationalist aspirations of interwar evangelicals. With memories of the Great War still fresh, they naturally feared the devastation and destruction war would bring. It would also mark the definitive failure of the vision for reconstruction they had espoused in 1919. Remarkably they still boldly asserted the responsibility and capacity of Christianity and their churches to be a transforming power in the life of the nations. A spirit of unselfishness in international relations, which only the influence of the gospel would effect, could remove the causes of war. By implication this view still placed evangelicals at the centre of world affairs. However unrealistically, they hoped the crisis of 1939 would provide an

---

73. E.g. *EC* (Sept.–Oct. 1938), 149; (Nov.–Dec. 1938), 179, 182–185.
74. 'Report of Commission No. 1. What Baptists Can Do to Avert War and Promote Peace', *WBC 1939*, 96–114.

opportunity for them to exercise a profound influence on the well-being and future of the world.[75] In 1919, as they sought to rebuild a Christian civilization, evangelicals could still anticipate broad acceptance in society; twenty years later, as they sought to preserve society from destruction, they had to reckon with widespread rejection. Even so, they remained committed to the task of bringing the gospel to bear in all of its implications for the benefit of the world and society as well as the individual.

Conclusion

When peace returned in 1919 evangelicals entered on the new era with a high hope of influencing the social and political arrangements of their communities towards the restoration of Christian civilization, the decline of which was dramatically highlighted by the War. Although what it might entail was adjusted in response to circumstances, this hope was never abandoned in the two ensuing decades. Right across the movement the evangelicals of this period, their differences notwithstanding, generally remained rhetorically and practically committed in some degree to social ministry and wider political and social action. Throughout they evinced an interest in world affairs, seeking above all the maintenance of peace and the moral order that would secure it. Domestically they engaged with a range of social issues with a moral and spiritual dimension such as temperance, the perceived preoccupation with pleasure and entertainment, Sabbath observance and race relations. They also remained concerned with the underlying social and economic structures of society, and continued to see in politics an avenue for pursuing the moral commitment inherent in evangelical conviction. Specific social ministries were maintained; and when the Depression struck, evangelicals responded to the suffering as best they could. As ever, they remained supporters of their societies, but worried about the rising power of the state as welfare policies were implemented. This worry was accentuated by events in Europe, where the potential for tyranny was starkly evident in the emerging dictatorships of Russia and Germany. Evangelical resistance to totalitarianism led to acceptance of the necessity of war when it loomed again in the late 1930s. If there was declension in evangelical social interest between the wars, it was from the zenith achieved in the *fin de siècle* era and the extraordinary commitment of the Great War years, and it was not the general experience of the movement.

---

75. E.g. S. W. Hughes, 'World Peace', *WBC 1939*, 221–225.

Commitment to social ministry abided because the underlying dynamic of evangelicalism did not change: contemporary evangelicals at large continued to think that Christian beliefs and values should shape social attitudes and behaviour in their communities. However, the interwar decades were not a period of great evangelical social and political attainment. For all of their commitment and effort, the evangelicals of this time won no lasting reforms of moment and failed to reverse the disturbing cultural trends of the day. Together with the outbreak of war in 1939, this inability to secure preferred social and political regulation in line with the expectations of the evangelical tradition marked the failure to restore the historic influence on English-speaking society envisaged in 1919. Differences about the priorities and functions of social ministry (as in other aspects of contemporary evangelicalism) further weakened the movement's attempts to demonstrate its realism and efficacy before the watching world. Division was also a reason for prophets from other expressions of Protestantism being seen to offer a more coherent and apt vision of a Christian society. But lack of impact is not the same thing as absence of interest. Interwar evangelicals had generally faced up to the very difficult social and political issues of their day and, in doing so, although it was a matter of contention, maintained the tradition of evangelical engagement with society. There had been no 'great reversal' in interwar evangelicalism.

EPILOGUE

On 3 September 1939 Britain declared war on Germany in response to its invasion of Poland. As in 1914, Britain's declaration brought the whole of the British Empire into the war. America's entry was again delayed, but it came as a result of the Japanese attack on Pearl Harbor on 7 December 1941. With large-scale fighting in South East Asia and the Pacific added to what was already taking place in Europe, North Africa and the Middle East, the conflict was more widespread than in the previous war. It also involved the home front much more extensively, particularly in Britain, which came under sustained enemy attack, especially between 1940 and 1942, the years of greatest peril. This war was more violent too, with three times as many casualties, the majority of them civilians. For the second time in a generation English-speaking evangelicals were caught up in a world war and suffered its disruptive effects.[1]

The response of evangelicals to what became the Second World War has been less studied than their responses to the First.[2] However, even a cursory

---

1. On the religious history of the war, see Andrew Chandler, 'Catholicism and Protestantism in the Second Word War in Europe', in *CHC9*, 262–284.
2. Useful sources include Stephen Parker, *Faith on the Home Front: Aspects of Church Life and Popular Religion in Birmingham 1939–1945* (Oxford: Peter Lang, 2005); Michael Snape, *God and the British Soldier: Religion and the British Army in the First and Second*

inspection of the evidence indicates that, although it was a very different kind of war, this response ran along broadly similar lines. Their own sustained commitment to Christian civilization through the interwar decades enabled evangelicals again to be in step with the broader community reaction to the outbreak of war.[3] Similarly their attitudes towards the totalitarian governments of the 1930s also readily aligned with the representation of the war as a straight-forward clash between good and evil on which the future of the world depended. But, as in the Great War, evangelicals went beyond the broad civil Christianity that facilitated identification of the national cause with the cause of Christ. While their spokespersons acknowledged the importance of other war aims – the destruction of Hitlerism, the salvation of democracy, the restoration of justice for the oppressed, and security for the future – they were referred to a frame-work of cosmological crisis in which the Allied cause was ranged against 'the principalities and powers'. Specifically, the war was a contest between 'godless materialism' and 'the Evangel of Christ' with 'the free course of the Gospel' to be decided.[4] As they were caught up in the conflict, evangelicals were in no doubt that this was a new war of religion in which their own cultural authority was at stake.

Their understanding of the war meant that for most evangelicals participation was again unproblematic. The peace churches maintained their historic position but members were usually prepared to engage in other forms of community service. The scruples of conscientious objectors were also largely respected, but there was something of a reaction against pacifism in the face of the evils of Nazism and Japanese imperialism. At almost every level of the evangelical movement the need to stand up to aggressors was accepted. A determination not to repeat the mistakes of the Great War meant that evangelicals' patriotism was duly cautious but no less definite.[5] Once more evangelical men and women were among those who readily enlisted and the clergy too came forward to serve as chaplains, although in this war their role was better understood and supported. Evangelicals also played a substantial part as non-combatants. Their churches joined with others and with established organizations such as the Salvation Army

World Wars (London: Routledge, 2005); Matthew Sutton, American Apocalypse: A History of Modern Evangelicalism (Cambridge, MA: Belknap Press, 2014), ch. 9.

3. Keith Robbins, 'Britain, 1940 and "Christian Civilization"', in his History, Religion and Identity in Modern Britain (London: Hambledon Press, 1993), 195–213.

4. E.g. 'The War and Anti-Christ', EC (Mar.–Apr. 1940), 55.

5. Gerald L. Sittser, A Cautious Patriotism: The American Churches and the Second World War (Chapel Hill: University of North Carolina Press, 1997).

and the YMCA (perhaps less thoroughly evangelical than in 1914–18) in providing a wide range of service ministries not only to service personnel but to those engaged in defence industries. As in the war of 1914–18, evangelicals were wholehearted in identifying with their societies in the hour of peril.

As well as the material means they could contribute, evangelicals once more mobilized the spiritual resources of the life of faith in support of the Allied cause. The Bible was again scanned for guidance and succour amid chaos and perplexity, and prophetic speculation found fresh stimulation in such apocalyptic developments as the advent of the atomic bomb. Advocacy of prayer was bolstered by invoking what prayer seemed to have accomplished in the previous conflict. The sacrifice of the cross still made sense of the pervasive suffering and furnished a power of endurance. Service personnel at all levels brought evangelical faith to their thinking and deportment as they played their various parts in the overall campaign. However, the power of the life of faith was nowhere seen to better effect than in the gut-wrenching despair of the Japanese prisoner-of-war camps in the South West Pacific region.[6] Here Bible reading, worship and hymn singing, fellowship and mutual service and support sustained evangelical conviction and enabled survival. As in the trenches during the Great War, the capacity of evangelical devotion to produce resilience and heroism was demonstrated in the most trying circumstances.

The spiritual battles fought by Second World War evangelicals were a powerful reminder that such a conflict also involved another 'war within'. Contemporary evangelicals felt the paradox of their nations fighting for Christian civilization when they were not truly Christian. The disparity between the ideal and the reality went beyond mere embarrassment as they again worried that the moral and spiritual condition of their societies was such that the Allies would be both incapable of winning the war and also unworthy of doing so. They acknowledged further that the signs of faithlessness such as drinking, gambling, pleasure seeking and (above all) desecration of Sunday were getting worse. While sensitive to the demands of wartime, they redoubled their critique of society and called on their communities to return to observing divine standards of conduct. They also lobbied governments to mitigate the worst of the abuses. If morale was to augment material superiority, the war was no time to go easy on the spiritual and ethical demands of the gospel.

As ever, the complement of bringing these demands to bear was the need to proclaim the gospel itself. With thousands facing the prospect of imminent

---

6. Robert D. Linder, 'The Fourth Tribe: Spiritual Mateship in the Japanese POW Camps in World War II, 1939–1945', *L* 2.7 (June 2014), 61–85.

death in the services and at home, the perennial task of presenting the message of salvation by faith through grace was urgent. But the spiritual crisis facing the world also required that large numbers of men and women should turn to God so that they, and society through them, would have the spiritual resources to meet the challenge and see the war through to victory. Of course those in the revivalist tradition hoped that the great need of the day would be met by mass repentance in revival. Whatever the inspiration, the result was an upsurge in evangelism. Indeed, the Southern Baptist chaplain L. G. Gatlin was discharged from the American army because of excessive zeal in evangelism.[7] The rising revivalist J. Edwin Orr was another who, building on his conversionist initiatives in the previous decade, grasped the opportunity to serve the men and women in the forces and reach them for Christ. Such established organizations as The Army Scripture Readers and Soldiers' and Airmen's Association (renamed to reflect new military arrangements) again called men in the British army and the Royal Air Force to 'REPENT AND TURN TO GOD'.[8] At home unexpected sites of evangelistic activity such as air-raid shelters were welcomed and new agencies such as Youth for Christ that were to have a significant post-war history also sprang to life.[9] Conversionism had performed many wider social functions during the early twentieth century. As during the Great War, between 1939 and 1945 it was part of the effort to win the war.

In seeking at once both to win men and women for evangelical Christianity and also to provide spiritual leadership to their communities, evangelicals were obliged to re-engage with the ethical issues raised by war. Why God allowed such conflict was a conundrum that attracted standard answers from new voices.[10] The unspeakable atrocities of the enemy were easily denounced, but this war was different in that English-speaking evangelicals had to face the moral dilemmas of their own war effort. The centre-left in particular worried about the violent and destructive methods used in the push for unconditional surrender, especially the relentless bombing of German cities. After two decades of demonizing communism, the alliance with the Soviet Union also caused some perplexity. At the end the atomic bombs dropped on Nagasaki and Hiroshima prompted great uneasiness. On all of these issues other

---

7. Sittser, *Cautious Patriotism*, 165.

8. See *WD* 19.3 (May–June 1941), n.p. (following 199).

9. Joel A. Carpenter, *Revive Us Again: The Reawakening of American Fundamentalism* (New York: Oxford University Press, 1997), ch. 9.

10. E.g. D. M. Lloyd-Jones, *Why Does God Allow War? A General Justification of the Ways of God* (London: Hodder & Stoughton, 1939).

evangelicals, particularly those on the right, tended to be more pragmatic in accepting what had to be done to force a righteous victory. If on specific issues there was a predictable diversity, evangelicals at large commended their creed to the world by holding that faith in Christ alone provided an alternative to war.

As the war developed, evangelicals evinced a growing concern for the kind of peace that might result. They readily embraced the ideal of total victory that was interpreted increasingly from their own point of view. Above all, it was imperative to defeat enemies such as Germany and Japan because of the danger they presented to the religious freedom required by evangelical religion to flourish. With the Vatican having apparently exploited wartime conditions to improve its position in European society, the same concern sustained the strident anti-Catholicism of the interwar years. Agitation for religious freedom to be a clearly stated war aim of the Allies was part of the preparation for the new period of reconstruction that would follow the cessation of hostilities. When that came in 1945, evangelicals added to general community rejoicing their own solemn thanksgiving and praise coupled with measured apprehension about the future. New causes of anxiety such as the spectre of nuclear warfare and the expansionist atheism of the Soviet Union added urgency to what appeared to be another opportunity to restore Christian civilization.[11] Even the response to the end of the fighting was similar to that of the Great War.

The second period of reconstruction in living memory brought to an end a half century in the history of evangelicalism that had passed through two distinct phases of roughly equal duration. From many angles, the first – the *fin de siècle* – has the appearance of one of the great ages in the history of the movement. Activism was dominant as contemporary evangelicals organized and laboured to evangelize the world in their generation. They were also energetic contributors to the social gospel as they sought to redeem their societies from the top down through politics and the bottom up by acts of service and relief. At the same time the movement's leaders and scholars produced an unprecedented quantum of high-quality theological writing in response to contemporary intellectual trends both to elaborate the meaning of and to uphold the warrants for evangelical belief and action. All was sustained by a strong devotional ethic that sought to keep men and women in close

---

11. E.g. 'Thanksgiving for Victory', *EC* (Apr.–June 1945), 40–42; 'Notes and Comments. End of the War. Atomic Bombs', *C* (16 Aug. 1945), 5; W. H. Tribble, 'Repentance the Need of the Hour', *RE* 43.1 (Jan. 1946), 30–39.

communion with God to complete the work of conversion in lives of total consecration. Moreover, evangelicals achieved historic levels of cooperation to claim, defend and exercise cultural authority in evangelistic outreach, theological explanation and community service. Such was the need for rational organization and joint effort that the ecumenist tendency was continually reaffirmed within the movement and commended to Protestant Christianity at large. With the conversionist-activist axis in the ascendant, the balance of elements in the evangelical synthesis was such as to achieve historic levels of aspiration and engagement with their world among *fin de siècle* evangelicals.

Beneath the surface appearance of strength and vitality there was also fragility in a time of transition as evangelicals adjusted to the unfavourable intellectual and social conditions of the modern world and declining influence in their communities. Their varying responses accelerated the diversification of an already highly variegated movement and generated countervailing pressures within the movement that pulled its adherents towards fundamentalist and liberal evangelical dispositions. In turn this diversity gave rise to disagreements and tensions over such matters as recruitment, devotional practices, biblical authority, the content and priority of key beliefs and the legitimacy of social ministry, which lessened the coherence of the movement. The inherent instability of the life of faith as experimental Christianity also continually undermined the disposition to solidarity stemming from a shared ecclesiology. If the evangelical coalition was intact and hard at work, by 1914 the underlying consensus was under increasing pressure and showing signs of fraying at the edges.

The interwar years were very different. Evangelicals began the post-war era confident that they offered a belief system and a way of life the world in the wake of the Great War would readily embrace as at once the answer to its bewilderment and the provision of its spiritual and moral needs. Probably always unrealistic, this hope for the restoration of Christian civilization soon proved to be unwarranted but was never really relinquished. While support for the churches seems to have held, the people of the English-speaking world did not come flocking back to evangelical Christianity and there was no great revival. Measured by their ability to affect political decisions and popular culture, evangelical influence on society also fell sharply, especially after the defeat of Prohibition. Three main patterns of thought and conduct came into sharp focus as evangelicals endeavoured to reverse this loss of sociocultural influence. Far from succeeding, they further weakened the movement by deepening the diversification of evangelicalism and by generating tensions that led in some cases to open conflict and schism, some marginalization of fundamentalists and a wariness of one another throughout the movement. These developments also changed the balance of the elements of the evangelical synthesis with the result that the movement as a whole became more inward looking as the biblicist-crucicentric axis became increasingly determinative. Their effect was to strengthen the separatist tendency in the evangelical tradition and to hamper attempts to instruct, convert and lead their communities in a 'new Reformation'. Interwar evangelicals did not restore Christian civilization; they failed to convince their communities of the realism and efficacy of their religion; and their movement became more divided, less coherent and less credible. In that these developments highlighted the loss of cultural authority and engendered significant changes in the hopes, expectations and strategies of evangelicals, this was the era of the disruption of evangelicalism.

The low point in the fortunes of the movement appears to have been in the 1920s when evangelicals encountered the harsh realities of the immediate post-war world. In the early 1930s they began taking steps that reflect an understanding of their predicament and what needed to be done to improve their fortunes. Centre-right evangelicals recognized that their influence was restricted by perceptions of obscurantism and devised measures to improve their intellectual standing. Fused with the theological reconstruction already underway by the centre-left, and favoured by changes in the theological and world settings, these measures began the intellectual recovery of evangelicalism. The conversionist impulse also produced fresh stirrings as the nature and need for evangelism at home and on the mission field were clarified following a period of confusion and weakness. Importantly too evangelicals took a leading part in the ecumenical movement. Broader than evangelicalism, it had a reflexive impact on the movement by reminding evangelicals not only of the benefits of unity and cooperation but also of the value of their own ecclesiology. Social ministry had never fallen away to the extent required by the 'great reversal' interpretation, but the rising power of the state and the drift to war in the later 1930s were powerful reminders to evangelicals of their importance to the causes of the religious freedom and well-being of their communities. These developments represented some reinvigoration of the conversionist-activist axis in the evangelical synthesis. They had not progressed very far by the outbreak of the Second World War and all were contested. But they do reveal that the other side of the disruption of evangelicalism was the operation of a normalizing tendency that pulled the movement back towards that configuration of the evangelical consensus that facilitated aspiration and community engagement.

While the *fin de siècle* and the interwar periods may be viewed discretely, they also belong together as successive phases of one half-century sequence in the history of evangelicalism. Viewing them in this way brings into deep relief the fluctuating fortunes of the evangelical movement between 1900 and around 1945. In turn apparent declension highlights the question of the impact of the First World War as the first and most significant of the three major world events that disturbed the lives of contemporary evangelicals. The standard view has been that the continuities from before 1914 are so significant that the War did not greatly alter the course of evangelicalism. While the importance of these continuities is undeniable, the difference in the temper and achievement between the two phases is so marked as to require an assessment of the War as the likely cause. Of course the basic consideration is the incalculable loss of evangelicals. High casualties in the context of the pattern of the evangelical response to the call to arms suggests that the movement lost many of those who, nurtured in *fin de siècle* evangelicalism, such as John Mott, Frank Buchman and T. C. Hammond, would have supported and led it in the difficult days of the 1920s and 1930s. Also important, however, was the apparent opportunity to recover cultural authority in response to which post-war evangelicals devised different – and often competing and incompatible – perspectives and strategies. When they proved to be largely ineffective, the War's stimulation to social activism looked to some evangelicals like a cause of weakness that had to be resisted. Given that the War had enforced the sense that high-minded cultural objectives were worth fighting for, the combative mentality it also nurtured brought the tensions arising from different aims and methods to open division and conflict. Mixed up in these differences too was a residual awareness of the need to fight 'the war within' that lies behind the new focus on doctrinal integrity among centre-right evangelicals and their more rigorous policing of the boundaries of belief and conduct. This brew of effects engendered the setting that increased the salience of the biblicist-crucicentric axis in the evangelical synthesis and so weakened the inherent ecumenism of the movement that it was unable to contain the equally congenital tendency to separatism. To the extent that it changed the character and dynamics of the movement, and thereby limited its capacity to re-establish its cultural authority, the Great War was largely if not solely responsible for the disruption of evangelicalism.

At the beginning of 1946 evangelicals tended to share in the widespread sense that the world was at another turning point at which it could start again. A sentiment of this order motivated the exhortation of Hugh Gough to English Anglican evangelicals at the first Islington Clerical Meeting after the War to cease from being hyphenated evangelicals and to present a united front as 'evangelicals pure and simple' as one of the essential conditions of a desperately needed 'new Evangelical Revival'. A similar assessment of the needs of the moment was behind the early post-war writings of Carl Henry and the efforts of the National Association of Evangelicals to draw evangelicals together to win back America

and the world beyond.[12] These prescriptions for strategy and process in a new
period of reconstruction presumed the diversification of the evangelical tradition
over the previous fifty years in response to the demands of the modern world
and the persistent hope of regaining the cultural authority of the mid-Victorian
era of 'dominance'. Such deep concern over the existence of liberal evangelical
and fundamentalist strands at opposite ends of an expanding centre (consisting
largely of the conservative evangelical/neo-evangelical bloc) as an impediment
to the effectiveness of the movement in the emerging world order was very
different from the confidence with which evangelicals had faced the new century
back in 1900. The change of outlook suggests that the disruption of evangelicalism was the principal legacy of the early twentieth century to the post-Second
World War generation of evangelicals.[13]

---

12. Ian Baruma, *Year Zero: The History of 1945* (New York: Penguin, 2013); Hugh Gough,
    'President's Address', *ICM 1947: Evangelical Essentials* (London: Church Book Room,
    n.d. [1947]), 13–14; Carpenter, *Revive Us Again*, chs. 8–11.
13. See Brian Stanley, *The Global Diffusion of Evangelicalism: The Age of Billy Graham and
    John Stott* (Nottingham: Inter-Varsity Press, 2013), ch. 2, esp. 27–28.

SELECT BIBLIOGRAPHY

Sources

Periodicals

Advent Witness

Australian Christian World

Baptist Magazine and Literary Review

Baptist Quarterly

Bible Student and Teacher

Biblical Review

Bibliotheca Sacra

Canadian Journal of Religious Thought

Christian

Christian World Pulpit

Church Quarterly Review

Churchman

Congregational Quarterly

Constructive Quarterly

Dawn: An Evangelical Magazine

Evangelical Christendom

Evangelical Christian

Evangelical Magazine

Evangelism: A Monthly Bulletin of Evangelistic Work in the Church of England
Free Church Chronicle
Holborn Review
Homiletic Review
Journal of the Wesley Bible Union
London Quarterly and Holborn Review
Modern Churchman
Outlook
Primitive Methodist Quarterly Review
Record of Christian Work
Southern Cross
Wesleyan Methodist Magazine
Witnessing for Christ in the Universities. A Terminal Magazine and Prayer Report
World Dominion

Reports and conference proceedings

Baptist World Congress, 1905, 1911, 1923, 1928, 1934, 1939, 1947.

Burleigh, J. H. S. et al. (eds.) (1938), *The Fourth Calvinistic Congress Held in Edinburgh 6th to 11th July 1938*, Edinburgh: Congress Executive.

Cairns, D. S. (ed.) (1919), *The Army and Religion: An Enquiry and Its Bearing upon the Religious Life of the Nation*, London: Macmillan.

Committee on the War and the Religious Outlook (1920), *Religion Among American Men As Revealed by a Study of Conditions in the Army*, New York: Association Press.

Ecumenical Methodist Conference, 1901, 1911, 1921, 1931.

Ecumenical Missionary Conference New York, 1900. Report of the Ecumenical Conference on Foreign Missions . . . April 21 to May 1, 2 vols., London: Religious Tract Society/American Tract Society.

Islington Clerical Meeting, 1900, 1902, 1904–15, 1918–39, 1947–8.

Proceedings of the . . . General Council of the Alliance of Reformed Churches Holding the Presbyterian System, 1896, 1904, 1909, 1913, 1921, 1925, 1929, 1933, 1937, 1948.

Proceedings of the . . . International Congregational Council, 1899, 1908, 1920, 1930, 1949.

Report of Sermons and Lectures. Westminster Bible Conference, Mundesley, 1906–16.

Towards Reunion: Being Contributions to Mutual Understanding by Church of England and Free Church Writers, London: Macmillan, 1919.

World Missionary Conference, 1910: The History and Records of the Conference Together with Addresses Delivered at the Evening Meetings, Edinburgh: Oliphant, Anderson & Ferrier [1910].

World Missionary Conference, 1910: Report of Commission IV. The Missionary Message in Relation to Non-Christian Religions, Edinburgh: Oliphant, Anderson & Ferrier, 1910.

World Missionary Conference, 1910: Report of Commission VI. The Home Base of Missions, Edinburgh: Oliphant, Anderson & Ferrier, n.d.

Other printed sources

Adeney, W. F. (1901), *A Century's Progress in Religious Life and Thought*, London: Methuen.

Alexander, Helen C. (1920), *Charles M. Alexander: A Romance of Song and Soul-Winning*, London: Marshall Brothers.

Anderson, Robert (1902), *The Bible and Modern Criticism*, London: Hodder & Stoughton.

—— (1904), *Pseudo-Criticism or the Higher Criticism and Its Counterfeit*, New York: Fleming H. Revell.

Austin, Percy (1930), *Letters to a Fundamentalist*, London: SCM Press.

Ballard, Frank (1914), *Britain Justified: The War from the Christian Standpoint*, London: Charles H. Kelley.

Balleine, G. R. (1908), *A History of the Evangelical Party in the Church of England*, London: Longmans, Green.

Bardsley, Cyril C. B., and T. Guy Rogers (eds.) (1915), *Studies in Revival*, London: Longmans, Green.

Bartleman, Frank (1982), *Azusa Street*, New Kensington, PA: Whitaker House.

Barton, James L. (1912), *Human Progress Through Missions*, New York: Fleming H. Revell.

Billington, Mary Frances (1915), *The Roll-Call of Serving Women: A Record of Woman's Work for Combatants and Sufferers in the Great War*, London: Religious Tract Society.

Black, Donald (1931), *Red Dust: An Australian Trooper in Palestine*, London: Jonathan Cape.

Boreham, Frank W. (1940), *My Pilgrimage: An Autobiography*, London: Epworth Press.

Brown, William Adams (1906), *Christian Theology in Outline*, New York: Charles Scribner's Sons.

Bruce, F. F. (1980), *In Retrospect: Remembrance of Things Past*, London: Pickering & Inglis.

Buchman, Frank N. D. (1942), *Remaking the World: Selections from the Speeches of Dr Frank N. D. Buchman*, London: Heinemann.

Cadoux, Cecil J. (1938), *The Case for Evangelical Modernism: A Study of the Relation Between Christian Faith and Traditional Theology*, London: Hodder & Stoughton.

Cairns, D. S. (1906), *Christianity in the Modern World*, London: Hodder & Stoughton.

Carnell, E. J. (1948), *An Introduction to Christian Apologetics: A Philosophic Defense of the Trinitarian–Theistic Faith*, Grand Rapids: Eerdmans.

Carter, Charles S., and G. E. A. Weeks (eds.) (1933), *The Protestant Dictionary: Containing Articles on the History, Doctrines and Practices of the Christian Church*, London: Harrison Trust, new ed.

Chapman, J. Wilbur (1900), *The Life and Work of Dwight L. Moody*, London: James Nisbet.

—— (1903), *Present-Day Evangelism*, New York: Baker & Taylor.

—— (1909), *Revival Addresses*, Melbourne: T. Shaw Fitchett.

—— (1922), *Evangelistic Sermons*, New York: Fleming H. Revell.

Clarke, William Newton (1907), *An Outline of Christian Theology*, Edinburgh: T. & T. Clark.

—— (1909), *Sixty Years with the Bible: A Record of Experience*, New York: Charles Scribner's Sons.

Coffin, Henry Sloane (1915), *The Practical Aims of a Liberal Evangelicalism: Closing Address, May 18th, 1915*, New York: Union Theological Seminary.

—— (1915), *Some Christian Convictions: A Practical Restatement in Terms of Present-Day Thinking*, New Haven: Yale University Press.

Coggan, Donald (ed.) (1934), *Christ and the Colleges: A History of the Inter-Varsity Fellowship of Evangelical Unions*, London: Inter-Varsity Fellowship.

Conn, J. C. M. (1939), *The Menace of the New Psychology*, London: Inter-Varsity Fellowship.

Dale, R. W. (1889), *The Old Evangelicalism and the New*, London: Hodder & Stoughton.

Darlow, T. H. (1925), *William Robertson Nicoll: Life and Letters*, London: Hodder & Stoughton.

Davenport, Frederick Morgan (1968 [1905]), *Primitive Traits in Religious Revivals: A Study in Mental and Social Evolution*, New York: Negro Universities Press.

Davies, David J. (1919), *The Church and the Plain Man*, Sydney: Angus & Robertson.

Davies, D. R. (1939), *On to Orthodoxy*, London: Hodder & Stoughton.

—— (1961), *In Search of Myself: The Autobiography of D. R. Davies*, London: Geoffrey Bles.

Davis, George T. B. (1905), *Torrey and Alexander: The Story of a World-Wide Revival*, New York: Fleming H. Revell.

Davison, W. T. (ed.) (1914), *The Chief Corner-Stone: Essays Towards an Exposition of the Christian Faith for To-day*, London: Charles H. Kelly.

Dennis, James S. (1899), *Christian Missions and Social Progress: A Sociological Study of Modern Missions*, 2 vols., Edinburgh: Oliphant, Anderson & Ferrier.

—— (1902), *Centennial Survey of Foreign Missions*, New York: Fleming H. Revell.

Drummond, Henry (1899), *The New Evangelism and Other Papers*, 2nd ed., London: Hodder & Stoughton.

Duncan, G. S. (1966), *Douglas Haig As I Knew Him*, London: George Allen & Unwin.

Eddy, Sherwood (1917), *With Our Soldiers in France*, New York: Association Press.

—— (1920), *Everybody's World*, New York: Association Press.

Erdman, Charles R. (1926), *The Spirit of Christ: Devotional Studies in the Doctrine of the Holy Spirit*, Chicago: Moody Press.

Fitchett, W. H. (1922), *Where the Higher Criticism Fails*, London: Epworth Press.

Fleming, Ambrose (1929), *The Christian Faith in Relation to Modern Thought*, Inter-Varsity Booklet 4, London: The Inter-Varsity Fellowship of Evangelical Unions.

—— (1930), *The Veracity of Holy Scripture*, Inter-Varsity Booklet 5, London: The Inter-Varsity Fellowship of Evangelical Unions.

Fletcher, Lionel B. (1932), *Effective Evangelism*, London: Religious Tract Society.

—— (1946), *Conquering Evangelism*, London: Marshall, Morgan & Scott.

Forsyth, Peter T. (1899), *Christian Perfection*, London: Hodder & Stoughton.

—— (1907), *Positive Preaching and Modern Mind*, London: Hodder & Stoughton.

—— (1910), *The Work of Christ*, London: Hodder & Stoughton.

—— (1916), *The Christian Ethic of War*, London: Longmans, Green.

—— (1916), *The Justification of God: Lectures for War-Time on a Christian Theodicy*, London: Duckworth.

Fosdick, Harry E. (1914), *The Manhood of the Master*, New York: Association Press.

—— (1915), *The Meaning of Prayer*, New York: Association Press.

—— (1918), *The Challenge of the Present Crisis*, New York: Association Press.

—— (1919), *The Church's Message to the Nation*, New York: Association Press.

—— (1926), *Adventurous Religion and Other Essays*, London: SCM Press.

—— (1957), *The Living of These Days: An Autobiography*, London: SCM Press.

French, E. Aldom (ed.) (1921), *Evangelism: A Reinterpretation*, London: Epworth Press.

Gairdner, W. H. T. (1910), *'Edinburgh 1910': An Account and Interpretation of the World Missionary Conference*, Edinburgh: Oliphant, Anderson & Ferrier.

Gray, A. Herbert (1918), *As Tommy Sees Us: A Book for Church Folk*, London: E. Arnold.

Gray, James M. (1907), *The Antidote to Christian Science, or How to Deal with It from the Bible and Christian Point of View*, 4th ed., New York: Fleming H. Revell.

Griffith-Jones, E. (1915), *The Challenge of Christianity to a World at War*, London: Duckworth.

Grubb, Kenneth (1971), *Crypts of Power: An Autobiography*, London: Hodder & Stoughton.

Grubb, Norman (1933), *C. T. Studd: Cricketer and Pioneer*, London: Religious Tract Society.

—— (1969), *Once Caught, No Escape: My Life Story*, London: Lutterworth Press.

Guinness, Howard (1978), *Journey Among Students*, Sydney: Anglican Information Office.

Hallock, G. B. F. (1922), *The Evangelistic Cyclopedia: A New Century Handbook of Evangelism*, New York: George H. Doran.

Hammond, Thomas C. (n.d. [1933]), *The Evangelical Revival and the Oxford Movement*, London: Church Book Room [= *Ch* 47.2, 79–86].

—— (1936), *'In Understanding Be Men': A Synopsis of Christian Doctrine for Non-Theological Students*, London: Inter-Varsity Fellowship.

—— (1938), *Perfect Freedom: An Introduction to Christian Ethics*, London: Inter-Varsity Fellowship.

—— (n.d. [1940]), *Fading Light: The Tragedy of Spiritual Decline in Germany*, London: Marshall, Morgan & Scott.

—— (1943), *Reasoning Faith: An Introduction to Christian Apologetics*, London: Inter-Varsity Fellowship.

Hankey, Donald (1916), *A Student in Arms*, London: Andrew Melrose.

Harford, John B., and Frederick C. MacDonald (n.d. [1922]), *Handley Carr Glyn Moule, Bishop of Durham: A Biography*, London: Hodder & Stoughton.

Harris, G. H. (1943), *Vernon Faithfull Storr: A Memoir*, London: SPCK.

Harrison, Marjorie (1934), *Saints Run Mad: A Criticism of the 'Oxford' Group Movement*, London: John Lane.

Henderson, Kenneth T. (1919), *Khaki and Cassock*, Melbourne: Melville & Mullen.

Henry, Carl (1946), *Remaking the Modern Mind*, Grand Rapids: Eerdmans.

Hooton, W. S. (1937), *Problems of Faith and Conduct*, London: Inter-Varsity Fellowship.

Howden, J. Russell (ed.) (n.d. [1925]), *Evangelicalism: By Members of the Fellowship of Evangelical Churchmen*, London: Thynne.

Jackson, George (1903), *The Teaching of Jesus*, London: Hodder & Stoughton.

—— (1908), *The Fact of Conversion*, New York: Fleming H. Revell.

Jackson, Gilbert (1935), *An Economist's Confession of Faith*, Toronto: Macmillan.

Jones, E. Stanley (1935), *Christ and Communism*, London: Hodder & Stoughton.

—— (1936), *Victorious Living*, London: Hodder & Stoughton.

Keeble, S. E. (1933), 'What the Churches Are Doing: Social Activities', in Percy Dearmer (ed.), *Christianity and the Crisis*, London: Victor Gollancz, 286–305.

Kincheloe, Samuel (1937), *Research Memorandum on Religion in the Depression. Bulletin 33*, New York: Social Science Research Council.

Knox, E. A. (1933), *The Tractarian Movement, 1833–1845*, London: Putnam.

Kraemer, Hendrik (1938), *The Christian Message in a Non-Christian World*, London: IMC.

Latourette, Kenneth S. (1936), *Missions Tomorrow*, New York: Harper & Brothers.

Lewis, Brian (1923), *Liberal Evangelicalism: Pamphlets*, 2 vols., London: Hodder & Stoughton.

—— (1980), *Our War: Australia During World War I*, Carlton: Melbourne University Press.

Lidgett, J. Scott (1936), *My Guided Life*, London: Methuen.

Lloyd-Jones, D. M. (1939), *Why Does God Allow War? A General Justification of the Ways of God*, London: Hodder & Stoughton.

Lyon, D. Willard (1915), *The Christian Equivalent of War*, London: Association Press.

McCullough, Hugh C. C. (1935), *The Call of the Sky*, London: Marshall, Morgan & Scott.

Machen, J. Gresham (1923), *Christianity and Liberalism*, New York: Macmillan.

—— (1925), *What Is Faith?* (London: Hodder & Stoughton).

Mackenzie, W. Douglas (1898), *Christianity and the Progress of Man As Illustrated by Modern Missions*, Edinburgh: Oliphant, Anderson & Ferrier.

—— (1918), *Christian Ethics in the World War*, New York: Association Press.

Mackintosh, H. R. (1964 [1937]), *Types of Modern Theology*, London: Fontana.

Maclean, Donald M. (1938), *The Revival of the Reformed Faith*, London: Inter-Varsity Fellowship.

Maclean, J. Kennedy (n.d.), *Triumphant Evangelism: The Three Years' Mission of Dr Torrey and Mr Alexander in Great Britain and Ireland*, London: Marshall Brothers.

McPherson, Aimee Semple (1919), *This Is That: Personal Experiences, Sermons and Writings of Aimee Semple McPherson, Evangelist*, Los Angeles: Bridal Call Publishing House.

Manley, G. T. (ed.) (1947), *The New Bible Handbook*, London: Inter-Varsity Christian Fellowship.

Marshall, Newton H. (1909), *Conversion, or the New Birth*, London: National Council of Evangelical Free Churches.

Mathews, Basil (ed.) (1919), *World Brotherhood*, London: Hodder & Stoughton.

—— (1924), *The Clash of Colour: A Study in the Problem of Race*, London: Edinburgh House Press.

Mee, Arthur, and J. Stuart Holden (n.d. [1917]), *Defeat or Victory? The Strength of Britain Book*, 2nd ed., Christchurch: L. M. Isitt.

Miller, Francis Pickens (1971), *Man from the Valley: Memoirs of a 20th-Century Virginian*, Chapel Hill: University of North Carolina Press.

Morgan, George (1909), *A Veteran in Revival: R. C. Morgan. His Life and Times*, London: Pickering & Inglis.

Morgan, J. Vyrnwy (1909), *The Welsh Religious Revival 1904–5: A Retrospect and a Criticism*, London: Chapman & Hall.

Mott, John R. (1900), *The Evangelization of the World in This Generation*, London: Student Volunteer Missionary Union.

—— (1905), *The Home Ministry and Modern Missions: A Plea for Leadership in World Evangelization*, London: Hodder & Stoughton.

—— (1910), *The Decisive Hour of Christian Missions*, London: CMS.

—— (1915), *The Present World Situation: With Special Reference to Demands Made upon the Christian Church in Relation to Non-Christian Lands*, London: SCM Press.

—— (1939), *Five Decades and a Forward View*, London: Harper & Brothers.

—— (n.d.), *The Morning Watch and Bible Study for Personal Spiritual Growth*, Melbourne: Student Movement Press.

Moule, Handley (1915), *Christus Consolator: Words for Hearts in Trouble*, London: SPCK.

—— (1916), *Christ and Sorrow: Thoughts for Stricken Hearts*, London: SPCK.

[Moulton, William F.] (1919), *James Hope Moulton, by His Brother*, London: Epworth Press.

Mulliner, H. G. (1936), *Arthur Burroughs: A Memoir*, London: James Nisbet.

Mullins, E. Y. (1924), *Christianity at the Cross Roads*, New York: George H. Doran.

Murdoch, Patrick J. (1915), *The Laughter and Tears of God and Other War Sermons*, Melbourne: Arbuckle, Waddell & Fawckner.

Murray, J. Lovell (1918), *The Call of a World Task in War Time*, rev. ed., New York: Association Press.

Neill, Stephen (1991), *God's Apprentice: The Autobiography of Stephen Neill*, ed. E. M. Jackson, London: Hodder & Stoughton.

(n.d. [1913]), *Old Paths in Perilous Times. An Account of the Cambridge Inter-Collegiate Christian Union*, n.p.

Oldham, J. H. (1916), *The World and the Gospel*, London: United Council for Missionary Education.

—— (1924), *Christianity and the Race Problem*, London: SCM Press.

Orr, James (1897), *The Ritschlian Theology and the Evangelical Faith*, London: Hodder & Stoughton.

Orr, James (ed.) (1915), *The International Standard Bible Encyclopaedia*, Chicago: Howard-Severance.

Orr, J. Edwin (n.d. [1937]), *Such Things Happen: 100,000 Miles Around the Globe*, London: Marshall, Morgan & Scott.

—— (n.d.), 'A Call for the Re-Study of Revival and Revivalism', http://www.jedwinorr. com/resources/pdf/Orr_Revival_and_Revivalism.pdf (accessed 13 July 2016).

Ottman, Ford C. (1920), *J. Wilbur Chapman: A Biography*, New York: Doubleday, Page.

Peake, Arthur S. (ed.) (1919), *A Commentary on the Bible*, London: Thomas Nelson & Sons.

—— (1938), *Recollections and Appreciations*, London: Epworth Press.

Pierson, A. T. (1905), *The Believer's Life: Its Past, Present and Future Tenses*, London: Morgan & Scott.

Rattenbury, J. Ernest (1932), *Evangelism: Its Shame and Glory*, London: Epworth Press.

Ridley, John G. (1941), *A Soldier's Testimony: Written for the Glory of God, the Honour of the Lord Jesus Christ, and the Help of Men, Especially Soldiers, and Veterans of the Great War*, 6th ed., Melbourne: Marshall, Morgan & Scott.

Rogers, T. Guy (ed.) (1923), *Liberal Evangelicalism: An Interpretation by Members of the Church of England*, London: Hodder & Stoughton.

—— (ed.) (1925), *The Inner Life: Essays in Liberal Evangelicalism Second Series By Members of the Church of England*, London: Hodder & Stoughton.

—— (1956), *A Rebel at Heart: The Autobiography of a Nonconforming Churchman*, London: Longmans, Green.

Scroggie, G. (n.d.), *Baptism with the Spirit. What Is It?* London: Pickering & Inglis.

Selbie, W. B. (ed.) (1911), *Evangelical Christianity: Its History and Witness*, London: Hodder & Stoughton.

Sellers, William E. (n.d. [1915]), *With Our Fighting Men: The Story of Their Faith, Courage, Endurance in the Great War*, London: Religious Tract Society.

—— (n.d. [1917]), *With Our Heroes in Khaki: The Story of Christian Work with Our Soldiers and Sailors – and Some of Its Results*, London: Religious Tract Society.

Shakespeare, J. H. (1918), *The Churches at the Cross Roads*, London: Williams & Norgate.

Shillito, Edward (1925), *Christian Citizenship: The Story of C.O.P.E.C.*, London: Longmans, Green.

Short, Arthur Rendle (n.d. [1930–1]), *The Bible and Modern Research*, London: Marshall, Morgan, & Scott.

Simpson, P. Carnegie (1934), *The Evangelical Church Catholic*, London: Hodder & Stoughton.

Smith, George A. (1899), *The Life of Henry Drummond*, London: Hodder & Stoughton.

—— (1901), *Modern Criticism and the Preaching of the Old Testament*, London: Hodder & Stoughton.

[Smith, Gipsy] (1906), *Gipsy Smith: His Life and Work by Himself*, London: National Council of the Evangelical Free Churches.

Snowden, James H. (1919), *The Coming of the Lord: Will It Be Premillennial?* New York: Macmillan.

Speer, Robert (1896), *Studies of the Man Christ Jesus*, New York: YMCA Press.

—— (1901), *Christ and Life*, New York: Fleming H. Revell.

—— (1919), *The Gospel and the New World*, New York: Fleming H. Revell.

—— (1919), *The New Opportunity of the Church*, New York: Macmillan.

Spurr, Frederic C. (n.d. [1916]), *Some Chaplains in Khaki: An Account of the Work of the Chaplains of the United Navy and Army Board*, London: H. R. Allenson & The Kingsgate Press.

Stamp, Josiah (1936), *Motive and Method in a Christian Order*, London: Epworth Press.

—— (1939), *Christianity and Economics*, London: Macmillan.

Stock, Eugene (1899), *A History of the Church Missionary Society: Its Environment, Its Men and Its Work*, 3 vols., London: CMS.

—— (1909), *My Recollections*, London: James Nisbet.

—— (1911), *A Plain Man's Thoughts on Biblical Criticism*, London: Longmans, Green.

Stoddart, Jane T. (1919), *The Case Against Spiritualism*, London: Hodder & Stoughton.

Storr, Vernon F. (1934), *Spiritual Liberty: A Study in Liberal Evangelicalism*, London: SCM Press.

Strong, Augustus H. (1908), *Outlines of Systematic Theology Designed for the Use of Theological Students*, Philadelphia: American Baptist Publication Society.

Strong, Josiah (1900), *Religious Movements for Social Betterment*, New York: Baker & Taylor.

—— (1902), *The Next Great Awakening*, New York: Baker & Taylor.

—— (1907), *The Challenge of the City*, New York: Young People's Missionary Movement.

Tatlow, Tissington (1933), *The Story of the Student Christian Movement of Great Britain and Ireland*, London: SCM Press.

Thomas, W. H. Griffith (n.d.), *Methods of Bible Study*, London: Marshall Brothers.

Thomson, D. P. (ed.) (1925), *The Modern Evangelistic Address*, New York: George H. Doran.

[Thomson, David P., and Hubert L. Simpson (eds.)] (1923), *Evangelism in the Modern World. Edited by Two University Men*, Glasgow: Thomson & Cowan.

—— (1924), *Modern Evangelistic Movements. Edited by Two University Men*, New York: George H. Doran.

Tiplady, Thomas (1917), *The Cross at the Front: Fragments from the Trenches*, New York: Fleming H. Revell.

—— (1918), *The Soul of the Soldier: Sketches of Life at the Front*, London: Methuen.

—— (1914), *To the Christian Scholars of Europe and America: A Reply from Oxford to the German Address to Evangelical Christians*, Oxford: Oxford University Press.

Torrey, R. A. (1898), *Ten Reasons Why I Believe the Bible Is the Word of God*, Chicago: Bible Institute Colportage Association.

—— (n.d. [1898]), *What the Bible Teaches: A Thorough and Comprehensive Study of All the Bible Has to Say Concerning the Great Doctrines of Which It Treats*, London: James Nisbet.

—— (1903), *Revival Addresses*, London: James Nisbet.

—— (1905), *Salvation and Whole Hearted Service*, New York: Fleming H. Revell.

—— (1917), *The Voice of God in the Present Hour*, New York: Fleming H. Revell.

—— (1918), *Peanut Patriotism and Pure Patriotism: Our Duty to God and Our Country in This Time of Crisis*, Los Angeles: BIOLA.

—— (1918), *Will Christ Come Again? An Exposure of the Foolishness and Falsehoods of Shailer Mathews*, Los Angeles: BIOLA.

—— (n.d.), *How to Make a Success of the Christian Life*, London: James Nisbet.

Torrey, R. A. (ed.) (1898), *How to Promote and Conduct a Successful Revival*, London: Andrew Melrose.

—— (1902), *The Torrey–Alexander Souvenir: A Complete Record of Their Work in Australia. A Special Souvenir Number of the 'Southern Cross'* (10 Sept. 1902).

Vine, Charles H. (ed.) (1907), *The Old Faith and the New Theology: A Series of Sermons and Essays on Some of the Truths Held by Evangelical Christians, and the Difficulties of Accepting Much of What Is Called the 'New Theology'*, London: Sampson Low, Marston.

Wace, Henry (1917), *The War and the Gospel*, London: Chas. J. Thynne.

Warfield, Benjamin B. (1931), *Perfectionism*, 2 vols., New York: Oxford University Press.

Warren, Max (n.d. [1944]), *What Is An Evangelical? An Enquiry*, London: Church Book Room.

—— (1974), *Crowded Canvas: Some Experiences of a Life-Time*, London: Hodder & Stoughton.

[Watts, Newman] (1932), *Why Sunday? By a London Journalist*, London: Lutterworth Press.

Webb, B. Linden (1915), *The Religious Significance of the War*, Sydney: Christian World.

Weber, H. C. (1929), *Evangelism: A Graphic Survey*, New York: Macmillan.

Whale, J. S. (1940), *Facing the Facts*, London: Hodder & Stoughton.

White, F. C. (n.d.), *Evangelism Today*, London: Marshall, Morgan & Scott.

Whitlow, Maurice (1938), *J. Taylor Smith: Everybody's Bishop*, London: Lutterworth Press.

Wilder, Robert (1902), *Missionary Principles and Practice*, New York: Fleming H. Revell.

Williams, T. Rhondda (1905), *The True Revival Versus Torreyism*, London.

Woods, C. Stacey (1978), *The Growth of a Work of God: The Story of the Early Days of the Inter-Varsity Christian Fellowship of the United States of America As Told by Its First General Secretary*, Downers Grove: InterVarsity Press.

Later editions of sources

Bickersteth, John (ed.) (1995), *The Bickersteth Diaries*, London: Leo Cooper.

Carpenter, Joel A. (ed.) (1988), *Conservative Call to Arms*, New York: Garland Publishing.

—— (1988), *God Hath Spoken: Twenty-Five Addresses Delivered at the World Conference on Christian Fundamentals May 25–June 1, 1919*, New York: Garland Publishing.

—— (1988), *A New Evangelical Coalition: Early Documents of the National Association of Evangelicals*, New York: Garland Publishing.

—— (1988), *The Premillennial Second Coming: Two Early Champions*, New York: Garland Publishing.

Clements, Keith (ed.) (2010), *The Moot Papers: Faith, Freedom and Society 1938–1944*, London: T. & T. Clark.

Davenport, Frederick Morgan (1968 [1905]), *Primitive Traits in Religious Revivals: A Study in Mental and Social Evolution*, New York: Negro Universities Press.

Dixon, A. C. (1988 [1905]), *Evangelism Old and New: God's Search for Man in All Ages*, New York: Garland Publishing.

Douglas, W. M. (1988 [1926]), *Andrew Murray and His Message*, Belfast: Ambassador Publications.

Hart, D. G. (ed.) (2004), *J. Gresham Machen: Selected Shorter Writings*, Phillipsburg: P&R Publishing.

Hutchison, William R. (ed.) (1968), *American Protestant Thought in the Liberal Era*, Lanham, MD: University Press of America.

Marsden, George (ed.) (1988 [1912–15]), *The Fundamentals: A Testimony to the Truth*, 12 vols. in 4, New York: Garland Publishing.

Noll, Mark (ed.) (1983), *The Princeton Theology 1812–1921: Scripture, Science, and Theological Method from Archibald Alexander to Benjamin Breckinridge Warfield*, Grand Rapids: Baker Books.

Pierson, A. T. (1984 [1905]), *Forward Movements of the Last Half Century*, London: Garland Publishing.

Stead, W. T. (1972 [1902]), *The Americanization of the World, or, the Trend of the Twentieth Century*, New York: Garland Publishing.

Torrey, R. A., and A. C. Dixon (eds.) (1996), *The Fundamentals*, 4 vols., Grand Rapids: Baker Books.

Secondary sources

Abrams, R. H. (1969 [1933]), *Preachers Present Arms: The Role of the American Churches and Clergy in World Wars I and II, With Some Observations on the War in Vietnam*, Scottdale, PA: Herald Press.

Airhart, Phyllis D. (2014), *A Church with the Soul of a Nation: Making and Remaking the United Church of Canada*, Montreal: McGill-Queen's University Press.

Akenson, Donald (1988), *Small Differences: Irish Catholics and Irish Protestants 1815–1922*, Montreal: McGill-Queen's University Press.

Allison, Neil (2013), 'Free Church Revivalism in the British Army During the First World War', in Michael Snape and Edward Madigan (eds.), *The Clergy in Khaki: New Perspectives on British Army Chaplaincy in the First World War*, Farnham: Ashgate, 41–55.

Anderson, Allan (2007), *Spreading Fires: The Missionary Nature of Early Pentecostalism*, London: SCM Press.

Anderson, Malcolm (1993), 'Economic Science in Evangelical Social Thought: A Missing Dimension of the English Christian Social Movement', *L* 15, 21–43.

Anderson, Richard James (1974), 'The Urban Revivalists, 1880–1910', PhD thesis, University of Chicago.

Anderson, Robert Mapes (1979), *Vision of the Disinherited: The Making of American Pentecostalism*, New York: Oxford University Press.

Appasamy, A. J. (1964), *Write the Vision: Edwin Orr's Thirty Years of Adventurous Service*, London: Marshall, Morgan & Scott.

Appelbaum, Patricia (2009), *Kingdom to Commune: Protestant Pacifist Culture Between World War I and the Vietnam Era*, Chapel Hill: University of North Carolina Press.

Askew, Thomas A. (2000), 'The New York 1900 Ecumenical Missionary Conference: A Centennial Reflection', *IBMR* 24.4, 146–154.

Atherstone, Andrew (2013), 'Evangelicals and the Oxford Movement Centenary', *JRH* 37.1, 98–117.

Atherstone, Andrew, and David Ceri Jones (eds.) (2011), *Engaging with Martyn Lloyd-Jones: The Life and Legacy of 'the Doctor'*, Nottingham: Apollos.

Atherstone, Andrew, and John Maiden (eds.) (2014), *Evangelicalism and the Church of England in the Twentieth Century: Reform, Resistance and Renewal*, Woodbridge: Boydell Press.

Bailey, Charles E. (1984), 'The British Protestant Theologians in the First World War: Germanophobia Unleashed', *HTR* 77.2, 195–221.

Baldwin, Ethel M., and David V. Benson (1967), *Henrietta Mears and How She Did It!*, Glendale: Regal Books.

Ballis, Peter H. (1986), 'Conscience and Compromise: New Zealand Adventists and Military Service During World War I', in Arthur J. Ferch (ed.), *Symposium on Adventist History in the South Pacific: 1885–1918*, Wahroonga, NSW: South Pacific Division of Seventh-Day Adventists, 40–52.

Barclay, Oliver R., and Robert M. Horn (2002), *From Cambridge to the World: 125 Years of Student Witness*, Leicester: Inter-Varsity Press.

Barfoot, Chas. H. (2011), *Aimee Semple McPherson and the Making of Modern Pentecostalism 1890–1926*, London: Equinox Publishing.

Barnes, John (1979), *Ahead of His Age: Bishop Barnes of Birmingham*, London: Collins.

Barnes, Kenneth C. (1991), *Nazism, Liberalism and Christianity: Protestant Social Thought in Germany and Great Britain 1925–1937*, Lexington: University Press of Kentucky.

Barrett, David et al. (2001), *World Christian Encyclopedia: A Comparative Survey of Churches and Religions in the Modern World*, 2nd ed., 2 vols., Oxford: Oxford University Press.

Baruma, Ian (2013), *Year Zero: The History of 1945*, New York: Penguin.

Baswick, Daryl (1997), 'Social Evangelism, the Canadian Churches, and the Forward Movement, 1919–1920', *OH* 89.4 (1997), 303–319.

Bayly, C. A. (2004), *The Birth of the Modern World 1780–1914*, Malden, MA: Blackwell Publishing.

Bebbington, David W. (1979), 'The City, the Countryside and the Social Gospel in Late Victorian Nonconformity', *SCH* 16, 415–426.

—— (1982), *The Nonconformist Conscience: Chapel and Politics 1870–1914*, London: George Allen & Unwin.

—— (1983), 'Baptists and Politics Since 1914', in K. W. Clements (ed.), *Baptists in the Twentieth Century*, London: Baptist Historical Society, 76–95.

—— (1984), 'The Persecution of George Jackson: A British Fundamentalist Controversy', *SCH* 21, 421–433.

—— (1986), 'Baptist Members of Parliament in the Twentieth Century', *BQ* 31.6, 252–287.

—— (1986), 'The Oxford Group Movement', *SCH* 23, 495–507.

—— (1989), *Evangelicalism in Modern Britain: A History from the 1730s to the 1980s*, London: Unwin Hyman.

—— (1993), 'Martyrs for the Truth: Fundamentalists in Britain', *SCH* 30, 417–451.

—— (1995), 'The Decline and Resurgence of Evangelical Social Concern 1918–1980', in John Wolffe (ed.), *Evangelical Faith and Public Zeal: Evangelicals and Society in Britain 1780–1980*, London: SPCK, 175–197.

—— (1996), 'Missionary Controversy and the Polarising Tendency in Twentieth-Century British Protestantism', *Anvil* 13.2, 141–157.

—— (2000), *Holiness in Nineteenth-Century England*, Carlisle: Paternoster Press.

—— (2003), 'Atonement, Sin and Empire, 1880–1914', in Andrew Porter (ed.), *The Imperial Horizons of British Protestant Missions, 1880–1914*, Grand Rapids: Eerdmans, 14–31.

—— (2003), 'Evangelism and Spirituality in Twentieth-Century Protestant Nonconformity', in Alan P. F. Sell and Anthony R. Cross (eds.), *Protestant Nonconformity in the Twentieth Century*, Carlisle: Paternoster Press, 184–215.

—— (2005), *The Dominance of Evangelicalism: The Age of Spurgeon and Moody*, Leicester: Inter-Varsity Press.

—— (2007), 'Baptist Members of Parliament: A Supplementary Note', *BQ* 42.2, pt. 2, 148–161.

—— (2008), 'Evangelicalism and Cultural Diffusion', in Mark Smith (ed.), *British Evangelical Identities Past and Present*, Eugene: Wipf & Stock, 18–34.

—— (2011), 'Lloyd-Jones and the Interwar Calvinist Resurgence', in Andrew Atherstone and David Ceri Jones (eds.), *Engaging with Martyn Lloyd-Jones: The Life and Legacy of 'the Doctor'*, Nottingham: Apollos, 38–58.

—— (2013), 'Baptists and Fundamentalism in Inter-War Britain', in David Bebbington and David Ceri Jones (eds.) (2013), *Evangelicalism and Fundamentalism in the United Kingdom During the Twentieth Century*, Oxford: Oxford University Press, 95–114.

Bebbington, David, and David Ceri Jones (eds.) (2013), *Evangelicalism and Fundamentalism in the United Kingdom During the Twentieth Century*, Oxford: Oxford University Press.

Bebbington, David, and Martin Sutherland (eds.) (2013), *Interfaces: Baptists and Others*, Milton Keynes: Paternoster Press.

Bederman, Gail (1989), '"The Women Have Had Charge of the Church Work Long Enough": The Men and Religion Forward Movement of 1911–1912 and the Masculinization of Middle-Class Protestantism', *AQ* 41.3, 432–465.

Bendroth, Margaret L. (2005), *Fundamentalists in the City: Conflict and Division in Boston's Churches, 1885–1920*, New York: Oxford University Press.

Bendroth, M., and L. Brereton (eds.) (2002), *Women and Twentieth-Century Protestantism*, Urbana: University of Illinois Press.

Binfield, Clyde (1984), *Pastors and People: The Biography of a Baptist Church, Queen's Road Coventry*, Coventry: Queen's Road Baptist Church.

Blocker, Jack S. (1989), *American Temperance Movements: Cycles of Reform*, Boston: Twayne Publishers.

Blocker, Jack S., Jr., David M. Fahey and Ian R. Tyrrell (eds.) (2003), *Alcohol and Temperance in Modern History: An International Encyclopedia*, 2 vols., Santa Barbara: ABC-CLIO.

Blumhofer, Edith L. (1989), *The Assemblies of God: A Chapter in the Story of American Pentecostalism*, 2 vols., Springfield: Gospel Publishing House.

—— (1993), *Aimee Semple McPherson: Everybody's Sister*, Grand Rapids: Eerdmans.

Bond, Brian, and Nigel Cave (eds.) (1999), *Haig: A Re-appraisal 70 Years On*, Barnsley: Leo Cooper.

Boone, Kathleen C. (1989), *The Bible Tells Them So: The Discourse of Protestant Fundamentalism*, Albany: State University of New York Press.

Bowler, Peter (2001), *Reconciling Science and Religion: The Debate in Early-Twentieth-Century Britain*, Chicago: University of Chicago Press.

Bowman, Matthew (2007), 'Sin, Spirituality, and Primitivism: The Theologies of the American Social Gospel, 1885–1917', *RAC* 17.1, 95–126.

—— (2014), *The Urban Pulpit: New York City and the Fate of Liberal Evangelicalism*, New York: Oxford University Press.

Boyd, Robin (2007), *The Witness of the Student Christian Movement: 'Church Ahead of the Church'*, Geneva: WCC Publications.

Brereton, Virginia L. (1990), *Training God's Army: The American Bible School, 1880–1940*, Bloomington: Indiana University Press.

Breward, Ian (1967), *Godless Schools? A Study of Protestant Reactions to Secular Schools in New Zealand*, Christchurch: Presbyterian Bookroom.

—— (2001), *A History of the Churches in Australasia*, Oxford: Clarendon Press.

Brown, Callum (2001), *The Death of Christian Britain: Understanding Secularisation 1800–2000*, London: Routledge.

—— (2006), *Religion and Society in Twentieth-Century Britain*, Harlow: Pearson Education.

Brown, Kenneth D. (1975), 'Non-Conformity and the British Labour Movement: A Case Study', *JSH* 8.2, 113–120.

—— (1988), *A Social History of Nonconformist Ministry in England and Wales, 1800–1930*, Oxford: Clarendon Press.

Brown, Stewart J. (1991), '"A Victory for God": The Scottish Presbyterian Churches and the General Strike of 1926', *JEH* 42.4, 596–617.

—— (1994), '"A Solemn Purification by Fire": Responses to the Great War in the Scottish Presbyterian Churches', *JEH* 45.1, 82–104.

Butler, Jonathan M. (1991), *Softly and Tenderly Jesus Is Calling: Heaven and Hell in American Revivalism, 1870–1920*, Brooklyn, NY: Carlson Publishing.

Campbell, Iain D. (2004), *Fixing the Indemnity: The Life and Work of Sir George Adam Smith (1856–1942)*, Carlisle: Paternoster Press.

Carey, Hilary (2011), *God's Empire: Religion and Colonialism in the British World, c. 1801–1908*, Cambridge: Cambridge University Press.

Carpenter, Joel A. (1990), 'Propagating the Faith Once Delivered: The Fundamentalist Missionary Enterprise, 1920–1945', in Joel A. Carpenter and Wilbert Shenk (eds.) (1990), *Earthen Vessels: American Evangelicals and Foreign Missions, 1880–1980*, Grand Rapids: Eerdmans, 92–132.

—— (1997), *Revive Us Again: The Reawakening of American Fundamentalism*, New York: Oxford University Press.

Carpenter, Joel A., and Wilbert Shenk (eds.) (1990), *Earthen Vessels: American Evangelicals and Foreign Missions, 1880–1980*, Grand Rapids: Eerdmans.

Cashdollar, Charles D. (2000), *A Spiritual Home: Life in British and American Reformed Congregations, 1830–1915*, University Park, PA: Pennsylvania State University Press.

Catterall, Peter (1993), 'Morality and Politics: The Free Churches and the Labour Party Between the Wars', *HJ* 36.3, 667–685.

Cauthen, Kenneth (1983), *The Impact of American Religious Liberalism*, 2nd ed., Lanham, MD: University Press of America.

Cave, Nigel (1999), 'Haig and Religion', in Brian Bond and Nigel Cave (eds.), *Haig: A Re-appraisal 70 Years After*, Barnsley: Leo Cooper, 240–260.

Ceadel, Martin (1980), *Pacifism in Britain 1914–1945: The Defining of a Faith*, Oxford: Clarendon Press.

Cerillo, Augustus, Jr. (1981), 'The Spanish–American War', in Ronald A. Wells (ed.), *The Wars of America: Christian Views*, Grand Rapids: Eerdmans, 91–125.

Chadwick, Owen (1975), *The Secularization of the European Mind in the Nineteenth Century*, Cambridge: Cambridge University Press.

Chandler, Andrew (2006), 'Catholicism and Protestantism in the Second World War in Europe', *CHC9*, 262–284.

Chant, Barry (2011), *The Spirit of Pentecost: The Origins and Development of the Pentecostal Movement in Australia 1870–1939*, Lexington: Emeth Press.

Chorley, E. Clowes (1946), *Men and Movements in the American Episcopal Church*, New York: Charles Scribner's Sons.

Christie, Nancy, and Michael Gauvreau (1996), *A Full-orbed Christianity: The Protestant Churches and Social Welfare in Canada 1900–1940*, Montreal: McGill-Queen's University Press.

—— (2010), *Christian Churches and Their Peoples, 1840–1965: A Social History of Religion in Canada*, Toronto: University of Toronto Press.

Clements, Keith (1999), *Faith on the Frontier: A Life of J. H. Oldham*, Edinburgh: T. & T. Clark.

Cochrane, J. R. (1994), 'Christianity During a Period of "National Consolidation"', in J. W. Hofmeyr and G. J. Pillay (eds.), *A History of Christianity in South Africa Volume I*, Pretoria: HAUM Tertiary, 200–245.

Cocksworth, Christopher J. (1993), *Evangelical Eucharistic Thought in the Church of England*, Cambridge: Cambridge University Press.

Cracknell, Kenneth (1995), *Justice, Courtesy, and Love: Theologians and Missionaries Encountering World Religions, 1846–1914*, London: Epworth Press.

Crago, T. Howard (1961), *The Story of F. W. Boreham*, London: Marshall, Morgan & Scott.

Creech, Joe (1996), 'Visions of Glory: The Place of the Azusa Street Revival in Pentecostal History', *CH* 65.3, 405–424.

Crerar, Duff (1995), *Padres in No Man's Land: Canadian Chaplains in the Great War*, Montreal: McGill-Queen's University Press.

Crouse, Eric R. (2005), *Revival in the City: The Impact of American Evangelists in Canada, 1884–1914*, Montreal: McGill-Queen's University Press.

Crunden, Robert M. (1982), *Ministers of Reform: The Progressives' Achievement in American Civilization 1889–1920*, New York: Basic Books.

Currie, Robert, Alan Gilbert and Lee Horsley (1977), *Churches and Churchgoers: Patterns of Church Growth in the British Isles Since 1700*, Oxford: Clarendon Press.

Danbom, David B. (1987), *'The World of Hope': Progressives and the Struggle for an Ethical Public Life*, Philadelphia: Temple University Press.

Davidson, Allan (2004), *Christianity in Aotearoa: A History of Church and Society in New Zealand*, 3rd ed., Wellington: Education for Ministry.

Dawson, David (1994), 'Funding Mission in the Early Twentieth Century', *IBMR* 24.4, 155–158.

—— (2002), 'Mission and Money in the Early Twentieth Century', *JPH* 80.1, 29–42.

Dayton, Donald (1987), *Theological Roots of Pentecostalism*, Metuchen, NJ: Scarecrow Press.

De Groot, Gerard J. (1991), '"We Are Safe Whatever Happens" – Douglas Haig, the Reverend George Duncan, and the Conduct of War, 1916–1918', in Norman MacDougall (ed.), *Scotland and War AD 79–1918*, Edinburgh: John Donald Publishers, 193–211.

De Gruchy, Steve (2006), 'Religion and Racism: Struggles Around Segregation, "Jim Crow" and Apartheid', *CHC* 9, 385–400.

Dickey, Brian (1988), *Holy Trinity Adelaide 1836–1988: The History of a City Church*, Adelaide: Trinity Church Trust.

Dickey, Brian (ed.) (1994), *The Australian Dictionary of Evangelical Biography*, Sydney: Evangelical History Association.

Dochuk, Darren (2000), 'Redeeming the City: Premillennialism, Piety and the Politics of Reform in Late-Nineteenth Century Toronto', *Historical Papers 2000: Canadian Society of Church History*, 53–72.

Dorsett, Lyle W. (1991), *Billy Sunday and the Redemption of Urban America*, Grand Rapids: Eerdmans.

Draney, Daniel W. (2008), *When Streams Diverge: John Murdoch MacInnis and the Origins of Protestant Fundamentalism in Los Angeles*, Milton Keynes: Paternoster Press.

Eason, Andrew Mark (2003), *Women in God's Army: Gender and Equality in the Early Salvation Army*, Waterloo: Wilfrid Laurier University Press.

Ebel, Jonathan H. (2010), *Faith in the Fight: Religion and the American Soldier in the Great War*, Princeton: Princeton University Press.

Eddison, John (ed.) (1983), *'Bash': A Study in Spiritual Power*, Basingstoke: Marshalls.

Edwards, Ben (2013), 'The Godless Congress of 1938: Christian Fears About Communism in Great Britain', *JRH* 37.1, 1–19.

Edwards, Mark T. (2012), *The Right of the Protestant Left: God's Totalitarianism*, New York: Palgrave Macmillan.

—— (2015), 'Can Christianity Save Civilisation? Liberal Protestant Anti-Secularism in Interwar America', *JRH* 39.1, 51–67.

Elliott, David (1993), 'Knowing No Borders: Canadian Contributions to American Fundamentalism', in George A. Rawlyk and Mark A. Noll (eds.), *Amazing Grace: Evangelicalism in Australia, Britain, Canada and the United States*, Grand Rapids: Baker Books, 349–374.

Ellis, William E. (2003), *'A Man of Books and a Man of the People': E. Y. Mullins and the Crisis of Moderate Southern Baptist Leadership*, Macon, GA: Mercer University Press.

Evans, Christopher H. (2004), *The Kingdom Is Always but Coming: A Life of Walter Rauschenbusch*, Grand Rapids: Eerdmans.

Evans, Elizabeth (1991), *The Wright Vision: The Story of the New England Fellowship*, Lanham, MD: Fellowship Press.

Evans, Robert (2007), *Emilia Baeyertz Evangelist*, Hazelbrook, NSW: Research in Evangelical Revivals.

Farley, A. Fay (2010), 'A Spiritual Healing Mission Remembered: James Moore Hickson's Christian Healing Mission at Palmerston North, New Zealand, 1923', *JRH* 34.1, 1–19.

Fea, John (1994), 'Power from On High in an Age of Ecclesiastical Impotence: The "Enduement of the Holy Spirit" in American Fundamentalist Thought, 1880–1936', *FH* 26.2, 23–35.

Fergusson, David (ed.) (1993), *Christ, Church and Society: Essays on John Baillie and Donald Baillie*, Edinburgh: T. & T. Clark.

Frank, Douglas W. (1986), *Less Than Conquerors: How Evangelicals Entered the Twentieth Century*, Grand Rapids: Eerdmans.

Furse-Roberts, David (2015), 'The Making of an Evangelical Tory: The Seventh Earl of Shaftesbury (1801–1885) and the Evolving Character of Victorian Evangelicalism', PhD thesis, University of New South Wales.

Gauvreau, Michael (1991), *The Evangelical Century: College and Creed in English Canada from the Great Revival to the Great Depression*, Montreal: McGill-Queen's University Press.

Gibbard, Noel (2002), *On the Wings of the Dove: The International Effects of the 1904–5 Revival*, Bridgend: Bryntirion Press.

Gilley, Sheridan, and Brian Stanley (eds.) (2006), *The Cambridge History of Christianity. Volume 8. World Christianities c.1815–c.1914*, Cambridge: Cambridge University Press.

Glass, William R. (1985), 'Fundamentalism's Prophetic Vision of the Jews: The 1930s', *JSS* 47.1, 63–76.

Gloege, Timothy E. W. (2007), 'Consumed: Reuben A. Torrey and the Construction of Corporate Fundamentalism', PhD thesis, Notre Dame University.

—— (2014), 'A Gilded Age Modernist: Reuben A. Torrey and the Roots of Contemporary Conservative Evangelicalism', in Darren Dochuk et al. (eds.), *American Evangelicalism: George Marsden and the State of American Religious History*, Notre Dame: University of Notre Dame Press, 199–229.

Goff, Phillip (1999), '"We Have Heard the Joyful Sound": Charles E. Fuller's Radio Broadcast and the Rise of Modern Evangelicalism', *RAC* 9.1, 67–95.

Gordon, James M. (2006), *James Denney (1856–1917): An Intellectual and Contextual Biography*, Carlisle: Paternoster Press.

Gorrell, Donald K. (1988), *The Age of Social Responsibility: The Social Gospel in the Progressive Era, 1900–1920*, Macon, GA: Mercer University Press.

Grass, Tim (2006), *Gathering to His Name: The Story of Open Brethren in Britain and Ireland*, Milton Keynes: Paternoster Press.

—— (2011), *F. F. Bruce: A Life*, Milton Keynes: Paternoster Press.

Green, S. J. D. (2011), *The Passing of Protestant England: Secularisation and Social Change c. 1920–1960*, Cambridge: Cambridge University Press.

Greenlee, James G., and Charles M. Johnston (1999), *Good Citizens: British Missionaries and Imperial States, 1870–1918*, Montreal: McGill-Queen's University Press.

Gribben, Crawford, and Andrew R. Holmes (eds.) (2006), *Protestant Millennialism, Evangelicalism and Irish Society, 1790–2005*, Houndmills: Palgrave Macmillan.

Grundy, Stanley N. (ed.) (1987), *Five Views on Sanctification*, Grand Rapids: Zondervan.

Hamilton, Michael (2014), 'The Interdenominational Evangelicalism of D. L. Moody and the Problem of Fundamentalism', in Darren Dochuk et al. (eds.), *American*

Evangelicalism: George Marsden and the State of American Religious History, Notre Dame: University of Notre Dame Press, 130–180.

Hammond, Sarah R. (2010), '"God's Business Men": Entrepreneurial Evangelicals in Depression and War', PhD thesis, Yale University.

—— (2011), '"God Is My Partner": An Evangelical Business Man Confronts Depression and War', *CH* 80.3, 498–519.

Hangen, Tona J. (2002), *Redeeming the Dial: Radio, Religion, and Popular Culture in America*, Chapel Hill: University of North Carolina Press.

Hankins, Barry (2010), *Jesus and Gin: Evangelicalism, the Roaring Twenties and Today's Culture Wars*, New York: Palgrave Macmillan.

—— (2011), 'The (Worst) Year of the Evangelical: 1926 and the Demise of American Fundamentalism', *FH* 43.1, 1–14.

Harris, Harriet A. (1998), *Fundamentalism and Evangelicals*, Oxford: Clarendon Press.

Harris, John (1994), *One Blood. 200 Years of Aboriginal Encounter with Christianity: A Story of Hope*, Sutherland: Albatross Books.

Hart, Daryl G. (1995), *Defending the Faith: J. Gresham Machen and the Crisis of Conservative Protestantism in Modern America*, Grand Rapids: Baker Books.

—— (2002), *That Old-Time Religion in Modern America: Evangelical Protestantism in the Twentieth Century*, Chicago: Ivan R. Dee.

Hart, D. G., and R. Albert Mohler (eds.) (1996), *Theological Education in the Evangelical Tradition*, Grand Rapids: Baker Books.

Harvey, Charles E. (1982), 'John D. Rockefeller, Jr., and the Interchurch World Movement of 1919–1920: A Different Angle on the Ecumenical Movement', *CH* 51.2, 198–209.

Harvey, Paul (2002), 'Saints but Not Subordinates: The Woman's Missionary Union of the Southern Baptist Convention', in M. Bendroth and L. Brereton (eds.), *Women and Twentieth-Century Protestantism*, Urbana: University of Illinois Press, 4–24.

Haykin, Michael A. G., and Kenneth J. Stewart (eds.) (2008), *The Emergence of Evangelicalism: Exploring Historical Continuities*, Nottingham: Apollos.

Hazelgrove, Jennifer (1999), 'Spiritualism After the Great War', *TCBH* 10.4, 404–430.

Heath, Gordon L. (2009), *A War with a Silver Lining: Canadian Protestant Churches and the South African War, 1899–1902*, Montreal: McGill-Queen's University Press.

Hedstrom, Matthew S. (2013), *The Rise of Liberal Religion: Book Culture and American Spirituality in the Twentieth Century*, New York: Oxford University Press.

Hempton, David (2005), *Methodism: Empire of the Spirit*, New Haven: Yale University Press.

Henry, S. D. (1985), 'Scottish Baptists and the First World War', *BQ* 31.2, 52–65.

Hilliard, David (1997), 'Intellectual Life in the Diocese of Melbourne', in Brian Porter (ed.), *Melbourne Anglicans: The Diocese of Melbourne 1847–1997*, Melbourne: Mitre Books, 27–48.

Hilton, Boyd (1988), *The Age of Atonement: The Influence of Evangelicalism on Social and Economic Thought, 1795–1865*, Oxford: Clarendon Press.

Hindmarsh, Bruce (2003), 'Is Evangelical Ecclesiology an Oxymoron? A Historical Perspective', in John G. Stackhouse (ed.), *Evangelical Ecclesiology: Reality or Illusion?*, Grand Rapids: Baker Academic, 15–37.

Hogg, William Richey (1952), *Ecumenical Foundations: A History of the International Missionary Council and Its Nineteenth-Century Background*, New York: Harper & Brothers.

Holmes, Andrew R. (2006), 'Biblical Authority and the Impact of Higher Criticism in Irish Presbyterianism, ca. 1850–1930', *CH* 75.2, 343–373.

Holmes, Janice (2000), *Religious Revivals in Britain and Ireland 1859–1905*, Dublin: Irish Academic Press.

Hopkins, C. Howard (1940), *The Rise of the Social Gospel in American Protestantism, 1865–1915*, Yale: Yale University Press.

—— (1951), *History of the Y.M.C.A. in North America*, New York: Association Press.

—— (1979), *John R. Mott 1865–1955: A Biography*, Grand Rapids: Eerdmans.

Hubbard, Nigel (1984), *'Almost a Martyr's Fire': Everard Digges La Touche (1883–1915)*, Canberra: National Library of Australia.

Hucker, Graham (2009), '"The Great Wave of Enthusiasm": New Zealand Reactions to the First World War in August 1914 – A Reassessment', *NZJH* 43.1, 59–75.

Hughes, Michael (2008), *Conscience and Conflict: Methodism, Peace and War in the Twentieth Century*, Werrington: Epworth Press.

Hunter, J. D. (1983), *American Evangelicalism: Conservative Evangelicalism and the Quandary of Modernity*, New Brunswick: Rutgers University Press.

Hutchinson, Mark, and Ogbu Kalu (eds.) (1998), *A Global Faith: Essays on Evangelicalism and Globalization*, Sydney: CSAC.

Hutchinson, Mark, and John Wolffe (2012), *A Short History of Global Evangelicalism*, Cambridge: Cambridge University Press.

Hutchison, William R. (1992), *The Modernist Impulse in American Protestantism*, Durham: Duke University Press.

Jacobsen, Douglas, and William V. Trollinger, Jr. (eds.) (1998), *Re-forming the Center: American Protestantism, 1900 to the Present*, Grand Rapids: Eerdmans.

James, Lawrence (1993), *Imperial Warrior: The Life and Times of Field-Marshall Viscount Allenby 1861–1936*, London: Weidenfeld & Nicolson.

Janda, Lance (2005), 'Casualties, Combatant and Non-Combatant', in Spencer C. Tucker (ed.), *The Encyclopedia of World War I*, 5 vols., Santa Barbara: ABC-CLIO, I, 272–273.

Jarlert, Anders (1995), *The Oxford Group, Group Revivalism, and the Churches of Northern Europe, 1930–1945, with Special Reference to Scandinavia and Germany*, Lund: Lund University Press.

Jenkins, Philip (2014), *The Great and Holy War: How World War I Became a Religious Crusade*, New York: HarperCollins.

Jeremy, David (2003), 'Twentieth-Century Protestant Nonconformists in the World of Business', in Alan P. F. Sell and Anthony R. Cross (eds.), *Protestant Nonconformity in the Twentieth Century*, Carlisle: Paternoster Press, 264–312.

Johnson, Dale A. (1999), *The Changing Shape of English Nonconformity, 1825–1925*, New York: Oxford University Press.

Johnson, Douglas (1979), *Contending for the Faith: A History of the Evangelical Movement in the Universities and Colleges*, Leicester: Inter-Varsity Press.

Johnson, Todd M., et. al. (2015), 'Christianity 2015: Religious Diversity and Personal Contact', *IBMR* 39.1, 28–29.

Joiner, Thekla E. (2007), *Sin in the City: Chicago and Revivalism 1880–1920*, Columbia: University of Missouri Press.

Jones, R. Tudur (2004), *Faith and the Crisis of a Nation: Wales 1890–1914*, ed. Robert Pope, trans. Sylvia Prys Jones, Cardiff: University of Wales Press.

Jordan, E. K. H. (1956), *Free Church Unity: History of the Free Church Council Movement 1896–1941*, London: Lutterworth Press.

Jordan, Philip D. (1982), *The Evangelical Alliance for the United States of America, 1847–1900: Ecumenism, Identity and the Religion of the Republic*, New York: Edwin Mellen Press.

Kalu, Ogbu (2014), 'Africa', in Donald M. Lewis and Richard V. Pierard (eds.), *Global Evangelicalism: Theology, History and Culture in Regional Perspective*, Downers Grove: InterVarsity Press, 125–165.

Katerberg, William H. (2001), *Modernity and the Dilemma of North American Anglican Identities, 1880–1950*, Montreal: McGill-Queen's University Press.

Kaye, Elaine (1988), *C. J. Cadoux: Theologian, Scholar, Pacifist*, Edinburgh: Cadoux Family and Edinburgh University Press.

Kazin, Michael (2006), *A Godly Hero: The Life of William Jennings Bryan*, New York: Alfred A. Knopf.

Kee, Kevin (2006), *Revivalists: Marketing the Gospel in English Canada, 1884–1957*, Montreal: McGill-Queen's University Press.

Killingray, David (2015), 'Hands Joined in Brotherhood: The Rise and Decline of a Movement for Faith and Social Change, 1875–2000', in Anthony Cross et al. (eds.), *Pathways and Patterns in History: Essays on Baptists, Evangelicals and the Modern World in Honour of David Bebbington*, London: Spurgeon's College; Didcot: Baptist Missional Society, 319–339.

Klauber, Martin I., and Scott M. Manetsch (eds.) (2008), *The Great Commission: Evangelicals and the History of World Missions*, Nashville: B&H Academic.

Koss, Stephen (1975), *Nonconformity in Modern British Politics*, London: B. T. Batsford.

Lake, Meredith (2013), *Faith in Action: Hammondcare*, Sydney: University of New South Wales Press.

Lange, Stuart (2013), *A Rising Tide: Evangelical Christianity in New Zealand 1930–65*, Dunedin: Otago University Press.

Larsen, Timothy (2002), *Christabel Pankhurst: Fundamentalism and Feminism in Coalition*, Woodbridge: Boydell Press.

Larsen, Timothy (ed.) (2003), *Biographical Dictionary of Evangelicals*, Downers Grove: InterVarsity Press; Leicester: Inter-Varsity Press.

Lawson, Tom (2003), 'The Anglican Understanding of Nazism 1933–1945: Placing the Church of England's Response to the Holocaust in Context', *TCBH* 14.2, 112–137.

Lean, Garth (1985), *Frank Buchman: A Life*, London: Constable.

Lewis, Donald M., and Richard V. Pierard (eds.) (2014), *Global Evangelicalism: Theology, History and Culture in Regional Perspective*, Downers Grove: IVP Academic.

Linder, Robert D. (1992), 'Australian Evangelicals in Politics in the Victorian Age: The Cases of J. D. Lang, W. G. Spence, and J. S. T. McGowen', *L* 13, 34–60.

—— (1993), '"Honest Jim" McGowen (1855–1922) as a Christian in Politics', *L* 15, 44–59.

—— (1997), 'Apostle to the Australians: The Rev. Dr Samuel Angus in Australia, 1915–1943', in Geoffrey R. Treloar (ed.), *The Furtherance of Religious Beliefs: Essays on the History of Theological Education in Australia*, Sydney: CSAC and EHA, 156–179.

—— (1997–8), 'The Methodist Love Affair with the Australian Labor Party, 1891–1929', *L* 23 and 24, 35–61.

—— (2000), *The Long Tragedy: Australian Evangelical Christians and the Great War, 1914–1918*, Adelaide: Openbook.

—— (2003), 'The Peaceful Evangelicals: Refusing to Take up the Sword, 1914–1918', *L* 33–34, 5–65.

—— (2004), 'William Henry Fitchett (1841–1928): Forgotten Methodist "Tall Poppy"', in Geoffrey R. Treloar and Robert D. Linder (eds.), *Making History for God: Essays on Evangelicalism, Revival and Mission in Honour of Stuart Piggin*, Sydney: Robert Menzies College, 197–238.

—— (2014), 'The Fourth Tribe: Spiritual Mateship in the Japanese POW Camps in World War II, 1939–1945', *L* 2.7, 61–85.

Livingstone, David N. (1987), *Darwin's Forgotten Defenders: The Encounter Between Evangelical Theology and Evolutionary Thought*, Grand Rapids: Eerdmans.

Livingstone, David N., et al. (eds.) (1999), *Evangelicals and Science in Historical Perspective*, New York: Oxford University Press.

Livingstone, David N., and Mark Noll (2002), 'B. B. Warfield (1851–1921): A Biblical Inerrantist as Evolutionist', *JPH* 80.3, 153–171.

Loane, Marcus L. (1960), *Archbishop Mowll: The Biography of Howard Kilvinton Mowll Archbishop of Sydney and Primate of Australia*, London: Hodder & Stoughton.

Lofton, Kathryn (2006), 'The Methodology of the Modernists: Process in American Protestantism', *CH* 75.2, 374–402.

Longfield, Bradley J. (1991), *The Presbyterian Controversy: Fundamentalists, Modernists and Moderates*, New York: Oxford University Press.

Lovegrove, Deryck W. (ed.) (2002), *The Rise of the Laity in Evangelical Protestantism*, London: Routledge.

Lyon, David (1998), 'Wheels Within Wheels: Glocalization and Contemporary Religion', in Mark Hutchinson and Ogbu Kalu (eds.), *A Global Faith: Essays on Evangelicalism and Globalization*, Sydney: Centre for the Study of Australian Christianity, 47–68.

McCabe, Michael A. (2000), '"Luther's Blunder": David Watson and Social Christianity in Early Twentieth-Century Scotland', *RSCHS* 30, 193–221.

McClymond, Michael J. (2004), 'Issues and Explanations in the Study of North American Revivalism', in Michael J. McClymond (ed.), *Embodying the Spirit: New Perspectives on North American Revivalism*, Baltimore: Johns Hopkins University Press, 1–46.

MacDonald, H. D. (1963), *Theories of Revelation: An Historical Study 1860–1960*, London: Allen & Unwin.

McGrath, Alister (1999), *T. F. Torrance: An Intellectual Biography*, Edinburgh: T. & T. Clark.

McIntosh, John (2014), 'Anglican Evangelicalism in Sydney 1897–1953: The Thought and Influence of Three Moore College Principals – Nathaniel Jones, D. J. Davies and T. C. Hammond', PhD thesis, University of New South Wales.

McKernan, Michael (1991), *Here Is Their Spirit: A History of the Australian War Memorial 1917–1990*, St Lucia: University of Queensland Press.

MacLeod, A. Donald (2007), *C. Stacey Woods and the Evangelical Rediscovery of the University*, Downers Grove: IVP Academic.

McLeod, Hugh (ed.) (2006), *The Cambridge History of Christianity*. Vol. 9: *World Christianities c. 1914–c. 2000*, Cambridge: Cambridge University Press.

McMaster, Richard (2006), *A Gentle Wind of God: The Influence of the East African Revival*, Scottdale, PA: Herald Press.

McNight, Edgar V. (1999), 'A. T. Robertson', in W. A. Elwell and J. D. Weaver (eds.), *Bible Interpreters of the Twentieth Century: A Selection of Evangelical Voices*, Grand Rapids: Baker Books, 93–104.

Madigan, Edward (2011), *Faith Under Fire: Anglican Army Chaplains and the Great War*, Houndmills: Palgrave Macmillan.

Magee, Malcolm D. (2008), *What the World Should Be: Woodrow Wilson and the Crafting of a Faith-Based Foreign Policy*, Waco: Baylor University Press.

Magnusson, Norris (1977), *Salvation in the Slums: Evangelical Social Work, 1865–1920*, Metuchen, NJ: Scarecrow Press and the American Theological Library Association.

Maiden, John (2009), *National Religion and the Prayer Book Controversy, 1927–1928*, Woodbridge: Boydell Press.

Malcolm, C. W. (1956), *Twelve Hours in the Day: The Life and Work of Rev. Lionel B. Fletcher*, London: Marshall, Morgan & Scott.

Maloney, John, and David Thompson, 'Christian Social Thought', *CHC8*, 142–153.

Mangum, R. Todd (2007), *The Dispensational–Covenantal Rift: The Fissuring of American Evangelical Theology from 1936 to 1944*, Milton Keynes: Paternoster Press.

Mangum, R. Todd, and Mark S. Sweetnam (2009), *The Scofield Bible: Its History and Impact on the Evangelical Church*, Colorado Springs: Paternoster Press.

Marsden, George M. (1977), 'Fundamentalism as an American Phenomenon', *CH* 46.2, 215–232.

—— (ed.) (1984), *Evangelicalism in Modern America*, Grand Rapids: Eerdmans.

—— (1987), *Reforming Fundamentalism: Fuller Seminary and the New Evangelicalism*, Grand Rapids: Eerdmans.

—— (2006), *Fundamentalism and American Culture: The Shaping of Twentieth-Century Evangelicalism 1870–1925*, rev ed., Oxford: Oxford University Press.

Marshall, David B. (1986), 'Methodism Embattled: A Reconsideration of the Methodist Church and World War I', *CHR* 66.1, 48–64.

Martin, Paul A. J. (1996), *Missionary of the Indian Road: The Theology of Stanley Jones*, Bangalore: Theological Book Trust.

Martin, Roger (1976), *R. A. Torrey: Apostle of Certainty*, Murfreesboro: Sword of the Lord Publishers.

Marty, Martin E. (1986–96), *Modern American Religion*, 3 vols., Chicago: University of Chicago Press.

Mews, Stuart (1977), 'Neo-Orthodoxy, Liberalism and War: Karl Barth, P. T. Forsyth and John Oman 1914–18', *SCH* 14, 361–375.

Miller, Robert M. (1958), *American Protestantism and Social Issues 1919–1939*, Chapel Hill: University of North Carolina Press.

—— (1985), *Harry Emerson Fosdick: Preacher, Pastor, Prophet*, New York: Oxford University Press.

Mitchell, Patrick (2003), *Evangelicalism and National Identity in Ulster, 1921–1998*, Oxford: Oxford University Press.

Moberg, David (1977), *The Great Reversal: Evangelism and Social Concern*, rev. ed., Philadelphia: J. B. Lippincott.

Moorhead, James H. (1999), *World Without End: Mainstream American Protestant Visions of the Last Things, 1880–1925*, Bloomington: Indiana University Press.

—— (2012), *Princeton Seminary in American Religion and Culture*, Grand Rapids: Eerdmans.

Morgan, D. Densil (2012), *Barth Reception in Britain*, London: T. & T. Clark.

Morrison, Hugh (2005), '"It Is Our Bounden Duty": Theological Contours of New Zealand's Missionary Movement, 1890–1930', *IBMR* 29.3, 123–128.

—— (2006), '"A Great Australasian Scheme": Australian Influences on New Zealand's Emerging Protestant Missionary Movement, 1885–1922', *FH* 38.2, 87–102.

Moses, John A. (1987), 'The British and German Churches and the Perception of War, 1908–1914', *WS* 5.1, 23–44.

Moynihan, Michael (ed.) (1983), *God on Our Side*, London: Secker & Warburg.

Mullin, Robert B. (1996), *Miracles and the Modern Religious Imagination*, New Haven: Yale University Press.

Muravchik, Stephanie (2011), *American Protestantism in the Age of Psychology*, Cambridge: Cambridge University Press.

Murch, James D. (1956), *Cooperation Without Compromise: A History of the National Association of Evangelicals*, Grand Rapids: Eerdmans.

Nelson, Warren (1994), *T. C. Hammond: His Life and Legacy in Ireland and Australia*, Edinburgh: Banner of Truth Trust.

Noble, T. A. (2006), *Tyndale House and Fellowship: The First Sixty Years*, Leicester: Inter-Varsity Press.

Noll, Mark A. (1988), *One Nation Under God? Christian Faith and Political Action in America*, San Francisco: Harper & Row.

—— (ed.) (1990), *Religion and American Politics: From the Colonial Period to the 1980s*, New York: Oxford University Press.

—— (1991), *Between Faith and Criticism. Evangelicals, Scholarship, and the Bible in America*, 2nd ed., Grand Rapids: Baker Book House.

—— (1992), *A History of Christianity in the United States and Canada*, Grand Rapids: Eerdmans.

—— (1994), *The Scandal of the Evangelical Mind*, Grand Rapids: Eerdmans.

—— (2001), *American Evangelical Christianity: An Introduction*, Oxford: Blackwell.

—— (2004), *The Rise of Evangelicalism: The Age of Edwards, Whitefield and the Wesleys*, Leicester: Apollos.

Noll, Mark A., David W. Bebbington and George A. Rawlyk (eds.) (1994), *Evangelicalism: Comparative Studies of Popular Protestantism in North America, the British Isles, and Beyond, 1700–1990*, New York: Oxford University Press.

Nolt, Steven M. (1998), '"Avoid Provoking the Spirit of Controversy": The Irenic Legacy of the Biblical Seminary in New York', in Douglas Jacobsen and William V. Trollinger, Jr. (eds.), *Re-forming the Center: American Protestantism, 1900 to the Present*, Grand Rapids: Eerdmans, 318–340.

Nutt, Rick L. (1997), *The Whole Gospel for the Whole World: Sherwood Eddy and American Protestant Mission*, Macon, GA: Mercer University Press.

Oakes, Peter (2004), 'F. F. Bruce and the Development of Evangelical Biblical Scholarship', *BJRULM* 86.3, 99–124.

O'Brien, Anne (2005), *God's Willing Workers: Women and Religion in Australia*, Sydney: University of New South Wales Press.

O'Brien, Glen (2012), '"The Empire's Titanic Struggle": Victorian Methodism and the Great War', *AP* 10, 50–70.

Opp, James (2005), *The Lord for the Body: Religion, Medicine, and Protestant Faith Healing in Canada, 1880–1930*, Montreal-Kingston: McGill-Queen's University Press.

Orrmont, Arthur (1972), *Requiem for War: The Life of Wilfred Owen*, New York: Four Winds Press.

Ostrander, Richard (1996), 'The Battery and the Windmill: Two Models of Protestant Devotionalism in Early-Twentieth-Century America', *CH* 65.1, 42–61.

Ostrander, Rick (2000), *The Life of Prayer in a World of Science: Protestants, Prayer and American Culture 1870–1930*, Oxford: Oxford University Press.

Paproth, Darrell (1997), *Failure Is Not Final: A Life of C. H. Nash*, Sydney: CSAC.

Parker, Michael (1998), *The Kingdom of Character: The Student Volunteer Movement for Foreign Missions (1886–1926)*, Lanham, MD: American Society of Missiology and University Press of America.

Parker, Stephen (2005), *Faith on the Home Front: Aspects of Church Life and Popular Religion in Birmingham 1939–1945*, Oxford: Peter Lang.

Patterson, James A. (1990), 'The Loss of a Protestant Missionary Consensus: Foreign Missions and the Fundamentalist–Modernist Conflict', in Joel A. Carpenter and Wilbert Shenk (eds.) (1990), *Earthen Vessels: American Evangelicals and Foreign Missions, 1880–1980*, Grand Rapids: Eerdmans, 73–91.

Phillips, Charlie, et al. (2015), 'Roundtable: Re-examining David Bebbington's "Quadrilateral Thesis"', *FH* 47.1, 44–96.

Phillips, Paul T. (1996), *A Kingdom on Earth: Anglo-American Social Christianity, 1880–1940*, University Park, PA: Pennsylvania State University Press.

Pierard, Richard V. (1986), 'John R. Mott and the Rift in the Ecumenical Movement During World War I', *JES* 23.4, 601–620.

—— (1998), 'Evangelical and Ecumenical: Missionary Leaders in Mainline Protestantism, 1900–1950', in Douglas Jacobsen and William V. Trollinger (eds.), *Re-forming the Center: American Protestantism, 1900 to the Present*, Grand Rapids: Eerdmans, 150–171.

—— (ed.) (2005), *Baptists Together in Christ 1905–2005: A Hundred Year History of the Baptist World Alliance*, Falls Church: Baptist World Alliance.

Pierard, Richard V., and Robert D. Linder (1988), *Civil Religion and the Presidency*, Grand Rapids: Academie Books.

Piercy, Karyn-Maree (2004), 'Patient and Enduring Love: The Deaconess Movement, 1900–1920', in John Stenhouse and Jane Thompson (eds.), *Building God's Own Country: Historical Essays on Religions in New Zealand*, Dunedin: University of Otago Press, 196–208.

Piggin, Stuart (1988), 'Towards a Bicentennial History of Australian Evangelicalism', *JRH* 15.1, 20–37.

—— (1994), 'Historical Streams of Influence on Evangelical Piety', *L* 18, 5–19.

—— (2012), *Spirit, Word and World: Evangelical Christianity in Australia*, rev. ed., Brunswick East: Acorn Press.

Piper, John F., Jr. (1987), *The American Churches in World War I*, Athens, OH: Ohio University Press.

—— (2000), *Robert E. Speer: Prophet of the American Church*, Louisville, KY: Geneva Press.

Pitts, Bill (2007), 'The Personal and the Social Christianity in Rauschenbusch's Thought', *ABQ* 26.2, 138–160.

—— (2009), 'Popular Reception of Rauschenbusch's *Christianity and the Social Crisis*, 1907–1909', *ABQ* 28.2, 162–179.

Pollock, J. C. (1953), *A Cambridge Movement*, London: John Murray.

Pope, Robert (1998), *Building Jerusalem: Nonconformity, Labour, and the Social Question in Wales, 1906–1939*, Cardiff: University of Wales Press.

Potter, Philip, and Thomas Wieser (1997), *Seeking and Serving the Truth: The First Hundred Years of the World Student Christian Federation*, Geneva: WCC Publications.

Price, Charles, and Ian Randall (2000), *Transforming Keswick*, Carlisle: OM Publishing.

Putney, Clifford (2001), *Muscular Christianity: Manhood and Sports in America, 1880–1920*, Cambridge, MA: Harvard University Press.

Ramsey, John C. (1962), *John Wilbur Chapman: The Man, His Methods and His Message*, Boston: The Christopher Publishing House.

Randall, Ian M. (1993), 'Spiritual Renewal and Social Reform: Attempts to Develop Social Awareness in the Early Keswick Movement', *VE* 23, 67–86.

—— (1999), *Evangelical Experiences: A Study in the Spirituality of English Evangelicalism 1918–1939*, Carlisle: Paternoster Press.

—— (2000), *Educating Evangelicalism: The Origins, Development and Impact of London Bible College*, Carlisle: Paternoster Press.

—— (2003), *Spirituality and Social Change: The Contribution of F. B. Meyer (1847–1929)*, Carlisle: Paternoster Press.

—— (2005), *What a Friend We Have in Jesus: The Evangelical Tradition*, London: Darton, Longman & Todd.

Randall, Ian M., and David Hilborn (2001), *One Body in Christ: The History and Significance of the Evangelical Alliance*, Carlisle: Evangelical Alliance and Paternoster Press.

Rapp, Dean R. (1993), 'The Reception of Freudianism by British Methodists During the "Psychoanalytic Craze" of the 1920s', *FH* 25.2, 23–46.

Rawlyk, George (1990), 'Politics, Religion, and the Canadian Experience: A Preliminary Probe', in Mark A. Noll (ed.), *Religion and American Politics: From the Colonial Period to the 1980s*, New York: Oxford University Press, 253–277.

—— (ed.) (1997), *Aspects of Canadian Evangelicalism*, Montreal: McGill-Queen's University Press.

Rawlyk, George A., and Mark Noll (eds.) (1993), *Amazing Grace. Evangelicalism in Australia, Britain, Canada, and the United States*, Grand Rapids: Baker Books.

Rennie, Ian S. (1994), 'Fundamentalism and the Varieties of North Atlantic Evangelicalism', in Mark Noll et al. (eds.), *Evangelicalism: Comparative Studies of Popular Protestantism in North America, the British Isles, and Beyond*, New York: Oxford University Press, 333–350.

Reynaud, Daniel (2015), *The Man the Anzacs Revered: William 'Fighting Mac' McKenzie Anzac Chaplain*, Warburton: Signs Publishing.

Reynolds, David (2014), *The Long Shadow: The Legacies of the Great War in the Twentieth Century*, New York: W. W. Norton.

Rhodes, Kenneth W. (2001), 'Ambivalent Fundamentalist: The Life and Ministry of Rev. Chester E. Tulga', PhD thesis, University of Akron.

Richey, Russell E. (1993), 'Revivalism: In Search of a Definition', *WTJ* 28.1–2, 165–175.

Robbins, Keith (1993), *History, Religion and Identity in Modern Britain*, London: Hambledon Press.

—— (2003), 'Protestant Nonconformists and the Peace Question', in Alan P. F. Sell and Anthony R. Cross (eds.), *Protestant Nonconformity in the Twentieth Century*, Carlisle: Paternoster Press, 216–239.

—— (2008), *England, Ireland, Scotland, Wales: The Christian Church 1900–2000*, Oxford: Oxford University Press.

Robert, Dana (1986), 'The Origin of the Student Volunteer Watchword: "The Evangelization of the World in This Generation"', *IBMR* 10.4, 146–149.

—— (2002), 'The First Globalization: The Internationalization of the Protestant Missionary Movement Between the World Wars', *IBMR* 26.2, 50–66.

Robins, Roger (1984), 'A Chronology of Peace: Attitudes Towards War and Peace in the Assemblies of God: 1914–1918', *Pn* 6.1, 3–25.

Robinson, James (2005), *Pentecostal Origins: Early Pentecostalism in Ireland in the Context of the British Isles*, Milton Keynes: Paternoster Press.

Rosell, Garth M. (2008), *The Surprising Work of God: Harold John Ockenga, Billy Graham, and the Rebirth of Evangelicalism*, Grand Rapids: Baker Academic.

Rouse, Ruth, and Stephen C. Neill (eds.) (1986), *A History of the Ecumenical Movement 1517–1948*, 3rd ed., Geneva: World Council of Churches.

Ruotsila, Markku (2008), *The Origins of Christian Anti-Internationalism: Conservative Evangelicals and the League of Nations*, Washington, DC: Georgetown University Press.

Russell, C. Allyn (1976), *Voices of Fundamentalism: Seven Biographical Studies*, Philadelphia: Westminster Press.

Sack, Daniel (2009), *Moral Re-Armament: The Reinventions of an American Religious Movement*, New York: Palgrave Macmillan.

Saler, Michael (2006), 'Modernity and Enchantment: A Historiographic Review', *AHR* 111.3, 692–716.

Sawatsky, Ronald (1985), '"Looking for That Blessed Hope": The Roots of Fundamentalism in Canada, 1878–1914', PhD thesis, University of Toronto.

Schmidt, William J. (1978), *Architect of Unity: A Biography of Samuel McCrae Cavert*, New York: Friendship Press.

Schultze, Quentin J. (1988), 'Evangelical Radio and the Rise of the Electronic Church, 1921–1948', *JBEM* 32.3, 289–306.

Schweitzer, Richard (2003), *The Cross and the Trenches: Religious Faith and Doubt Among British and American Great War Soldiers*, Westport, CT: Praeger Publishers.

Scorgie, Glen C. (1988), *A Call for Continuity: The Theological Contribution of James Orr*, Macon, GA: Mercer University Press.

Sell, Alan P. F. (1991), *A Reformed, Evangelical, Catholic Theology: The Contribution of the World Alliance of Reformed Churches, 1875–1982*, Grand Rapids: Eerdmans.

—— (2006), *Nonconformist Theology in the Twentieth Century*, Milton Keynes: Paternoster Press.

Sell, Alan P. F., and Anthony R. Cross (eds.) (2003), *Protestant Nonconformity in the Twentieth Century*, Carlisle: Paternoster Press.

Shepherd, Peter (2001), *The Making of a Modern Denomination: John Howard Shakespeare and the English Baptists 1898–1924*, Carlisle: Paternoster Press.

Shils, Edward (1981), *Tradition*, London: Faber & Faber.

Showalter, Nathan D. (1998), *The End of a Crusade: The Student Volunteer Movement for Foreign Missions and the Great War*, Lanham, MD: Scarecrow Press.

Shuff, Roger (2005), *Searching for the True Church: Brethren and Evangelicals in Mid-Twentieth-Century England*, Carlisle: Paternoster Press.

Simpson, Jane (1989), 'Joseph W. Kemp: Prime Interpreter of American Fundamentalism in New Zealand in the 1920s', in Douglas Pratt (ed.), *'Rescue the Perishing': Comparative Perspectives on Evangelism and Revivalism*, Auckland: College Communications, 23–41.

Sittser, Gerald L. (1997), *A Cautious Patriotism: The American Churches and the Second World War*, Chapel Hill: University of North Carolina Press.

Smith, Eric (1991), *Another Anglican Angle. Liberal Evangelicalism: The Anglican Evangelical Group Movement 1906–1967*, Oxford: The Amate Press.

Smith, Gary Scott (2000), *The Search for Social Salvation: Social Christianity and America, 1880–1925*, Lanham, MD: Lexington Books.

Smith, Mark (ed.) (2008), *British Evangelical Identities Past and Present*. Vol. 1: *Aspects of the History and Sociology of Evangelicalism in Britain and Ireland*, Eugene: Wipf & Stock.

Snape, Michael (2005), *God and the British Soldier: Religion and the British Army in the First and Second World Wars*, London: Routledge.

—— (2006), 'The Great War', *CHC9*, 131–150.

—— (2011), 'Church of England Army Chaplains in the First World War: Goodbye to "Goodbye to All That"', *JEH* 62.2, 318–345.

Stackhouse, John G., Jr. (1993), *Canadian Evangelicalism in the Twentieth Century: An Introduction to Its Character*, Toronto: University of Toronto Press.

Staggers, Kermit L. (1986), 'Reuben A. Torrey: American Fundamentalist, 1856–1928', PhD thesis, Claremont Graduate School.

Stanley, Brian (1990), *The Bible and the Flag*, Leicester: Apollos.

—— (1990), 'Evangelical Social and Political Ethics: An Historical Perspective', *EvQ* 62.1, 19–36.

—— (2006), 'Defining the Boundaries of Christendom: The Two Worlds of the World Missionary Conference, 1910', *IBMR* 30.4, 171–176.

—— (2009), *The World Missionary Conference, Edinburgh 1910*, Grand Rapids: Eerdmans.

—— (2013), *The Global Diffusion of Evangelicalism: The Age of Billy Graham and John Stott*, Nottingham: Inter-Varsity Press.

Stenhouse, John (1992), 'Fundamentalism and New Zealand Culture', in Bryan Gilling (ed.), *Be Ye Separate*: *Fundamentalism and the New Zealand Experience*, Hamilton: University of Waikato and Colcom Press, 1–23.

Stephenson, Alan M. G. (1984), *The Rise and Decline of English Modernism*, London: SPCK.

Stonehouse, Ned B. (1987 [1954]), *J. Gresham Machen: A Biographical Memoir*, 3rd ed., Edinburgh: Banner of Truth Trust.

Sutherland, M. P. (1996), 'Pulpit or Podium? J. K. Archer and the Dilemma of Christian Politics in New Zealand', *NZJBR* 1, 26–46.

Sutherland, Philomena (2013), 'Sectarianism and Evangelicalism in Birmingham and Liverpool', in John Wolffe (ed.), *Protestant–Catholic Conflict from the Reformation to the Twenty-First Century*, Houndmills: Palgrave Macmillan, 132–165.

Sutton, Matthew A. (2007), *Aimee Semple McPherson and the Resurrection of Christian America*, Cambridge, MA: Harvard University Press.

—— (2014), *American Apocalypse: A History of Modern Evangelicalism*, Cambridge, MA: Belknap Press.

Synan, Vincent (2001), *The Century of the Holy Spirit: 100 Years of Pentecostal and Charismatic Renewal, 1901–2000*, Nashville: Thomas Nelson.

Szasz, Ferenc (1982), *The Divided Mind of Protestant America, 1880–1930*, Tuscaloosa: University of Alabama Press.

Taves, Ann (1999), *Fits, Trances, and Visions: Experiencing Religion and Explaining Experience from Wesley to James*, Princeton: Princeton University Press.

—— (2002), 'Feminization Revisited. Protestantism and Gender at the Turn of the Century', in M. Bendroth and L. Brereton (eds.), *Women and Twentieth-Century Protestantism*, Urbana: University of Illinois Press, 304–324.

Thompson, David M. (1983), 'War, the Nation and the Kingdom of God: The Origins of the National Mission of Repentance and Hope', *SCH* 20, 337–350.

—— (1993), 'The Christian Socialist Revival in Britain: A Reappraisal', in J. Garnett and C. Matthew (eds.), *Revival and Religion Since 1700: Essays for John Walsh*, London: Hambledon Press, 273–295.

Thorne, Phillip R. (1995), *Evangelicalism and Karl Barth: His Reception and Influence in North American Evangelical Theology*, Allison Park: Pickwick Publications.

Tomkins, Oliver (1957), *The Life of Edward Woods*, London: SCM Press.

Toone, Mark J. (1988), 'Evangelicalism in Transition: A Comparative Analysis of the Work and Theology of D. L. Moody and His Protégés, Henry Drummond and R. A. Torrey', PhD thesis, University of St Andrews.

Tooze, Adam (2014), *The Deluge: The Great War and the Remaking of Global Order, 1916–1931*, London: Allen Lane.

Travell, John (1999), *Doctor of Souls: A Biography of Dr Leslie Dixon Weatherhead*, Cambridge: Lutterworth Press.

Treloar, Geoffrey R. (2006), 'The Cambridge Triumvirate and the Acceptance of New Testament Higher Criticism in Britain, 1850–1900', *JAS* 4.1, 19–32.

—— (2006), 'T. C. Hammond the Controversialist', *AHSDSJ* 51.1, 20–35.

—— (2013), 'Baptists and the World 1900–1940: A "Great Reversal"?', in David Bebbington and Martin Sutherland (eds.), *Interfaces: Baptists and Others*, Milton Keynes: Paternoster Press, 177–198.

—— (2013), 'The British Contribution to *The Fundamentals*', in David Bebbington and David Ceri Jones (eds.), *Evangelicalism and Fundamentalism in the United Kingdom During the Twentieth Century*, Oxford: Oxford University Press, 15–34.

—— (2014), 'The Word Disputed: The Crisis of Evangelical Biblicism in the 1920s and 1930s', *L* 2.7, 105–122.

Turner, Frank M. (1993), *Contesting Cultural Authority: Essays in Victorian Intellectual Life*, Cambridge: Cambridge University Press.

—— (2002), *John Henry Newman: The Challenge to Evangelical Religion*, New Haven: Yale University Press.

Tyrrell, Ian (1991), *Woman's World/Woman's Empire: The Woman's Christian Temperance Union in International Perspective, 1880–1930*, Chapel Hill: University of North Carolina Press.

—— (2010), *Reforming the World: The Creation of America's Moral Empire*, Princeton: Princeton University Press.

Utzinger, J. Michael (2006), *Yet Saints Their Watch Are Keeping: Fundamentalists, Modernists, and the Development of Evangelical Ecclesiology, 1887–1937*, Macon, GA: Mercer University Press.

Vollmer, Hendrik (2013), *The Sociology of Disruption, Disaster and Social Change*, Cambridge: Cambridge University Press.

Wacker, Grant (1985), 'The Holy Spirit and the Spirit of the Age in American Protestantism, 1880–1910', *JAH* 72, 45–62.

—— (1996), 'Travail of a Broken Family: Evangelical Responses to Pentecostalism in America, 1906–1916', *JEH* 47.3, 505–528.

—— (2001), *Heaven Below: Early Pentecostals and American Culture*, Cambridge, MA: Harvard University Press.

Wakefield, Gordon S. (1971), *Robert Newton Flew, 1886–1962*, London: Epworth Press.

Walls, Andrew (2002), *The Cross-Cultural Process in Christian History*, New York: Orbis Books.

Walsh, Timothy B. (2005), '"Signs and Wonders That Lie": Unlikely Polemical Outbursts Against the Early Pentecostal Movement in Britain', *SCH* 41, 410–422.

—— (2012), *To Meet and Satisfy a Very Hungry People: The Origins and Fortunes of English Pentecostalism, 1907–1925*, Milton Keynes: Paternoster Press.

Ward, W. R. (1992), *The Protestant Evangelical Awakening*, Cambridge: Cambridge University Press.

—— (2006), *Early Evangelicalism: A Global Intellectual History, 1670–1789*, Cambridge: Cambridge University Press.

Warner, Rob (2007), *Reinventing English Evangelicalism, 1966–2001: A Theological and Sociological Study*, Milton Keynes: Paternoster Press.

Warren, Heather A. (1997), *Theologians of a New World Order: Reinhold Niebuhr and the Christian Realists 1920–1948*, New York: Oxford University Press.

Wearmouth, Robert F. (1957), *The Social and Political Influence of Methodism in the Twentieth Century*, London: Epworth Press.

Wellings, Martin (1993), 'The First Protestant Martyr of the Twentieth Century: The Life and Significance of John Kensit (1853–1902)', *SCH* 30, 347–358.

—— (2003), *Evangelicals Embattled: Responses of Evangelicals in the Church of England to Ritualism, Darwinism and Theological Liberalism 1890–1930*, Carlisle: Paternoster Press.

—— (2013), 'Methodist Fundamentalism Before and After the First World War', in David Bebbington and David Ceri Jones (eds.), *Evangelicalism and Fundamentalism in the United Kingdom During the Twentieth Century*, Oxford: Oxford University Press, 76–94.

—— (2014), 'The Anglican Evangelical Group Movement', in Andrew Atherstone and John Maiden (eds.), *Evangelicalism and the Church of England in the Twentieth Century: Reform, Resistance and Renewal*, Woodbridge: Boydell Press, 68–88.

Weston, William J. (1997), *Presbyterian Pluralism: Competition in a Protestant House*, Knoxville: University of Tennessee Press.

—— (2003), *Leading from the Center: Strengthening the Pillars of the Church*, Louisville: Geneva Press.

White, Ronald C., Jr., and C. Howard Hopkins (1976), *The Social Gospel: Religion and Reform in Changing America*, Philadelphia: Temple University Press.

Wilhoit, Mel R. (1995), 'Alexander the Great: Or, Just Plain Charlie', *Hymn* 46.2, 20–28.

Wilkinson, Alan (1978), *The Church of England and the First World War*, London: SPCK.

Wilkinson, J. T. (1971), *Arthur Samuel Peake: A Biography*, London: Epworth Press.

Wilkinson, Michael (ed.) (2009), *Canadian Pentecostalism: Transition and Transformation*, Montreal: McGill-Queen's University Press.

Williams, Sarah C. (2014), 'Evangelicals and Gender', in Donald M. Lewis and Richard V. Pierard (eds.), *Global Evangelicalism: Theology, History and Culture in Regional Perspective*, Downers Grove: IVP Academic, 270–295.

Wilson, Paul (2001), 'Central Canadian Baptists and the Role of Cultural Factors in the Fundamentalist–Modernist Schism of 1927', *BHH* winter–spring, 61–81.

Wolfe, Kenneth M. (1984), *The Churches and the British Broadcasting Corporation 1922–1956: The Politics of Broadcast Religion*, London: SCM Press.

Wolffe, John (1994), *God and Greater Britain: Religion and National Life in Britain and Ireland, 1843–1945*, London: Routledge.

—— (2006), *The Expansion of Evangelicalism: The Age of Wilberforce, More, Chalmers and Finney*, Leicester: Inter-Varsity Press.

—— (2015), 'A Comparative Historical Categorisation of Anti-Catholicism', *JRH* 39.2, 182–202.

Wood, H. G. (1953), *Terrot Reaveley Glover: A Biography*, Cambridge: Cambridge University Press.

Wright, Robert (1991), *A World Mission: Canadian Protestantism and the Quest for a New International Order, 1918–1939*, Montreal: McGill-Queen's University Press.

INDEX